T0255673

Deep Reinforcement Learning with Python

With PyTorch, TensorFlow and OpenAI Gym

Nimish Sanghi

Apress®

Deep Reinforcement Learning with Python

Nimish Sanghi
Bangalore, India

ISBN-13 (pbk): 978-1-4842-6808-7   ISBN-13 (electronic): 978-1-4842-6809-4
https://doi.org/10.1007/978-1-4842-6809-4

Managing Director, Apress Media LLC: Welmoed Spahr
Acquisitions Editor: Celestin Suresh John
Development Editor: James Markham
Coordinating Editor: Aditee Mirashi

Cover designed by eStudioCalamar

Cover image designed by Freepik (www. freepik.com)

Distributed to the book trade worldwide by Springer Science+Business Media New York, 1 New York Plaza, Suite 4600, New York, NY 10004-1562, USA. Phone 1-800-SPRINGER, fax (201) 348-4505, e-mail orders-ny@springer-sbm.com, or visit www.springeronline.com. Apress Media, LLC is a California LLC and the sole member (owner) is Springer Science + Business Media Finance Inc (SSBM Finance Inc). SSBM Finance Inc is a **Delaware** corporation.

For information on translations, please e-mail booktranslations@springernature.com; for reprint, paperback, or audio rights, please e-mail bookpermissions@springernature.com.

Apress titles may be purchased in bulk for academic, corporate, or promotional use. eBook versions and licenses are also available for most titles. For more information, reference our Print and eBook Bulk Sales web page at www.apress.com/bulk-sales.

Any source code or other supplementary material referenced by the author in this book is available to readers on GitHub via the book's product page, located at www.apress.com/978-1-4842-6808-7. For more detailed information, please visit www.apress.com/source-code.

Printed on acid-free paper

This book is dedicated to my wife Suman and children,
Harsh and Yash, who allowed their time
to be stolen for writing this book.

Table of Contents

About the Author

 **Nimish Sanghi** is a passionate technical leader who brings extreme focus to the use of technology for solving customer problems. He has more than 25 years of work experience in software and consulting. Nimish has held leadership roles with P&L responsibilities at PwC, IBM, and Oracle. In 2006 he set out on his entrepreneurial journey in software consulting at SOAIS with offices in Boston, Chicago, and Bangalore. Today the firm provides automation and digital transformation services to Fortune 100 companies, helping them make the transition from on-premise applications to the cloud.

He is also an angel investor in the space of AI and automation-driven startups. He has cofounded Paybooks, a SaaS HR and payroll platform for the Indian market. He has also cofounded a Boston-based startup that offers ZipperAgent and ZipperHQ, a suite of AI-driven workflow and video marketing automation platforms. He currently holds the positions of CTO and chief data scientist for both these platforms.

Nimish has an MBA from the Indian Institute of Management in Ahmedabad, India, and a BS in electrical engineering from the Indian Institute of Technology in Kanpur, India. He holds multiple certifications in AI and deep learning.

About the Technical Reviewer

**Akshay Kulkarni** is an artificial intelligence and machine learning evangelist, an author, a speaker, and a mentor.

He has consulted with several Fortune 500 and global enterprises to drive AI and data science–led strategic transformation. Akshay has rich experience in building and scaling AI and machine learning businesses. Currently he is part of Publicis Sapient's core data science team where he takes part in strategy and transformation interventions through AI and works on various machine learning, deep learning, natural language processing, and artificial intelligence engagements by applying state-of-the-art techniques in this space.

Akshay has been awarded as one of "top 40 under 40 data scientists in India" by AIM. He is a regular speaker at major AI and data science conferences and has published books on data science/machine learning. He has delivered 500+ tech talks on data science and AI in various conferences, technical institutions, and community-arranged forums. Also, he is a well-known speaker at O'Reilly AI conferences.

He is passionate about teaching and acts as a data science mentor at various organizations. He is also a visiting faculty (industry expert) at a few of the top graduation (IIT, RIT, etc.) and business (IIM, etc.) institutes/universities in India. In his spare time, he enjoys reading, writing, coding, and helping aspiring data scientists.

Acknowledgments

I would like to thank the team at Apress, especially editors James Markham, Aditee Mirashi, and Celestin John who believed in me and helped me refine the drafts with numerous valuable suggestions. I would like to thank technical reviewer Akshay Kulkarni who reviewed the drafts for its correctness, checked my code, and helped me improve the readability of the book. I would also like to thank everyone else at Apress who played a role in making this book a reality.

I would like to thank my wife Suman who, during the pandemic time when this was written, single-handedly took charge of keeping the family healthy, giving me space, and giving me time to write this book.

Lastly, I would like to thank you, the reader, who has decided to invest valuable time reading this book. Please provide your feedback, letting me know if this book met your expectations and what could be better. Nothing would make me happier than knowing that I was able to play a role in expanding your knowledge. I can be reached at `nimish.sanghi@gmail.com`.

Introduction

This book is about reinforcement learning and takes you from the basics through advanced topics. Though this book assumes no prior knowledge of the field of reinforcement learning, it expects you to be familiar with the basics of machine learning and specifically supervised learning. Have you coded in Python before? Are you comfortable working with libraries such as NumPy and scikit-learn? Have you heard of deep learning and explored basic build blocks of training simple models in PyTorch or TensorFlow? You should answer yes to all of these questions to get the best out of this book. If not, I suggest you review these concepts first; reviewing any introductory online tutorial or book from Apress on these topics would be sufficient.

This book walks you through the basics of reinforcement learning, spending lot of time explaining the concepts in initial chapters. If you have prior knowledge of reinforcement learning, you can go through the first four chapters at a fast pace. Starting in Chapter 5, the book picks up the pace as it starts exploring advanced topics that combine deep learning with reinforcement learning. The accompanying code hosted on GitHub forms an integral part of this book. While the book includes listings of the relevant code, Jupyter notebooks in the code repository provide additional insights and practical tips on coding these algorithms. You will be best served by reading the chapter and going through the explanations first and then working through the code in Jupyter notebooks. You are also encouraged to try to rewrite the code, training agents for different additional environments found in the OpenAI Gym library.

For a subject like this, math is unavoidable. However, we have tried our best to keep it minimal. The book quotes a lot of research papers that give short explanations of the approach taken. Readers wanting to gain a deeper understanding of the theory should go through these research papers. This book's purpose is to introduce practitioners to the motivation and high-level approach behind many of the latest techniques in this field. However, by no means is it meant to provide a complete theoretical understanding of these techniques, which is best gained by reading the original papers.

The book is organized into ten chapters.

Chapter 1, "Introduction to Deep Reinforcement Learning," introduces the topic, setting the background and motivating readers with real-world examples of how reinforcement learning is changing the landscape of intelligent machines. It also covers the installation of Python and related libraries so you can run the code accompanying this book.

Chapter 2, "Markov Decision Processes," defines the problem in detail that we are trying to solve in the field of reinforcement learning. We talk about the agent and environment. We go in depth about what constitutes a reward, value functions, model, and policy. We look at various flavors of Markov processes. We establish the equations by Richard Bellman as part of dynamic programming.

Chapter 3, "Model-Based Algorithms," focuses on the setup for a model and how the agent plans its action for optimal outcome. We also explore the OpenAI Gym environment library, which implements many of the common environments that we will use for coding and testing algorithms throughout the book. Finally, we explore "value" and "policy iteration" approaches to planning.

Chapter 4, "Model-Free Approaches," talks about the model-free learning methods. Under this setup, the agent has no knowledge of the environment/model. It interacts with the environment and uses the rewards to learn an optimal policy through a trial-and-error approach. We specifically look at the Monte Carlo (MC) approach and the temporal difference (TD) approach to learning. We first study them individually and then combine the two under the concept of n-step returns and eligibility traces.

Chapter 5, "Function Approximation," looks at setups in which the state of the system changes from being discrete (as will be the case until Chapter 4) to being continuous. We study how to use parameterized functions to represent the state and bring scalability. First, we talk about the traditional approach of handcrafted function approximation, especially the linear approximators. Then, we introduce the concept of using a deep learning–based model as nonlinear function approximators.

Chapter 6, "Deep Q-Learning," dives deep into DeepMind to successfully demonstrate how to use deep learning and reinforcement learning together to design agents that can learn to play video games such as Atari games. In this chapter, we explore how DQN works and what tweaks are required to make it learn. We then survey the various flavors of DQN, complete with detailed code examples, both in PyTorch and TensorFlow.

Chapter 7, "Policy Gradient Algorithms," switches focus to explore the approach of learning a good policy directly in a model-free setup. The approaches in the preceding chapters are based on first learning value functions and then using these value functions to optimize the policy. In this chapter, we first talk about the theoretical foundations of the direct policy optimization approach. After establishing the foundations, we discuss various approaches including some very recent and highly successful algorithms, complete with implementations in PyTorch and TensorFlow.

Chapter 8, "Combining Policy Gradients and Q-Learning," as the name suggests, covers how to combine the value-based DQN and policy gradients methods to leverage the advantages of both the approaches. It also enables us to design agents that can operate in continuous action spaces, which is not easily feasible under approaches until Chapter 7. We specifically look at three popular ones: deep deterministic policy gradients (DDPG), twin delayed DDPG (TD3), and soft actor critic (SAC). Like before, we have comprehensive implementations in PyTorch and TensorFlow to help readers master the subject.

Chapter 9, "Integrated Planning and Learning," is all about combining the model-based approach from Chapter 3 and model-free approach from Chapters 4 to 8. We explore the general framework under which such integrations can be made possible. Finally, we explain Monte Carlo tree search (MCTS) and how it was used to train AlphaGo, which could beat champion Go players.

Chapter 10, "Further Exploration and Next Steps," surveys various other extensions of reinforcement learning, including concepts such as scalable model-based approaches, imitation and inverse learning, derivative-free methods, transfer and multitask learning, as well as meta learning. The coverage here is from 30,000 feet to expose readers to new and related concepts without getting lost in the details. We conclude by talking about the way you should continue to explore and learn beyond what is covered in this book.

## CHAPTER 1

Introduction to Reinforcement Learning

Reinforcement learning is one of the fastest growing disciplines and is helping to make AI real. Combining deep learning with reinforcement learning has led to many significant advances that are increasingly getting machines closer to acting the way humans do. In this book, we will start with the basics and finish up with mastering some of the most recent developments in the field. There will be a good mix of theory (with minimal mathematics) and code implementations using PyTorch as well as TensorFlow.

In this chapter, we will set the context and get everything prepared for you to follow along in the rest of the book.

Reinforcement Learning

All intelligent beings start with some knowledge. However, as they interact with the world and gain experiences, they learn to adapt to the environment and become better at doing things. To quote a 1994 op-ed statement in the *Wall Street Journal*,[1] intelligence can be defined as follows:

> *A very general mental capability that, among other things, involves the ability to reason, plan, solve problems, think abstractly, comprehend complex ideas, learn quickly and learn from experience. It is not merely book learning, a narrow academic skill, or test-taking smarts. Rather, it reflects a broader and deeper capability for comprehending our surroundings—"catching on," "making sense" of things, or "figuring out" what to do.*

---

[1]https://en.wikipedia.org/wiki/Mainstream_Science_on_Intelligence

© Nimish Sanghi 2021
N. Sanghi, *Deep Reinforcement Learning with Python*, https://doi.org/10.1007/978-1-4842-6809-4_1

Intelligence in the context of machines is called *artificial intelligence*. Oxford Languages defines artificial intelligence (AI) as follows:

> *The theory and development of computer systems able to perform tasks normally requiring human intelligence, such as visual perception, speech recognition, decision-making, and translation between languages.*

This is what we will study in this book: the theory and design of algorithms that help machines (agents) gain the capability to perform tasks by interacting with the environment and continually learning from its successes, failures, and rewards. Originally AI revolved around designing solutions as a list of formal rules that could be expressed using logic and mathematical notations. These rules consisted of a collection of information codified into a knowledge base. The design of these AI systems also consisted of an inference engine that enabled users to query the knowledge base and combine the individual strands of rules/knowledge to make inferences. These systems were also known as *expert systems*, *decision support systems*, etc. However, soon people realized that these systems were too brittle. As the complexity of problems grew, it became exponentially harder to codify the knowledge or to build an effective inference system.

The modern concept of reinforcement learning is a combination of two different threads through their individual development. First is the concept of optimal control. Among many approaches to the problem of optimal control, in 1950 Richard Bellman came up with the discipline of *dynamic programming*, which we will be using extensively in this book. Dynamic programming, however, does not involve learning. It is all about planning through the space of various options using Bellman recursive equations. We will have a lot to say about these equations in Chapters 2 and 3.

The second thread is that of learning by trial and error, which finds its origin in the psychology of animal training. Edward Thorndike was the first one to express the concept of *trial and error* in clear terms. In his words:

> *Of several responses made to the same situation, those which are accompanied or closely followed by satisfaction to the animal will, other things being equal, be more firmly connected with the situation, so that, when it recurs, they will be more likely to recur; those which are accompanied or closely followed by discomfort to the animal will, other things being equal, have their connections with that situation weakened, so that, when it recurs, they will be less likely to occur. The greater the satisfaction or discomfort, the greater the strengthening or weakening of the bond.*

The concept of increasing the occurrence of good outcomes and decreasing the occurrence of bad outcomes is something we will see in use in Chapter 7 on policy gradients.

In the 1980s, these two fields merged to give rise to the field of modern reinforcement learning. In the last decade, with the emergence of powerful deep learning methods, reinforcement learning when combined with deep learning is giving rise to very powerful algorithms that could make artificial intelligence real in coming times. Today's reinforcement systems interact with the world to acquire experience and learn to optimize their actions based on the outcomes of their interactions with the world by generalizing its experience. There is no explicit coding of expert knowledge.

Machine Learning Branches

Machine learning involves learning from the data presented to the system so that the system can perform a specified task. The system is not explicitly told how to do the task. Rather, it is presented with the data, and the system learns to carry out some task based on a defined objective. We will not say more about it as we assume that you are familiar with the concept of machine learning.

Machine learning approaches are traditionally divided into three broad categories, as shown in Figure 1-1.

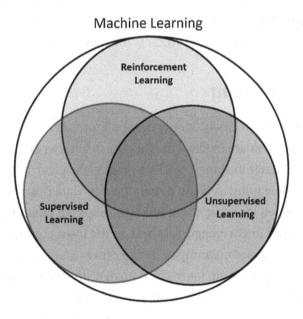

Figure 1-1. *Branches of machine learning*

The three branches of machine learning differ in the sense of the "feedback" available to the learning system. They are discussed in the following sections.

Supervised Learning

In supervised learning, the system is presented with the labeled data, and the objective is to generalize the knowledge so that new unlabeled data can be labeled. Consider that images of cats and dogs are presented to the system along with labels of which image shows a cat or a dog. The input data is represented as a set of data $D = (x_1, y_1), (x_2, y_2), \dots (x_n, y_n)$, where $x_1, x_2, \dots, x_n$ are the pixel values of individual images and $y_1, y_2, \dots, y_n$ are the labels of the respective images, say, a value of 0 for an image of a cat and a value of 1 for an image of a dog. The system/model takes this input and learns a mapping from image x_i to label y_i. Once trained, the system is presented with a new image x' to get a prediction of the label $y' = 0$ or 1 depending on whether the image is that of a cat or that of a dog.

This is a classification problem where the system learns to classify an input into a correct class. The other problem type is that of regression where we want to predict the price of a house based on the features of the house. The training data is again represented as $D = (x_1, y_1), (x_2, y_2), \dots (x_n, y_n)$. The inputs are $x_1, x_2, \dots, x_n$ where each input x_i is a vector of certain attributes, e.g., number of rooms in a house, its area and size of front lawn, etc. The system is given as label y_i, the market value of the house. The system uses the input data from many houses to learn the mapping of input features x_i to the value of a house y_i. The trained model is then presented with a vector x', which consists of the features of a new house, and the model predicts the market value y' of this new house.

Unsupervised Learning

Unsupervised learning has no labels. It only has the inputs $D = x_1, x_2, \dots, x_n$ and no labels. The system uses this data to learn the hidden structure of the data so that it can cluster/categorize the data into some broad categories. Post learning, when the system is presented with a new data point x', it can match the new data point to one of the learned clusters. Unlike supervised learning, there is no well-defined meaning to each category. Once the data is clustered into a category, based on the most common attributes within a cluster, we could assign some meaning to it. The other use of unsupervised learning is to leverage underlying input data to learn the data distribution so that the system can be subsequently queried to produce a new synthetic data point.

Many times unsupervised learning is used for feature extraction, which is then fed to a supervised learning system. By clustering data, we can first identify the hidden structure and remap the data to a lower dimensional form. With this lower dimensional data, supervised learning is able to learn faster. Here we are using unsupervised learning as a feature extractor.

There is yet another way to leverage unsupervised learning approach. Consider the case when you have a small amount of labeled data and a large amount of unlabeled data. Both the labeled data and the unlabeled data are first clustered together. Next, in each such cluster, the unlabeled data is assigned the labels based on the strength of labeled data in that cluster. We are basically leveraging labeled data to assign labels to the unlabeled data. The completely labeled data is next fed into the supervised learning algorithm to train a classification system. This approach of combining supervised and unsupervised learning together is known as *semisupervised learning*.

Reinforcement Learning

Let's first look at an example. We are trying to design an autonomous vehicle that can drive on its own. We have a car that we will call the *agent*, i.e., a system or an algorithm that is learning to drive on its own. It is learning a *behavior* to drive. Its current coordinates, speed, and direction of motion when combined as a vector of numbers is known as its *current state*. The agent uses its current state to make a decision to either apply the brake or press on the gas pedal. It also uses this information to turn the steering to change the direction of the car's motion. The combined decision of "breaking/accelerating" and "steering the car" is known as an *action*. The mapping of a specific current state to a specific action is known as a *policy*. The agent's action when good will yield a happy outcome, and when an action is bad, it will result in an unhappy outcome. The agent uses this feedback of the outcome to assess the effectiveness of its action. The outcome as a feedback is known as a *reward* that the agent gets for acting in a particular way in a specific state. Based on the current state and its action, the car reaches a new set of coordinates, speed, and direction. This is the *new state* that the agent finds itself in based on how it acted in the previous step. Who provides this outcome and decides the new state? It is the surroundings of the car, and it is something that the car/agent has no control over. Everything else that the agent does not control is known as the *environment*. We will have a lot more to say about each of these terms throughout the book.

In this setup, the data provided by the system in the form of state vectors, actions taken, and rewards obtained is sequential and correlated. Based on the action the agent takes, the next state and reward obtained from the environment could change drastically. In the previous example of the autonomous car, imagine there is a pedestrian who is crossing the road in front of the car. In this situation, the action of accelerating the car versus breaking the car would have very different outcomes. Accelerating the car could lead to injuring the pedestrian as well as damage to the car and its occupants. Braking the car could lead to avoiding any damages and the car continuing on its onward journey after the road is clear.

In reinforcement learning, the agent does not have prior knowledge of the system. It gathers feedback and uses that feedback to plan/learn actions to maximize a specific objective. As it does not have enough information about the environment initially, it must explore to gather insights. Once it gathers "enough" knowledge, it needs to exploit that knowledge to start adjusting its behavior to maximize the objective it is chasing. The difficult part is that there is no way to know when the exploration is "enough." If the agent continues to explore even after it has gotten perfect knowledge, it is wasting resources trying to gather new information of which there is none left. On the other hand, if the agent prematurely assumes that it has gathered enough knowledge, it may end up optimizing based on incomplete information and may perform poorly. This dilemma of when to explore and when to exploit is the core recurring theme of reinforcement learning algorithms. As we go through different behavior optimization algorithms in this book, we will see this issue play out again and again.

Core Elements

A reinforcement learning system can be broken into four key components: policy, rewards, value functions, and model of the environment.

Policy is what forms the intelligence of the agent. An agent gets to interact with the environment to sense the current state of the environment, e.g., a robot getting visual and other sensory inputs from the system, also known as the *current state* of the environment or the current observation data being perceived by the robot. The robot, like an intelligent entity, uses the current information and possibly the past history to decide on what to do next, i.e., what *action* to perform. The policy maps the state to the action that the agent takes. Policies can be *deterministic*. In other words, for a given state of environment, there is a fixed action that the agent takes. Sometimes the policies can be *stochastic*; in other words, for a given state, there are multiple possible actions that the agent can take.

Reward refers to the goal/objective that the agent is trying to achieve. Consider a robot trying to go from Point A to Point B. It senses the current position and takes an action. If that action brings it near to its goal B, we would expect the reward to be positive. If it takes the robot away from Point B, it is an unfavorable outcome, and we would expect the reward to be negative. In other words, the reward is a numerical value indicating the goodness of the action taken by the agent based on the objective/goal it is trying to achieve. The reward is the primary way for the agent to assess if the action was good or bad and use this information to adjust its behavior, i.e., optimizing the policy that it is learning.

Rewards are an intrinsic property of the environment. The reward obtained is a function of the current state the agent is in and the action it takes while in that state. Rewards and the policy being followed by the agent define the *value functions*.

- *Value* in a state is the total cumulative reward an agent is expected to get based on the state it is in and policy it is following.

- *Rewards* are immediate feedback from the environment based on the state and action taken in that state. Unlike value, rewards do not change based on an agent's actions. Taking a specific action in a specific state will always produce the same reward.

Value functions are like long-term rewards that are influenced not only by the environment but also by the policy the agent is following. Value exists because of the rewards. The agent accumulates rewards as it follows a policy and uses these cumulative rewards to assess the value in a state. It then makes changes to its policy to increase the value of the state.

We can connect this idea to the *exploration-exploitation dilemma* we talked about earlier. There may be certain states in which an optimal action may bring an immediate negative reward. However, such an action may still be optimal as it may put the agent in a new state from which it can get to its goal a lot faster. An example would be crossing over a hump or taking a detour to have a shorter path to the goal.

Unless the agent explores enough, it may not uncover these shorter paths and may end up settling for a less than optimal path. However, having discovered the shorter path, it has no way of knowing if it still needs more exploration to find yet another quicker path to a goal or it is better to just exploit its prior knowledge to race toward the goal.

The initial five chapters of the book focus on algorithms that use the previously described value functions to find optimal behavior/policy.

The last component is model of the environment. In some approaches of finding optimal behavior, agents use the interactions with the environment to form an internal model of the environment. Such an internal model helps the agent to plan, i.e., consider one or more chain of actions to assess the best sequence of actions. This method is called *model-based* learning. At the same time, there are other methods that are completely based on trial and error. Such methods do not form any model of the environment. Hence, these are called *model-free* methods. The majority of the agents use a combination of model-based and model-free methods for finding the optimal policy.

Deep Learning with Reinforcement Learning

In recent years, a sub-branch of machine learning involving models based on neural networks has exploded. With the advent of powerful computers, abundance of data, and new algorithms, it is now possible to train models to generalize based on raw inputs like images, text, and voice similar to way humans operate. The need of domain-specific handcrafted features to train the models is getting replaced with powerful neural-network-based models under the sub-branch of deep learning.

In 2014, DeepMind successfully combined deep learning techniques with reinforcement learning to learn from the raw data collected from an environment without any domain-specific processing of the raw input. Its first success was converting the conventional Q-learning algorithm under reinforcement learning to a deep Q-learning approach that was named Deep Q Networks (DQN). Q-learning involves an agent following some policy to gather experiences of its actions in the form of a tuple of the current state, the action it took, the reward it got, and the next state it found itself in. The agent then uses these experiences with Bellman equations in an iterative loop to find an optimal policy so that the value function (as explained earlier) of each state increases.

Earlier attempts to combine deep learning with reinforcement learning had not been successful due to the unstable performance of the combined approach. DeepMind made some interesting and smart changes to overcome instability issues. It first applied the combined approach of traditional reinforcement learning and deep learning for developing game-playing agents for Atari games. The agent would get the snapshot of the game and have no prior knowledge of the rules of the game. The agent would use this raw visual data to learn to play games such as Atari video games. In many cases, it achieved human-level performance. The company subsequently extended the approach to develop agents that could defeat champion human players in a game like Go. The use of deep learning with reinforcement learning has given rise to robots that act a lot more intelligently without the need to handcraft domain-specific knowledge. It is an exciting and fast-growing field. We will visit this in Chapter 5. Most of the algorithms that we study from Chapter 6 onward will involve a combination of deep learning with reinforcement learning.

Examples and Case Studies

To motivate you, we will look at various uses of reinforcement learning and how it is helping solve some real-world problems today.

Autonomous Vehicles

First, we look at the field of autonomous vehicles (AVs). AVs have sensors like LiDAR, radar, cameras, etc., that sense their nearby environment. These sensors are then used to carry out object detection, lane detection, etc. The raw sensory data and object detection are combined to get a unified scene representation that is used for planning a path to a destination. The planned path is next used to feed inputs to the controls to make the system/agent follow that path. The motion planning is the part in which trajectories are planned.

A concept like inverse reinforcement learning in which we observe an expert and learn the implied objective/reward based on the expert's interaction can be used to optimize cost functions to come up with smooth trajectories. Actions such as overtaking, lane changing, and automated parking also leverage various parts of reinforcement learning to build intelligence into the behavior. The alternative would be to handcraft various rules, and that can never be exhaustive or flexible.

Robots

Using computer vision and natural language processing or speech recognition using deep learning techniques has added human-like perceptions to autonomous robots. Further, combined deep learning and reinforcement learning methods have resulted in teaching robots to learn human-like gaits to walk, pick up and manipulate objects, or observe human behavior through cameras and learn to perform like humans.

Recommendation Systems

Today we see recommender systems everywhere. Video sharing/hosting applications YouTube, TikTok, and Facebook suggest to us the videos that we would like to watch based on our viewing history. When we visit any e-commerce site, based on the current product we are viewing and our past purchase patterns or based on the way other users have acted, we are presented with other similar product recommendations.

All such recommender engines are increasingly driven by reinforcement learning–based systems. These systems continually learn from the way users respond to the suggestions presented by the engine. A user acting on the recommendation reinforces these actions as good actions given the context.

Finance and Trading

Because of its sequential action optimization focus wherein past states and actions influence the future outcomes, reinforcement learning finds significant use in time-series analysis, especially in the field of finance and stock trading. Many automated trading strategies use a reinforcement learning approach to continually improve and fine-tune the trading algorithms based on the feedback from past actions. Banks and financial institutions use chatbots that interact with the users to provide effective, low-cost user support and engagement. These bots again use reinforcement learning to fine-tune its behavior. Portfolio risk optimization and credit scoring systems have also benefitted from RL-based approaches.

Healthcare

Reinforcement learning finds significant use in healthcare, be it generating predictive signals and enabling medical intervention at early stages or be it robot-assisted surgeries or managing the medical and patient data. It is also used to refine the interpretation of imaging data, which is dynamic in nature. RL-based systems provide recommendations learned from its experiences and continually evolve.

Game Playing

Finally, we cannot stress enough the way RL-based agents are able to beat human players in many board games. While it may seem wasteful to design agents that can play games, there is a reason for that. Games offer a simpler idealized world, making it easier to design, train, and compare approaches. Approaches learned under such idealized environment/setup can be subsequently enhanced to make agents perform well in real-world situations. Games provide a well-controlled environment to research deeper into the field.

As we said before, deep reinforcement learning is a fascinating and rapidly evolving field, and we hope to provide you with a solid foundation to get started in your journey to master this field.

Libraries and Environment Setup

All the code examples in this book are in Python with PyTorch, TensorFlow, and OpenAI Gym libraries. While there are many ways to set up the environment, we will use the conda environment. These are the steps to get a complete environment:

1. Visit `https://docs.conda.io/en/latest/miniconda.html` and choose the Miniconda install for your platform to install Miniconda. Please choose the latest Python3.x version. If you already have Anaconda or Miniconda installed, you can skip this step.

2. We will create a new environment to run the code accompanying this book. Open a command terminal and type the following:

    ```
    conda create -n apress python=3.8
    ```

    where `apress` is the name of the environment and we are using Python 3.8.x. Answer yes to all the prompts.

3. Switch to the new environment you created using the following:

    ```
    conda activate apress
    ```

Make sure that all the commands that we ask you to run in upcoming steps are carried out in the same terminal where you have activated the new conda environment.

4. Install TensorFlow 2.x. You can refer to https://www.tensorflow.org/install for further details, or you can run the following command in the conda shell:

```
pip install tensorflow
```

Follow the prompts and answer appropriately (mostly as yes).

5. We will now install PyTorch. Visit https://pytorch.org/get-started/locally/ and choose the environment setup you have. You do not need a GPU-enabled machine. Most of the examples in this book will run fine on a CPU except one example in Chapter 6 where we train an agent to play an Atari game. Even with a GPU, training an Atari game-playing agent may take a long time.

At the time of writing this book, we chose the following combination on the previous page:

```
PyTorch build: Stable (1.7.0)
Your OS: Windows or Mac
Package: Conda
Language: Python
CUDA: None
```

With these choices, the command generated was as follows:

```
conda install pytorch torchvision torchaudio cpuonly -c
pytorch
```

Copy and paste the generated command from the web page into your conda terminal where you have apress as the current active conda environment (step 3).

Make sure that you generate the command for your local machine using the link https://pytorch.org/get-started/locally/ and making the appropriate choices.

6. Next, we will install a Jupyter notebook. At the previous terminal, run the following in the terminal:

```
conda install -c conda-forge jupyter notebook
```

Please note that we are using a classic Jupyter notebook. However, if you prefer you can install a JupyterLab interface instead, you can find more details at `https://jupyter.org/install`.

7. We will now install the OpenAI Gym library, which contains various reinforcement learning environments that we will use to train the agents on. Please type the following on the command line:

```
pip install gym
```

You can refer to `https://gym.openai.com/docs/#installation` for further details.

8. Next in the line is `matplotlib`, which has routines to plot graphs. Please run the following command in the previous terminal. Please note that all commands have to be run in the command shell where `apress` is the current active `conda` environment.

```
conda install -c conda-forge matplotlib
```

You can read more about `matplotlib` at `https://matplotlib.org/`.

9. Let's also install another plotting library named `seaborn`. It is built on top of `matplotlib` and helps install nicely formatted graphic routines. Run the following command in the terminal:

```
conda install -c anaconda seaborn
```

You can read more about Seaborn at `https://seaborn.pydata.org/index.html`.

10. We will install a small library to provide progress bars for training. Run the following at the terminal:

```
conda install -c conda-forge tqdm
```

11. Let's install a few additional dependencies for OpenAI Gym. We
     will install Atari-related dependencies so that Atari games can
     be trained through OpenAI Gym interfaces. We will also install
     Box2D to allow the continuous control dependencies that we will
     use in Chapter 8. Finally, we will install pygame, which allows us to
     play Atari games and interact with it using a keyboard. Please use
     the following commands in the terminal:

```
pip install gym[atari]
```

On a Mac you may need to run pip install 'gym[atari]'. Please
make note of the single quotes.

Next run the following two commands at the terminal:

```
conda install -c conda-forge pybox2d
```

```
pip install pygame
```

If you are on Windows, you may need to reinstall the Atari simulator.
The direct install from pip install gym[atari] does not seem
to work with Windows and gives a dll not found error. However,
please do not skip running pip install gym[atari]. It is required to
install a few other dependencies to run the Atari simulator. Run the
following two commands to fix this problem and run it *only* after you
have executed pip install gym[atari]:

```
pip unistall atari-py
```

```
pip install -f https://github.com/Kojoley/atari-py/
releases atari_py
```

12. Finally, we install stable-baselines3, which has delivered
     implementations of many popular RL algorithms. To install it, run
     the following command in the terminal:

```
pip install stable-baselines3
```

You can read more about this library at https://github.com/DLR-
RM/stable-baselines3.

13. Now you download and unzip the code file accompanying this book. Open a terminal and navigate inside that unzipped folder. Switch to the previously installed conda environment using the following:

conda activate apress

Next start the Jupyter notebook with the following command at the terminal:

jypyter notebook

At this point, you will see your default browser open, and you are all set to navigate to the respective chapters (Figure 1-2).

Figure 1-2. *You can open the notebooks to run and play around with the code.*

Figure 1-3 shows one of the notebooks from Chapter 2 opened.

Figure 1-3. *Sample notebook open*

Alternate Way to Install Local Environment

Once you unzip the code folder, you will see a folder named environments. It contains two YML environment files. One is for Windows and is named environment_win.yml, and the other is for macOS and is named environment_mac.yml. You can use these files to replicate the environment on your machine locally. Navigate to this folder and run the following.

On Windows:

```
conda env create -f environment_win.yml
```

On macOS:

```
conda env create -f environment_mac.yml
```

Using this approach will take care of the previous steps 2 to 12.

Summary

In this chapter, we started by introducing the field of reinforcement learning and the history of how it has evolved from a rigid rule-based decision-making system to a flexible optimal behavior learning system, learning on its own from prior experiences.

We talked about the three sub-branches of machine learning, i.e., supervised learning, unsupervised learning, and reinforcement learning. We compared the three approaches to elaborate on the problem context for which each of these makes sense. We also talked about the subcomponents and terms that comprise a reinforcement setup. These are agent, behavior, state, action, policy, reward, and environment. We used the example of a car and a robot to show how these subcomponents interact and what each of these terms means.

We talked about the concept of reward and value functions. We discussed that rewards are short-term feedback and that value functions are long-term feedback of the agent's behavior. Finally, we introduced model-based and model-free learning approaches. Next, we talked about the influence of deep learning in the field of reinforcement learning and how DQN started the trend of combining deep learning with reinforcement learning. We also discussed how the combined approach has resulted in scalable learning including from unstructured inputs such as images, text, and voice.

We moved on to talk about the various use cases of reinforcement learning citing examples from the fields of autonomous vehicles, intelligent robots, recommender systems, finance and trading, healthcare, and video/board games. Finally, we walked through the steps required to set up a Python environment and be able to run the code examples accompanying this book.

## CHAPTER 2

Markov Decision Processes

As discussed in Chapter 1, reinforcement learning involves sequential decision-making. In this chapter, we will formalize the notion of using stochastic processes under the branch of probability that models sequential decision-making behavior. While most of the problems we study in reinforcement learning are modeled as *Markov decision processes* (MDP), we start by first introducing Markov chains (MC) followed by Markov reward processes (MRP). We finish up by discussing MDP in-depth while covering model setup and the assumptions behind MDP.

We then discuss related concepts such as value functions of state and action value functions of state-action pairs. Finally, we conclude the chapter with a detailed discussion of the various forms of Bellman equations like Bellman expectation equations and Bellman optimality equations as well a quick introduction to various types of learning algorithms.

While the chapter's focus will be theoretical foundations of reinforcement learning, we will have examples and exercises to help cement the concepts. There is no better way to learn than to code yourself, which is a recurring theme of this book.

Definition of Reinforcement Learning

In the previous chapter we talked about the cycle of an agent interacting with the environment by taking an action based on its current state, getting a numerical reward, and finding itself in a new state.

Figure 2-1 illustrates this concept.

© Nimish Sanghi 2021
N. Sanghi, *Deep Reinforcement Learning with Python*, https://doi.org/10.1007/978-1-4842-6809-4_2

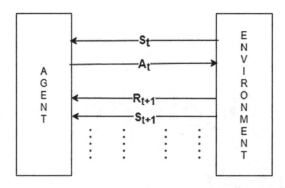

Figure 2-1. *The cycle of agent environment interaction*

The agent at time t is in a state S_t. From the set of actions the agent can take in this state, it takes a specific action A_t. At this point, the system transitions to the next time period (t+1). The environment responds to the agent with a numerical reward R_{t+1} as well as puts the agent in a new state of S_{t+1}. The cycle of "state to action to reward and next state" goes on until the time agent reaches some end-goal state like the end of a game, the completion of a task, or the end of a specified number of time steps.

Agent acts   Environment reacts

S_t --------> A_t --------> R_{t+1}, S_{t+1}

Current state   Action taken   reward and new state

$S_0, A_0, R_1, S_1, A_1, R_2, S_2, A_2, R_3, S_3, A_3, R_4, S_4$............

There is a cycle of state, action, reward, and state (S, A, R, S).

The agent takes an action based on the state it finds itself in; i.e., the agent "acts" by taking an action. The environment "reacts" to the agent's action by rewarding the agent with some numeric reward and also transitioning the agent into a new state. The agent's objective is to take a sequence of actions that maximize the sum total of rewards it gets from the environment.

The purpose of reinforcement learning is to have the agent learn the best possible action for each of the states it could find itself in, keeping in mind the cumulative reward maximization objective.

As an example, consider the game of chess. The position of a piece on the board could form the current state $(\mathbf{S_t})$. The agent (player) takes an action $(\mathbf{A_t})$ by moving a chess piece. The agent gets a reward $(\mathbf{R_{t+1}})$, let's say 0 for a safe move and -1 for a move leading to checkmate. The game also moves to a new state, $(\mathbf{S_{t+1}})$.

At times, in literature, states are also referred as *observations* to distinguish between the fact that in some situations the agent may get to see only partial details of the actual state. This partially observable state is known as *observation*. The agent has to use the full or partial state information to make decisions with respect to the action it should take. It is an important aspect in real-life implementations to understand what will be observed by the agent and how detailed it will be. The choice and theoretical guarantee of the learning algorithm can be significantly influenced by the level of partial observability. We will initially focus on situations where state and observations are the same; in other words, the agent knows every possible detail of the current state. But starting in Chapter 5, we will start looking at situations where the state is either not fully known or even if fully known needs to be summarized using some kind of approximation.

Let's now go through a couple of examples to understand in depth the cycle of state/observation to action to reward to next state. Throughout the book, we will be using a Python library by OpenAI called Gym, which implements some common simple environments. Let's look at the first environment: MountainCar. Start your Jupyter notebook and navigate to listing_2_1.ipynb.

In the MountainCar environment, there is a hill that the car is trying to climb with the the end goal of reaching the flag on the top-right side of hill. The car is not powerful enough, so the car needs to swing to the left and then accelerate to the right to reach the goal. This back and forth swing needs to happen multiple times so that the car can gain enough momentum and reach the flag at the top of the right valley. See Figure 2-2.

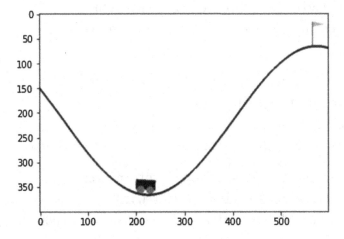

Figure 2-2. *MountainCar-v0 environment. This enviroment has a two-dimensional state and a set of three discrete actions*

Listing 2-1 shows the code to test the `MountainCar` environment.

Listing 2-1. MountainCar Environment

```
import gym
env = gym.make('MountainCar-v0')

# reset environment and get initial observation/state
# Observation/state is a tuple of (position, velocity)
obs = env.reset()
print("initial observation:", obs)

# possible 3 actions
# {0: "accelerate to left", "1": "do nothing", "2": "accelerate to right"}
print("possible actions:", env.action_space.n)

# reinforcement learning is all
# about learing to take good actions
# from a given state/observation
# right now taking a random action
def policy(observation):
    return env.action_space.sample()

# take 5 random actions/steps
for _ in range(5):

    # to render environment for visual inspection
    # when you train, you can skip rendering to speed up
    env.render()

    # based on curret policy, use the current observation
    # to find the best action to take.
    action = policy(obs)
    print("\ntaking action:", action)

    # pass the action to env which will return back
    # with new state/"observation" and "reward"
    # there is a "done" flag which is true when game ends
```

```
    # "info" provides some diagnostic information
    obs, reward, done, info = env.step(action)
    print("got reward: {0}. New state/observation is: {1}".format(reward, obs))
# close the enviroment
env.close()
```

Let's walk through the code line by line. We first import the OpenAI gym library with import gym. OpenAI Gym has multiple environments implemented for reinforcement learning. We will be using some of these environments as we go through the chapters of this book.

Moving on, we instantiate the MountainCar environment with env = gym. make('MountainCar-v0'). This is followed by initializing the environment through obs = env.reset(), which returns the initial observation. In the case of MountainCar, the observation is a tuple of two values: (x-position, x-velocity). The agent uses observation to find the best action: action = policy(obs).

In Listing 2-1, the agent is taking random actions. However, as we progress through the book, we will learn different algorithms that would be used to find reward-maximizing policies. For the MountainCar environment, there are three possible actions: accelerate left, do nothing, and accelerate right. The agent passes the action to the environment. At this point, the system conceptually takes a time step moving from time t to time t+1.

The environment executes the action and returns a tuple of four values: new observation at time (t+1), reward (r_{t+1}), done flag, and some debug info. These values are stored locally with obs, reward, done, info = env.step(action).

Next, the agent uses the new observation to again take a next step getting back a new tuple of four values, i.e., next state, reward, done flag, and debug info. This cycle of "state to action to reward to new state" goes on until the game ends or until it is terminated in the code. In this setup, the agent gets a reward of -1 at each time step, with a reward of 0 when the game ends. Accordingly, the agent's objective is to reach the flag in the shortest possible number of steps.

Let's look at yet another environment. Replace the line env = gym. make('MountainCar-v0') with env = gym.make('CartPole-v1') and again run the code in Listing 2-1. See Figure 2-3.

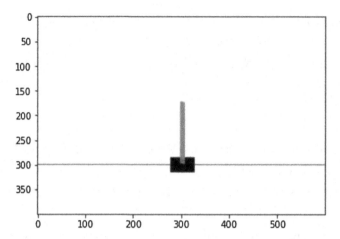

Figure 2-3. *CartPole-v1 environment. This objective is to balance the pole upright for the longest possible time*

The CartPole environment has an observation space consisting of four values. The cart's position on the x-axis and velocity along the x-axis are the first two values. The tilt angle of the pole is the third value in the observation tuple that has to be between -24° to 24°. The fourth value in the observation tuple is the angular velocity of the pole.

Possible actions are 0 and 1, which push the cart to the left or right, respectively. The agent keeps getting the reward of 1 at each time step, thereby incentivizing the agent to balance the pole for the longest possible duration and earn as many points as possible. The game ends if the pole tilts more than 12° on either side or if the cart moves more than 2.4 on either side, i.e., the cart reaches either ends or if 200 steps have been taken.

You may have noticed that the code setup is the same in both cases. We just changed one code line to instantiate different environments. The rest of the code to step through the environment and receive feedback remains the same. The abstraction provided by the OpenAI Gym library makes it easier for us to test a particular algorithm across many environments. Further, we can also create our own custom environment based on the problem at hand.

This section covered a brief definition of reinforcement learning and the basics of OpenAI Gym environment that we will be using. In the upcoming sections, we will go over the different components of the reinforcement learning (RL) setup in detail.

Agent and Environment

The setup of the agent and environment is a flexible one. The agent is a closed system that gets the state/observation details from outside the system. It uses a given policy or learns a policy to maximize some goal that has been provided to it. It also gets the reward from the environment based on the current observation/state and the action the agent takes. The agent has no control on what those rewards will be. The agent also does not control the transition from state to state. The transition depends on the environment, and the agent can only influence the outcome indirectly by deciding which action to take in a given state it finds itself in.

On the other hand, the environment is everything that is outside the agent. In other words, it could be the rest of whole world. However, the environment is usually defined in a much narrow way: to comprise information that could influence the reward. The environment receives the action the agent wants to take. It provides feedback to the agent in the form of reward as well as a transition to a new state based on the action the agent took. Next, the environment provides part of the revised state information to the agent that becomes the agent's new observation/state.

The boundary between the agent and the environment is an abstract one. It is defined based on the task at hand and the goal we are trying to achieve in a particular case. Let's look at some examples.

Consider the case of an autonomous car. The agent state could be the visuals from multiple cameras, light detection and ranging (LiDAR), and the other sensor readings as well as geocoordinates. While the "environment" is everything outside the agent, i.e., the whole world, the agent's relevant state/observation is only those parts of the world that are relevant for the agent to take an action. The position and actions of a pedestrian two blocks away may not be relevant for an autonomous car to make decisions and hence do not need to be part of the observation/state of the agent. The action space of an autonomous car could be defined in terms of gas-pedal value, breaks, and steering controls. The actions taken by the vehicle result in transitioning the car into a new observation state. This cycle goes on. The agent (i.e., autonomous car) is expected to take actions that maximize the reward based on a specific goal, e.g., going from Point A to Point B.

Let's consider another example of a robot trying to solve a Rubik's Cube. The observation/state in this case would the configuration of the Rubik Cube's six faces, and the actions would be the manipulations that can be performed on the Rubik's Cube.

The reward could be -1 for each time step and 0 at the end of a successful solution, i.e., on termination. Such a reward setup will incentivize the agent to find the least number of manipulations to solve the puzzle.

In our setup where we will be using the OpenAI Gym environment, observations will always be a tuple of various values with the exact composition dependent on the specific Gym environment. Actions will be dependent on the specific environment. Rewards will be provided by the environment with the exact real number numerical value dependent on the specific Gym environment. The agent in this case will be the software program that we write. The agent's (software program) main job will be to receive the observation from the OpenAI Gym environment, take an action, and wait for the environment to provide feedback in terms of reward and next state.

While we talk of discrete steps, i.e., the agent in state (S_t) taking action (A_t) and, in the next time step, receiving reward (R_{t+1}) and the next state (St+1), many times the nature of the real-life problem would be continuous one. In such cases, we could conceptually divide the time into small discrete time steps, thereby modeling the problem back into the discrete time-step environment and solving using the familiar setup as shown earlier.

At the most general level, when the agent finds itself in state S, it can take one of the many possible actions with some probability distribution over the space of actions. Such policies are known as *stochastic policies*. Further, in some cases the agent may take only one specific action for a given state every time the agent finds itself in that state. Such policies are known as *deterministic policies*. A policy is defined as follows:

$$\pi = p(a|s) \tag{2.1}$$

i.e., the probability of taking an action a when the agent is in state s.

Similarly, at a most general level, the reward received and the next state of the agent would be a probability distribution over the possible values of rewards and next states. This is known as *transition dynamics*.

$$p(s',r) = Pr\{S_t = s', R_t = r \mid S_{t-1} = s, A_{t-1} = a\} \tag{2.2}$$

where S_t and S_{t-1} belong to all possible states. A_t belongs to all possible actions, and reward r is a numerical value. The previous equation defines the probability of the next state being s' and the reward being r when the last state was s and agent took an action a.

Rewards

In reinforcement learning, a reward is a signal from the environment to the agent to let the agent know how good or bad the action was. The agent uses this feedback to fine-tune its knowledge and learn to take good actions that maximize the rewards. It gives rise to some important questions, such as what do you maximize, the immediate reward for the last action or the reward over the complete life history? What happens when the agent does not know enough about the environment? How much should it explore the environment by taking some random steps before it starts? This dilemma is known as the *exploration versus exploitation dilemma*. We will keep coming back to this point as we go through various algorithms. The objective of the agent to maximize the cumulative total rewards is known as the *reward hypothesis*.

To reiterate, a reward is a signal, or a single numerical value that the environment sends back to the agent to inform the agent of the quality of the action. Please note that observations could be multidimensional like two-dimensional for `MountainCar` and four-dimensional for `CartPole`. Similarly, actions can be multidimensional, e.g., acceleration value and steering angle for the autonomous car scenario. However, in each such case, the reward is always a scalar real number. It may seem limiting to have only a single value, but it is not. At the end, the agent is trained for the purpose of reaching a goal, and rewards codify that progress.

Let's look at a maze example where the agent is trying to find its way out. We could formulate the reward as the agent getting a reward of -1 at each time step and a reward of 0 at the end of episode. Such a reward setup incentivizes the agent to come out of maze with the least possible number of steps and minimize the sum total of a negative one (-1). An alternate reward setup could be an agent getting a reward of 0 in all time steps and a reward of 1 at the end of episode when the agent is out of the maze. What do you think will happen to the agent's behavior in the later setup? The agent has a reason to get out of the maze to collect a reward of +1, but it is in no hurry. It will get the same +1 whether it comes out after 5 steps or after 500 steps. How do we modify the situation to push the agent to not focus just on reward collection but to do so in the fastest possible time?

This question leads naturally to the concept of *discounting*. What carries more utility? A reward "x" after five timesteps or the same reward "x" after 500 timesteps? Of course, the earlier the better, and hence a reward of +1 after 5 steps is more valuable as compared to +1 reward after 500 steps. We induce this behavior by discounting the rewards from the future to present. A reward of "R" from the next time step is discounted to the current time by a discount factor "γ" (gamma). The discount factor is a value between 0 and 1. In the maze example, the reward with maze completion in five steps would mean a reward of γ^5. (+1) versus a reward of γ^{500}. (+1) for 500 steps to complete. The "return" at time "t" is defined as follows:

$$G_t = R_{t+1} + \gamma R_{t+2} + \gamma^2 R_{t+3} + \ldots\ldots + \gamma^{T-t+1} R_T \tag{2.3}$$

The discount factor is similar to what we see in the financial world. It is the same concept as the money now being more valuable than money later.

The discount factor also serves an important mathematical purpose of making sure that total return G_t is bounded for continuing tasks. Consider a scenario of a continuing task where each state gives some positive reward. As it is a continuing task that has no logical end, the total reward will keep adding and explode to infinity. However, with a discounting factor, the total cumulative reward will get capped. Therefore, discounting is always introduced in continuing tasks and is optional in episodic tasks.

It is interesting to note the effect of the discounting factor on the horizon over which the agent tries to maximize the cumulative reward. Consider a discount factor of 0. If you use this discount value in (2.3), you will see that cumulative reward is equal to just the reward at the next instant reward. This in turn would lead the agent to become short-sighted and greedy with respect to the next time step reward only. Next, consider the other extreme with a discount factor approaching a value of 1. In this case, the agent will become more and more far-sighted since, using a discount factor of 1, we can see that the cumulative reward as defined in (2.3) will give equal importance to all the future rewards. The whole sequence of actions from the current time step until the end becomes important and not just the immediate next timestep reward.

The previous discussion should emphasize the importance of designing an appropriate reward based on the behavior the agent needs to optimize. The reward is the signal that the agent uses to decide between a good or bad state and/or action. For example, in a game of chess, if you design the reward as the number of opponent pieces captured, the agent may learn to play dangerous moves just to maximize rewards from immediate actions instead of sacrificing one of its own pieces to get into a position of strength and a possible win in a future move. The field of reward design is an open area of research. Having said that, the examples in the book will use fairly simple and intuitive reward definitions.

The reward design is not an easy task, especially in the field of continuous control and robotics. Consider the task of a humanoid where the objective of training is, say, to make the agent learn to run for as long as possible. How will the agent know the way that arms and legs need to be moved in coordination to learn the task of running? Specific measures such as the distance of the center of gravity of the agent from the ground, the energy spent in making action, and the torso angle to the ground are combined with trial and error to make the agent learn a good policy. In the absence of a good reward signal shaping the behavior we want the agent to learn, it will take a long time for agent to learn. Even worse, the agent sometimes may learn counterintuitive behavior. A good example is that of OpenAI's agent to play the video game CoastRunners that had the objective of finishing the boat race quickly and ahead of other players. The game provided a score for hitting the targets in the way, and there is no explicit score for finishing the game. The agent learned a hilarious and destructive behavior of repeatedly hitting a set of targets and not progressing through the race but scoring 20 percent higher than human players. You can read more about it in the OpenAI blog[1] and see a video of the behavior in action. Rewards need to be designed with care to ensure that autonomous RL agents do not learn potentially dangerous behaviors.

In other cases, it is not at all clear how to model the reward function. Consider a robot trying to learn human-like behavior or, say, pouring water in a glass from a jug o without spilling water or breaking the glass tumbler due to excessive grip force. In such cases, an extension of reinforcement learning known as *inverse reinforcement learning* is used to learn the implicit reward function based on observations from watching a human expert perform the task. We will briefly talk about it in Chapter 10. However, a detailed study of reward shaping and discovery could take a book of its own.

So, in a nutshell, just like the quality of data is important for supervised learning, an appropriate reward function is important to make algorithms train the agent for a desired behavior.

Markov Processes

The field of reinforcement learning is based on the formalism of Markov processes. Before we dive deep into learning (behavior optimization) algorithms, we need to have a good grasp of this fundamental theoretical construct. In this section, we will go over Markov chains followed by Markov reward processes and lastly Markov decision processes.

---

[1]https://openai.com/blog/faulty-reward-functions/

Markov Chains

Let's first talk about what a Markov property is. Consider the diagram in Figure 2-4. We are trying to model the rain status of a city on a daily basis. It has two states; i.e., on any given day either it rains or it does not. The arrows from one state to another indicate the probability of being in one of the two states the next day based on the current state. For example, if it rains today, the chance of rain the next day is 0.3, and the chance it will not rain the next day is 0.7. Similarly, if there is no rain today, the chance it will continue to be dry tomorrow is 0.8, while there is a 0.2 chance that it will rain tomorrow.

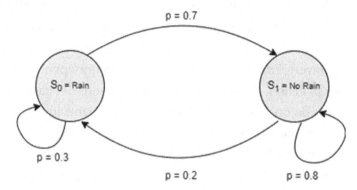

Figure 2-4. *A simple two-state Markov chain. One state is "rain," and second state is "no rain"*

In this model, we assume that rain on a given day depends on the state of the previous day; i.e., the chance of rain tomorrow is 0.3 if it also rained today, and the chance of rain tomorrow is 0.2 if it did not rain today. Whether it rained yesterday or before that has no impact on the probability of rain tomorrow. This is an important concept. It is known as *independence*; i.e., knowing the present (present state at time t) makes the future (future state at time t+1) independent of the past (all past states at time 0 , 1, ..., t-1). Mathematically, we can express this as follows:

$$P(S_{t+1} = s' | S_0, S_1, \ldots\ldots S_{t-1}, S_t = \mathrm{s}) = P(S_{t+} = s' | S_t = \mathrm{s}) \tag{2.4}$$

It simply means that the probability of being in a state at time t+1 depends only on the state at time t. The state at time (t+1) has no dependence on the states before time (t), i.e., no dependence on the states S_0 to S_{t-1}.

If the environment provides observations to the agent that is detailed enough, then the agent can know what is to be known from its current state and does not need to remember the chain of states/events it had to go through in the past to reach the present. This *Markov independence* is an important assumption that is required to prove the theoretical soundness of reinforcing learning algorithms. In practice, many times we still get fairly good results for non-Markov systems. However, it is important to remember that in the absence of the Markov property, the results cannot be evaluated for theoretical worst-case bounds.

Going back to the Markov chain diagram in Figure 2-3, we can define transition probability as the probability of moving to state S_{t+1} from state S_t in the prior time step. If a system has m states, the transition probabilities will be a square matrix with m rows and m columns. The transition probability matrix for Figure 2-3 will look like this:

$$P = \begin{bmatrix} 0.3 & 0.7 \\ 0.2 & 0.8 \end{bmatrix}$$

The sum of values in every row will be 1. The row values indicate the probability of going from one given state to all the states in the system. For example, row 1 indicates that the probability from s_1 to s_1 is 0.3 and from s_1 to s_2 is 0.7.

The previous Markov chain will have a steady state in which there is a defined probability of being in one of the two states on a given day. Let's say that the probability of being in state s_1 and s_2 is given by a vector $S = [s_1 \ s_2]^T$. From Figure 2-4 we can see that

$$s_1 = 0.3 \times s_1 + 0.2 \times s_2 \text{ (a)}$$
$$s_2 = 0.7 \times s_1 + 0.8 \times s_2 \text{ (b)}$$

We also know that

$$s_1 + s_2 = 1 \text{ (c)}$$

as the system must be in one of the two states at any point in time.

The equations in (a), (b), and (c) form a consistent and solvable system of equations. From (a), $0.7 \times s_1 = 0.2 \times s_2$. Or, $s_1 = (0.2/0.7) s_2$.

Substituting a value of s_1 from previously in (c), we get this:

$$0.2/0.7 \ s_2 + s_2 = 1$$

which gives $s_2 = 0.7/0.9 = 0.78$, which turn gives $s_1 = 0.2/0.9 = 0.22$.

In vector algebra notations, we can specify the relationship at steady state as follows:

$$S^T = S^T \cdot P \ \dots\dots(c)$$

This relationship can be used to solve for steady-state probability iteratively using. Listing 2-2 gives a code snippet for this.

Listing 2-2. Markov Chain Example and Its Solution by Iterative Method

```python
# import numpy library to do vector algebra
import numpy as np

# define transition matrix
P = np.array([[0.3, 0.7], [0.2, 0.8]])
print("Transition Matrix:\n", P)

# define any starting solution to state probabilities
# Here we assume equal probabilities for all the states
S = np.array([0.5, 0.5])

# run through 10 iterations to calculate steady state
# transition probabilities
for i in range(10):
    S = np.dot(S, P)
    print("\nIter {0}. Probability vector S = {1}".format(i, S))

print("\nFinal Vector S={0}".format(S))
```

When we run the program in listing_2_2.ipynb, the output produced is given below, which matches with the values we got from solving equations (a), (b), and (c) together:

```
Final Vector S=[0.22222222 0.77777778]
```

The formulation in Figure 2-3 has no start and end state. This is an example of a *continuing task*. There is another class of formulation that has one or more end states. Let's look at Figure 2-4. This is known as an *episodic task* in which the agent starts in some state and goes through many transitions to eventually reach an end state. There could one or more end states with different outcomes. In Figure 2-5, the end state is the successful completion of an exam resulting in a certificate. In a game of chess there could be three end states: win, loss, or draw.

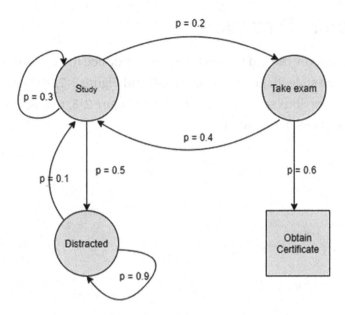

Figure 2-5. *An example of an episodic Markov chain with one end state depicted by way of a square box*

Like the continuing formulation, there is a concept of a transition probability matrix. For Figure 2-4 it will look like this:

s_1 = "Study"; s_2="Distracted"; s_3="Take exam"; s_4="Certificate"

$$P = \begin{bmatrix} 0.3 & 0.5 & 0.2 & 0 \\ 0.1 & 0.9 & 0 & 0 \\ 0.4 & 0 & 0 & 0.6 \\ 0 & 0 & 0 & 1 \end{bmatrix}$$

In the case of the episodic task as shown earlier, we can look at multiple runs with each run called an *episode.* Let the start state always be s_1. Examples of multiple episodes could look like. In the previous example, we have only one end state, and hence episodes will always end in s_4 as shown below:

$$s_1, s_2, s_2, s_1, s_3, s_4$$
$$s_1, s_2, s_2, s_1, s_3, s_1, s_2, s_3, s_4$$
$$s_1, s_2, s_2, s_2, s_2, s_2, s_2, s_2, s_2, s_2, s_2, s_2, s_2, s_2, s_2, s_1, s_3, s_4$$

In episodic tasks, we do not have a concept of steady state. Eventually the system will transition to one of the end states no matter what the order of transition that takes place.

Markov Reward Processes

Moving on to the Markov reward process, we now introduce the concept of rewards. Look at the modified state diagrams in Figure 2-6 and Figure 2-7. They are the same problems as in the previous section (Figure 2-4 and Figure 2-5, respectively) with the addition of rewards at each transition.

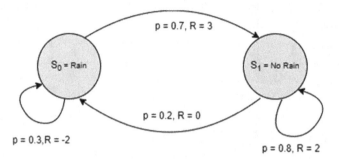

Figure 2-6. *Continuing Markov reward process. This is similar to the Markov chain in Figure 2-4 with an addition of reward R for each transition arrow*

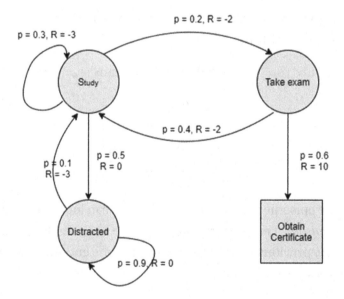

Figure 2-7. *The episodic Markov reward process similar to Figure 2-5 with additional rewards R for each transition*

In the previous two MRP setups, we can compute transition probabilities similar to that in MC as before. In addition, we can calculate the value of a state v(s), which is the cumulative reward that the agent gets when it is in state S=s at time t and it follows the dynamics of the system.

$$v(s) = E[G_t \mid S_t = s] \tag{2.5}$$

where G_t is defined in (2.3).

$$G_t = R_{t+1} + \gamma R_{t+2} + \gamma^2 R_{t+3} + \dots$$

The notation $E[G_t \mid S_t = s]$ is read as an expectation of return G_t when the starting state at time t is $S_t = s$. The word *expectation* means the average value of G_t when the simulation is performed a large number of times. The expectation operator ($E[\bullet]$) is used to derive formulae and to prove theoretical results. However, in practice, it is replaced by averages over many sample simulations and is also known as *Monte Carlo simulation*.

We also notice the use of γ as the discount factor. As explained earlier, γ captures the notion that the reward today is better than the reward tomorrow. It is also important mathematically to avoid unbounded returns for continuing tasks. We will not go into the mathematical details here beyond mentioning this fact.

A value of $\gamma = 1$ implies that the agent is far-sighted, and it cares as much about future rewards as it does for immediate rewards. A value of $\gamma = 0$ implies that an agent is short-sighted and cares only about immediate reward in the next time step. You can check this concept by putting different values of γ in the equation $G_t = R_{t+1} + \gamma R_{t+2} + \gamma^2 R_{t+3} + \dots$.

To summarize, up to now we have introduced the concept of transition probability P, return G_t, and value of a state $v(s) = E[G_t \mid S_t = s]$.

Markov Decision Processes

Markov decision processes extend reward processes by bringing the additional concept of "action." In MRP, the agent had no control on the outcome. Everything was governed by the environment. However, under the MDP regime, the agent can choose actions based on the current state/observation. The agent can learn to take actions that maximize the cumulative reward, i.e., total return G_t.

Let's look at an extension of the episodic MRP from Figure 2-7. Looking at Figure 2-8, one can see that in state Learning, the agent can take one of the two actions, either to study more or to take exam. The agent chooses the two actions with an equal probability of 0.5. The action influences the probabilities of the next state and reward values. If the agent decides to study more, there is a 0.7 chance that the agent will get distracted and get busy with social media, and there is a 0.3 chance that the agent will continue to stay focused on learning. However, the decision of "take exam" leads to two outcomes. Either the agent fails with a probability of 0.4 going back to Learning with a reward of -2, or with a probability of 0.6, the agent successfully completes the exam, "obtaining certificate" and getting a reward of 10.

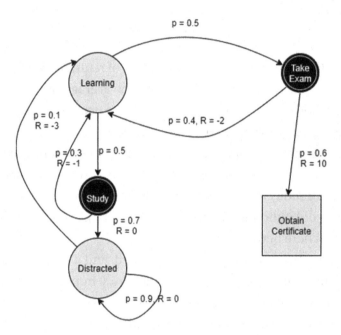

Figure 2-8. *Episodic Markov decision process as an extension of Markov reward process given in Figure 2-7. Black filled circles are the decisions that the agent can take*

The transition function is now a mapping from the current state and action to the next state and reward. It defines the probability of getting a reward **r** with a transition to the next state **s′** whenever the agent takes action **a** in state **s**.

$$p(s',r\,|\,s,a)=\Pr\{\,S_t=s',\,R_t=r\,|\,S_{t-1}=s,\,A_{t-1}=a\} \tag{2.6}$$

We can use (2.6) to derive many useful relations. Transition probability can be derived from the previous transition function. Transition probability defines the probability of the agent finding itself in state **s′** when it takes action **a** while in state **s**. It is defined as follows:

$$p(s'|s,a) = \Pr\{S_t = s'|S_{t-1} = s, A_{t-1} = a\} = \sum_{r \in R} p(s', r|s, a) \qquad (2.7)$$

(2.7) has been obtained by averaging over all the possible rewards that the agent could get while transitioning from **(s,a)** to **s′**.

Let's look at a different example of MDP, one that is a continuing task. Think of an electric van at the airport to ferry passengers from one terminal to another. The van has two states, "High charge" and "Low charge." In each state, the van can "stay idle," "charge by connecting to charging station," or "ferry passengers." If the van ferries passengers, it gets a reward of "b," but there is a chance that in a "low charge" state ferrying passengers may drain the battery completely and the van would need to be rescued, resulting in a reward of -10. Figure 2-9 shows the MDP.

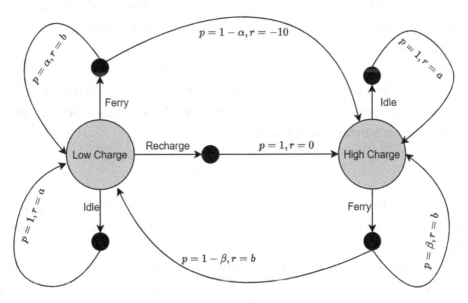

Figure 2-9. *Electric van: continuing Markov decision process with two states. Each state has three actions: idle, ferry, or recharge*

In the "Low" state, the van can take an action from the set of possible actions, {recharge, idle, ferry}. In the "High" state, the van can take an action from {idle, ferry}. All other transitions are zero. With p(s′, r | s, a) given as shown earlier, p(s′ | s, a) can be calculated. In this case, it is the same as p(s′, r | s, a). This is because for each transition from (s ,a) to (s′) there is only one fixed reward. In other words, there is no uncertainty or a probability distribution for rewards. The reward is the same fixed value every time the agent in state **s** takes an action **a** and finds itself in the next state **s′**. The previous setup is one of the most common ones encountered in practical problems. However, theoretically in most general cases, the reward could be a probability distribution like a "ferry" action reward being linked to the number of passengers ferried by the van.

We will continue to use this example in the following sections of this chapter.

Policies and Value Functions

As shown earlier, MDP has states, and the agent can take actions that transition the agent from the current state to the next state. In addition, the agent gets feedback from the environment in the form of a "reward." The dynamics of MDP are defined as $p(S_t = s'$, $R_t = r \mid S_{t-1} = s, A_{t-1} = a)$. We have also seen "cumulative return" G_t, which is the sum total of all rewards received from time t. The agent has no control on transition dynamics. It is outside the agent's control. However, the agent can control the decision, i.e., what action to take in which state.

This is exactly what the agent tries to learn based on the transition dynamics of the system. The agent does so with an objective to maximize the G_t for each state S_t that can be expected on average across multiple runs. The mapping of states to actions is known as *policy*. It is formally defined as follows:

$$\pi(A_t = a \mid S_t = s) \tag{2.8}$$

Policy is defined as the probability of taking action a at time t when the agent is in state s at time t. The agent tries to learn the mapping function from the state to actions to maximize the total return.

Policies can be of two types. See Figure 2-10. The first type of policies are stochastic policies in which $\pi(a \mid s)$ is a probability function. For a given state, there are multiple actions that the agent can take, and the probability of taking each such action is defined by $\pi(a \mid s)$. The second type is *deterministic policies* where there is only one unique action for a given state. In other words, the probability function $\pi(A_t = a \mid S_t = s)$ becomes a simple mapping function with the value of a function being 1 for some action $A_t = a$ and 0 for all other actions A_t.

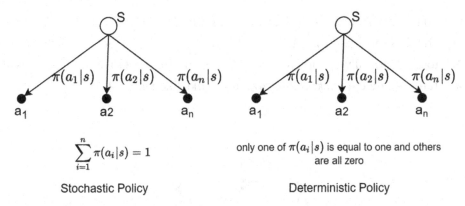

$$\sum_{i=1}^{n} \pi(a_i|s) = 1$$

only one of $\pi(a_i|s)$ is equal to one and others are all zero

Stochastic Policy   Deterministic Policy

Figure 2-10. *Types of policies. (a) Stochastic poliocy in which agent can take one of the many actions based on probability distribution. (b) Deterministic policy in which agent learns to take only one action that is most optimal*

The cumulative reward G_t (i.e., return) that the agent can get at time t while in state S_t is dependent on the state S_t, and the policy agent is the following. It is known as a *state value function*. The value of G_t is dependent on the trajectory of states that the agent will see after time t, which in turn depends on the policy the agent will follow. Hence, the value function is always defined in the context of the policy the agent is following. It is also referred to as the agent's *behavior*. It is formally defined as follows:

$$v_{\pi}(s) = E_{\pi}[G_t | S_t = s] \tag{2.9}$$

Let's try to break this down a little bit. $v_{\pi}(s)$ specifies the "state value" of state s when the agent is following a policy π. $E_{\pi}[\bullet]$ signifies that whatever comes inside the square bracket is an average taken over many samples. While it is mathematically known as the *expectation* of the expression inside the square brackets under policy π, in reality we usually calculate these values using simulation. We carry out the calculation over multiple iterations and then average the value. As per one of the fundamental law of statistics, averages converge to expectations under general conditions. This concept is significantly used in computing and goes under the name of Monte Carlo simulations. Coming to the final part, the expression inside the square brackets is $G_t | S_t = s$, i.e., the average return G_t over many runs that the agent can get at time t while in state s at time t under the agent's behavior of following policy π.

At this point, let's introduce the term *backup diagrams*. It shows the path from time t when the agent is in state S_t to its successor states that the agent can find itself in at time t+1. It depends on the action the agent takes at time t, i.e., $\pi(A_t = a|S_t = s)$. Further, it depends on the environment/model transition function $\Pr\{ S_{t+1} = s', R_{t+1} = r \mid S_t = s, A_t = a \}$, which takes the agent to state S_{t+1} with a reward of R_{t+1} based on state S_t and the action A_t it took. Pictorially, a one-step transition from the current state to the possible successor states is called a *backup diagram* and looks like Figure 2-11.

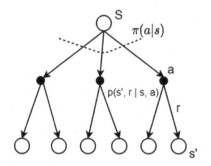

Figure 2-11. *Backup diagram starting from state, taking an action. Empty circles signify states, and dark circles signify actions*

We will make extensive use of backup diagrams especially when we talk about Bellman equations in the next section. Backup diagrams are helpful in conceptualizing and reasoning about the equations as well working out the proofs for various learning algorithms. They are also helpful in reasoning about data collection required to train agents.

Another related concept to value functions is the concept of action value functions. A value function is the expected cumulative reward the agent gets when it takes actions based on the policy π. However, suppose that the agent is free to take any action at this first-time step t with the condition that it must follow policy π on all the following time steps t+1 onward. The expected return that the agent gets at time t is now known as action value function $q_\pi(s, a)$. Formally it is defined as follows:

$$q_\pi(s,a) = E_\pi[G_t \mid S_t = s, A_t = a] \tag{2.10}$$

There is a simple and subtle relationship between v (state value) and q-values (state action value), which will be explored in detail in next section.

This pretty much completes the definition of various components of an MDP. In the next section, we explore the recursive relationship between v and q values of state/state action at time t to that of successor values at time t+1. Almost all the learning algorithms exploit this recursive relationship.

Bellman Equations

Let's look again at (2.9), which defines the value function. Let's look at the definition of G_t defined in (2.3); both are reproduced here:

$$G_t = R_{t+1} + \gamma R_{t+2} + \gamma^2 R_{t+3} + \dots + \gamma^{T-t+1} R_T \qquad (2.11)$$

$$v_\pi(s) = E_\pi[G_t \mid S_t = s] \qquad (2.12)$$

In other words, the value of a state is the expectation/average of the cumulative reward if an agent in that state s follows a policy π. The state that the agent finds itself in and the reward it gets from the environment are dependent on the policy it is following, i.e., the action it takes in a given state. There is a recursive relationship in which the expression for G_t can be written in terms of G_{t+1}.

$$G_t = R_{t+1} + \gamma \left[R_{t+2} + \gamma R_{t+3} + \gamma^2 R_{t+4} + \dots + \gamma^{T-t+1-1} R_T \right] \qquad (2.13)$$

Let's concentrate on the expression inside the square brackets.

$$R_{t+2} + \gamma R_{t+3} + \gamma^2 R_{t+4} + \dots + \gamma^{T-t+1-1} R_T$$

Next, we do a change of variable from t to t' where $t' = t + 1$. The previous expression can be rewritten as follows:

$$R_{t'+1} + \gamma R_{t'+2} + \gamma^2 R_{t'+3} + \dots + \gamma^{T-t'+1} R_T \qquad (2.14)$$

Comparing (2.14) to the expression of G_t as given in (2.11), we see that

$$R_{t'+1} + \gamma R_{t'+2} + \gamma^2 R_{t'+3} + \dots + \gamma^{T-t'+1} R_T = G_{t'} = G_{t+1} \qquad (2.15)$$

Next, we substitute (2.15) in (2.13), to get this:

$$G_t = R_{t+1} + \gamma G_{t+1} \qquad (2.16)$$

We can now substitute this recursive definition of G_t in the expression for $v_\pi(s)$ in (2.12) to get this:

$$v_\pi(s) = E_\pi[R_{t+1} + \gamma G_{t+1} \mid S_t = s] \qquad (2.17)$$

The expectation E_π is over all possible actions a that the agent can take in state $S_t = s$ as well as all over the new states the environment transitions the agent to defined by the transition function $p(s', r \mid s, a)$. The expanded form of expectation leads to the revised expression of $v_\pi(s)$ as follows:

$$v_\pi(s) = \sum_a \pi(a|s) \sum_{s', r} p(s', r|s, a)\left[r + \gamma\, v_\pi(s')\right] \tag{2.18}$$

The way to interpret this equation is that the state value for **s** is the average over all the rewards and state values for successor states **s'**. The averaging is done based on the policy $\pi(a|s)$ of taking an action **a** in state **s** followed by the environment transition probability $p(s', r|s, a)$ of the agent transitioning to **s'** with reward **r** based on the state-action pair (s, a). The equation in (2.18) shows the recursive nature of linking the state value of the current state (s) with the state values of the successor states (s').

A similar relationship exists for action value functions. Let's start from (2.10) and walk through the derivation of the recursive relationship between q-values.

$$q_\pi(s,a) = E_\pi\left[G_t \mid S_t = s, A_t = a\right]$$

$$= E_\pi\left[R_t + \gamma\, G_{t+1} \mid S_t = s, A_t = a\right]$$

Expanding the expectation with summing over all possibilities, we get this:

$$q_\pi(s, a) = \sum_{s', r} p(s', r|s, a)\left[r + \gamma\, v_\pi(s')\right] \tag{2.19}$$

Let's now look at the relationship of $v_\pi(s)$ and $q_\pi(s, a)$. They are related through the policy $\pi(s|a)$ the agent is following. The q-value is the value of the tuple (s, a), and the state value is the value for a state (s). The policy links the state to the possible set of actions through a probability distribution. Combing these results in the relationship, we get this:

$$v_\pi(s) = \sum_a \pi(a|s).q_\pi(s, a) \tag{2.20}$$

The previous relationship can also be inferred from equations (2.18) and (2.19) taken together, wherein we replace part of the right-side expression in (2.18) with $q_\pi(s, a)$ as per equation (2.19).

Just like equation (2.18) gives a recursive relationship of $v_\pi(s)$ in terms of the state values of the next state $v_\pi(s')$, we could also express $q_\pi(s, a)$ in (2.19) in terms of the pairs $q_\pi(s', a')$. This is achieved by replacing $v_\pi(s')$ in (2.1) with the expression in (2.20). This manipulation gives us a recursive relationship between q-values.

$$q_\pi(s, a) = \sum_{s', r} p(s', r|s, a)\left[r + \gamma \sum_{a'} \pi(a'|s') q_\pi(s', a') \right] \qquad (2.21)$$

The equations (2.18) and (2.21) that link the current state-values or q-values with successive values can be represented by way of backup diagrams. We now expand the back diagram in Figure 2-12 to cover both the previous cases. The diagram follows the standard convention: states **s** are shown as outlined circles, and action nodes representing **a** are shown as filled black circles.

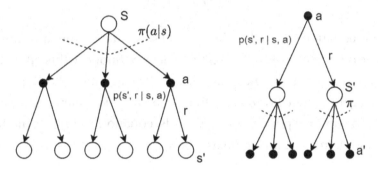

Figure 2-12. *Backup diagram for state values and action values. Outline circles represent states, and filled circles represent actions*

Equation (2.18) is the Bellman equation for $v_\pi(s)$, and equation (2.21) is the Bellman equation for $q_\pi(s, a)$. These equations formalize the recursive relationship in a sequential decision-making setup like reinforcement learning. All the algorithms in reinforcement learning are based on variations of these two equations with the purpose of maximizing the value functions under different assumptions and approximations. As we go through these algorithms, we will keep highlighting the parts of the equation being approximated under certain assumptions along with the pros and cons of individual approaches.

A large part of your expertise as a practitioner of reinforcement learning will revolve first around formulating a real-life problem into an RL setup and second choosing the right set of algorithms based on constraints and assumptions. Accordingly, the emphasis of this book will be on the conditions and assumptions required to make a technique work best, choosing using a specific technique makes sense, and the pros and cons of competing options available for a given problem. We will present mathematical equations to formalize the relationship, but the core focus will be to help you gain an intuitive sense of what is going on and when a given approach/algorithm makes sense.

Optimality Bellman Equations

Solving a reinforcement learning problem means finding (learning) a policy that maximizes the state value functions. Suppose you have a set of policies. The objective then would be to choose the policy that maximizes the state value $v_\pi(s)$. The optimal value function for a state is defined as $v_x(s)$. The relation for optimal state value can be stated as follows:

$$v_*(s) = max_\pi \, v_\pi(s) \tag{2.22}$$

The previous equation shows that the optimal state value is the maximum state value that can be obtained across all possible policies π. Suppose this optimal policy is denoted by a superscript (*) to the policy, i.e., π^*. If an agent is following the optimal policy, then the agent in state (s) will take that action a, which maximizes the q(s, a) obtained under the optimal policy. In other words, equation (2.20) gets modified from being an expectation to a maximization as follows:

$$v_*(s) = max_a \, q_{\pi^*}(s, a) \tag{2.23}$$

Further, similar to equations (2.18) and (2.22), the recursive form of optimal state and action value functions is given as follows:

$$v_*(s) = max_a \sum_{s',r} p(s', r \,|\, s, a) \big[r + \gamma \, v_*(s') \big] \tag{2.24}$$

$$q_*(s, a) = \sum_{s',r} p(s', r \,|\, s, a) \big[r + \gamma \, max_{a'} \, q_*(s', a') \big] \tag{2.25}$$

These optimal equations can be represented using backup diagrams as shown in Figure 2-13, highlighting the recursive relationship between the current and successor values.

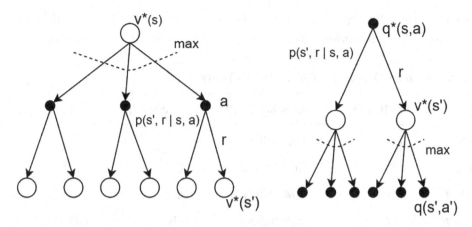

Figure 2-13. *Backup diagram for optimal state values and action values. Policy π is replaced by the "max" operation*

If you have all the **v*** values, then it is easy to find the optimal policy. We use a one-step backup diagram as shown in Figure 2-12 to find the **a*** that resulted in the optimal value **v***. It can be seen as a one-step search. Finding the optimal policy is even easier if we are given an optimal q*(s, a). In a state **s**, we just choose the action **a**, which has the highest value of **q**. This is evident from equation (2.23). Let's apply these concepts to the problem of the electric van introduced in Figure 2-9, which is reproduced in Figure 2-14.

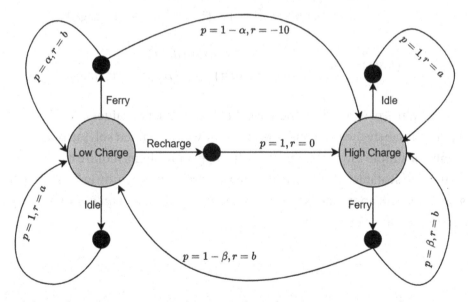

Figure 2-14. *Electric van: continuing Markov decision process with two states. Each state has three actions: idle, ferry, or recharge. Reproduction of Figure 2-9*

45

Let's draw the table depicting various values, as shown in Table 2-1. In this table we list all the *possible combinations of* (s, a, s', r) as well as probability $p(s', r \mid s, a)$.

Table 2-1. *System Dynamics for MDP in Figure 2-14*

State (s)	Action (a)	New State (s')	Reward (r)	P(s', r I s, a)
Low battery	Idle	Low battery	a	1.0
Low battery	Charge	High battery	0	1.0
Low battery	Ferry	Low battery	b	α
Low battery	Ferry	High battery	-10	1- α
High battery	Idle	High battery	a	1.0
High battery	Ferry	High battery	b	β
High battery	Ferry	Low battery	b	1-β

Let's use Table 2-1 to calculate the optimal state values using equation (2.24).

$$v_*(low) = max \begin{cases} a + \gamma \, v_*(low) \\ \gamma \, v_*(high) \\ \alpha \left[b + \gamma v_*(low) \right] + (1-\alpha).\left[-10 + \gamma \, v_*(high) \right] \end{cases}$$

$$v_*(high) = max \begin{cases} a + \gamma \, v_*(high) \\ \beta \left[b + \gamma \, v_*(high) \right] + (1-\beta).\left[b + \gamma \, v_*(low) \right] \end{cases}$$

For given values of a, b, α, β, γ, there will be a unique set of values of $v*(high)$ and $v*(low)$ that will satisfy the previous equations. However, explicit solving of equations is feasible only for simple toy problems. Real-life bigger problems require the use of other methods that are scalable. This is exactly what we are going to study in rest of the book: various methods and approaches to solve Bellman equations for an optimal policy that the agent should follow in a given context.

Types of Solution Approaches with a Mind-Map

With the background of reinforcement learning setup and Bellman equations, it is time to look at the landscape of algorithms in the reinforcement learning world. Figure 2-15 from OpenAI shows a high-level landscape of the various types of learning algorithms in the RL space.

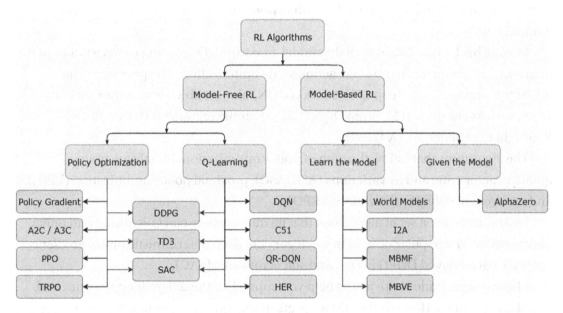

Figure 2-15. *Mind-map of algorithms in reinforcement learning. This is a high-level map showing only broad categorizations (refer to* `https://spinningup.openai.com/en/latest/spinningup/rl_intro2.html`*)*

As seen in Bellman equations, the system transition dynamics $p(s', r \mid s, a)$ forms a central part. The transition dynamics describes the model of environment. However, transition dynamics is not always known. Accordingly, the first broad categorization of learning algorithms can be done based on the knowledge (or lack thereof) of the model, i.e., categories of model-based and model-free algorithms.

Model-based algorithms can be further classified into two categories: one where we are given the model, e.g., the game of Go or chess, and the second category being the one where the agent needs to explore and learn the model. Some popular approaches under "learn the model" are world models, imagination augmented agents (I2A), model-based RL with model-free fine tuning (MBMF), and model-based value exploration (MBVE).

Moving back to the model-free setup, we note that Bellman equations provide us with a way to find the state/action values and use them to find the optimal policies. Most of these algorithms take an approach of iterative improvement. Eventually we want the agent to have an optimal policy, and algorithms use Bellman equations to evaluate the goodness of a policy and also to guide the improvement in the right direction. However, there is another way. Why not improve the policy directly instead of the indirect way of values to policies? Such an approach of direct policy improvement is known as *policy optimization.*

Moving back to the category of the model-free world, Q-learning forms a major part of model-free Bellman-driven state/action value optimization. The popular variants under this approach are Deep Q-Networks (DQN) along with various minor variants of DQN, such as categorical 51-Atom DQN (C51), quantile regression DQN (QR-DQN), and hindsight experience replay (HER).

The algorithms that follow the path of policy optimization directly are policy gradient, actor critic and its variations (A2C/A3C), proximal policy optimization (PPO), and trust region policy optimization (TRPO).

Finally, there are a set of algorithms that lie midway between Q-learning and policy optimization. The popular ones in this category are deep deterministic policy gradient (DDPG), twin delayed DDPG (TD3), and soft actor-critic (SAC).

These categorizations are just to help you appreciate the different approaches and popular algorithms. However, the list and categorization are not exhaustive. The field of reinforcement learning is evolving rapidly with new approaches being added on a regular basis. Please use the previous mind-map only as high-level guidance.

Summary

This chapter set the context for what is reinforcement learning, the setup, and the various definitions. It then talked about Bellman equations and optimality equations along with the state/action value functions and backup diagrams. The chapter then concluded with a view of the algorithm landscape.

The following chapters will delve deeper into many of these algorithms starting with dynamic programming in the next chapter.

CHAPTER 3

Model-Based Algorithms

In Chapter 2, we talked about the parts of the setup that form the agent and the part that forms the environment. The agent gets the state $S_t = s$ and learns a policy $\pi(s|a)$ that maps states to actions. The agent uses this policy to take an action $A_t = a$ when in state $S_t = s$. The system transitions to the next time instant of $t+1$. The environment responds to the action $(A_t = a)$ by putting the agent in a new state of $S_{t+1} = s'$ and providing feedback to the agent in terms of a reward, R_{t+1}. The agent has no control over what the new state S_{t+1} and reward R_{t+1} will be. This transition from $(S_t = s, A_t = a) \rightarrow (R_{t+1} = r, S_{t+1} = s')$ is governed by the environment. This is known as *transition dynamics*. For a given pair of (s, a), there could be one or more pairs of (r, s'). In a deterministic world, we would have a single pair of (r, s') for a fixed combination of (s, a). However, in stochastic environments, i.e., environments with uncertain outcomes, we could have many pairs of (r, s') for a given (s, a).

In this chapter, we will focus on algorithms in which the transition dynamics $\Pr\{ S_{t+1} = s', R_{t+1} = r \mid S_t = s, A_t = a\}$ are known. The agent will use this knowledge to "plan" a policy that maximizes the cumulative return of the state value $v_\pi(s)$. All these algorithms will be based on dynamic programming, which allows us to break the problem into smaller subproblems and use the recursive relationship of Bellman equations explained in Chapter 2. Along the way, you will be introduced to the other concepts of how to improve a policy in the general sense.

However, before we dive into the algorithms, we will take a short detour to study the RL environments that will be used in this chapter. Once we get that out of the way, we will focus on the model-based algorithms.

OpenAI Gym

The coding exercises are based on the OpenAI Gym environment that was introduced in the previous chapter briefly. Gym is a library developed by OpenAI for comparing reinforcement learning (RL) algorithms. It provides a set of standardized environments

49

© Nimish Sanghi 2021
N. Sanghi, *Deep Reinforcement Learning with Python*, https://doi.org/10.1007/978-1-4842-6809-4_3

that can be used to develop and compare various RL algorithms. All these environments have a shared interface that allows us to write general algorithms.

The installation of Gym is easy and has already been explained in the setup section of Chapter 1. In Chapter 2, we covered two popular environments that are used while learning about reinforcement learning: MountainCar-v0 and CartPole-v1. In this chapter, we are going to use an even simpler environment to talk about dynamic programming. It is a 4x4 grid, as shown in Figure 3-1. The top-left and bottom-right positions are terminal states shown as shaded cells in the figure. In a given cell, the agent can move in any of the four directions: UP, RIGHT, DOWN, and LEFT. The actions deterministically move the agent in the direction of the action unless there is a wall. In the case of hitting a wall, the agent stays in the current position. The agent gets a reward of -1 every timestep until it reaches the terminal state.

0	1	2	3
4	5	6	7
8	9	10	11
12	13	14	15

Figure 3-1. *Grid world environment. It is a 4×4 grid with terminal states at the top left and bottom right. Numbers in the grid represent the state S*

This environment is not provided in the Gym library. We will be creating a custom environment in OpenAI Gym. While there is a documented (https://github.com/openai/gym/blob/master/docs/creating-environments.md) file structure that needs to be followed if we want to publish the environment to the outside world, we will follow a simpler single-file structure to define the grid world environment since it is only for our personal use. An environment must implement the following functions: step(action), reset(), and render().

We will take an approach of extending one of the template environments provided in Gym: DiscreteEnv. It already implements the step and reset functions. We only have to provide nA (number of actions in each state), nS (total number of states), and a dictionary

P in which P[s][a] gives a list of tuples with values (probability, next_state, reward, done). In other words, it provides the transition dynamics. In other words, for a given state s and action a, it gives a list of tuples consisting of possible next states s', reward r, and probability $p(s', r|s, a)$. The fourth value in the tuple is a Boolean flag done indicating if the next state s' is a terminal state or not a terminate state.

The transition dynamics P is known under the current setup of model-based learnings, which is the focus of this chapter. However, P should not be directly used in model-free algorithms, i.e., algorithms that learn without the knowledge of the model (transition dynamics). We will study model-free algorithms in subsequent chapters. Listing 3-1 shows the script file gridworld.py.

Listing 3-1. Grid World Environment

```
import numpy as np
import sys
from gym.envs.toy_text import discrete
from contextlib import closing
from io import StringIO

# define the actions
UP = 0
RIGHT = 1
DOWN = 2
LEFT = 3

class GridworldEnv(discrete.DiscreteEnv):
    """

    A 4x4 Grid World environment from Sutton's Reinforcement
    Learning book chapter 4. Termial states are top left and
    the bottom right corner.

    Actions are (UP=0, RIGHT=1, DOWN=2, LEFT=3).
    Actions going off the edge leave agent in current state.
    Reward of -1 at each step until agent reaches a terminal state.
    """

    metadata = {'render.modes': ['human', 'ansi']}
```

```python
def __init__(self):
    self.shape = (4, 4)
    self.nS = np.prod(self.shape)
    self.nA = 4

    P = {}
    for s in range(self.nS):
        position = np.unravel_index(s, self.shape)
        P[s] = {a: [] for a in range(self.nA)}
        P[s][UP] = self._transition_prob(position, [-1, 0])
        P[s][RIGHT] = self._transition_prob(position, [0, 1])
        P[s][DOWN] = self._transition_prob(position, [1, 0])
        P[s][LEFT] = self._transition_prob(position, [0, -1])

    # Initial state distribution is uniform
    isd = np.ones(self.nS) / self.nS

    # We expose the model of the environment for dynamic programming
    # This should not be used in any model-free learning algorithm
    self.P = P

    super(GridworldEnv, self).__init__(self.nS, self.nA, P, isd)

def _limit_coordinates(self, coord):
    """

    Prevent the agent from falling out of the grid world
    :param coord:
    :return:
    """

    coord[0] = min(coord[0], self.shape[0] - 1)
    coord[0] = max(coord[0], 0)
    coord[1] = min(coord[1], self.shape[1] - 1)
    coord[1] = max(coord[1], 0)
    return coord

def _transition_prob(self, current, delta):
    """

    Model Transitions. Prob is always 1.0.
```

```
    :param current: Current position on the grid as (row, col)
    :param delta: Change in position for transition
    :return: [(1.0, new_state, reward, done)]
    """

    # if stuck in terminal state
    current_state = np.ravel_multi_index(tuple(current), self.shape)
    if current_state == 0 or current_state == self.nS - 1:
        return [(1.0, current_state, 0, True)]

    new_position = np.array(current) + np.array(delta)
    new_position = self._limit_coordinates(new_position).astype(int)
    new_state = np.ravel_multi_index(tuple(new_position), self.shape)

    is_done = new_state == 0 or new_state == self.nS - 1
    return [(1.0, new_state, -1, is_done)]

def render(self, mode='human'):
    outfile = StringIO() if mode == 'ansi' else sys.stdout

    for s in range(self.nS):
        position = np.unravel_index(s, self.shape)
        if self.s == s:
            output = " x "
        # Print terminal state
        elif s == 0 or s == self.nS - 1:
            output = " T "
        else:
            output = " o "

        if position[1] == 0:
            output = output.lstrip()
        if position[1] == self.shape[1] - 1:
            output = output.rstrip()
            output += '\n'

        outfile.write(output)
    outfile.write('\n')
```

```
# No need to return anything for human
if mode != 'human':
    with closing(outfile):
        return outfile.getvalue()
```

GridworldEnv is created by extending the template environment discrete. DiscreteEnv provided in the Gym library. In __init__(self), we define nA, nS, and transition function P as per the dynamics depicted in Figure 3-1. Listing 3-1 completely describes the custom Gym environment that will be used in the rest of the chapter.

Let's now focus on the model-free algorithms, which is what we intend to study in this chapter in the "Dynamic Programming" section.

Dynamic Programming

Dynamic programming is an optimization technique that was developed by Richard Bellman in 1950s. It refers to breaking down a complex problem into simpler subproblems, finding optimal solutions to the subproblems, and then combining the subproblem optimal solutions to obtain the optimal solution of the original problem. Let's take a look at the Bellman equation (2.18) that expresses the value of a state $v_\pi(s)$ in terms of the policy $(a|s)$, system dynamics $p(s',r|s, a)$, and state value of successor states $v_\pi(s')$.

$$v_\pi(s) = \sum_a \pi(a|s) \sum_{s',r} p(s',r|s,a) \left[r + \gamma \, v_\pi(s') \right]$$

We are expressing the value $v_\pi(s)$ in terms of other state values $v_\pi(s')$, all of which are unknown. If we could somehow get all the successor state values for the current state, we will be able to calculate $v_\pi(s)$. This shows the recursive nature of the equation.

We also note that a particular value $v_\pi(s')$ would be needed multiple times wherever s' is a successor state of some state s. Because of this nature, we can cache (i.e., store) the value $v_\pi(s')$ and use it multiple times to avoid recalculating $v_\pi(s')$ again and again, every time it was needed.

Dynamic programming is an extensively used optimization technique for a varied class of problems that allow decomposition of complex problems into smaller problems. Some common applications are scheduling algorithms, graph algorithms like shortest path, graphical models like Viterbi algorithms, and lattice models in bioinformatics.

As this book is about reinforcement learning, we will restrict the use of dynamic programming for solving the Bellman expectation and Bellman optimality equations, both for value and action-value functions. These equations are given in (2.18), (2.21), (2.24), and (2.25), and they are reproduced for ready reference.

Here is the Bellman expectation equation for the value function:

$$v_\pi(s) = \sum_a \pi(a|s) \sum_{s',r} p(s',r|s,a)\left[r + \gamma\, v_\pi(s')\right] \tag{3.1}$$

Here is the Bellman expectation equation for the action-value function:

$$q_\pi(s,a) = \sum_{s',r} p(s',r|s,a)\left[r + \gamma \sum_{a'} \pi(a'|s')\, q(s',a')\right] \tag{3.2}$$

Here is the Bellman optimality equation for the value function:

$$v_*(s) = max_a \sum_{s',r} p(s',r|s,a)\left[r + \gamma\, v_*(s')\right] \tag{3.3}$$

Here is the Bellman optimality equation for the action-value function:

$$q_*(s,a) = \sum_{s',r} p(s',r|s,a)\left[r + \gamma\, max_{a'}\, q_*(s',a')\right] \tag{3.4}$$

Each of these four equations represents the v or q-value of a state or state-action pair in terms of the value of successor states or state actions meeting the recursive nature of dynamic programming. In the following sections, we will first use expectation equations to evaluate a policy, which is known as *evaluation* or *prediction*. We will then make use of optimality equations to find an optimal policy that maximizes the state values and state-action values. This will be followed by a section on a generalized setup, an extensively used generalized framework for policy improvement. We will conclude the chapter by talking about the practical challenges in large-scale problem setups and various approaches to optimizing dynamic programming in that context.

This chapter will mostly focus on the class of problems where we have a finite set of states the agent can find itself in as well as a finite set of actions in each state. Problems with continuous state and continuous actions can technically be solved using dynamic programming by first discretizing the states and actions. You can see an example of such an approach toward the end of Chapter 4. It will also form the bulk of Chapter 5.

Policy Evaluation/Prediction

We will now make use of equation (3.1) to derive the state values using its iterative nature and the concepts of dynamic programming. Equation (3.1) represents the state value for a state **s** in terms of its successor states. The values of states also depend on the policy the agent is following, which is defined as policy $\pi(a|s)$. Because of this dependence of value on policy, all the state values are subscripted with π to signify that state values in (3.1) are the ones obtained by following a specific policy $\pi(a|s)$. Please note that changing the policy π will produce a different set of values $v_\pi(s)$ and $q_\pi(s,a)$.

The relationship in (3.1) can be graphically represented by a backup diagram, as shown in Figure 3-2.

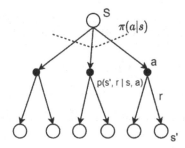

Figure 3-2. *Backup digaram of Bellman expectation equation for state-value functions. Empty circles signify states, and dark circles signify actions*

The agent starts in state **s**. It takes as action **a** based on its current policy $\pi(a|s)$. The environment transitions the agent to a new state s' along with the reward r based on the system dynamics $p(s', r|s, a)$. As you can see, equation (3.1) is a system of equations, one equation for each state. If there are $|S|$ states, we will have $|S|$ such equations. The number of equations equals $|S|$ and is the same as the number of unknown v(s), one for each $S = s$. Thus, (3.1) represents a system of $|S|$ equations with $|S|$ unknowns. We could solve the system of equations using any linear programming techniques. However, it will involve the inversion of a matrix and is therefore not very practical for most of the RL problems in real life.

Instead, we will resort to the use of iterative solutions. This is achieved by starting with some random state values $v_0(s)$ at first iteration $k = 0$ and using them on the right side of (3.1) to obtain the state values at the next iteration step.

$$v_{k+1}(s) \leftarrow \sum_a \pi(a|s) \sum_{s',r} p(s',r|s,a)\left[r + \gamma\, v_k(s')\right] \qquad (3.6)$$

Notice the change of subscript from π to (k) and $(k+1)$. Also notice the change of equality (=) to assignment ($\leftarrow$). We are now representing the state values at iteration $(k+1)$ in terms of the state values in previous iteration k, and there will be $|S|$ (total number of states) such updates in each iteration. It can be shown that as k increases and goes to infinity (∞), V_k will converge to V_π. The previous approach of finding the values of all the states for a given policy is known as *policy evaluation*. We start from an arbitrarily chosen value of V_0 at $k = 0$ and iterate over the state values using equation (3.6), until the state values V_k stop changing. The other name for policy evaluation is *Prediction*, i.e., predicting the state values for a given policy.

Usually, in each iteration, we create a new copy of the existing state values v and update all the values in a new array from the values of all the states in a previous array. We maintain two sets of arrays for state values, V_k and V_{k+1}. This is known as *synchronous* update, i.e., updating all the state values based on the state values from the previous iteration. However, there is an alternate approach. One could maintain only one array of state values and do updates *in place* where each new value immediately overwrites the old one. In-place updates help in faster convergence provided each state is updated enough times. This kind of in-place update is called *asynchronous* updates. We have a section, later in this chapter, devoted to various types of in-place updates.

Figure 3-3 gives the pseudocode for iterative policy evaluation.

ITERATIVE POLICY EVALUATION

Input π, the policy to be evaluated and convergence threshold θ.

Initialize state values $V(s) = 0$ or to any arbitrary values for all states s ∈ S. However, terminal state values should always be initialized to 0.

Make a copy: $V'(s) \leftarrow V(s)$ for all s.

Loop:

$\Delta = 0$

Loop for each s ∈ S:

$$V'(s) \leftarrow \sum_{a} \pi(a|s) \sum_{s',r} p(s',r|s,a)\left[r + \gamma\, V(s')\right]$$

$$\Delta = \max(\Delta, |V(s) - V'(s)|$$

$V(s) \rightarrow V'(s)$ for all s ∈ S; i.e., make a copy of V(s)
until $\Delta < \theta$.

Figure 3-3. *Policy evaluation algorithm*

Let's now apply the previous algorithm to the grid world given in Figure 3-1. We will assume a random policy $\pi(a|s)$ where each of the four actions (UP, RIGHT, DOWN, LEFT) have an equal probability of 0.25. Listing 3-2 shows the code for policy evaluation applied to the grid world. This is from the file listing3_2.ipynb.

Note   The code listings in this book will show only relevant code in the context of discussion. Please view the Python script files and/or Python notebooks for the complete implementation.

Listing 3-2. Policy Evaluation/Policy Planning: listing3_2.ipynb

```
def policy_eval(policy, env, discount_factor=1.0, theta=0.00001):
    """
    Evaluate a policy given an environment and
    a full description of the environment's dynamics.

    Args:
        policy: [S, A] shaped matrix representing the policy. Random in our case
        env: OpenAI env. env.P -> transition dynamics of the environment.
            env.P[s][a] [(prob, next_state, reward, done)].
            env.nS is number of states in the environment.
            env.nA is number of actions in the environment.
        theta: Stop evaluation once value function change is
            less than theta for all states.
        discount_factor: Gamma discount factor.

    Returns:
        Vector of length env.nS representing the value function.
    """
    # Start with a (all 0) value function
    V = np.zeros(env.nS)
    V_new = np.copy(V)
    while True:
        delta = 0
        # For each state, perform a "backup"
        for s in range(env.nS):
            v = 0
            # Look at the possible next actions
            for a, pi_a in enumerate(policy[s]):
                # For each action, look at the possible next states...
                for prob, next_state, reward, done in env.P[s][a]:
                    # Calculate the expected value as per backup diagram
                    v += pi_a * prob * \
                        (reward + discount_factor * V[next_state])
            # How much our value function changed (across any states)
            V_new[s] = v
            delta = max(delta, np.abs(V_new[s] - V[s]))
```

```
    V = np.copy(V_new)
    # Stop if change is below a threshold
    if delta < theta:
        break
return np.array(V)
```

When we run the code against the grid world with the agent following a random policy, we see the state values $v_\pi(s)$ for each grid cell given in Figure 3-4.

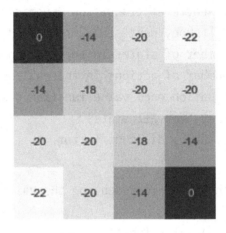

Figure 3-4. *Policy evaluation $v_\pi(s)$ for the grid world from Figure 3-1 with the agent following a random policy. Each of the four actions UP, DOWN, LEFT, and RIGHT have an equal probability of 0.25*

We can see that the values have converged. Let's take a look at the third row in the last column with a state value of $v_\pi(s) = -14$. In this state, the action UP will take the agent to a cell with a state value of -20, the action LEFT takes the agent to a cell with a state value of -18, the action DOWN takes the agent to a terminal state with a value of 0, and the action RIGHT hits the wall, leaving the agent in same state. Let's apply equation (3.1). We will expand the right side of equation (3.1) with actions applied in order—TOP, RIGHT, DOWN, LEFT:

-14 = 0.25*(-1+(-20)) + 0.25*(-1+(-14)) + 0.25*(-1+0) + 0.25*(-1+(-18))

-14 = -14

The values on both sides are matching, which confirms convergence. Accordingly, the values shown in Figure 3-4 are the state values when the agent follows a random policy. Please note that we have considered a discount factor of $\gamma = 1.0$.

Having understood policy evaluation, in the next section we will talk about how to improve the policy for a given environment.

Policy Improvement and Iterations

The previous section showed how to iterate to get state values $v_\pi(s)$ for a given policy. We could use this information to improve upon the policy. In our grid world, we have four actions that we could take from any state. Instead of following a random policy $\pi(a|s)$, we now look at the value of taking all four actions individually and then following policy π after that step. This will give us four values of $q(s, a)$ action values, which are the action values of taking each of the four possible actions in the grid world.

$$q(s, a) = \sum_{s', r} p(s', r|s, a) \left[r + \gamma v_\pi(s') \right]$$

Note that $q(s, a)$ has no subscript of π. We are evaluating $q(s, a)$ for all possible actions while in state $S = s$. If any of the $q(s, a)$ is greater than the current state value $v_\pi(s)$, it means that current policy $\pi(a|s)$ is not taking the optimal action, and we could improve on the policy in current state $S = s$. Taking the q-value maximizing action $A = a$ and defining this to be the policy in state $S = s$ will give a higher state value compared to the current policy $\pi(a|s)$. In other words, we define the following:

$$\pi'(a|s) = \underset{a}{argmax}\, q(s, a) \tag{3.7}$$

Because of a general result called the *policy improvement theorem*, which we will not go into here, the values for all states under the new policy π' are going to be equal to or greater than the state values under policy π. In other words, while choosing a maximizing action in a specific state $S = s$ improves the state value of that state, it cannot reduce the values of other states. It can either leave them unchanged or improve those other states that depend on $S = s$. Mathematically, we can express this as follows:

$$v_\pi'(s) \geq v_\pi(s) \quad s \in S$$

The previous maximizing step (greedy step) of maximization could be applied to all the states based on their current q-values. Such an extension of maximizing action across all states is known as a *greedy policy*, and the recursive state value relation is given by Bellman's optimality equation (3.4).

We now have a framework to improve the policy. For a given MDP, we first do policy evaluation iteratively to obtain state values $v(s)$, and then we apply the greedy selection of action maximizing the q values as per (3.7). This results in state values going out of sync with Bellman equations as the maximization step is applied to each individual state without flowing it through all the successor states. Therefore, we again carry out the policy iteration under the new policy π' to find the state/action values under the improved policy. Once the state values are obtained, the maximizing action could again be applied to further improve the policy to π''. The cycle goes on until no further improvement is observed. This sequence of action can be depicted as follows:

$$\pi_0 \xrightarrow{\text{evaluate}} v_{\pi_0} \xrightarrow{\text{improve}} \pi_1 \xrightarrow{\text{evaluate}} v_{\pi_1} \xrightarrow{\text{improve}} \pi_2 \dots \xrightarrow{\text{improve}} \pi_* \xrightarrow{\text{evaluate}} v_*$$

From the policy improvement theorem, we know that each swipe of greedy improvement and policy evaluation, $v_\pi \xrightarrow{\text{improve}} \pi' \xrightarrow{\text{evaluate}} v_{\pi'}$ gives us a policy that is better than the previous one with $v'_\pi(s) \geq v_\pi(s)$ $s \in S$. For an MDP that has a finite number of discrete states and finite number of actions in each state, with each swipe leading to an improvement, an optimal policy would be found once we stop observing any further improvement in state values. This is bound to happen within a finite number of cycles of improvement.

This approach of finding an optimal policy is called *policy iteration*. Figure 3-5 shows the pseudocode for policy iteration.

POLICY ITERATION

Initialize state values V(s) and policy π arbitrarily.

For example, V(s) = 0 s € S, and π(a I s) as random define convergence threshold θ.

Policy Evaluation

Loop:

   $\Delta = 0$

   Loop for each s € S:

$$V'(s) \leftarrow \sum_a \pi(a|s) \sum_{s',r} p(s',r|s,a)\left[r + \gamma V(s')\right]$$

$$\Delta = \max(\Delta, |V(s) - V'(s)|)$$

V(s) ← V'(s) for all s € S; i.e., make a copy of V(s)
until $\Delta < \theta$.

Policy Improvement

policy-changed ← false

Loop for each s € S:

      old-action ← π(s)

$$\pi(s) \leftarrow argmax_a \sum_{s',r} p(s',r|s,a)\left[r + \gamma V(s')\right]$$

      If π(s) ≠ old-action, then policy-changed = true.

  If policy-changed = true, then go to step 2.

Otherwise, return V(s) as v* and π(s) as π*.

Figure 3-5. *Policy iteration algorithm for finite MDP*

Let's apply the previous algorithm to the grid world from Figure 3-1. Listing 3-3 shows the code for the policy iteration applied to the grid world. The complete code is given in `listing3_3.ipynb`. The function `policy_evaluation` remains the same as Listing 3-2. There is a new function, `policy_improvement`, which applies greedy maximization to return a policy that improves upon the existing one. `policy_iteration` is a function that runs `policy_evaluation` followed by `policy_improvement` in a loop until the state values stop increasing and converge to a fixed point.

Listing 3-3. Policy Iteration: listing3_3.ipynb

```
# Policy Improvement

def policy_improvement(policy, V, env, discount_factor=1.0):
    """

    Improve a policy given an environment and a full description
    of the environment's dynamics and the state-values V.

    Args:
        policy: [S, A] shaped matrix representing the policy.
        V: current state-value for the given policy
        env: OpenAI env. env.P -> transition dynamics of the environment.
            env.P[s][a] [(prob, next_state, reward, done)].
            env.nS is number of states in the environment.
            env.nA is number of actions in the environment.
        discount_factor: Gamma discount factor.

    Returns:
        policy: [S, A] shaped matrix representing improved policy.
        policy_changed: boolean which has value of `True` if there
                        was a change in policy
    """

    def argmax_a(arr):
        """
        Return idxs of all max values in an array.
        """

        max_idx = []
        max_val = float('-inf')
```

```
            for idx, elem in enumerate(arr):
                if elem == max_val:
                    max_idx.append(idx)
                elif elem > max_val:
                    max_idx = [idx]
                    max_val = elem
            return max_idx

    policy_changed = False
    Q = np.zeros([env.nS, env.nA])
    new_policy = np.zeros([env.nS, env.nA])

    # For each state, perform a "greedy improvement"
    for s in range(env.nS):
        old_action = np.array(policy[s])
        for a in range(env.nA):
            for prob, next_state, reward, done in env.P[s][a]:
                # Calculate the expected value as per backup diagram
                Q[s,a] += prob * (reward + discount_factor * V[next_state])

        # get maximizing actions and set new policy for state s
        best_actions = argmax_a(Q[s])
        new_policy[s, best_actions] = 1.0 / len(best_actions)

    if not np.allclose(new_policy[s], policy[s]):
        policy_changed = True

    return new_policy, policy_changed
# Policy Iteration
def policy_iteration(env, discount_factor=1.0, theta=0.00001):

    # initialize a random policy
    policy = np.ones([env.nS, env.nA]) / env.nA
    while True:
        V = policy_evaluation(policy, env, discount_factor, theta)
        policy, changed = policy_improvement(policy, V, env, discount_factor)
```

```
    if not changed: #terminate iteration once no improvement is observed
        V_optimal = policy_evaluation(policy, env, discount_factor, theta)
        print("Optimal Policy\n", policy)
        return np.array(V_optimal)
```

Figure 3-6 shows the state values for each grid cell as a result of running `policy_iteration` on the grid world.

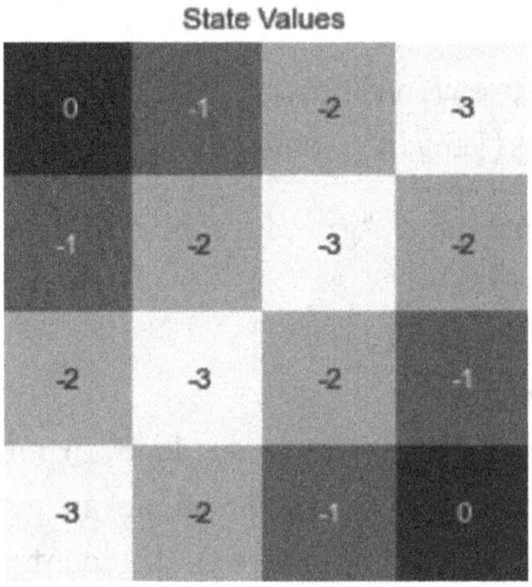

Figure 3-6. *Policy iteration $v_*(s)$ for the grid world from Figure 3-1. The agent is following an optimal policy as found by applying policy_iteration from Listing 3-3*

We see that the optimal state values are a negative of number of steps required to reach the closest terminal state. As the reward is -1 for each time step until the agent reaches the terminal state, the optimal policy would take the agent to the terminal state in the minimal number of possible steps. For some states, more than one action could lead to the same number of steps to reach the terminal state. For example, looking at the top-right state with state value = -3, it takes three steps to reach the terminal state at the top left or the terminal state at the bottom right. In other words, the state value is the negative of the Manhattan distance between the state and nearest terminal state.

We can also extract the optimal policy, as shown in Figure 3-7. The left of the figure shows the policy as extracted from the code in Listing 3-3, and the right side of the diagram shows the same policy graphically superimposed on the grid.

```
Optimal Policy
[[0.25 0.25 0.25 0.25]
 [0.   0.   0.   1.  ]
 [0.   0.   0.   1.  ]
 [0.   0.   0.5  0.5 ]
 [1.   0.   0.   0.  ]
 [0.5  0.   0.   0.5 ]
 [0.   0.   0.5  0.5 ]
 [0.   0.   1.   0.  ]
 [1.   0.   0.   0.  ]
 [0.5  0.5  0.   0.  ]
 [0.   1.   0.   0.  ]
 [0.   0.   1.   0.  ]
 [1.   0.   0.   0.  ]
 [0.   1.   0.   0.  ]
 [0.   1.   0.   0.  ]
 [0.25 0.25 0.25 0.25]]
```

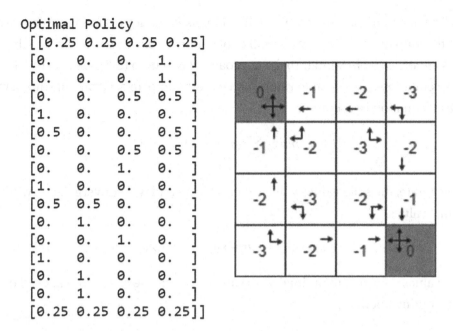

Figure 3-7. *Policy Iteration* $v_*(s)$ *for the grid world from Figure 3-1 as shown in Figure 3-6. Left: optimal policy with probability of action for each cell in the grid. Right: grid superimposed with the optimal policy*

Policy evaluation is also known as *prediction* as we are trying to find the state values consistent with the current policy the agent is following. Similarly, using policy iteration to find an optimal policy is also known as *control*: to control the agent and find an optimal policy.

Value Iteration

Let's look at policy iteration and try to assess how many passes we need to find an optimal policy. Policy iteration has two steps that go in a cycle. The first is policy evaluation, which is run for the current policy and requires multiple passes over the state space so that state values converge and become consistent with the current policy. The second part of the loop is policy improvement, which requires one pass over the state space to find the best action for each state, i.e., greedy improvement with respect to the current state action values. From this, it is evident that a large part of time is spent in policy evaluation and letting values converge.

An alternate approach is to truncate the loop inside policy evaluation. When we truncate the loop inside policy evaluation to only one loop, we have an approach known as *value iteration*. Similar to the approach of equation (3.6), we take the Bellman optimality equation (3.3) for state value and convert it into an assignment with iteration. The revised equation is as follows:

$$v_{k+1}(s) \leftarrow max_a \sum_{s',r} p(s', r|s, a)\left[r + \gamma\, v_k(s')\right] \qquad (3.8)$$

As we iterate, the state values will keep improving and will converge to v*, which are the optimal values.

$$v_0 \rightarrow v_1 \rightarrow \ldots v_k \rightarrow v_{k+1} \rightarrow \ldots \rightarrow v_*$$

Once values converge to optimal state values, we can use a one-step backup diagram to find the optimal policy.

$$\pi_*(a|s) = \underset{a}{argmax} \sum_{s',r} p(s', r|s, a)\left[r + \gamma\, v_*(s')\right] \qquad (3.9)$$

The previous procedure to iterate over values taking a max at each step is known as *value iteration*. Figure 3-8 shows the pseudocode.

VALUE ITERATION

Initialize state values V(s) (terminal states are always initialized to 0), e.g. V(s) = 0 s € S. Define convergence threshold θ.

Make a copy: V'(s) ← V(s) for all s.

Loop:

Δ ← 0

Loop for each s € S:

$$V'(s) \leftarrow max_a \sum_{s',r} p(s',r|s,a)\left[r + \gamma V(s')\right]$$

$$\Delta = \max(\Delta, |V(s) - V'(s)|)$$

V(s) ← V'(s) for all s € S, i.e., make a copy of V(s)
until Δ < θ.

Output a deterministic policy, breaking ties deterministically.

Initialize π(s), an array of length |S|.

Loop for each s € S.

$$\pi(s) \leftarrow argmax_a \sum_{s',r} p(s',r|s,a)\left[r + \gamma V(s')\right]$$

Figure 3-8. *Value iteration algorithm for a finite MDP*

Let's apply the previous value iteration algorithm to the grid world given in Figure 3-1. Listing 3-4 contains the code for value iteration applied to the grid world. You can check out file `listing3_4.ipynb` for a detailed implementation. Function `value_iteration` is the straight implementation of the pseudocode in Figure 3-8.

Listing 3-4. Value Iteration: listing3_4.ipynb

```
# Value Iteration
def value_iteration(env, discount_factor=1.0, theta=0.00001):
    """

    Varry out Value iteration given an environment and a full description
    of the environment's dynamics.
```

```
    Args:
        env: OpenAI env. env.P -> transition dynamics of the environment.
            env.P[s][a] [(prob, next_state, reward, done)].
            env.nS is number of states in the environment.
            env.nA is number of actions in the environment.
        discount_factor: Gamma discount factor.
        theta: tolernace level to stop the iterations

    Returns:
        policy: [S, A] shaped matrix representing optimal policy.
        value : [S] length vector representing optimal value
    """

    def argmax_a(arr):
        """
        Return idx of max element in an array.
        """
        max_idx = []
        max_val = float('-inf')
        for idx, elem in enumerate(arr):
            if elem == max_val:
                max_idx.append(idx)
            elif elem > max_val:
                max_idx = [idx]
                max_val = elem
        return max_idx

    optimal_policy = np.zeros([env.nS, env.nA])
    V = np.zeros(env.nS)
    V_new = np.copy(V)

    while True:
        delta = 0
        # For each state, perform a "greedy backup"
        for s in range(env.nS):
            q = np.zeros(env.nA)
            # Look at the possible next actions
```

```
    for a in range(env.nA):
        # For each action, look at the possible next states
        # to calculate q[s,a]
        for prob, next_state, reward, done in env.P[s][a]:

            # Calculate the value for each action as per backup diagram
            if not done:
                q[a] += prob * (reward + discount_factor * V[next_
                state])
            else:
                q[a] += prob * reward

        # find the maximum value over all possible actions
        # and store updated state value
        V_new[s] = q.max()
        # How much our value function changed (across any states)
        delta = max(delta, np.abs(V_new[s] - V[s]))

    V = np.copy(V_new)

    # Stop if change is below a threshold
    if delta < theta:
        break

# V(s) has optimal values. Use these values and one step backup
# to calculate optimal policy
for s in range(env.nS):
    q = np.zeros(env.nA)
    # Look at the possible next actions
    for a in range(env.nA):
        # For each action, look at the possible next states
        # and calculate q[s,a]
        for prob, next_state, reward, done in env.P[s][a]:

            # Calculate the value for each action as per backup diagram
            if not done:
                q[a] += prob * (reward + discount_factor * V[next_state])
            else:
                q[a] += prob * reward
```

```
# find the optimal actions
# We are returning stochastic policy which will assign equal
# probability to all those actions which are equal to maximum value
best_actions = argmax_a(q)
optimal_policy[s, best_actions] = 1.0 / len(best_actions)

return optimal_policy, V
```

The output of running the value algorithm against the grid world will produce the optimal state values $v*(s)$ and optimal policy $v_{\pi}.(a|s)$ with exactly similar values and policy, as shown in Figures 3-7 and 3-8.

Before moving forward, let's summarize. What we have looked at up until now is classified as *synchronous dynamic programming algorithms*, as summarized in Table 3-1.

Table 3-1. *Synchronous Dynamic Programming Algorithms*

Algorithm	Bellman Equation	Type of Problem
Iterative policy evaluation	Expectation equations	Prediction
Policy iteration	Expectation equations and greedy improvement	Control
Value iteration	Optimality equations	Control

Generalized Policy Iteration

The policy iteration described earlier has two steps: policy evaluation, which gets the state values in sync with the policy the agent is following, requiring multiple passes over all states for values to converge to v_{π}, and greedy action selection to improve the policy. As explained, the second step of improvement results in the current state of values going out of sync with the new policy. Therefore, we are required to carry out yet another round of policy evaluation to bring the state values back into sync with the new policy. The cycle of evaluation followed by improvement stops when there is no further change in state values. This happens when the agent has reached optimal policy and state values are also optimal and in sync with the optimal policy. The convergence to the optimal policy (fixed point) v_{π} can be depicted visually, as shown in Figure 3-9.

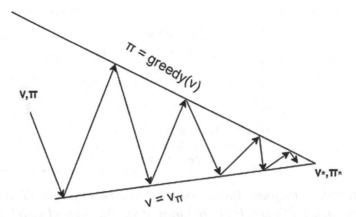

Figure 3-9. *Iteration between the two steps. The first step is evalaution to get the state values in sync with the policy being followed. The second step is that of policy improvement to do a greedy maximization for actions*

We have seen two extremes for the number of loops to iterate inside the policy evaluation step. Also, every iteration, be it policy evaluation or policy improvement, covered all the states in the model. However, even within an iteration, we could visit only a partial set of states to evaluate and/or improve the state action by greedy selection. The *policy improvement theorem* guarantees that even a partial coverage of all the states will lead to an improvement unless the agent is already following an optimal policy. In other words, the state value sync does not need to be complete. It may terminate midway, which results in the arrow in Figure 3-9 stopping short of touching the bottom line of $v = v_\pi$. Similarly, the step of policy improvement may not carry out improvement for all the states, which again leads to arrows in Figure 3-9 stopping short of the upper line of $\pi = greedy(v)$.

In summary, these two steps of policy evaluation and policy improvement with all their variations of how many states to sweep or after how many iterations to stop within evaluation step lead to convergence as long as each state is visited enough times in both evaluation and improvement. This is known as *generalized policy iteration* (GPI). Most of the algorithms that we will study can be classified as some form of GPI. When we go through various algorithms, please keep in mind the picture given in Figure 3-10.

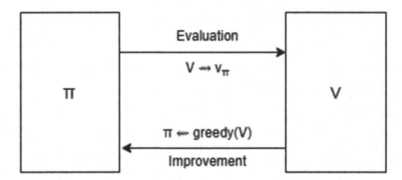

Figure 3-10. *Iteration between the two steps. The first step is evalaution to get state values in sync with the policy being followed. The second step is that of policy improvement to do a greedy maximization for actions*

Asynchronous Backups

Dynamic programming–based algorithms have scalability issues. The dynamic programming approach is much better and scalable than direct solution methods such as linear programing, which involves solving a matrix equation. However, dynamic programming still does not scale well for real-life problems. Consider a single sweep under policy iteration. It requires a visit to each state, and under each state, you need to consider all the actions possible. Further, each action involves a calculation that may theoretically involve all the states again depending on the state transition function $p(s',$ $r|s, a)$. In other words, every iteration has a complexity of $O(|A| * |s|^2)$. We started with policy iteration under which we carried out multiple iterations as part of evaluation step for the state values to converge. The second control method we looked at was value iteration. We reduced the evaluation iterations to only one step by leveraging Bellman optimality equations. All these were synchronous dynamic programming algorithms under which all states are updated using Bellmen backup equations (3.1) to (3.4).

However, there is no need to update each state in every iteration. We could update and/or optimize in any order covering only partial parts of the total states in the system. All such methods to sweep over states yield optimal state values and optimal policies as long as each state is visited often enough. There are various approaches to making a sweep.

The first one is *in-place dynamic programming.* Up until now we have been maintaining two copies of the state. The first copy holds the existing state values, and the second copy holds the new state values being updated. An *in-place* strategy uses only a copy of state value array. The same array is used for reading old and updating new state values. As an example, let's look at value iteration equation from (3.8). Note the subtle difference in the subindices on state values on the right and left sides of original value iteration equation as compared to those in-place versions. The original version uses array V_k to update a new array V_{k+1}, while the in-place edit updates the same array.

Here is the original:

$$v_{k+1}(s) \leftarrow max_a \sum_{s',r} p(s',r|s,a)\left[r + \gamma\, v_k(s')\right]$$

Here it is with in-place updates: it's same array of v(s) on both sides of the arrow.

$$v(s) \leftarrow max_a \sum_{s',r} p(s',r|s,a)\left[r + \gamma\, v(s')\right]$$

Experiments have shown that in-place edits offer faster convergence as the values move up even midway of an iteration.

The second idea revolves around the order in which states should be updated. In synchronous programing, we update all the states in a single iteration. However, values may converge faster if we use *prioritized sweeping*. Prioritized sweeping requires knowledge of the predecessors of a state. Suppose we have just updated a state $S = s$ and the value changed by an amount Δ. All the predecessor states of state $S = s$ are added to a priority queue with a priority of Δ. If a predecessor state is already there in the priority queue with a priority more than Δ, it is left untouched. In the next iteration, a new state with the highest priority is taken out of the queue and updated, taking us back to the beginning of the loop. The strategy of priority sweeping *requires knowledge of reverse dynamics*, i.e., the predecessors of a given state.

The third idea is *real-time dynamic programming*. With this approach, we only update the value of the states that the agent has currently seen, i.e., the states that are relevant to the agent and use its current path of exploration to prioritize the updates. The approach avoids wasteful updates to the states that are not on the horizon of the agent's current path and hence mostly irrelevant.

Dynamic programming, both synchronous and asynchronous, uses full-width backups like the one shown in Figure 3-2. For a given state, we need to know every action possible and every successor state $S = s'$. We also need to know the environment dynamics $p(s', r|s, a)$. However, using an asynchronous approach does not completely solve the scalability issue. It only extends the scalability a bit. In other words, dynamic programming is feasible only for midsize problems even with asynchronous updates.

Starting in the next chapter, we will consider a more scalable approach to solving reinforcement learning problems using sample-based methods. Under sample-based methods, we do not know about environment dynamics nor do we carry out full-width sweeps.

Summary

In this chapter, we introduced the concept of dynamics programming and how it is applied in the field of reinforcement learning. We looked at policy evaluation for prediction followed by policy iteration for control. We then looked at value iteration. These discussions led to generalized policy iteration. The chapter concluded with a quick review of asynchronous variants for a more efficient approach to state updates.

CHAPTER 4

Model-Free Approaches

In the previous chapter, we looked at dynamic programming where we knew the model dynamics $p(s', r|s, a)$, and this knowledge was used to "plan" the optimal actions. This is also known as the *planning problem*. In this chapter, we will shift our focus and look at *learning problems*, i.e., a setup where the model dynamics are not known. We will learn value and action-value functions by sampling, i.e., collecting experience by following some policy in the real world or by running the agent through a policy in simulation. There is another class of problems where we find the model-free approach more applicable. In some problems, it is easier to sample than to calculate the transition dynamics, e.g., consider solving a problem of finding the best policy to play a game like blackjack. There are many combinations to reach a score that depend on the cards seen so far and the cards still in the deck. It is almost impossible to calculate the exact transition probabilities from one state to another state but easy to sample states from an environment. To summarize, we use model-free methods when either we do not know the model dynamics or we know the model, but it is much more practical to sample than to calculate the transition dynamics.

In this chapter, we will look at two broad classes of model-free learning: Monte Carlo (MC) methods and temporal difference (TD) methods. We will first understand how policy evaluation works in a model-free setup and then extend our understanding to look at control, i.e., to find the optimal policy. We will also touch upon the important concept of bootstrapping and the exploration-versus-exploitation dilemma as well as off-policy versus on-policy learning. Initially, the focus will be to look at the MC and TD methods individually, after which we will look into additional concepts like n-step returns, importance sampling, and eligibility traces in a bid to combine the MC and TD methods into a common, more generic approach called TD(λ).

77

© Nimish Sanghi 2021
N. Sanghi, *Deep Reinforcement Learning with Python*, https://doi.org/10.1007/978-1-4842-6809-4_4

Estimation/Prediction with Monte Carlo

When we do not know the model dynamics, what do we do? Think back to a situation when you did not know something about a problem. What did you do in that situation? You experiment, take some steps, and find out how the situation responds. For example, say you want to find out if a die or a coin is biased or not. You toss the coin or throw the die multiple times, observe the outcome, and use that to form your opinion. In other words, you sample. The law of large numbers from statistics tell us that the average of samples is a good substitute for the averages. Further, these averages become better as the number of samples increase. If you look back at the Bellman equations in the previous chapter, you will notice that we had expectation operator $E[\bullet]$ in those equations; e.g., the value of a state being $v(s) = E[G_t|S_t = s]$. Further, to calculate $v(s)$, we used dynamic programming requiring the transition dynamics $p(s', r \mid s, a)$. In the absence of the model dynamics knowledge, what do we do? We just sample from the model, observing returns starting from state $S = s$ and until the end of the episode. We then average the returns from all episode runs and use that average as an estimate of $v_\pi(s)$ for the policy π that the agent is following. This in a nutshell is the approach of *Monte Carlo methods*: replace expected returns with the average of sample returns.

There are a few points to note. MC methods do not require knowledge of the model. The only thing required is that we should be able to sample from it. We need to know the return of starting from a state until termination, and hence we can use MC methods only on episodic MDPs in which every run finally terminates. It will not work on nonterminating environments. The second point is that for a large MDP we can keep the focus on sampling only that part of the MDP that is relevant and avoid exploring irrelevant parts of the MDP. Such an approach makes MC methods highly scalable for very large problems. A variant of the MC method called *Monte Carlo tree search* (MCTS) was used by OpenAI in training a Go game-playing agent.

The third point is about Markov assumption; i.e., the past is fully encoded in the present state. In other words, knowing the present makes the future independent of the past. We talked about this property in Chapter 2. This property of Markov independence forms the basis of the recursive nature of Bellman equations where a state just depends on the successor state values. However, under the MC approach, we observe the full return starting from a state S and until termination. We are not depending on the value of successor states to calculate the current state value. There is no Markov property assumption being made here. A lack of Markov assumption in MC methods make them much more feasible for the class of MDPs known as POMDPs (for "partially observable

MDP"). In a POMDP environment, we get only partial-state information, which is known as *observation*.

Moving on, let's look at a formal way to estimate the state values for a given policy. We let the agent start a new episode and observe that the return from the time agent is in state $S = s$ for the first time in that episode and until the episode ends. Many episode runs are carried out, and an average of return across episodes is taken as an estimate of $v_\pi(S = s)$. This is known as the *first-visit MC method*. Please note that, depending on the dynamics, an agent may visit the same state $S = s$ in some later step within the same episode before termination. However, in the first-visit MC method, we take the total return only from the first visit in an episode until the end of the episode. There is another variant in which we take the average of returns from every visit to that state until the end of the episode. This is known as the *every-visit MC method*.

Figure 4-1 shows the backup diagram for the MC method. In DP we take a full swipe to cover all the actions possible from a state as well as all the possible transitions to a new state from the state-action pair $(S = s, A = a)$. We go only one level deep from state $S = s$ to $A = a$ and then to the next state $S = s'$. Compared to this, in the MC method, the backup covers a full sample trajectory from the current state $S = s$ to the terminal state. It does not cover all the branching possibilities; rather, it covers only one single path that got sampled from the start state $S = s$ to the terminal state.

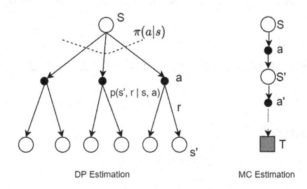

DP Estimation   MC Estimation

Figure 4-1. *Backup diagram of MC methods as compared to Bellman equation–based DP backup*

Let's now look at the pseudocode for the first-visit version, which is given in Figure 4-2. We input the policy π that the agent is currently following. We initialize two arrays: one to hold the current estimate of $V(s)$ and the second to hold the number of visits $N(s)$ to a state $S = s$. Multiple episodes are executed, and we update $V(s)$ as well as $N(s)$ for the state agent visits in every episode, updating only for the first visit in the "first visit version" and updating for every visit in the "every visit version." The pseudocode covers only the "first visit variant." The "every visit" variant is easy to implement, just dropping the condition "*Unless S_t appears in S_0, S_1, ...*" As per the law of large numbers, the statistical law on which Monte Carlo simulations are based, $V(s)$ will converge to true $v_\pi(s)$ when the number of visits to each state goes to infinity.

FIRST VISIT MC PREDICTION

Input:

   π, the policy to be evaluated

Initialize:

   Cumulative state values $S(s) = 0$ for all $s \in S$

   Estimated state values $V(s) = 0$ for all $s \in S$

   Visit count $N(s) = 0$ for all $s \in S$

Loop:

   Sample episode following policy π : S_0, A_0, R_1, S_1, A_1, R_2, ... A_{t-1}, R_T, S_T

   $G \leftarrow 0$

   Loop backward for each step of episode, $t = T - 1, T - 2, ..., 1, 0$

      $G \leftarrow \gamma.G + R_{t+1}$

      Unless S_t appears in S_0, S_1, ..., S_{t-1}

$$N(s) \leftarrow N(s)+1$$
$$S(s) \leftarrow S(s)+G$$
$$V(s) \leftarrow S(s)/N(s)$$

Figure 4-2. *First-visit MC prediction for estimating $v_\pi(s)$. The pseudocode uses the online version to update the values as samples are received*

We store the cumulative total and the count of first visits to a state. The average is calculated by dividing the total by the count. Every time a state is visited, the following update is carried out:

$$N(s) = N(s) + 1; \quad S(s) = S(s) + G; \quad V(s) = S(s) / N(s)$$

With a minor change, we could look at the update in another way, without needing the cumulative totals $S(s)$. In this alternate formulation, we will have one array $V(s)$ that gets updated for every visit directly without needing to divide the total by the count. The derivation of this updated rule is as follows:

$$N(s)_{n+1} = N(S)_n + 1$$

$$V(s)_{n+1} = \left[S(s)_n + G \right] / N(s)_{n+1}$$

$$= \left[V(s)_n * N(s)_n + G \right] / N(s)_{n+1}$$

$$= V(s)_n + 1 / N(s)_{n+1} * \left[G - V(s)_n \right] \tag{4.1}$$

The difference $[G - V(s)_n]$ can be viewed as an error between the latest sampled value G and the current estimate $V(s)_n$. The difference/error is then used to update the current estimate by adding $1/N * error$ to the current estimate. As the number of visits increases, the new sample has increasingly low influence in revising the estimate of $V(s)$. This is because the multiplication factor $1/N$ reduces to zero as N becomes very large.

Sometimes, instead of using a diminishing factor $1/N$, we can use a constant α as the multiplication factor in front of the difference $[G - V(s)_n]$.

$$V_{n+1} = V_n + \alpha (G - V_n) \tag{4.2}$$

The constant multiplication factor approach is more appropriate for problems that are nonstationary or when we want to give a constant weight to all the errors. A situation like this can happen when the old estimate V_n may not be very accurate.

Let's now look at the implementation of MC value prediction. Listing 4-1 shows the code, and the full code is available in file `listing4_1.ipynb`.

Listing 4-1. MC Value Prediction Algorithm for Estimation

```python
def mc_policy_eval(policy, env, discount_factor=1.0, episode_count=100):

    # Start with (all 0) state value array and a visit count of zero
    V = np.zeros(env.nS)
    N = np.zeros(env.nS)
    i = 0

    # run multiple episodes
    while i < episode_count:

        #collect samples for one episode
        episode_states = []
        episode_returns = []
        state = env.reset()
        episode_states.append(state)
        while True:
            action = np.random.choice(env.nA, p=policy[state])
            (state, reward, done, _) = env.step(action)
            episode_returns.append(reward)
            if not done:
                episode_states.append(state)
            else:
                break

        #update state values
        G = 0
        count = len(episode_states)
        for t in range(count-1, -1, -1):
            s, r = episode_states[t], episode_returns[t]
            G = discount_factor * G + r
            if s not in episode_states[:t]:
                N[s] += 1
                V[s] = V[s] + 1/N[s] * (G-V[s])

        i = i+1

    return np.array(V)
```

The code in Listing 4-1 is a straight implementation of the pseudocode in Figure 4-2. The code implements the online version of update as explained in equation (4.1), i.e., `N[s]+=1; V[s]=V[s]+1/N[s]*(G-V[s])`. The code also implements the "first-visit" version but can be converted to "every visit" with a very small tweak. We just need to drop the "if" check, i.e., "`if s not in episode_states[:t]`" to carry out the updates at every step.

To ensure convergence to the true state values, we need to ensure each state is visited enough times, being infinite in limit. As shown in the results at the end of the Python notebook, state values do not converge very well for 100 episodes. However, with 10,000 episodes, the values have converged well and match those produced with the DP method given in Listing 3-2.

Bias and Variance of MC Predication Methods

Let's now look at the pros and cons of "first visit" versus "every visit." Do both of them converge to the true underlying $V(s)$? Do they fluctuate a lot while converging? Does one converge faster to true value? Before we answer this question, let's first review the basic concept of bias-variance trade-off that we see in all statistical model estimations, e.g., in supervised learning.

Bias refers to the property of the model to converge to the true underlying value that we are trying to estimate, in our case $v_\pi(s)$. Some estimators are biased, meaning they are not able to converge to the true value due to their inherent lack of flexibility, i.e., being too simple or restricted for a given true model. At the same time, in some other cases, models have bias that goes down to zero as the number of samples grows.

Variance refers to the model estimate being sensitive to the specific sample data being used. This means the estimate value may fluctuate a lot and hence may require a large data set or trials for the estimate average to converge to a stable value.

The models, which are very flexible, have low bias as they are able to fit the model to any configuration of a data set. At the same time, due to flexibility, they can overfit to the data, making the estimates vary a lot as the training data changes. On the other hand, models that are simpler have high bias. Such models, due to the inherent simplicity and restrictions, may not be able to represent the true underlying model. But they will also have low variance as they do not overfit. This is known as *bias-variance trade-off* and can be presented in a graph as shown in Figure 4-3.

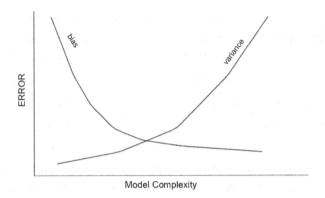

Figure 4-3. *Bias variance trade-off. Model complexity is increasing toward the right on the x-axis. Bias starts off high when the model is restricted and drops off as the model becomes flexible. Variance shows a reverse trend with model complexity*

Comparing "first visit" to "every visit," *first visit* is unbiased but has high variance. *Every visit* has bias that goes down to zero as the number of trials increases. In addition, *every visit* has low variance and usually converges to the true value estimates faster than *first visit*.

Control with Monte Carlo

Let's now talk about control in a model-free setup. We need to find the optimal policy in this setup without knowing the model dynamics. As a refresher, let's look at the generalized policy iteration (GPI) that was introduced in Chapter 3. In GPI, we iterate between two steps. The first step is to find the state values for a given policy, and the second step is to improve the policy using greedy optimization. We will follow the same GPI approach for control under MC. We will have some tweaks, though, to account for the fact that we are in model-free world with no access/knowledge of transition dynamics.

In Chapter 3, we looked at state values, $v(s)$. However, in the absence of transition dynamics, state values alone will not be sufficient. For the greedy improvement step, we need access to the action values, $q(s, a)$. We need to know the q-values for all possible actions, i.e., all $q(S = s, a)$ for all possible actions a in state $S = s$. Only with that information will we be able to apply a greedy maximization to pick the best action, i.e., $\text{argmax}_a q(s, a)$.

We have another complication *when* compared to DP. The agent follows a policy at *the* time of generating the samples. However, such a policy may result in many state-action pairs never being visited, and even more so if the policy is a deterministic one. If *the* agent does not visit a state-action pair, it does not know all $q(s, a)$ for a given state, and hence it cannot find the maximum q-value yielding *an* action. One way to solve the issue is to ensure enough exploration by exploring starts, i.e., ensuring that *the* agent starts an episode from a random state-action pair and over the course of many episodes covers each state-action pair enough time*s, in fact,* infinite in limit.

Figure 4-4 shows the GPI diagram with the change of *v*-values to *q*-values. The evaluation step now is the MC prediction step that was introduced in *the previous* section. Once *the q*-values stabilize, greedy maximization can be applied to obtain a new policy. *The p*olicy *i*mprovement theorem ensures that *the* new policy will be better or at least as good as *the* old policy. The *previous* approach of GPI will *be* a recurring theme. Based on the setup, *the* evaluation steps will change, and *the* improvement step invariably will continue to be greedy maximization.

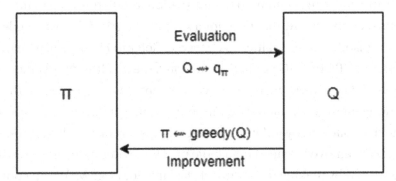

Figure 4-4. *Iteration between the two steps. The first step is evaluation to get the state-action values in sync with the policy being followed. The second step is that of policy improvement to do a greedy maximization for actions*

The assumption of "exploring starts" is not very practical and efficient. It's not practical, as in many scenarios, because *the* agent does not get to choose the start condition, e.g., while training a self-driving car. It's not efficient, as it may not be feasible, and it may also be wasteful for *the* agent to visit each state-action pair infinite (in limit) times. We still need continued exploration for *the* agent to visit all the actions in the states that are visited by the current policy. This is achieved by using a ε-*greedy policy.*

CHAPTER 4   MODEL-FREE APPROACHES

In a ε-greedy policy, agent takes the action with *the* maximum q-value with *the* probability 1-ε, and it takes any action randomly with probability ε/|A|. In other words, the remaining probability of ε is divided equally across all actions to ensure that *the* agent continues to explore nonmaximizing actions. In other words, *the* agent *exploits* the knowledge with probability 1-ε, and it *explores* with probability ε.

$$\pi(a|s) = \begin{cases} 1 - \varepsilon + \dfrac{\varepsilon}{|A|} & \textit{for } a = argmax_a \; Q(s,a) \\ \dfrac{\varepsilon}{A} & \textit{otherwise} \end{cases} \tag{4.3}$$

The action with a maximum q-value gets picked with probability 1-ε from greedy max and ε/|A| as part of random exploration. All other actions are picked up with probability ε/|A|. As the agent learns over multiple episodes, *the* value of ε can be reduced slowly to zero to reach optimal greedy policy.

Let's make one more refinement to the estimation/prediction step of the iteration. In the previous section, we saw that even for a simple 4×4 grid MDP, we needed an order of 10,000 episodes for the values to converge. Refer to Figure 3-9, which shows the convergence of GPI: the MC prediction step puts the *v*-values or *q*-values in sync with the current policy. However, in the previous chapter, we also saw that there was no need for the agent to go all the way to the convergence of values. Similarly, we could run MC prediction followed by policy improvement on an episode-by-episode basis. This approach will remove the need for a large number of iterations in the estimation/ prediction step, thereby making the approach scalable for large MDPs. In contract to the convergence diagram in Figure 3-9, such an approach will produce convergence as shown in Figure 4-5.

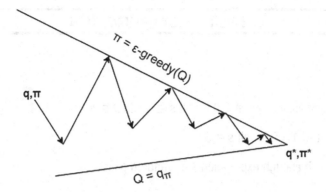

Figure 4-5. *Iteration between the two steps. The first step is the MC prediction/ evaluation for a single step to move the q-values in the direction of the current policy. The second step is that of policy improvement to do a ε-greedy maximization for actions*

Combining all the previous tweaks, we have a practical algorithm for Monte Carlo–based control for optimal policy learning. This is called *greedy* in the limit with infinite exploration (GLIE). We will use the every-visit version in the q-value prediction step. But it takes a minor tweak, just like the one in MC prediction in Figure 4-6 to make it the first-visit variant.

GLIE FOR POLICY OPTIMIZATION

Initialize:

State-action values $Q(s, a) = 0$ for all $s \in S$ and $a \in A$.

Visit count $N(s) = 0$ for all $s \in S$.

Policy π with enough exploration e.g., random policy

Loop:

Sample episode (k) following policy π : $S_0, A_0, R_1, S_1, A_1, R_2, \ldots . A_{t-1}, R_T, S_T$

$G \leftarrow 0$

Loop backward for each step of episode, $t = T - 1, T - 2, \ldots , 1, 0$

$$G \leftarrow \gamma. \, G + R_{t+1}$$

$$N(s,a) \leftarrow N(s,a) + 1$$

$$Q(s,a) \leftarrow Q(s,a) + 1/N(s,a) * \left[G - Q(s,a) \right]$$

Reduce ε using $\varepsilon = 1/k$

Update policy using ε-greedy using updated $Q(s, a)$

Figure 4-6. *Every-visit (GLIE) MC control for policy optimization*

Let's now look at the actual implementation given in `listing4_2.ipynb`. Listing 4-2 reproduces the relevant parts of the code. The implementation follows the pseudocode. We have some extra functions like `argmax_a()` that help us find the action with `max Q(s,a)` for a given state. Another function, `get_action(state)`, returns a ε-greedy action for the current policy. You are encouraged to make tweaks and convert it into the "first visit" variant. You may also want to then compare the result of "first visit" versus "every visit" MC control.

Listing 4-2. GLIE MC Control Algorithm

```python
def GLIE(env, discount_factor=1.0, episode_count=100):
    """
    Find optimal policy given an environment.
    Returns:
        Vector of length env.nS representing the value function.
        policy: [S, A] shaped matrix representing the policy. Random in our case

    """
    # Start with (all 0) state value array and state-action matrix.
    # also initialize visit count to zero for the state-action visit count.
    V = np.zeros(env.nS)
    N = np.zeros((env.nS, env.nA))
    Q = np.zeros((env.nS, env.nA))
    #random policy
    policy = [np.random.randint(env.nA) for _ in range(env.nS)]
    k = 1
    eps = 1

    def argmax_a(arr):
        """
        Return idx of max element in an array.
        Break ties uniformly.
        """
        max_idx = []
        max_val = float('-inf')
        for idx, elem in enumerate(arr):
            if elem == max_val:
                max_idx.append(idx)
            elif elem > max_val:
                max_idx = [idx]
                max_val = elem
        return np.random.choice(max_idx)

    def get_action(state):
        if np.random.random() < eps:
            return np.random.choice(env.nA)
```

```
    else:
        return argmax_a(Q[state])

# run multiple episodes
while k <= episode_count:

    #collect samples for one episode
    episode_states = []
    episode_actions = []
    episode_returns = []
    state = env.reset()
    episode_states.append(state)
    while True:
        action = get_action(state)
        episode_actions.append(action)
        (state, reward, done, _) = env.step(action)
        episode_returns.append(reward)
        if not done:
            episode_states.append(state)
        else:
            break

    #update state-action values
    G = 0
    count = len(episode_states)
    for t in range(count-1, -1, -1):
        s, a, r = episode_states[t], episode_actions[t], episode_
        returns[t]
        G = discount_factor * G + r
        N[s, a] += 1
        Q[s, a] = Q[s, a] + 1/N[s, a] * (G-Q[s, a])

    #Update policy and optimal value
    k = k+1
    eps = 1/k
    #uncomment this to have higher exploration initially
    #and then let epsilon decay after 5000 episodes
```

```
#if k <=100:
#     eps = 0.02

for s in range(env.nS):
    best_action = argmax_a(Q[s])
    policy[s] = best_action
    V[s] = Q[s,best_action]

return np.array(V), np.array(policy)
```

So far in this chapter we have studied on-policy algorithms for prediction and control. In other words, the same policy is used to generate samples as well as policy improvement. Policy improvement is done with respect to q-values of the same ε-greedy policies. We need exploration to find $Q(s, a)$ for all state-action pairs, which is achieved by using ε-greedy policies. However, as we progress, the ε-greedy policy with a limit is suboptimal. We need to exploit more as our understanding of the environment grows with more and more episodes. We have also seen that while theoretically the policy will converge to an optimal policy, at times it requires careful control of the ε value. The other big disadvantage of MC methods is that we need the episodes to finish before we can update q-values and carry out policy optimization. Therefore, MC methods can only be applied to environments that are episodic and where the episodes terminate. Starting in the next section, we will start looking at a different class of algorithms called *temporal difference* methods that combine the advantages of DP (single time-step updates) and MC (i.e., no need to know system dynamics). However, before we dive deep into TD methods, let's go through a short section to introduce and then compare on-policy versus off-policy learning.

Off-Policy MC Control

In GLIE, we saw that to explore enough, we needed to use ε-greedy policies so that all state actions are visited often enough in limit. The policy learned at the end of the loop is used to generate the episodes for the next iteration of the loop. We are using the same policy to explore as the one that is being maximized. Such an approach is called *on-policy* where samples are generated from the same policy that is being optimized.

There is another approach in which the samples are generated using a policy that is more exploratory with a higher ε, while the policy being optimized is the one that may have a lower ε or could even be a fully deterministic one. Such an approach of using a different policy to learn than the one being optimized is called *off-policy* learning. The policy being used to generate the samples is called the *behavior policy*, and the one being learned (maximized) is called the *target policy*. Let's look at Figure 4-7 for the pseudocode of the off-policy MC control algorithm.

OFF POLICY MC CONTROL OPTIMIZATION

Initialize:

    State-action values $Q(s, a) = 0$ for all $s \in S$ and $a \in A$.

    Visit count $N(s) = 0$ for all $s \in S$.

    Policy $\pi = argmax_a Q(S, a)$

Loop:

    $b \leftarrow$ a "behavior policy" with enough exploration

    Sample episode (k) following policy b : $S_0, A_0, R_1, S_1, A_1, \dots . A_{T-1}, R_T, S_T$

    $G \leftarrow 0$

    Loop backward for each step of episode, $t = T - 1, T - 2, \dots, 1, 0$

$$G \leftarrow \gamma.G + R_{t+1}$$
$$N(s,a) \leftarrow N(s,a) + 1$$
$$Q(s,a) \leftarrow Q(s,a) + 1/N(s,a) * \left[G - Q(s,a)\right]$$

    $\pi = argmax_a Q(S, a)$

Figure 4-7. Off-policy MC control for policy optimization

Temporal Difference Learning Methods

Refer to Figure 4-1 to study the backup diagrams of the DP and MC methods. In DP, we back up the values over only one step using values from the successor states to estimate the current state value. We also take an expectation over action probabilities based on the policy being followed and then from the (s, a) pair to all possible rewards and successor states.

$$v_\pi(s) = \sum_a \pi(a|s) \sum_{s',r} p(s',r|s,a)\left[r + \gamma v_\pi(s')\right]$$

The value of a state $v_\pi(s)$ is estimated based on the current estimate of the successor states $v_\pi(s')$. This is known as *bootstrapping*. The estimate is based on another set of estimates. The two sums are the ones that are represented as branch-off nodes in the DP backup diagram in Figure 4-1. Compared to DP, MC is based on starting from a state and sampling the outcomes based on the current policy the agent is following. The value estimates are *averages over multiple runs*. In other words, the sum over model transition probabilities is replaced by averages, and hence the backup diagram for MC is a single long path from one state to the terminal state. The MC approach allowed us to build a scalable learning approach while removing the need to know the exact model dynamics. However, it created two issues: the MC approach works only for episodic environments, and the updates happen only at the end of the termination of an episode. DP had the advantage of using an estimate of the successor state to update the current state value without waiting for an episode to finish.

Temporal difference learning is an approach that combines the benefits of both DP and MC, using bootstrapping from DP and the sample-based approach from MC. The update equation for TD is as follows:

$$V(s) = V(s) + \alpha\left[R + \gamma * V(s') - V(s)\right] \tag{4.4}$$

The current estimate of the total return for state $S = s$, i.e., G_t, is now given by bootstrapping from the current estimate of the successor state (s') shown in the sample run. In other words, G_t in equation (4.2) is replaced by $R + \gamma * V(s')$, an estimate. Compared to this, in the MC method, G_t was the discounted total return for the sample run.

The TD approach described is known as TD(0), and it is a one-step estimate. The reason for calling it TD(0) will become clearer toward the end of the chapter when we talk about TD(λ). For clarity's sake, let's look at the pseudocode for value estimation using TD(0) given in Figure 4-8.

TD(0) FOR ESTIMATION

Input: π, the policy for which state values need to be estimated

Initialize:

    State values $V(s) = 0$ for all $s \in S$

    α – step size

Loop for each episode:

    Choose a start state S

    Loop for each step in the episode:

        Take action A as per state S and policy π

        Observe reward R and next state S'

$$V(s) \leftarrow V(s) + \alpha \left[R + \gamma * V(s') - V(s) \right]$$

$$S \leftarrow S'$$

Figure 4-8. *TD(0) policy estimation*

Having seen all three approaches, DP, MC, and TD, let's put the backup diagrams of all three approaches together, as shown in Figure 4-9. TD(0) is similar to DP as it uses bootstrapping, which is an estimate of the next state values to estimate the current state values. TD(0) is similar to MC as it samples the episodes and uses the observed reward and the next state to update the estimates.

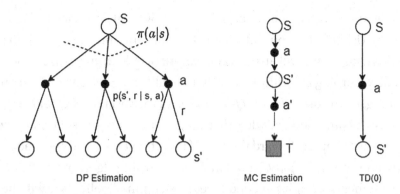

Figure 4-9. *Backup diagram of DP, MC, and TD(0) compared*

Let's now introduce another quantity that you are likely to see again and again in reinforcement learning literature. In equation (4.4), the quantity $[R + \gamma * V(s')]$ is the revised estimate of the total return from state $S = s$, and it is based on a one-step backup from successor states. Further, in equation (4.4), $V(s)$ on the right side of assignment is the current estimate. The update is moving the estimate from $V(s)$ to $V(s) + \alpha$ (*Difference*) where the difference δ_t is given by the following expression:

$$\delta_t = R_{t+1} + \gamma * V(S_{t+1}) - V(S_t) \tag{4.5}$$

The difference δ_t is known as *TD error*. It represents the error (difference) in the estimate of $V(s)$ based on reward R_{t+1} plus the discounted next time-step state value $V(S_{t+1})$ and the current estimate of $V(s)$, i.e., $V(S_t)$. The value of the state is moved by a proportion (learning rate, step rate α) of this error δ_t.

TD has an advantage over DP as it does not require the model knowledge (transition function). A TD method has an advantage over MC as TD methods can update the state value at every step; i.e., they can be used in an online setup through which we learn as the situation unfolds without waiting for the end of episode.

Temporal Difference Control

This section will start taking you into the realm of the real algorithms used in the RL world. In the remaining sections of the chapter, we will look at various methods used in TD learning. We will start with a simple one-step on-policy learning method called *SARSA*. This will be followed by a powerful off-policy technique called *Q-learning*. We will study some foundational aspects of Q-learning in this chapter, and in the next chapter we will integrate deep learning with Q-learning, giving us a powerful approach called Deep Q Networks (DQN). Using DQN, you will be able to train game-playing agents on an Atari simulator. In this chapter, we will also cover a variant of Q-learning called *expected SARSA*, another off-policy learning algorithm. We will then talk about the issue of maximization bias in Q-learning, taking us to *double Q-learning*. All the variants of Q-learning become very powerful when combined with deep learning to represent the state space, which will form the bulk of next chapter. Toward the end of this chapter, we will cover additional concepts such as *experience replay*, which make off-learning algorithms efficient with respect to the number of samples needed to learn an optimal policy. We will then talk about a powerful and a bit involved approach called TD(λ) that tries to combine MC and TD methods on a continuum. Finally, we will look at an environment that has continuous state space and how we can binarize the state values and apply the previously mentioned TD methods. The exercise will demonstrate the need for the approaches that we will take up in the next chapter, covering functional approximation and deep learning for state representation. After Chapters 5 and 6 on deep learning and DQN, we will show another approach called *policy optimization* that revolve around directly learning the policy without needing to find the optimal state/action values.

We have been using the 4×4 grid world so far. We will now look at a few more environments that will be used in the rest of the chapter. We will write the agents in an encapsulated way so that the same agent/algorithm could be applied in various environments without any changes.

The first environment we will use is a variant of the grid world; it is part of the Gym library called the *cliff-walking* environment. In this environment, we have a 4×12 grid world, with the bottom-left cell being the start state *S* and the bottom-right state being the goal state *G*. The rest of the bottom row forms a cliff; stepping on it earns a reward of -100, and the agent is put back to start state again. Each time a step earns a reward of -1 until the agent reaches the goal state. Similar to the 4×4 grid world, the agent can take a step in any direction [UP, RIGHT, DOWN, LEFT]. The episode terminates when the agent reaches the goal state. Figure 4-10 depicts the setup.

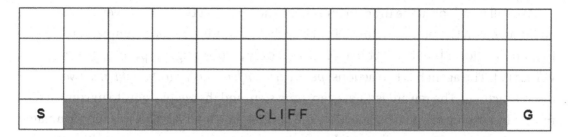

reward = -1 for all transitions. Stepping on cliff has reward of -100

Figure 4-10. *4×10 cliff world. There is a reward of -100 for stepping on the cliff and -1 for other transitions. The goal is to start from S and reach G with the best possible reward*

The next environment we will look at is the "taxi problem." There are four locations marked R, G, Y, and B. When an episode starts, a passenger is randomly standing in one of these four locations. One of the four squares is chosen randomly as the destination location. There are 25 possible locations for a taxi to be found. The passenger has five locations: a start position or an inside taxi. There are four destinations. All these combinations take the possible values of state space to be 500 different combinations. The state value is expressed as a tuple of (taxi_row, taxi_col, passenger_location, destination). There are six actions that can be taken deterministically. The taxi can move *North, South, West, East,* and then there are two actions of *pick* or *drop* passenger. The rewards are -1 per time step, +20 for successful pick/drop, and -10 for pick/drop from the wrong locations. The episode ends when the passenger is picked up and dropped off successfully. Figure 4-11 shows the schematic of the environment.

Figure 4-11. *5×5 taxi problem. There is a reward of -1 for all transitions. An episode ends when the passenger is dropped off at the destination*

We will now look at the third environment known as CartPole. We covered this environment in Chapter 2. In this state, the space is a continuous one comprising four observations: [Cart position, Car velocity, Pole angle, pole angular velocity]. The agent has two actions: *push cart to left* or *push cart to right*, i.e., two discrete actions. The reward is +1 at every time step, and the agent wants to maximize the reward by keeping the pole balanced for the longest time interval. The episode terminates once the pole angle is more than 12 degrees in either direction or the cart position is beyond 2.4 from the center, i.e., either < -2.4 or > 2.4 or if the agent is able to balance the pole for 200 time steps. Figure 4-12 shows a snapshot of the environment in action.

Figure 4-12. *Cart pole problem. The objective is to balance the pole vertically for the maximum number of time steps with a reward of +1 for every time step*

Having explained the various environments, let's now jump into solving these with TD algorithms, starting first with SARSA, an on-policy method.

On-Policy SARSA

Like the MC control methods, we will again leverage GPI. We will use a TD-driven approach for the policy value estimation/prediction step and will continue to use greedy maximization for the policy improvement. Just like with MC, we need to explore enough and visit all the states an infinite number of times to find an optimal policy. Similar to the MC method, we can use a ε-greedy policy and slowly reduce the ε value to zero, i.e., for the limit bring down the exploration to zero.

TD setup is model-free; i.e., we have no prior comprehensive knowledge of transitions. At the same time, to be able to maximize the return by choosing the right actions, we need to know the state-action values $Q(S, A)$. We can reformulate TD estimation from equation (4.4) to the one in (4.6), essentially replacing $V(s)$ with $Q(s, a)$. Both the setups are Markov processes, with equation (4.4) focusing on state-to-state transitions and now the focus being state-action to state-action.

$$Q(S_t,A_t)=Q(S_t,A_t)+\alpha * \left[R_{t+1} +\gamma * Q(S_{t+1},A_{t+1})-Q(S_t,A_t) \right] \qquad (4.6)$$

Similar to equation (4.5), the TD error is now given in context of q-values.

$$\delta_t = R_{t+1} +\gamma * Q(S_{t+1},A_{t+1})-Q(S_t,A_t) \qquad (4.7)$$

To carry out an update as per equation (4.6), we need all the five values S_t, A_t, R_{t+1}, S_{t+1}, and A_{t+1}. This is the reason the approach is called SARSA (state, action, reward, state, action). We will follow a ε-greedy policy to generate the samples, update the q-values using (4.6), and then based on the updated q-values create a new ε-greedy. The policy improvement theorem guarantees that the new policy will be better than the old policy unless the old policy was already optimal. Of course, for the guarantee to hold, we need to bring down the exploration probability ε to zero in the limit.

Please also note that for all episodic policies, the terminal states have $Q(S,A)$ equal to zero; i.e., once in terminal state, the person cannot transition anywhere and will keep getting a reward of zero. This is another way of saying that the episode ends and $Q(S,A)$ is zero for all terminal states. Therefore, when S_{t+1} is a terminal state, equation (4.6) will have $Q(S_{t+1},A_{t+1}) = 0$, and the update equation will look like this:

$$Q(S_t,A_t)=Q(S_t,A_t)+\alpha * \left[R_{t+1} -Q(S_t,A_t) \right] \qquad (4.8)$$

Let's now look at the pseudocode of the SARSA algorithm; see Figure 4-13.

SARSA ON-POLICY TD CONTROL

Initialize:

    State-action values $Q(s, a) = 0$ for all $s \in S$ and $a \in A$.

    Policy $\pi = \varepsilon$-greedy policy with some small $\epsilon \in [0, 1]$

    Learning rate (step size) $\alpha \in [0, 1]$

    Discount factor $\gamma \in [0, 1]$

Loop for each episode:

    Start state S, choose action A based on ε-greedy policy

    Loop for each step until episode end:

        Take action A and observe reward R and next state S'

        Choose action A' using ε-greedy policy using current Q values

        If S' not terminal:

$$Q(S,A) \leftarrow Q(S,A) + \alpha * \left[R + \gamma * Q(S',A') - Q(S,A) \right]$$

        Else:
$$Q(S,A) \leftarrow Q(S,A) + \alpha * \left[R - Q(S,A) \right]$$

        $S \leftarrow S'; A \leftarrow A'$

        [optionally reduce ε periodically toward zero]

    Return policy π based on final Q values.

Figure 4-13. *SARSA, on-policy TD control*

Let's now walk through the code from listing4_3.ipynb, which implements SARSA. The code has a class named SARSAAgent that implements the SARSA learning agent. It has two key functions: update(), which takes the values of state, action, reward, next_state, and next_action, as well as the done flag. It updates the q-value using the TD update equations (4.6) and (4.8). The other function is get_action(state), which returns a random action with probability ε and argmax Q(S,A) with probability

1-ε. There is a generic function `train_agent()` outside the class that trains the agent in a given environment. There are two helper functions: `plot_rewards()` to plot the reward per episode as the training progresses and `print_policy()` to print the optimal policy learned. The listing shows only the code for `SARSAAgent`. For the rest of the code, refer to `listing4_3.ipynb` (Listing 4-3).

Listing 4-3. SARA On-Policy TD Control

```
# SARSA Learning agent class
from collections import defaultdict

class SARSAAgent:
    def __init__(self, alpha, epsilon, gamma, get_possible_actions):
        self.get_possible_actions = get_possible_actions
        self.alpha = alpha
        self.epsilon = epsilon
        self.gamma = gamma
        self._Q = defaultdict(lambda: defaultdict(lambda: 0))

    def get_Q(self, state, action):
        return self._Q[state][action]

    def set_Q(self, state, action, value):
        self._Q[state][action] = value

    # carryout SARSA updated based on the sample (S, A, R, S', A')
    def update(self, state, action, reward, next_state, next_action, done):
        if not done:
            td_error = reward + self.gamma * self.get_Q(next_state, next_
            action) /
- self.get_Q(state,action)
        else:
            td_error = reward - self.get_Q(state,action)

        new_value = self.get_Q(state,action) + self.alpha * td_error
        self.set_Q(state, action, new_value)

    # get argmax for q(s,a)
    def max_action(self, state):
```

```
    actions = self.get_possible_actions(state)
    best_action = []
    best_q_value = float("-inf")

    for action in actions:
        q_s_a = self.get_Q(state, action)
        if q_s_a > best_q_value:
            best_action = [action]
            best_q_value = q_s_a
        elif  q_s_a == best_q_value:
            best_action.append(action)
    return np.random.choice(np.array(best_action))

# choose action as per ε-greedy policy
def get_action(self, state):
    actions = self.get_possible_actions(state)

    if len(actions) == 0:
        return None

    if np.random.random() < self.epsilon:
        a = np.random.choice(actions)
        return a
    else:
        a = self.max_action(state)
        return a
```

Figure 4-14 shows the graph of per-episode-reward as learning progresses and the optimal policy learned. We can see that the reward soon gets close to the optimal value. The policy learned is to avoid the cliff by first going all the way up and then taking a right turn to walk toward the goal. This is surprising as we would have expected the agent to learn the policy to skirt over the cliff and reach the goal, which would have been the shortest path by four steps as compared to the one learned by agent.

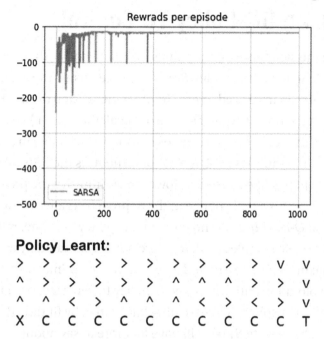

Policy Learnt:

>	>	>	>	>	>	>	>	>	>	v	v
^	>	>	>	>	>	^	^	^	>	>	v
^	^	<	>	^	^	^	<	>	<	>	v
X	C	C	C	C	C	C	C	C	C	C	T

Figure 4-14. *Reward graph during learning under SARSA and policy learned by agent*

However, as our policy continues to explore using ε-greedy, there is always a small chance that in a state when the agent is next to a cliff cell, it takes a random action and falls off into the cliff. It demonstrates the issue of continued exploration even when enough has been learned about the environment, i.e., when the same ε-greedy policy is used for sampling as well as for improvement. We will see how this issue is avoided in Q-learning in which off-policy learning is carried out using an exploratory behavior policy to generate training samples and a deterministic policy is learned as the optimal target policy.

Next, we will study our first off-policy TD algorithm called *Q-learning*.

Q-Learning: An Off-Policy TD Control

In SARSA, we used the samples with the values S, A, R, S', and A' that were generated by the following policy. Action A' from state S' was produced using the ε-greedy policy, the same policy that was then improved in the "improvement" step of GPI. However, instead of generating A' from the policy, what if we looked at all the $Q(S', A')$ and chose the action A', which maximizes the value of $Q(S',A')$ across actions A' available in state S'? We could continue to generate the samples (S, A, R, S') (notice no A' as the fifth value in this tuple) using an exploratory policy like ε-greedy. However, we improve the policy by choosing A' to be $argmax_{A'}Q(S', A')$. This small change in the approach creates a new way to learn the optimal policy called *Q-learning*. It is no more an on-policy learning, rather an off-policy control method where the samples (S, A, R, S') are being generated by an exploratory policy, while we maximize $Q(S', A')$ to find a deterministic optimal target policy.

We are using exploration with the ε-greedy policy to generate the samples (S, A, R, S'). At the same time, we are exploiting the existing knowledge by finding the Q maximizing action $argmax_{A'}Q(S', A')$ in state S'. We will have lot more to say about these trade-offs between exploration and exploitation in Chapter 9.

The update rule for q-values is now defined as follows:

$$Q(S_t, A_t) \leftarrow Q(S_t, A_t) + \alpha * \left[R_{t+1} + \gamma * max_{A_{t+1}} Q(S_{t+1}, A_{t+1}) - Q(S_t, A_t) \right] \quad (4.10)$$

Comparing the previous equation with equation (4.8), you will notice the subtle difference between the two approaches and how that makes Q-learning an off-policy method. The off-policy behavior of Q-learning is handy, and it makes the sample efficient. We will touch upon this in a later section when we talk about *experience replay* or *replay buffer*. Figure 4-15 gives the pseudocode of Q-learning.

Q-LEARNING OFF-POLICY TD CONTROL

Initialize:

    State-action values $Q(s, a) = 0$ for all $s \in S$ and $a \in A$.

    Policy $\pi = \varepsilon$-greedy policy with some small $\epsilon \in [0,1]$

    Learning rate (step size) $\alpha \in [0,1]$

    Discount factor $\gamma \in [0,1]$

Loop for each episode:

    Start state S

    Loop for each step until episode end:

        Choose action A based on ε-greedy policy

        Take action A and observe reward R and next state S'

        If S' not terminal:

$$Q(S,A) \leftarrow Q(S,A) + \alpha * \left[R + \gamma * max_A Q(S',A') - Q(S,A) \right]$$

        Else:

$$Q(S,A) \leftarrow Q(S,A) + \alpha * \left[R - Q(S,A) \right]$$

        $S \leftarrow S'$

Return policy π based on final Q values.

Figure 4-15. *Q-learning, off-policy TD control*

The code in `listing4_4.ipynb` implements Q-learning. Like SARSA, it has a Q-learning agent that is similar to the SARSA agent in Listing 4-3 except for the change in the update rule, which follows (4.10) for Q-learning. The learning function also has a minor change from SARSA. We do not need the fifth value anymore in SARSA, i.e., the next_action A' from S'. We now choose the best action A' while in state S' to improve the policy similar to the Bellman optimality equation. The rest of the implementation from SARSA is carried over to Q-learning. Listing 4-4 shows the implementation of

QLearningAgent. Please note carefully the changes in the update rule as compared to that of the SARSA agent.

Listing 4-4. Q Learning Off-Policy TD Control

```
# Q- Learning agent class
from collections import defaultdict

class QLearningAgent:
    def __init__(self, alpha, epsilon, gamma, get_possible_actions):
        self.get_possible_actions = get_possible_actions
        self.alpha = alpha
        self.epsilon = epsilon
        self.gamma = gamma
        self._Q = defaultdict(lambda: defaultdict(lambda: 0))

    def get_Q(self, state, action):
        return self._Q[state][action]

    def set_Q(self, state, action, value):
        self._Q[state][action] = value

    # Q learning update step
    def update(self, state, action, reward, next_state, done):
        if not done:
            best_next_action = self.max_action(next_state)
            td_error = reward + self.gamma * self.get_Q(next_state, best_
            next_action) - self.get_Q(state,action)
        else:
            td_error = reward - self.get_Q(state,action)

        new_value = self.get_Q(state,action) + self.alpha * td_error
        self.set_Q(state, action, new_value)

    # get best A for Q(S,A) which maximizes the Q(S,a) for actions in state S
    def max_action(self, state):
        actions = self.get_possible_actions(state)
        best_action = []
```

```
    best_q_value = float("-inf")

    for action in actions:
        q_s_a = self.get_Q(state, action)
        if q_s_a > best_q_value:
            best_action = [action]
            best_q_value = q_s_a
        elif  q_s_a == best_q_value:
            best_action.append(action)
    return np.random.choice(np.array(best_action))

# choose action as per ε-greedy policy for exploration
def get_action(self, state):
    actions = self.get_possible_actions(state)

    if len(actions) == 0:
        return None

    if np.random.random() < self.epsilon:
        a = np.random.choice(actions)
        return a
    else:
        a = self.max_action(state)
        return a
```

Let's look at Q-learning being applied on the cliff world environment. The reward per episode improves with training and reaches the optimal value of -13 as compared to that of -17 under SARSA. As shown in Figure 4-16, a better policy under Q-learning is evident. Under Q-learning, the agent learns to navigate to the goal through the cells in the second row just above the cliff. Under Q-learning, the agent is learning a deterministic policy, and our environment is also deterministic. In other words, if the agent takes an action to move right, it will definitely move right and has zero chance of taking any random step in any other direction. Therefore, the agent learns the most optimal policy of going toward the goal by just grazing over the cliff.

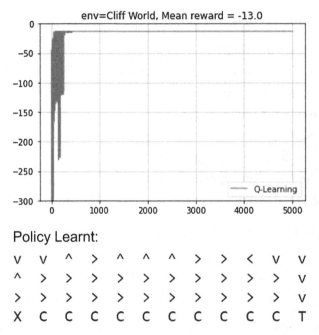

Policy Learnt:

V	V	^	>	^	^	^	>	>	<	V	V
^	>	>	>	>	>	>	>	>	>	>	V
>	>	>	>	>	>	>	>	>	>	>	V
X	C	C	C	C	C	C	C	C	C	C	T

Figure 4-16. *Reward graph during learning under Q-learning and policy learned by agent*

The file listing4_4.ipynb also shows the learning curve when the Q-agent is applied to the taxi world environment. We will be revisiting Q-learning in next chapter on the deep learning approach to the state value approximation. Under that setup, Q-learning is called DQN. DQN with its variants will be used to train a game-playing agent on some Atari games.

To conclude the discussion on Q-learning, let's look at a particular issue that Q-learning may introduce, that of maximization bias.

Maximization Bias and Double Learning

If you look back at equation (4.10), you will notice that we are maximizing over A' to get the max value $Q(S', A')$. Similarly, in SARSA, we find a new ε-greedy policy that is also maximizing over Q to get the action with highest q-value. Further, these q-values are estimates themselves of the true state-action values. In summary, we are using a max over the q-estimate as an "estimate" of the maximum value. Such an approach of "max of estimate" as an "estimate of max" introduces a +ve bias.

To see this, consider a scenario where the reward in some transition takes three values: 5, 0, +5 with an equal probability of 1/3 for each value. The expected reward is zero, but the moment we see a +5, we take that as part of the maximization, and then it never comes down. So, +5 becomes an estimate of the true reward that otherwise in expectation is 0. This is a positive bias introduced due to maximization step.

One of the ways to remove the +ve bias is to use a set of two q-values. One q-value is used to find the action that maximizes the q-value, and the other set of q-values is then used to find the q-value for that max action. Mathematically, it can be represented as follows:

Replace $maxAQ(S, A)$ with $Q_1(S, argmaxAQ_2(S, A))$.

We are using Q_2 to find the maximizing action A, and then Q_1 is used to find the maximum q-value. It can be shown that such an approach removes the +ve or maximization bias. We will revisit this concept when we talk about DQN.

Expected SARSA Control

Let's look at another method that is kind of a hybrid between Q-learning and SARSA; it's called *expected SARSA*. It is similar to Q-learning except that "max" in (4.10) is replaced with an expectation, as shown here:

$$Q(S_t, A_t) \leftarrow Q(S_t, A_t) + \alpha * \left[R_{t+1} + \gamma * \sum_a \pi(a|S_{t+1}).Q(S_{t+1}, a) - Q(S_t, A_t) \right] \qquad (4.11)$$

Expected SARSA has a lower variance as compared to the variance seen in SARSA due to the random selection of A_{t+1}. In expected SARSA, instead of sampling, we take the expectation over all possible actions.

In the cliff world problem, we have deterministic actions, and hence we can set the learning rate $\alpha = 1$ without any major impact on the learning quality. We give the pseudocode for the algorithm. It mirrors Q-learning except for the update logic of taking *expectation* instead of *maximization*. We can run expected SARSA as on-policy, which is what we will do while testing it against the cliff and taxi worlds. It can also be run off-policy where the behavior policy is more exploratory and the target policy π follows a deterministic greedy policy. See Figure 4-17.

EXPECTED SARSA TD CONTROL

Initialize:

> State-action values $Q(s, a) = 0$ for all $s \in S$ and $a \in A$.
>
> Policy $\pi = \varepsilon$-greedy policy with some small $\epsilon \in [0, 1]$
>
> Learning rate (step size) $\alpha \in [0, 1]$
>
> Discount factor $\gamma \in [0, 1]$

Loop for each episode:

> Start state S
>
> Loop for each step until episode end:
>
>> Choose action A based on ε-greedy policy
>>
>> Take action A and observe reward R and next state S'
>>
>> If S' not terminal:
>>
>> $$Q(S,A) \leftarrow Q(S,A) + \alpha * \left[R + \gamma * max_{A'} Q(S',A') - Q(S,A) \right]$$
>>
>> Else:
>>
>> $$Q(S,A) \leftarrow Q(S,A) + \alpha * \left[R - Q(S,A) \right]$$
>
> $S \leftarrow S'$

Return policy π based on final Q values.

Figure 4-17. *Expected SARA TD control*

The file `listing4_5.ipynb` shows the code for the expected SARSA agent. It is similar to the Q-agent except for the replacement of the maximization by the expectation. This change increases the computational complexity of the algorithm a bit but offers faster convergence than SARSA and Q-learning. Listing 4-5 reproduces the code for the expected SARSA agent class.

Listing 4-5. Expected SARSA TD Control

```
# Expected SARSA Learning agent class

class ExpectedSARSAAgent:
    def __init__(self, alpha, epsilon, gamma, get_possible_actions):
        self.get_possible_actions = get_possible_actions
        self.alpha = alpha
        self.epsilon = epsilon
        self.gamma = gamma
        self._Q = defaultdict(lambda: defaultdict(lambda: 0))

    def get_Q(self, state, action):
        return self._Q[state][action]

    def set_Q(self, state, action, value):
        self._Q[state][action] = value

    # Expected SARSA Update
    def update(self, state, action, reward, next_state, done):
        if not done:
            best_next_action = self.max_action(next_state)
            actions = self.get_possible_actions(next_state)
            next_q = 0
            for next_action in actions:
                if next_action == best_next_action:
                    next_q += (1-self.epsilon+self.epsilon/len(actions))*
                    self.get_Q(next_state, next_action)
                else:
                    next_q += (self.epsilon/len(actions))* self.get_Q(next_
                    state, next_action)

            td_error = reward + self.gamma * next_q - self.
            get_Q(state,action)
        else:
            td_error = reward - self.get_Q(state,action)

        new_value = self.get_Q(state,action) + self.alpha * td_error
        self.set_Q(state, action, new_value)
```

```python
# get best A for Q(S,A) which maximizes the Q(S,a) for actions in state S
def max_action(self, state):
    actions = self.get_possible_actions(state)
    best_action = []
    best_q_value = float("-inf")

    for action in actions:
        q_s_a = self.get_Q(state, action)
        if q_s_a > best_q_value:
            best_action = [action]
            best_q_value = q_s_a
        elif  q_s_a == best_q_value:
            best_action.append(action)
    return np.random.choice(np.array(best_action))

# choose action as per ε-greedy policy for exploration
def get_action(self, state):
    actions = self.get_possible_actions(state)

    if len(actions) == 0:
        return None

    if np.random.random() < self.epsilon:
        a = np.random.choice(actions)
        return a
    else:
        a = self.max_action(state)
        return a
```

Figure 4-18 shows the result of training the expected SARSA agent for the cliff world. It has the fastest convergence to the optimal value compared to SARSA and Q-learning. You can experiment and see that the changing learning rate α has no major impact on the convergence in the limit. It is also interesting to note that the policy learned by the expected SARA falls between Q-learning and SARSA. The agent under this policy goes through the middle row of the maze to reach the goal. In our case, we are using the expected SARSA as on-policy, i.e., using the same ε-greedy policy to explore and improve. But possibly due to the expectation, it learns to improve from regular SARSA and finds it safe enough to go through the middle row. In the Python notebook, you can also see the result of running this algorithm against the taxi world.

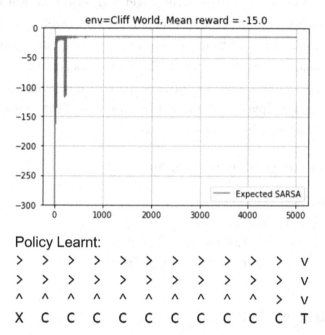

Figure 4-18. *Reward graph with expected SARSA in the cliff world and policy learned by the agent*

Replay Buffer and Off-Policy Learning

Off-policy learning involves two separate policies: behavior policy $b(a|s)$ to explore and generate examples; and $\pi(a|s)$, the target policy that the agent is trying to learn as the optimal policy. Accordingly, we could use the samples generated by the behavior policy again and again to train the agent. The approach makes the process sample efficient as a single transition observed by the agent can be used multiple times.

This is called *experience replay*. The agent is collecting experiences from the environment and replaying those experiences multiple times as part of the learning process. In experience replay, we store the samples (s, a, r, s', done) in a buffer. The samples are generated using an exploratory behavior policy while we improve a deterministic target policy using q-values. Therefore, we can always use older samples from a behavior policy and apply them again and again. We keep the buffer size fixed to some predetermined size and keep deleting the older samples as we collect new ones. The process makes learning sample efficient by reusing a sample multiple time. The rest of the approach remains the same as an off-policy agent.

Let's apply this approach to the Q-learning agent. This time we will skip giving the pseudocode as there is hardly any change except for using samples from the replay buffer multiple times in each transition. We store a new transition in the buffer and then sample `batch_size` samples from the buffer. These samples are used to train the Q-agent in the usual way. The agent then takes another step in the environment, and the cycle begins again. `Listing4_6.ipynb` gives the implementation of the replay buffer and how it is used in the learning algorithm. See Listing 4-6.

Listing 4-6. Q-Learning with Replay Buffer

```
class ReplayBuffer:
    def __init__(self, size):
        self.size = size #max number of items in buffer
        self.buffer =[] #array to hold buffer

    def __len__(self):
        return len(self.buffer)

    def add(self, state, action, reward, next_state, done):
        item = (state, action, reward, next_state, done)
        self.buffer = self.buffer[-self.size:] + [item]

    def sample(self, batch_size):
        idxs = np.random.choice(len(self.buffer), batch_size)
        samples = [self.buffer[i] for i in idxs]
        states, actions, rewards, next_states, done_flags =
        list(zip(*samples))
        return states, actions, rewards, next_states, done_flags

# training algorithm with reply buffer
def train_agent(env, agent, episode_cnt=10000, tmax=10000,
anneal_eps=True, replay_buffer = None, batch_size=16):

    episode_rewards = []
    for i in range(episode_cnt):
        G = 0
```

```
        state = env.reset()
        for t in range(tmax):
            action = agent.get_action(state)
            next_state, reward, done, _ = env.step(action)
            if replay_buffer:
                replay_buffer.add(state, action, reward, next_state, done)
                states, actions, rewards, next_states, done_flags = replay_
                buffer(batch_size)
                for i in range(batch_size):
                    agent.update(states[i], actions[i], rewards[i], next_
                    states[i], done_flags[i])
            else:
                agent.update(state, action, reward, next_state, done)

            G += reward
            if done:
                episode_rewards.append(G)
                # to reduce the exploration probability epsilon over the
                # training period.
                if anneal_eps:
                    agent.epsilon = agent.epsilon * 0.99
                break
            state = next_state
    return np.array(episode_rewards)
```

The Q-agent with the replay buffer is supposed to improve the initial convergence by sampling repeatedly from the buffer. The sample efficiency will become more apparent when we look at DQN. Over the long run, there won't be any significant difference between the optimal values learned with or without the replay buffer. It has another advantage of breaking the correlation between samples. This aspect will also become apparent when we look at deep learning with Q-learning, i.e., DQN.

Q-Learning for Continuous State Spaces

Until now all the examples we have looked at had discrete state spaces. All the methods studied so far could be categorized as tabular methods. The state action space was represented as a matrix with states along one dimension and actions along the cross-axis.

We will soon transition to continuous state spaces and make heavy use of deep learning to represent the state through a neural net. However, we can still solve many of the continuous state problems with some simple approaches. In preparation for the next chapter, let's look at the simplest approach of converting continuous values into discrete bins. The approach we will take is to round off continuous floating-point numbers with some precision, e.g., for a continuous state space value between -1 to 1 being converted into -1, -0.9, -0.8, ... 0, 0.1, 0.2, ... 1.0.

`listing4_7.ipynb` shows this approach in action. We will continue to use the Q-learning agent, experience reply, and learning algorithm from `listing4_6`. However, this time we will be applying the learning on a continuous environment, that of `CartPole`, which was described in detail at the beginning of the chapter. The key change that we need is to receive the state values from environment, discretize the values, and then pass this along to the agent as observations. The agent only gets to see the discrete values and uses these discrete values to learn the optimal policy using QAgent. We reproduce in Listing 4-7 the approach used for converting continuous state values into discrete ones. See Figure 4-19.

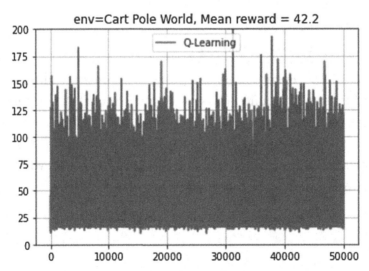

Figure 4-19. *Reward graph with Q-learning on CartPole continuous state space environment*

Listing 4-7. Q-Learning (Off-Policy) on Continuous State Environment

```
# We will use ObservationWrapper class from gym to wrap our environment.
# We need to implement observation() method which will receive the
# original state values from underlying environment
# In observation() we will discretize the state values
# which then will be passed to outside world by env
# the agent will use these discrete state values
# to learn an effective policy using q-learning
from gym.core import ObservationWrapper

class Discretizer(ObservationWrapper):
    def observation(self, state):
        discrete_x_pos = round(state[0], 1)
        discrete_x_vel = round(state[1], 1)
        discrete_pole_angle = round(state[2], 1)
        discrete_pole_ang_vel = round(state[3], 1)

        return (discrete_x_pos, discrete_x_vel,
                discrete_pole_angle, discrete_pole_ang_vel)
```

The Q-agent with discrete discretization of states is able to get about 50 rewards compared to the maximum reward of 200. In subsequent chapters, we will study other more powerful methods to obtain more rewards.

n-Step Returns

In this section, we will unify the MC and TD approaches. MC methods sample the return from a state until the end of the episode, and they do not bootstrap. Accordingly, MC methods cannot be applied for continuing tasks. TD, on the other hand, uses one-step return to estimate the value of the remaining rewards. TD methods take a short view of the trajectory and bootstrap right after one step.

Both the methods are two extremes, and there are many situations when a middle-of-the-road approach could produce lot better results. The idea in *n-step* is to use the rewards from the next n steps and then bootstrap from n+1 step to estimate the value of the remaining rewards. Figure 4-20 shows the backup diagrams for various values of n. On one extreme is one-step, which is the TD(0) method that we just saw in the context of SARSA, Q-learning, and other related approaches. At the other extreme is the ∞-step TD, which is nothing but an MC method. The broad idea is to see that the TD and MC methods are two extremes of the same continuum.

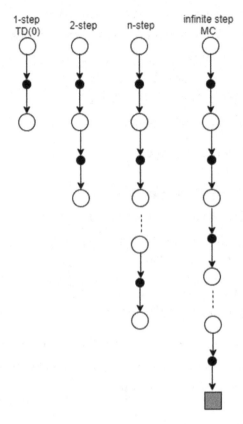

Figure 4-20. *Backup diagrams of n-step methods with TD(0) and MC at two extremes, n=1 and n=∞ (end of episode)*

The approach of n-step can be used in an on-policy setting. We can have n-step SARSA and n-step expected SARSA, and these are natural extensions of what we have learned so far. However, using an n-step approach in off-policy learning would require us to factor one more concept, the relative difference of observing a specific n-step transition across states under behavior policy versus that under target-policy. To use the data from behavior policy $b(a|s)$ for optimizing target policy $\pi(a|s)$, we need to multiply the n-step returns observed under the behavior policy with a ratio called *importance sampling ratio*.

Consider a starting state S_t and the trajectory of action and state sequences until the end of the episode, $A_t, S_{t+1}, A_{t+1}, ..., S_T$. The probability of observing the sequence under a policy π is given by the following:

$$\Pr\{trajectory\} = \pi(A_t|S_t.p(S_{t+1}|S_t,A_t.\pi(A_{t+1}|S_{t+1}.......p(S_T|S_{T-1},A_{T-1}$$

The importance sampling ratio is the ratio of the probability of trajectory under the target policy π and the probability of trajectory under behavior policy b.

$$\rho_{t:T-1} = \frac{\Pr_\pi\{trajectory\}}{\Pr_b\{trajectory\}} = \prod_{k=t}^{T-1} \frac{\pi(A_k \vee S_k)}{b(A_k \vee S_k)} \tag{4.12}$$

The importance sampling ratio ensures that the return of a trajectory observed under the behavior policy is adjusted up or down based on the relative chance of observing a trajectory under the target policy versus the chance of observing the same trajectory under the behavior policy.

Nothing comes for free, which is the case with importance sampling. The importance sampling ratio can cause wide variance. Plus, these are not computationally efficient. There are many advanced techniques like *discount-aware importance sampling* and *per-decision importance sampling*, which look at the importance sampling and rewards in various different ways to reduce the variance and also to make these algorithms efficient.

We will not be going into the details of implementing these algorithms in this book. Our key focus was to introduce these at a conceptual level and make you aware of the advanced techniques.

Eligibility Traces and TD(λ)

Eligibility traces unify the MC and TD methods in an algorithmically efficient way. TD methods when combined with eligibility trace produce TD(λ) where $\lambda = 0$, making it equivalent to the one-step TD that we have studied so far. That's the reason why one-step TD is also known as TD(0). The value of $\lambda = 1$ makes it similar to the regular ∞-step TD or in other words an MC method. Eligibility trace makes it possible to apply MC methods on nonepisodic tasks. We will cover only high-level concepts of eligibility trace and TD(λ).

In the previous section, we looked at n-step returns with n=1 taking us to the regular TD method and n=∞ taking us to MC. We also touched upon the fact that neither extreme is good. An algorithm performs best with some intermediate value of

n. n-step offered a view on how to unify TD and MC. What eligibility does is to offer an efficient way to combine them without keeping track of the n-step transitions at each step. Until now we have looked at an approach of updating a state value based on the next n transitions in the future. This is called the *forward view*. However, you could also look backward, i.e., at each time step t, and see the impact that the reward at time step t would have on the preceding n states in past. This is known as *backward view* and forms the core of TD(λ). The approach allows an efficient implementation of integrating n-step returns in TD learning.

Look back at Figure 4-20. What if instead of choosing different values of n, we combined all the n-step returns with some weight? This is known as λ-return, and the equation is as follows:

$$G_t^\lambda = (1-\lambda) \sum_{n=1}^{T-t-1} \lambda^{n-1} G_{t:t+n} + \lambda^{T-t-1} G_t \tag{4.13}$$

Here, $G_{t:t+n}$ is the n-step return which uses bootstrapped value of remaining steps at the end of the nth step. It is defined as follows:

$$G_{t:t+n} = R_{t+1} + \gamma R_{t+2} + \ldots + \gamma^{n-1} R_{t+n} + \gamma^n V(S_{t+n}) \tag{4.14}$$

If we put $\lambda = 0$ in (4.13), we get the following:

$$G_t^0 = G_{t:t+1} = R_{t+1} + \gamma V(S_{t+1})$$

The previous expression is similar to the target value for state-action updates of TD(0) in (4.7).

On other hand, putting $\lambda = 1$ in (4.13) makes G_t^1 mimic MC and return G_t as follows:

$$G_t^1 = G_t = R_{t+1} + \gamma R_{t+2} + \ldots + \gamma^{T-t-1} R_T$$

The TD(λ) algorithm uses the previous λ-return with a trace vector known as *eligibility trace* to have an efficient online TD method using the "backward" view. Eligibility trace keeps a record of how far in the past a state was observed and by how much would that state's estimate would be impacted by the current return observed.

We will stop here with the basic introduction of λ-returns, eligibility trace, and TD(λ). For a detailed review of the mathematical derivations as well as the various algorithms based on them, refer to the book Reinforcement Learning: An Introduction by Barto and Sutton, 2nd edition.

Relationships Between DP, MC, and TD

At the beginning of the chapter, we talked about how the DP, MC, and TD methods compare. We introduced the MC methods followed by the TD methods, and then we used n-step and TD(λ) to combine MC and TD as two extremes of the sample-based model-free learning.

To conclude the chapter, Table 4-1 summarizes the comparison of the DP and TD methods.

Table 4-1. *Comparison of DP and TD Methods in the Context of Bellman Equations*

	Full Backup (DP)	Sample Backup (TD)
Bellman expectation equation for $v_\pi(s)$	Iterative policy evaluation	TD prediction
Bellman expectation equation for $q_\pi(s, a)$	Q-policy iteration	SARSA
Bellman optimality equation for $q\pi(s, a)$	Q-value iteration	Q-learning

Summary

In this chapter, we looked at the model-free approach to reinforcement learning. We started by estimating the state value using the Monte Carlo approach. We looked at the "first visit" and "every visit" approaches. We then looked at the bias and variance trade-off in general and specifically in the context of the MC approaches. With the foundation of MC estimation in place, we looked at MC control methods connecting it with the GPI framework for policy improvement that was introduced in Chapter 3. We saw how GPI could be applied by swapping the estimation step of the approach from DP-based to an MC-based approach. We looked in detail at the exploration exploitation dilemma that needs to be balanced, especially in the model-free world where the transition probabilities are not known. We then briefly talked about the off-policy approach in the context of the MC methods.

TD was the next approach we looked into with respect to model-free learning. We started off by establishing the basics of TD learning, starting with TD-based value estimation. This was followed by a deep dive into SARSA, an on-policy TD control method. We then looked into Q-learning, a powerful off-policy TD learning approach, and some of its variants like expected SARSA.

In the context of TD learning, we also introduced the concept of state approximation to convert continuous state spaces into approximate discrete state values. The concept of state approximation will form the bulk of the next chapter and will allow us to combine deep learning with reinforcement learning.

Before concluding the chapter, we finally looked at n-step returns, eligibility traces, and TD(λ) as ways to combine TD and MC into a single framework.

CHAPTER 5

Function Approximation

In the previous three chapters, we looked at various approaches to planning and control, first using dynamic programming (DP), then using the Monte Carlo approach (MC), and finally using the temporal difference (TD) approach. In all these approaches, we always looked at problems where the state space and actions were both discrete. Only in the previous chapter toward the end did we talk about Q-learning in a continuous state space. We discretized the state values using an arbitrary approach and trained a learning model. In this chapter, we are going to extend that approach by talking about the theoretical foundations of approximation and how it impacts the setup for reinforcement learning. We will then look at the various approaches to approximating values, first with a linear approach that has a good theoretical foundation and then with a nonlinear approach specifically with neural networks. This aspect of combining deep learning with reinforcement learning is the most exciting development that has moved reinforcement learning algorithms to scale.

As usual, the approach will be to look at everything in the context of the *prediction/ estimation* setup where the agent tries to follow a given policy to learn the state value and/or action values. This will be followed by talking about *control*, i.e., to find the optimal policy. We will continue to be in a model-free world where we do not know the transition dynamics. We will then talk about the issues of convergence and stability in the world of function approximation. So far, the convergence has not been a big issue in the context of the exact and discrete state spaces. However, function approximation brings about new issues that need to be considered for theoretical guarantees and practical best practices. We will also touch upon batch methods and compare them with the incremental learning approach discussed in the first part of this chapter.

We will close the chapter with a quick overview of deep learning, basic theory, and the basics of building/training models using PyTorch and TensorFlow.

© Nimish Sanghi 2021
N. Sanghi, *Deep Reinforcement Learning with Python*, https://doi.org/10.1007/978-1-4842-6809-4_5

Introduction

Reinforcement learning can be used to solve very big problems with many discrete state configurations or problems with continuous state space. Consider the game of backgammon, which has close to 10^{20} discrete states, or consider the game of Go, which has close to 10^{170} discrete states. Also consider environments like self-driving cars, drones, or robots: these have a continuous state space.

Up to now we saw problems where the state space was discrete and also small in size, such as the grid world with ~100 states or the taxi world with 500 states. How do we scale the algorithms we have learned so far to bigger environments or environments with continuous state spaces? All along we have been representing the state values $V(s)$ or the action values $Q(s, a)$ with a table, with one entry for each value of state s or a combination of state s and action a. As the numbers increase, the table size is going to become huge, making it infeasible to be able to store state or action values in a table. Further, there will be too many combinations, which can slow down the learning of a policy. The algorithm may spend too much time in states that are very low probability in a real run of the environment.

We will take a different approach now. Let's represent the state value (or state-action value) with the following function:

$$\hat{v}(s;w) \approx v_\pi(s)$$

$$\hat{q}(s, a; w) \approx q_\pi(s, a) \tag{5.1}$$

Instead of representing values in a table, they are now being represented by the function $\hat{v}(s;w)$ or $\hat{q}(s, a; w)$ where the parameter w is dependent on the policy being followed by the agent, and where s or (s, a) are the inputs to the state or state-value functions. We choose the number of parameters $|w|$ which is lot smaller than the number of states $|s|$ or the number of state-action pairs ($|s| \times |a|$). The consequence of this approach is that there is a generalization of representation of state of the state-action values. When we update the weight vector w based on some update equation for a given state s, it not only updates the value for that specific s or (s, a), but also updates the values for many other states or state actions that are close to the original s or (s, a) for which the update has been carried out. This depends on the geometry of the function. The other values of states near s will also be impacted by such an update as shown previously. We are approximating the values with a function that is a lot more restricted than the number of states. Just to be specific, instead of updating $v(s)$ or $q(s, a)$ directly, we now update the parameter set w of the function, which in turn impacts the value estimates $\hat{v}(s;w)$ or $\hat{q}(s, a; w)$. Of course, like before, we carry out the w update using the MC or TD approach. There are various approaches to function approximation. We could feed the state vector (the values of all the variables that signify the state, e.g., position, speed, location, etc.) and get $\hat{v}(s;w)$, or we could feed state and action vectors and get $\hat{q}(s, a; w)$ as an output. An alternate approach that is very dominant in the case of actions being discrete and coming from a small set is to feed state vector s and get $|A|$ number of $\hat{q}(s, a; w)$, one for each action possible ($|A|$ denotes the number of possible actions). Figure 5-1 shows the schematic.

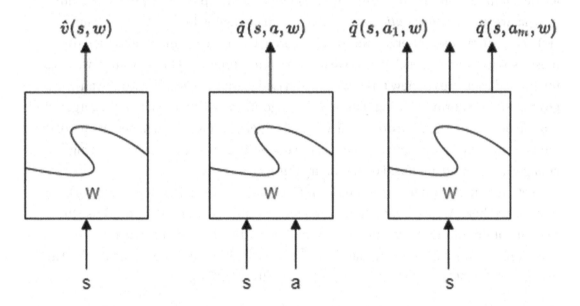

Figure 5-1. *Ways to represent $\hat{v}(s;w)$ or $\hat{q}(s, a; w)$ using the function approximation approach. The first and last ones are the most common ones we will be using in this chapter*

There are various approaches to building such functional approximators, but we will be exploring two common approaches: linear approximators using tiling and nonlinear approximators using neural networks.

However, before we do so, we need to revisit theoretical foundations to see what operations are required to make w move such that we successively reduce the error between target values and the current estimates of state or state-action values, $v(s)$ or $q(s, a)$.

Theory of Approximation

Function approximation is a topic studied extensively in the field of supervised learning wherein based on training data we build a generalization of the underlying model. Most of the theory from supervised learning can be applied to reinforcement learning with functional approximation. However, RL with functional approximation brings to fore new issues such as how to bootstrap as well as its impact on nonstationarity. In supervised learning, while the algorithm is learning, the problem/model from which the training data was generated does not change. However, when it comes to RL with function approximation, the way the target (labeled *output* in supervised learning) is formed, it induces nonstationarity, and we need to come up with new ways to handle it. What we mean by *nonstationarity* is that we do not know the actual target values of $v(s)$ or $q(s, a)$. We use either the MC or TD approach to form estimates and then use these estimates as "targets." And as we improve our estimates of target values, we used the revised estimates as new targets. In supervised learning it is different; the targets are given and fixed during training. The learning algorithm has no impact on the targets. In reinforcement learning, we do not have actual targets, and we are using estimates of the target values. As these estimates change, the targets being used in the learning algorithm change; i.e., they are not fixed or stationary during the learning.

Let's revisit the update equations for MC (equation 4.2) and TD (equation 4.4), reproduced here. We have modified the equations to make both MC and TD use the same notations of subscript t for the current time and $t + 1$ for the next instant. Both equations carry out the same update to move $V_t(s)$ closer to its target, which is $G_t(s)$ in the case of the MC update and $R_{t+1} + \gamma * V_t(s')$ for the TD(0) update.

$$V_{t+1}(s) = V_t(s) + \alpha \left[G_t(s) - V_t(s) \right] \tag{5.2}$$

$$V_{t+1}(s) = V_t(s) + \alpha \left[R_{t+1} + \gamma * V_t(s') - V_t(s) \right] \tag{5.3}$$

This is similar to what we do in supervised learning, especially in linear least square regression. We have the output values/targets $y(t)$, and we have the input features $x(t)$, together called *training data*. We can choose a model $Model_w[x(t)]$ like the polynomial linear model, decision tree, or support vectors, or even other nonlinear models like neural nets. The training data is used to minimize the error between what the model is predicting and what the actual output values are from the training set. The is called the *minimizing loss function* and is represented as follows:

$$J(w) = \left[y(t) - \hat{y}(t;w) \right]^2 ; where\ \hat{y}(t;w) = Model_w \left[x(t) \right] \tag{5.4}$$

When $J(w)$ is a differentiable function, which will be the case in this book, we can use gradient descent to tweak the weights/parameters w of the model to minimize the error/loss function $J(w)$. Usually, the update is carried out in batches multiple times using the same training data until the loss stops reducing further. The model with weights w has now learned the underlying mapping from input $x(t)$ to output $y(t)$. The way the delta update is carried out is given in the following equations:

$$\text{Gradient of } J(w) \text{ wrt } w \ : \ = \nabla_w J(w)$$

$$\text{For given loss function: } \Delta_w J(w) = -2 * \left[y(t) - \hat{y}(t;w) \right] * \nabla_w \hat{y}(t;w).$$

To adjust w, we take a small step in the negative direction of $\Delta_w J(w)$, which will reduce the error.

$$w_{t+1} = w_t - \alpha . \nabla_w J(w) \tag{5.5}$$

The weights move in the direction that minimize the loss, i.e., the difference between the actual and predicted output values. Moving on, let's spend some time talking about the various approaches to function approximation. The most common approaches are as follows:

- Linear combination of features. We combine the features (such as speed, velocity, position, etc.) weighted by vector w and use the computed value as the state value. Common approaches are as follows:

  - Polynomials

  - Fourier basis functions

  - Radial basis functions

  - Coarse coding

  - Tile coding

- Nonlinear but differentiable approaches, with neural networks being the most popular and currently trending one.

- Nonparametric, memory-based approaches.

In this book, we will mostly talk about deep learning–based neural network approaches that suit unstructured inputs such as images captured by the agent's vision system or freeform texts using natural language processing (NLP). Later parts of this chapter and the next chapter will be devoted to using deep learning–based function approximation, and we will see many variations with full code examples using PyTorch and TensorFlow. But we are getting ahead of ourselves. Let's first examine a few common linear approximation approaches such as coarse coding and tile coding. As the focus of this book is on the use of deep learning in reinforcement learning, we will not be devoting a lot of time to various other linear approximation approaches. Also, just because we are not devoting time to all the linear approaches, it does not mean that they lack power of effectiveness. Depending on the problem at hand, the linear approximation approach may be the right way to go; it's effective, fast, and with convergence guarantees.

Coarse Coding

Let's look at the mountain car problem that was discussed in Figure 2-2. The car has a two-dimensional state, a position, and a velocity. Suppose we divide the two-dimensional state space into overlapping circles with each circle representing a feature. If state S lies inside a circle, that particular feature is present and has a value of 1; otherwise, the feature is absent and has a value of 0. The number of features is the number of circles. Let's say we have p circles; then we have converted a two-dimensional continuous state space to a p-dimensional state space where each dimension can be 0 or 1. In other words, each dimension can belong to {0,1}.

Note   {0,1} represents the set of possible values, i.e., either 0 or 1. (0,1) with regular brackets represents the range of values, i.e., any value from 0 to 1 with both 0 and 1 excluded. [0,1) represents the range of values between 0 to 1 as well as the value on left; i.e., 0 is included in the range.

All those features represented by circles in which the state S lies will be "on" or equal to 1. Figure 5-2 shows an example. Two states are shown in the diagram, and depending on the circles that these points lie inside, the corresponding features will be turned on, while other features will be turned off. The generalization will depend on the size of circles and how densely the circles are packed together. If the circles are replaced by an ellipses, the generalization will be more in the direction of the elongation. We could also choose shapes other than circles to control the amount of generalization.

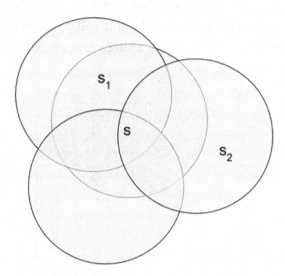

Figure 5-2. *Coarse coding in two dimensions using circles. The generalization depends on the size of circles as well as the density with which the circles are put together*

Now consider the case with large, densely packed circles. A large circle makes the initial generalization wide where two faraway states are connected because they fall inside at least one common circle. However, the density (i.e., number of circles) allows us to control the fine-grained generalization. By having many circles, we ensure that even nearby states have at least one feature that is different between two states. This will hold even when each of the individual circles is big. With the help of experiments with varying configurations of the circle size and number of circles, one can fine-tune the size and number of circles to control the generalization appropriate for the problem/domain in question.

Tile Encoding

Tile encoding is a form of coarse coding that can be programmatically planned. It works well over multidimensional space, making it much more useful than generic coarse coding.

Let's consider a two-dimensional space like the mountain car we just talked about. We divide the space into nonoverlapping grids covering the whole space. Each such division is calling *tiling*, as shown in the left diagram of Figure 5-3. The *tiles* are square

129

here, and depending the location of state S on this 2D space, only one tile is 1, while all other tiles are 0.

We then have a number of such *tiling* offset from each other. Suppose we use n tilings; then for a state, only one tile from each tiling will be on. In other words, if there are n tilings, then exactly n features will be 1, a single feature from each of the n tilings. Figure 5-3 shows an example.

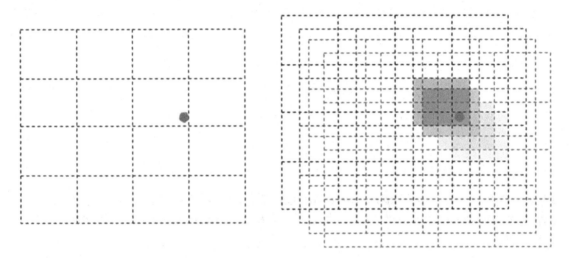

Figure 5-3. *Tile coding. We have 4×4=16 tiles in a single tiling as shown in the left figure. And we have four tilings overlapping each other as shown in four different colors in the right figure. A state (green color dot) lights up a single tile from each tiling. The generalization is controlled by the number of tiles in a single tiling as well as the total number of tilings*

Note that if the learning rate of step size were α(alpha) in equations (5.1) and (5.2), we would now replace it with $\frac{\alpha}{n}$ where n is the number of tilings. This is to make the algorithm scale free of the number of tilings. As both coarse coding and tile encoding use binary features, digital computers can speed up computations.

The nature of generalization now depends on the following factors:

- The number of tiles in a single tiling (the left figure in Figure 5-3)

- The number of tilings (the right figure in Figure 5-4 showing four tilings in four different colors)

- The nature of offset, whether uniform and symmetric or asymmetric

There are some general strategies to decide the previous numbers. Consider the situation where each tile in a single tiling is a square of width w. For a continuous space of k dimensions, it will be a k-dimensional square with each side of width w. Suppose we have n tilings, and hence the tilings need to be offset from each other by a distance of $\dfrac{w}{n}$ in all dimensions. This is known as a *displacement vector*. The first heuristic is to choose n such that $n = 2^i \geq 4k$. And the displacement in each direction is an odd multiple (1, 3, 5, 7, ..., $2k - 1$) of displacement vector $\dfrac{w}{n}$. In our upcoming example, we will be using a library to help us divide the two-dimensional mountain car state space into appropriate tilings. We will provide the 2D state vector, and the library will give us back the active tiles vector.

Challenges in Approximation

While we leverage the knowledge of supervised learning–based methods like gradient descent explained earlier, we have to keep two things in mind that make gradient-based methods harder to work in reinforcement learning as compared to the supervised learning.

First, in supervised learning, the training data is held constant. The data is generated from the model, and while we do, the model does not change. It is a ground truth that is given to us and that we are trying to approximate by using the data to learn about the way inputs are mapped to outputs. The data provided to the training algorithm is external to the algorithm, and it does not depend on the algorithm in any way. It is given as constant and independent of the learning algorithm. Unfortunately, in RL, especially in a model-free setup, such is not the case. The data used to generate training samples are based on the policy the agent is following, and it is not a complete picture of the underlying model. As we explore the environment, we learn more, and a new set of training data is generated. We either use the MC-based approach of observing an actual trajectory or bootstrap under TD to form an estimate of the target value, the $y(t)$. As we explore and learn more, the target $y(t)$ changes, which is not the case in supervised learning. This is known as the problem of *nonstationary targets*.

Second, supervised learning is based on the theoretical premise of samples being uncorrelated to each other, mathematically known as i.i.d. (for "independent identically distributed") data. However, in RL, the data we see depends on the policy that the agent followed to generate the data. In a given episode, the states we see are dependent on the policy the agent is following at that instant. States that come in later time steps depend on the action (decisions) the agent took earlier. In other words, the data is *correlated*. The next state s_{t+1} we see depends on the current state s_t and the action a_t agent takes in that state.

These two issues make function approximation harder in an RL setup. As we go along, we will see the various approaches that have been taken to address these challenges.

With a broad understanding of the approach, it is time now to start with our usual course of first looking at value *prediction/estimate* to learn a function that can represent the value functions. We will then look at the *control* aspect, i.e., the process of the agent trying to optimize the policy. It will follow the usual pattern of using Generalized Policy Iteration (GPI), just like the approach in the previous chapter.

Incremental Prediction: MC, TD, TD(λ)

In this section, we will look at the prediction problem, i.e., how to estimate the state values using function approximation.

Following along, let's try to extend the supervised training process of finding a model using training data consisting of inputs and targets to function approximation under RL using the loss function in (5.4) and weight update in (5.5). If you compare the loss function in (5.4) and MC/TD updates in (5.2) and (5.3), you can draw a parallel by thinking of MC and TD updates as operations, which are trying to minimize the error between the actual target $v_\pi(s)$ and the current estimate $v(s)$. We can represent the loss function as follows:

$$J(w) = E_\pi \left[V_\pi(s) - V_t(s) \right]^2 \tag{5.6}$$

Following the same derivation as in (5.5) and using stochastic gradient descent (i.e., replacing expectation with update at each sample), we can write the update equation for weight vector $\boldsymbol{w}$ as follows:

$$w_{t+1} = w_t - \alpha . \nabla_w J(w)$$

$$w_{t+1} = w_t + \alpha . \left[V_\pi(s) - V_t(s;w) \right] . \nabla_w V_t(s;w) \tag{5.7}$$

However, unlike supervised learning, we do not have the actual/target output values $V_\pi(s)$; rather, we use estimates of these targets. With MC, the estimate/target of $V_\pi(s)$ is $G_t(s)$, while the estimate/target under TD(0) is $R_{t+1} + \gamma * V_t(s')$. Accordingly, the updates under MC and TD(0) with functional approximation can be written as follows.

Here is the MC update:

$$w_{t+1} = w_t + \alpha.\left[G_t(s) - V_t(s;w)\right].\nabla_w V_t(s;w) \tag{5.8}$$

Here is the TD(0) update:

$$w_{t+1} = w_t + \alpha.\left[R_{t+1} + \gamma * V_t(s';w) - V_t(s;w)\right].\nabla_w V_t(s;w) \tag{5.9}$$

A similar set of equations can be written for q-values. We will see that in the next section. This is along the same lines of what we did for the MC and TD control sections in the previous chapter.

Let's first consider the setup of linear approximation where the state value $\hat{v}(s;w)$ can be expressed as a dot product of state vector $x(s)$ and weight vector w:

$$\hat{v}(s;w) = x(s)^T.w = \sum_i x_i(s) * w_i \tag{5.10}$$

The derivative of $\hat{v}(s;w)$ with respect to w will now be simply state vector $x(s)$.

$$\Delta_w V_t(s;w) = x(s) \tag{5.11}$$

Combining (5.11) with equation (5.7) gives us the following:

$$w_{t+1} = w_t + \alpha.\left[V_\pi(s) - V_t(s;w)\right].x(s) \tag{5.12}$$

As discussed, we do not know the true state value $V_\pi(s)$, and hence we use an estimate $G_t(s)$ in the MC approach and an estimate $R_{t+1} + \gamma * V_t(s')$ in the TD(0) approach. This gives us the weight update rules for MC and TD in the linear approximation case as follows.

Here is the MC update:

$$w_{t+1} = w_t + \alpha.\left[G_t(s) - V_t(s;w)\right].x(s) \tag{5.13}$$

Here is the TD(0) update:

$$w_{t+1} = w_t + \alpha.\left[R_{t+1} + \gamma * V_t(s';w) - V_t(s;w) \right].x(s) \tag{5.14}$$

In simple terms, the update to weights, the second term on the right side of (5.14), can be expressed as follows:

Update = learning rate x prediction error x feature value

Let's tie this back to the table-based approach for the discrete states that we saw in the previous chapter. We will show that table lookup is a special case of the linear approach. Consider that each component of x(s) is either one or zero and only one of them can have a value of 1 with all rest of the features being zero. $x^{table}(s)$ is a column vector of size p in which only one element can have a value of 1 at any point with the rest of the elements equal to 0. Depending on the state the agent is in, the corresponding element would be 1.

$$x^{table}(s) = \begin{pmatrix} 1(s=s_1) \\ .. \\ .. \\ 1(s=s_p) \end{pmatrix}$$

The weight vector comprises the values of state v(s) for each s = s_1, s_2, ... s_p.

$$\begin{pmatrix} w_1 \\ .. \\ .. \\ w_p \end{pmatrix} = \begin{pmatrix} v(s_1) \\ .. \\ .. \\ v(s_1) \end{pmatrix}$$

Using these expressions in (5.10), we get the following:

$$\hat{v}(s=s_k;w) = x(s)^T.w = v(s_k)$$

We use this expression in the linear update equations (5.13) and (5.14) to get the familiar update rules from Chapter 4:

Here is the MC update:

$$v_{t+1}(s) = v_t(s) + \alpha.\left[G_t(s) - V_t(s)\right], \; s \in s_1, s_1, \dots, s_p \qquad (5.15)$$

Here is the TD(0) update:

$$v_{t+1}(s) = v_t(s) + \alpha.\left[R_{t+1} + \gamma * V_t(s') - V_t(s)\right], \; s \in s_1, s_1, \dots, s_{p.} \qquad (5.16)$$

The previous derivation was to tie back the table lookup back as a special case of a more general linear function approximation.

One more point to note that we glossed over while deriving the update equations was that the point of target estimate $G_t(s)$ in MC and $R_{t+1} + \gamma * V_t(s')$ in TD(0) depending on the current policy, which in turn depends on the current weight vector w. As an example, let's revisit (5.6) and replace $V_\pi(s)$ with the TD target and then take the gradient.

$$loss: \quad J(w) = \left[V_\pi(s) - V_t(s)\right]^2$$

$$or, \; J(w) = \left[R_{t+1} + \gamma * V_t(s'; w) - V_t(s; w)\right]^2$$

If we take the derivative of $J(w)$ with respect to w, we will actually get two terms, one due to the derivative of $V_t(s'; w)$, the next state, and another term due to the derivative of $V_t(s; w)$. Such an approach of taking both gradient contributions $\nabla V_t(s'; w)$ and $\nabla V_t(s; w)$ worsens the speed of learning. First, the reason is that we want the targets to stay constant, and hence we need to ignore the contribution due to $\nabla V_t(s'; w)$. Second, conceptually with gradient descent we are trying to pull the value of the current state $V_t(s'; w)$ toward its target. Taking the second contribution term $\nabla V_t(s'; w)$ means that we are trying to move the value of the next state $S=s'$ toward the value of the current state $S=s$.

In summary, we take only the derivative of the current state value $V_t(s; w)$ and ignore the derivative of the next state value $V_t(s'; w)$. The approach makes the value estimation look similar to the approach used with supervised learning with stationary targets. This is also the reason why sometimes the gradient descent method used in (5.8) and (5.9) are also called *semi-gradient* methods.

As we touched upon earlier, the convergence of algorithms is not guaranteed anymore, unlike the guarantee we had in the tabular setup due to contraction theorems. However, most of the algorithms with some careful considerations do converge in practice. Table 5-1 shows the convergence of various prediction/estimation algorithms. We will not be going into the detailed explanation of these convergence properties. Such a discussion is more suited for a book with a focus on the theoretical aspects of learning. Ours is a practical one, with enough theory to understand the background and appreciate the nuances of algorithms, with the core focus being on coding these algorithms in PyTorch or TensorFlow.

Table 5-1. *Convergence of Prediction/Estimation Algorithms*

Policy Type	Algorithm	Table Lookup	Linear	Nonlinear
On-policy	MC	Y	Y	Y
	TD(0)	Y	Y	N
	TD(λ)	Y	Y	N
Off-policy	MC	Y	Y	Y
	TD(0)	Y	N	N
	TD(λ)	Y	N	N

In a later section, we will see that the combination of bootstrapping (e.g., TD), function approximation, and off-policy all present together can impact stability adversely unless careful consideration is given to the learning process.

Let's now look at the control problem, i.e., how to optimize the policy with function approximation.

Incremental Control

Just like in the previous chapter, we will follow a similar approach. We start with function approximation to estimate the q-values.

$$\hat{q}(s, a; w) \approx q_{\pi}(s, a) \tag{5.17}$$

Like before, we form a loss function between the target and current value.

$$J(w) = E_\pi \left[\left(q_\pi(s,a) - \hat{q}(s,a;w) \right)^2 \right]$$ (5.18)

Loss is minimized with respect to w to carry out stochastic gradient descent:

$$w_{t+1} = w_t - \alpha . \nabla_w J(w)$$

where,

$$\nabla_w J(w) = \left(q_\pi(s,a) - \hat{q}(s,a;w) \right) . \nabla_w \hat{q}(s,a;w)$$ (5.19)

Like before, we can simplify the equation when $\hat{q}(s,a;w)$ uses linear approximation with $\hat{q}(s,a;w) = x(s,a)^T . w$. The derivative $\nabla_w \hat{q}(s,a;w)$, in a linear case as shown previously, will become $\nabla_w \hat{q}(s,a;w) = x(s,a)$.

Next, as we do not know the true q-value $q_\pi(s,a)$, we replace it with the estimates using either MC or TD, giving us a set of equations.

Here is the MC update:

$$w_{t+1} = w_t + \alpha . \left[G_t(s) - q_t(s,a;w) \right] . \nabla_w q_t(s,a)$$ (5.20)

Here is the TD(0) update:

$$w_{t+1} = w_t + \alpha . \left[R_{t+1} + \gamma * q_t(s',a';w) - q_t(s,a;w) \right] . \nabla_w q_t(s;a;w)$$ (5.21)

These equations allow us to carry out q-value estimation/prediction. This is the *evaluation* step of Generalized Policy Iteration where we carry out multiple rounds of gradient descent to improve on the q-value estimates for a given policy and get them close to the actual target values.

Evaluation is followed by greedy policy maximization to improve the policy. Figure 5-4 shows the process of iteration under GPI with function approximation.

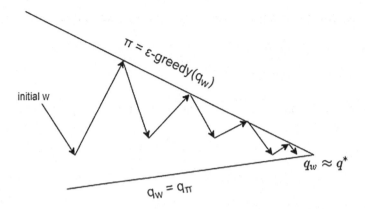

Figure 5-4. *Generalized Policy Iteration with function approximation*

Semi-gradient N-step SARSA Control

Let's use equation (5.9) with the TD target in a SARSA on-policy control regime. The agent samples the environment using the current policy and observes the state, action, reward, next state, next action $(s_t, a_t, r_{t+1}, s_{t+1}, a_{t+1})$ and uses these sets of observations to carry out a weight update using equation (5.20). Figure 5-5 shows the complete algorithm.

SEMI-GRADIENT N-STEP SARSA CONTROL (EPISODIC)

Input:

A differentiable function $\hat{q}(s,a;w)\colon |S| \cdot |A| \cdot R^d \to R$

Other parameters: step size α, exploration prob ε, number of steps: n

Initialize:

Initialize weights $\boldsymbol{w}\colon R^d$ arbitrarily like $\boldsymbol{w} = \boldsymbol{0}$

Three arrays to store (S_t, A_t, R_t) with access using "$mod\ n + 1$"

Loop for each episode:

Start episode with S_0 (non terminal)

Select and store A_0, ε-greedy action using $\hat{q}(S_0, \bullet; w)$

$T \leftarrow \infty$

Loop for $t = 1, 2, 3, \ldots$:

| If $t < T$, then :

| Take action A_t

| Observe and store R_{t+1} and S_{t+1}

| If S_{t+1} is terminal then:

| $T \leftarrow t + 1$

| else:

| select and store A_t using ε-greedy $\hat{q}(S_0, \bullet; w)$

|

| $\tau \leftarrow t - n + 1$ (τ is index whose estimate is being updated)

| If $\tau \geq 0$:

| $G \leftarrow \displaystyle\sum_{i=\tau+1}^{\min(\tau+n,T)} \gamma^{i-\tau-1} R_i$

| If $\tau + n < T$, then $G \leftarrow G + \gamma^n \hat{q}(S_{\tau+n}, A_{\tau+n}, w)$

| $w \leftarrow w + \alpha\left[G - \hat{q}(S_\tau, A_\tau, w)\right]\nabla \hat{q}(S_\tau, A_\tau, w)$ (5.20 with n-step estimate)

Until $\tau = T - 1$

Figure 5-5. *N-step semi-gradient SARSA for episodic control*

The w update is equation (5.20) with the target being G, the n-step return. In our example of n-step SARSA for the mountain car, we will be using tile encoding, a binary feature approximator. In our setup:

$$\hat{q}(S, A; w) = x(S, A)^T .w \text{ ; where } x(S, A) \text{ is the tile encoded feature vector}$$

Accordingly, $\nabla \hat{q}(S_\tau, A_\tau, w) = x(S, A)$

In Listing 5-1, we have a class QEstimator to hold the weights and also carry out tiling. Function get_active_features takes as input continuous two-dimensional values of S and the discrete input action A to return the tile-encoded active_feature $x(S, A)$, i.e., binary tiling features that are active for a given (S, A). Function q_predict also takes as input (S, A) and returns the estimate $\hat{q}(S, A; w) = x(S, A)^T. w$. It internally calls get_active_features to first get features and carries out a dot product with the weight vector. The weight update equation shown toward the end of the algorithm in Figure 5-5 is what the function q_update carries out. Function get_eps_greedy_action carries out action selection using ε-greedy $\hat{q}(S_0, \bullet; w)$.

The other function sarsa_n implements the algorithm given in Figure 5-5, calling functions from QEstimator as required. Similar to many examples in the previous chapter, we also have a helper function plot_rewards to plot the per-episode rewards as the training progresses. Listing 5-1 gives the code (listing5_1.ipynb).

Listing 5-1. N-Step SARA Control: Mountain Car

```
class QEstimator:

    def __init__(self, step_size, num_of_tilings=8, tiles_per_dim=8,
    max_size=2048, epsilon=0.0):
        self.max_size = max_size
        self.num_of_tilings = num_of_tilings
        self.tiles_per_dim = tiles_per_dim
        self.epsilon = epsilon
        self.step_size = step_size / num_of_tilings

        self.table = IHT(max_size)

        self.w = np.zeros(max_size)

        self.pos_scale = self.tiles_per_dim / (env.observation_space.high[0] \
                                    - env.observation_space.low[0])
```

```python
        self.vel_scale = self.tiles_per_dim / (env.observation_space.high[1] \
                                            - env.observation_space.low[1])

    def get_active_features(self, state, action):
        pos, vel = state
        active_features = tiles(self.table, self.num_of_tilings,
                    [self.pos_scale * (pos - env.observation_space.low[0]),
                     self.vel_scale * (vel- env.observation_space.low[1])],
                    [action])
        return active_features

    def q_predict(self, state, action):
        pos, vel = state
        if pos == env.observation_space.high[0]:  # reached goal
            return 0.0
        else:
            active_features = self.get_active_features(state, action)
            return np.sum(self.w[active_features])

    # learn with given state, action and target
    def q_update(self, state, action, target):
        active_features = self.get_active_features(state, action)
        q_s_a = np.sum(self.w[active_features])
        delta = (target - q_s_a)
        self.w[active_features] += self.step_size * delta

    def get_eps_greedy_action(self, state):
        pos, vel = state
        if np.random.rand() < self.epsilon:
            return np.random.choice(env.action_space.n)
        else:
            qvals = np.array([self.q_predict(state, action) for action in
            range(env.action_space.n)])
            return np.argmax(qvals)
```

```
#########################
def sarsa_n(qhat, step_size=0.5, epsilon=0.0, n=1, gamma=1.0,
episode_cnt = 10000):
    episode_rewards = []
    for _ in range(episode_cnt):
        state = env.reset()
        action = qhat.get_eps_greedy_action(state)
        T = float('inf')
        t = 0
        states = [state]
        actions = [action]
        rewards = [0.0]
        while True:
            if t < T:
                next_state, reward, done, _ = env.step(action)
                states.append(next_state)
                rewards.append(reward)

                if done:
                    T = t+1
                else:
                    next_action = qhat.get_eps_greedy_action(next_state)
                    actions.append(next_action)

            tau = t - n + 1

            if tau >= 0:
                G = 0
                for i in range(tau+1, min(tau+n, T)+1):
                    G += gamma ** (i-tau-1) * rewards[i]
                if tau+n < T:
                    G += gamma**n * qhat.q_predict(states[tau+n],
                    actions[tau+n])
                qhat.q_update(states[tau], actions[tau], G)

            if tau == T - 1:
                episode_rewards.append(np.sum(rewards))
                break
```

```
        else:
            t += 1
            state = next_state
            action = next_action

    return np.array(episode_rewards)
```

Figure 5-6 shows the result of running this algorithm to train the mountain car. We can see that within 50 episodes the agent reaches a steady state, and it is able get to the goal of hitting the flag on the right side of the valley in about 110 time steps.

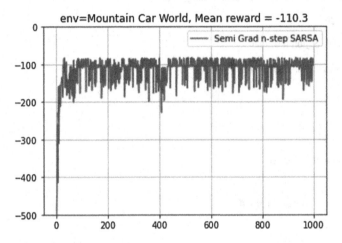

Figure 5-6. *N-step semi-gradient SARSA with MountainCar*

Semi-gradient SARSA(λ) Control

Next, we will look at the semi-gradient SARSA(λ) algorithm with eligibility traces. SARSA(λ) further generalizes the n-step SARSA. When the state or state-action values are represented by binary features with linear function approximation like in the case of the mountain car with tile encoding, we get the algorithm as given in Figure 5-7. This algorithm introduces a concept of eligibility trace that has the same number of components as the weight vector. *Weight vector* is a long-term memory over many episodes to generalize from all the examples shown. *Eligibility trace* is a short-term memory lasting less than the length of episode. It helps in the learning process by having an effect on weight. We will not go into the detailed derivations of the update rules. You can refer to `http://incompleteideas.net/book/the-book.html` for a detailed explanation of the concepts and mathematical derivations.

SEMI-GRADIENT SARSA(Λ) CONTROL (EPISODIC)

Input:

A tile function $F(s, a)$ giving the active tile indices (i) for a given s, a

Other parameters: step size α, trace decay $\lambda \in [0, 1]$

Initialize:

Initialize weights w: R^d arbitrarily like $w = 0$

Initialize eligibility trace z: R^d arbitrarily like $w = 0$

Three arrays to store (S_t, A_t, R_t) with access using "$mod\ n + 1$"

Loop for each episode:

Start episode with S (non terminal)

Select A, ε-greedy action using $\hat{q}(S, \bullet; w)$

$z \leftarrow 0$

$T \leftarrow \infty$

Loop for each step:

Take action A and observe R, S

$\delta \leftarrow R$

Loop for active indices i in $F(S, A)$

$\delta \leftarrow \delta - w_i$

$z_i \leftarrow z_i + 1$ (accumulating trace)

$or, z_i \leftarrow 1$ (replacing trace)

If S' terminal:

$w \leftarrow w + \alpha\delta z$

Go to next episode

Select A using ε-greedy $\hat{q}(S', \bullet; w)$

Loop for active indices i in $F(S', A)$:

$\delta \leftarrow \delta + \gamma\, w_i$

$w \leftarrow w + \alpha\delta z$

$z \leftarrow \gamma\lambda z$

$S \leftarrow S'; A \leftarrow A'$

Figure 5-7. *Semi-gradient SARSA(λ) for episodic control when features are binary and the value function is a linear combination of the feature vector and weight vector*

Let's look at running the previous algorithm on the mountain car. `Listing5_2.ipynb` has the full code. In Listing 5-2, we highlight the important parts of the code. Like `listing5_1. ipynb`, we have a class called `QEstimator` with some minor modifications to store the trace values and also to use the trace in the weight update function `q_update`. We also have two helper functions: `accumulating_trace` and `replacing trace` to implement the tracking of the two variants of traces. Function `sarsa_lambda` implements the overall learning algorithm given in Figure 5-7. We also have a function to run the trained agent through some episodes and record the behavior. Once you have trained the agent and generated the animation, you can run the MP4 file and see the strategy that the agent follows to reach the goal.

Listing 5-2. SARSA (λ) Control: Mountain Car

```
def accumulating_trace(trace, active_features, gamma, lambd):
    trace *= gamma * lambd
    trace[active_features] += 1
    return trace

def replacing_trace(trace, active_features, gamma, lambd):
    trace *= gamma * lambd
    trace[active_features] = 1
    return trace

# code omitted as it largely similar to listing 5-1
# except for adding trace vector to init fn and to q_update fn
class QEstimator:

def sarsa_lambda(qhat, episode_cnt = 10000, max_size=2048, gamma=1.0):
    episode_rewards = []
    for i in range(episode_cnt):
        state = env.reset()
        action = qhat.get_eps_greedy_action(state)
        qhat.trace = np.zeros(max_size)
        episode_reward = 0

        while True:
            next_state, reward, done, _ = env.step(action)
            next_action = qhat.get_eps_greedy_action(next_state)
            episode_reward += reward
            qhat.q_update(state, action, reward, next_state, next_action)
```

145

```
    if done:
        episode_rewards.append(episode_reward)
        break
    state = next_state
    action = next_action
return np.array(episode_rewards)
```

Figure 5-8 shows the result of running the SARSA(λ) algorithm to train the mountain car. We can see that the results are similar to those in Figure 5-6. This is too small a problem, but for larger problems, eligibility trace–driven algorithms will show better and faster convergence.

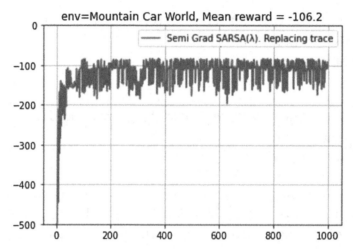

Figure 5-8. *Semi-gradient SARSA(λ) with the mountain car*

Convergence in Functional Approximation

Let's start exploring convergence by looking at an example. As shown in Figure 5-9, let's consider a two-state transition as part of some MDP. Let's assume we will use function approximation with the value of the first state being w and the value of the second state being $2w$. Here, w is a single number and not a vector.

Figure 5-9. *Two-step transition under functional approximation*

Let's assume that $w = 10$ and the agent transitions from the first state to the second state, i.e., from the state with the value 10 to the state with the value 20. We are also assuming that the transition from the first state to the second state is the only possible transition in the first state, and the reward for this transition is zero every time. Let the learning rate be $\alpha = 0.1$.

Let's now apply equation (5.14) to the previous one.

$$w_{t+1} = w_t + \alpha . \left[R_{t+1} + \gamma * V_t(s';w) - V_t(s;w) \right] . x(s)$$

$$w_{t+1} = w_t + 0.1 * \left[0 + \gamma * 2 w_t - w_t \right] . 1$$

i.e.; $w_{t+1} = w_t + 0.1 * w_t * (2\gamma - 1)$

Let's assume that λ is close to 1, and the current weight is 10. The updated weight will look like this: $w_{t+1} = 10 + 0.1 * 10 * (2 - 1) = 11$.

As long as $(2\gamma - 1) > 0$, every update will lead to the divergence of weight. It goes to show that function approximation can cause divergence. This is because of the value generalization where updating the value of a given state also updates the value of nearby or related states. There are three angles to the instability issue as listed.

- *Function approximation*: A way to generalize for a very large state space using weights, a smaller-sized vector as compared to the total number of states

- *Bootstrapping*: Forming target values using estimates of state values, e.g., in TD(0) the target being the estimate $R_{t+1} + \gamma * V_t(s';w)$

- *Off-policy learning*: Training the agent using a behavior policy but learning a different optimal policy

The presence of these three components together significantly increases the chances of divergence even in a simple prediction/estimation scenario. The control and optimization problems are even more complex to analyze. It has also been shown that instability can be avoided as long as all three are not present together. That brings us to the question, could we drop any of the three and assess the impact of such a drop?

Function approximation especially using neural networks has made RL practical for large real-world problems. Other alternatives are not practical. Bootstrapping has made the process sample efficient. The alternative of forming targets by watching the whole episode, while feasible, is not very practical. Off-policy learning can be replaced with on-policy, but again for RL to become close to the way humans learn, we need off-policy to learn about some problem/situation by exploring another, similar problem. Therefore, there are no easy answers to this. We cannot drop any of the three requirements with low impact. That's the theoretical side. In practice, most of the time, algorithms converge with some careful monitoring and tweaking.

Gradient Temporal Difference Learning

The semi-gradient TD learning with the update equation as shown in equation (5.9) does not follow a true gradient. While taking the gradient of a loss function, we kept the estimate of the target, i.e., $R_{t+1} + \gamma * V_t(s'; w)$, constant. It did not appear in the derivative with respect to the weight w. The real Bellman error is $R_{t+1} + \gamma * V_t(s'; w) - V_t(s; w)$, and the derivative of it ideally should have had gradient terms for both $V_t(s; w)$ and $V_t(s'; w)$.

There is a variation of this known as *gradient temporal difference learning* that follows the true gradient and offers convergence in all the cases of table lookup, linear and nonlinear functional approximation, and both the under on-policy and off-policy methods. Adding this to the mix of algorithms, Table 5-1 can be modified as shown in Table 5-2. We will not go into the mathematical proof of it in this book because the focus of the book is on the practical implementations of the algorithms.

Table 5-2. *Convergence of Prediction/Estimation Algorithms*

Policy Type	Algorithm	Table Lookup	Linear	Nonlinear
On-policy	MC	Y	Y	Y
	TD(0)	Y	Y	N
	TD(λ)	Y	Y	N
	Gradient TD	Y	Y	Y
Off-policy	MC	Y	Y	Y
	TD(0)	Y	N	N
	TD(λ)	Y	N	N
	Gradient TD	Y	Y	Y

Continuing, we give the convergence of control algorithms in Table 5-3.

Table 5-3. *Convergence of Control Algorithms*

Algorithm	Table Lookup	Linear	Nonlinear
MC control	Y	(Y)	N
On-policy TD (SARSA)	Y	(Y)	N
Off-policy Q-learning	Y	N	N
Gradient Q-learning	Y	Y	N

(Y): fluctuates around the near-optimal value function. A guarantee of convergence is off in all nonlinear cases.

Batch Methods (DQN)

Up to now we have been focusing on algorithms that were incremental; i.e., we sampled transition and then using the values we updated the weight vector w with the help of stochastic gradient descent. But this approach is not sample efficient. We discard a sample after using it only once. However, with nonlinear function approximation, especially with neural networks, we need multiple passes over the network to make the network weights converge to true values. Further, in many real-life scenarios like robotics, we need sample efficiency on two counts: neural networks with the slow convergence and hence the need for multiple passes, and generating samples in real life being very slow. In this section on batch reinforcement methods, we take you through the use of batch methods specifically with Deep Q Networks, which are the deep network version of the off-policy Q-learning.

Like before, we estimate the state value using function approximation, as shown in equation (5.1): $\hat{v}(s,w) \approx v_\pi(s)$.

Consider that we somehow know the actual state value $v_\pi(s)$, and we are trying to learn the weight vector w to arrive at a good estimate $\hat{v}(s,w) \approx v_\pi(s)$. We collect a batch of experiences.

$$D = \left\{ <s_1, v_1^\pi>, <s_2, v_2^\pi>, \ldots, <s_T, v_T^\pi> \right\}$$

We form a least squares loss as the average of the difference between the true value and the estimate and then carry out gradient descent to minimize error. We use a mini-batch gradient descent to take a sample of past experiences and use that to move the weight vector using a learning rate α.

$$LS(w) = E_D\left[\left(v_\pi(s) - \hat{v}(s;w)\right)^2\right].$$

We approximate it using samples.

$$LS(w) = \frac{1}{N}\sum_{i=1}^{N}\left(v_\pi(s_i) - \hat{v}(s_i;w)\right)^2 \tag{5.22}$$

Taking gradient of $LS(w)$ with respect to w and using the negative gradient to adjust w, we get equation (5.23), which is similar to equation (5.7).

$$w_{t+1} = w_t + \alpha.\frac{1}{N}\sum_{i=1}^{N}\left[v_\pi(s_i) - \hat{v}(s_i;w)\right].\nabla_w \hat{v}(s_i;w) \tag{5.23}$$

Like before, we can carry out a similar update with q-values.

$$w_{t+1} = w_t + \alpha.\frac{1}{N}\sum_{i=1}^{N}\left[q_\pi(s_i,a_i) - \hat{q}(s_i, a_i;w)\right].\nabla_w \hat{q}(s_i, a_i;w) \tag{5.24}$$

However, we do not know the true value functions, $v_\pi(s_i)$ or $q_\pi(s_i, a_i)$. Like before, we replace the true values with the estimates using either the MC or TD approach. Let's now look at a flavor of this called DQN, the deep learning version of Q-learning shown in Chapter 4. In DQN, an off-policy algorithm, we sample the current state s, take a step a as per the current behavior policy, an ε-greedy policy using current q-values. We observe the reward r and next state s'. We use $\max \hat{q}(s',.;w)$ for all actions a' possible in the state s' to form the target.

$$q_\pi(s_i,a_i) = r_i + \gamma\, max_{a'} q\left(s_i', a_i'; w_t^-\right)$$

Here we have used a different weight vector **$wt-$** to calculate the estimate of the target. Esentially we have two networks, one called *online* with weights w, which is being updated as per equation (5.24), and a second similar network called *target network* but with a copy of the weight called w^-. Weight vector w^- is updated less frequently, say after every 100 updates of online network weight w. This approach keeps the target network constant and allows us to use the machinery of supervised learning. Please also note that we are using subscript i to denote the sample in the mini-batch and t to denote the index at which weights are updated. The final update equation with all this put together can be written as follows:

$$w_{t+1} = w_t + \alpha. \frac{1}{N} \sum_{i=1}^{N} \left[r_i + \gamma \, max_{a_i} \tilde{q}\left(s_i', a_i'; w_t^-\right) - \hat{q}\left(s_i, a_i; w\right) \right] . \nabla_w \, \hat{q}\left(s_i, a_i; w\right) \qquad (5.25)$$

In a nutshell, we run the agent through environment using the ε-greedy policy and collect experiences in a buffer called replay buffer D. We carry out the weight update for online network using (5.25). We also update target network weights once in a while (say after every 100 batch updates of w). We use the updated q-values with ε-exploration to add more experiences to the replay buffer and carry out the whole cycle once again. This in essence is the DQN approach. We have a lot more to say about it in the next chapter, which is completely devoted to DQN and its variants. For now, we leave the topic here and move on.

Linear Least Squares Method

Experience replay as used in the batch method finds the least square solution, minimizing the error between the target as estimated using TD or MC and the current value function estimate. However, it takes many iterations to converge. However, if we use linear function approximation for value function $\hat{v}(s;w) = x(s)^T w$ for prediction and $\hat{q}(s,a; w) = x(s, a)^T w$ for control, we can find the least square solution directly. Let's look at prediction first.

We start with equation (5.22), substituting $\hat{v}(s;w) = x(s)^T w$ to get this:

$$LS(w) = \frac{1}{N} \sum_{i=1}^{N} \left(v_\pi(s_i) - x(s_i)^T . w \right)^2$$

Taking gradient of $LS(w)$ with respect to w and setting it to zero, we get the following:

$$\sum_{i=1}^{N} x(s_i) v_\pi(s_i) = \sum_{i=1}^{N} x(s_i) . x(s_i)^T w$$

Solving for w gives the following:

$$w = \left(\sum_{i=1}^{N} x(s_i).x(s_i)^T \right)^{-1} \sum_{i=1}^{N} x(s_i)v_\pi(s_i) \tag{5.26}$$

The previous solution involves the inversion of a $N \cdot N$ matrix that requires $O(N_3)$ computations. However, using Shermann-Morrison, we can solve this in $O(N_2)$ time. As before, we do not know the true value $v_\pi(s_i)$. We replace the true value with its estimate using MC, TD(0), or TD(λ) estimates giving us linear least square MC (LSMC), LSTD, or LSTD(λ) prediction algorithms.

$$\text{LSMC}: v_\pi(s_i) \approx G_i$$

$$\text{LSTD}: v_\pi(s_i) \approx R + \gamma \, \hat{v}(s_i';w)$$

$$\text{LSTD}(\lambda): v_\pi(s_i) \approx G_i^\lambda$$

All these prediction algorithms have good convergence both for off-policy or for on-policy.

Moving ahead, we extend the analysis to control using the q-value linear function approximation and GPI where the pervious approach is used for the q-value prediction, followed by the greedy q-value maximization in the policy improvement step. This is known as *linear least square policy iteration* (LSPI). We iterate through these cycles of prediction followed by improvement until the policy converges, i.e., until the weights converge. We give here the final result of linear least square Q-learning (LSPI) without going through the derivation.

Here is the Prediction Step:

$$w = \left(\sum_{i=1}^{N} x(s_i,a_i).(x(s_i,a_i)+\gamma \, x(s_i',\pi(s_i')))^T \right)^{-1} \sum_{i=1}^{N} x(s_i,a_i)r_i$$

where (i) is the ith sample (s_i, a_i, r_i, s'_i) from experience replay D and $\pi(s_i') = argmax_{a'} \, \hat{q}(s_i', a';w)$, i.e., the action with maximum q-value in state s'.

And here is the Control Step:

For each state **s**, we change the policy that maximizes the q-value after the weight update w carried out in the previous prediction step.

$$\pi'(s_i) = argmax_a \,\hat{q}(s_i, a; w^{updated})$$

Earlier, we covered most of the variants of policy iteration with function approximation: incremental, batch, and linear methods. Let's take a short detour to introduce the PyTorch and TensorFlow libraries.

Deep Learning Libraries

Previous sections in the chapter showed us that by using the function approximation approach, we need to have an efficient way to calculate the derivatives of state-value function $\nabla_w \hat{v}(s_i; w)$ or the action-value function $\nabla_w \hat{q}(s_i, a_i; w)$. If we are using neural networks, we need to use back propagation to calculate these derivatives at each layer of the network. This is where libraries like PyTorch and TensorFlow come into the picture. Similar to the NumPy library, these also carry out vector/matrix computations in an efficient manner. Further, these are highly optimized to handle tensors (arrays with more than two dimensions).

In neural networks, we need to be able to back-propagate errors to calculate the gradients of error with respect to the weights of layers at all levels. Both these libraries are highly abstracted and optimized to handle this for us behind the scenes. We just need to build the forward computation, taking input through all the computations to give us the final output. The libraries keep track of the computation graph and allow us to carry out the gradient update to weights with just one function call.

To refresh your knowledge of both these libraries, we have included two Python notebooks that take you through training a simple model for the classification of digits using the MNIST data set. `listing5_3_pytorch_intro.ipynb` is for the code using PyTorch, and `listing5_4_tensorflow.ipynb` walks through the same thing using TensorFlow. We are not reproducing the code in the text here as these notebooks are just meant for you to refresh your knowledge on PyTorch and TensorFlow.

Summary

In this chapter, the primary focus was to look at the use of function approximation for very large or continuous state spaces that cannot be handled using the approach of table-based learning that we saw in previous chapters.

We talked about what it means to carry out optimization with function approximation. We also showed how the concepts of training in supervised learning, training a model to produce values close to targets, can be applied in reinforcement learning with proper handling for moving targets and the sample interdependence shown in RL.

We then looked at various strategies of functional approximation, including linear and nonlinear ones. We also saw how table-based methods are just special cases of linear approximation. This was followed by a detailed discussion of incremental methods for prediction and control. We saw these being applied on the mountain car to build training agents using n-step SARSA and SARSA(λ).

Next, we talked about batch methods in general and explored the complete derivation of the update rule for DQN, a popular algorithm from the family of batch methods. We then looked at linear least squares methods for prediction and control. Along the way, we kept highlighting the convergence issues in general as well as convergence in the specific methods being discussed.

We finally concluded the chapter with a brief introduction to deep learning frameworks like PyTorch and TensorFlow.

CHAPTER 6

Deep Q-Learning

In this chapter, we will do a deep dive into Q-learning combined with function approximation using neural networks. Q-learning in the context of deep learning using neural networks is also known as *Deep Q Networks* (DQN). We will first summarize what we have talked about so far with respect to Q-learning. We will then look at code implementations of DQN on simple problems followed by training an agent to play Atari games. Following this, we will extend our knowledge by looking at various modifications that can be done to DQN to improve the learning, including some very recent and state-of-the-art approaches. Some of these approaches may involve a bit of math to understand the rationale for these approaches. However, we will try to keep the math to a minimum and include just the required details to appreciate the background and reasoning. All the examples in this chapter will be coded using either the PyTorch or TensorFlow library. Some code walk-throughs will have the code for both PyTorch and TensorFlow, while others will be discussed using only PyTorch.

Deep Q Networks

In Chapter 4 we talked about Q-learning as a model-free off-policy TD control method. We first looked at the online version where we used an exploratory behavior policy (ε-greedy) to take a step (action A) while in state S. The reward R and next state S' were then used to update the q-value $Q(S, A)$. Figure 4-14 and Listing 4-4 detailed the pseudocode and actual implementation. The update equation used in this context is given here. You may want to revisit this before you move forward.

$$Q(S_t,A_t) \leftarrow Q(S_t,A_t) + \alpha * \left[R_{t+1} + \gamma * \max_a Q(S_{t+1},A_{t+1}) - Q(S_t,A_t) \right] \qquad (6.1)$$

155

© Nimish Sanghi 2021
N. Sanghi, *Deep Reinforcement Learning with Python*, https://doi.org/10.1007/978-1-4842-6809-4_6

We briefly talked about maximization bias and the approach of double Q-learning wherein we use two tables of q-values. We will have more to say about it in this chapter when we look at double DQN.

Following this, we looked at the approach of using a sample multiple times to convert online TD updates to batch TD updates, making it more sample efficient. It introduced us to the concept of a replay buffer. While it was only about sample efficiency in the context of discrete state and state-action spaces, with function approximation with neural networks, it becomes pretty much a must-have to make deep learning neural networks converge. We will revisit this again, and when we talk about prioritized replay, we will look at other options to sample transitions/experiences from the buffer.

Moving along, in Chapter 5, we looked at various approaches of function approximation. We looked at tile encoding as a way to achieve linear function approximation. We then talked about DQN, i.e., batch Q-learning with neural networks as function approximators. We went through a long derivation to arrive at a weight (with neural network parameters) update equation as given in equation (5.25). This is reproduced here:

$$w_{t+1} = w_t + \alpha.\frac{1}{N}\sum_{i=1}^{N}\left[r_i + \gamma \; max_{a_i'}\; \tilde{q}\left(s_i',a_i';w_t^-\right) - \hat{q}(s_i,a_i;w)\right].\nabla_w\,\hat{q}(s_i,a_i;w) \qquad (6.2)$$

Please also note that we are using subscript i to denote the sample in the mini-batch and i to denote the index at which the weights are updated. Equation (6.2) is the one we will be using extensively in this chapter. We will make various adjustments to this equation as we talk about different modifications and study their impact.

We also talked about not having a theoretical guarantee of convergence under nonlinear function approximation with a gradient update. We will have more to say about that in this chapter. The Q-learning approach was for discrete states and actions where the update to the q-value was using (6.1) as compared to adjusting the weight parameters for the deep learning–based approach in DQN. The Q-learning case had guarantees of convergence, while with DQN we had no such guarantee. DQN is computationally intensive as well. However, despite these shortcomings in DQN, DQN makes it possible to train agents using raw images, something not at all conceivable in the case of plain Q-learning. Let's now put equation (6.2) to practice to train the DQN agents in various environments.

Let's revisit the CartPole problem, which has a four-dimensional continuous state with values for the current cart position, velocity, angle of the pole, and angular velocity of the pole. The actions are of two types: push the cart to the left or push the cart to the right with the aim of keeping the pole balanced for as long as possible. The following are the details of the environment:

```
Observation:
    Type: Box(4)
    Num  Observation              Min                     Max
    0    Cart Position            -4.8                    4.8
    1    Cart Velocity            -Inf                    Inf
    2    Pole Angle               0.418 rad (-24 deg)     0.418 rad (24 deg)
    3    Pole Angular Velocity    -Inf                    Inf
Actions:
    Type: Discrete(2)
    Num    Action
    0      Push cart to the left
    1      Push cart to the right
```

We will build a small neural network with 4 as the input dimension, three hidden layers, followed by an output layer of dimension 2 being the number of possible actions. Figure 6-1 shows the network diagram.

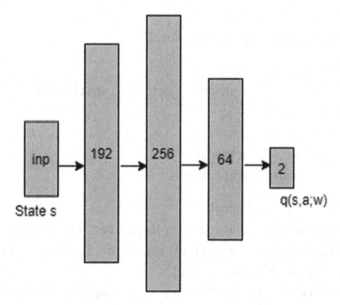

Figure 6-1. *Simple neural network*

We will use PyTorch's `nn.Module` class to build the network. We will also implement some additional functions. Function `get_qvalues` takes a batch of states as input, i.e., a tensor of dimension (N×4) where N is the number of samples. It passes the state values through the network to produce the q-values. The output vector has size (N×2); i.e., one row for each input. Each row has two q-values, one for the left-push action and another for the right-push action. Function `sample_actions` in the same class takes in a batch of q-values (N×2). It uses the ε-greedy policy (equation 4.3) to choose an action. The output is the (N×1) vector. Listing 6-2 shows the code for this in PyTorch. Listing 6-3 shows the same code in TensorFlow 2.0's eager execution mode. You can find the complete PyTorch implementation in file `listing6_1_dqn_pytorch.ipynb` and for TensorFlow in file `listing6_1_dqn_tensorflow.ipynb`.

Note   While not essential, you will gain more from the code discussions with some prior knowledge of PyTorch or TensorFlow. You should be able to create basic networks, define loss functions, and carry out basic training steps for optimization. TensorFlow's new eager execution model is similar to PyTorch. For this reason, we will provide the code in both libraries for a limited set of examples to get you started. Otherwise, most of the code in the book will be in PyTorch.

Listing 6-1. A Simple DQN Agent in PyTorch

```
class DQNAgent(nn.Module):
    def __init__(self, state_shape, n_actions, epsilon=0):
        super().__init__()
        self.epsilon = epsilon
        self.n_actions = n_actions
        self.state_shape = state_shape

        state_dim = state_shape[0]
        # a simple NN with state_dim as input vector (inout is state s)
        # and self.n_actions as output vector of logits of q(s, a)
        self.network = nn.Sequential()
        self.network.add_module('layer1', nn.Linear(state_dim, 192))
        self.network.add_module('relu1', nn.ReLU())
        self.network.add_module('layer2', nn.Linear(192, 256))
```

```
        self.network.add_module('relu2', nn.ReLU())
        self.network.add_module('layer3', nn.Linear(256, 64))
        self.network.add_module('relu3', nn.ReLU())
        self.network.add_module('layer4', nn.Linear(64, n_actions))
        #
        self.parameters = self.network.parameters

    def forward(self, state_t):
        # pass the state at time t through the newrok to get Q(s,a)
        qvalues = self.network(state_t)
        return qvalues

    def get_qvalues(self, states):
        # input is an array of states in numpy and outout is Qvals as numpy
        array
        states = torch.tensor(states, device=device, dtype=torch.float32)
        qvalues = self.forward(states)
        return qvalues.data.cpu().numpy()

    def sample_actions(self, qvalues):
        # sample actions from a batch of q_values using epsilon greedy policy
        epsilon = self.epsilon
        batch_size, n_actions = qvalues.shape
        random_actions = np.random.choice(n_actions, size=batch_size)
        best_actions = qvalues.argmax(axis=-1)
        should_explore = np.random.choice(
            [0, 1], batch_size, p=[1-epsilon, epsilon])
        return np.where(should_explore, random_actions, best_actions)
```

Listing 6-2 shows the same code in TensorFlow 2.x using the Keras interface. We are using the new eager execution model, which is similar to the approach that PyTorch takes. TensorFlow used to have a different model in earlier versions, which was a little bit hard to conceptualize with two separate phases: one of symbolic graphs to build all the network operations and then a second phase of training of the model by passing data as tensors into the model build in the first phase.

Listing 6-2. A Simple DQN Agent in TensorFlow

```
class DQNAgent:
    def __init__(self, state_shape, n_actions, epsilon=0):
        self.epsilon = epsilon
        self.n_actions = n_actions
        self.state_shape = state_shape

        state_dim = state_shape[0]
        self.model = tf.keras.models.Sequential()
        self.model.add(tf.keras.Input(shape=(state_dim,)))
        self.model.add(tf.keras.layers.Dense(192, activation='relu'))
        self.model.add(tf.keras.layers.Dense(256, activation='relu'))
        self.model.add(tf.keras.layers.Dense(64, activation='relu'))
        self.model.add(tf.keras.layers.Dense(n_actions))

    def __call__(self, state_t):
        # pass the state at time t through the newrok to get Q(s,a)
        qvalues = self.model(state_t)
        return qvalues

    def get_qvalues(self, states):
        # input is an array of states in numpy and outout is Qvals as numpy
        array
        qvalues = self.model(states)
        return qvalues.numpy()

    def sample_actions(self, qvalues):
        # sample actions from a batch of q_values using epsilon greedy policy
        epsilon = self.epsilon
        batch_size, n_actions = qvalues.shape
        random_actions = np.random.choice(n_actions, size=batch_size)
        best_actions = qvalues.argmax(axis=-1)
        should_explore = np.random.choice(
            [0, 1], batch_size, p=[1-epsilon, epsilon])
        return np.where(should_explore, random_actions, best_actions)
```

The code for the replay buffer is simple. We have a buffer called self.buffer to hold the previous examples. Function add takes in (state, action, reward, next_state, done), the values from a single step/transition by the agent, and adds that to the buffer. If the buffer has already reached full length, it discards the oldest transition to make space for the new addition. Function sample takes an integer batch_size and returns batch_size samples/transitions from the buffer. In this vanilla implementation, each transition stored in the buffer has equal probability of getting sampled. Listing 6-3 shows the code for the replay buffer.

Listing 6-3. Replay Buffer (Same in PyTorch or TensorFlow)

```
class ReplayBuffer:
    def __init__(self, size):
        self.size = size #max number of items in buffer
        self.buffer =[] #array to hold samples
        self.next_id = 0

    def __len__(self):
        return len(self.buffer)

    def add(self, state, action, reward, next_state, done):
        item = (state, action, reward, next_state, done)
        if len(self.buffer) < self.size:
            self.buffer.append(item)
        else:
            self.buffer[self.next_id] = item
        self.next_id = (self.next_id + 1) % self.size

    def sample(self, batch_size):
        idxs = np.random.choice(len(self.buffer), batch_size)
        samples = [self.buffer[i] for i in idxs]
        states, actions, rewards, next_states, done_flags = list(zip(*samples))
        return np.array(states),
                    np.array(actions),
        np.array(rewards),
        np.array(next_states),
        np.array(done_flags)
```

Moving ahead, we have a utility function, play_and_store, that takes in an env (e.g., CartPole), an agent (e.g., DQNAgent), an exp_replay (ReplayBuffer), the agent's start_state, and n_steps (i.e., number of steps/actions to take in the environment). The function makes the agent take n_steps number of steps starting from the initial state start_state. The steps are taken based on the current ε-greedy policy that the agent is following using agent.sample_actions and records these n_steps transitions in the buffer. Listing 6-4 shows the code.

Listing 6-4. Implementation of Function play_and_record

```
def play_and_record(start_state, agent, env, exp_replay, n_steps=1):

    s = start_state
    sum_rewards = 0

    # Play the game for n_steps and record transitions in buffer
    for _ in range(n_steps):
        qvalues = agent.get_qvalues([s])
        a = agent.sample_actions(qvalues)[0]
        next_s, r, done, _ = env.step(a)
        sum_rewards += r
        exp_replay.add(s, a, r, next_s, done)
        if done:
            s = env.reset()
        else:
            s = next_s

    return sum_rewards, s
```

Next, we look at the learning process. We first build the loss, L, that we want to minimize. It is the averaged squared error between the target value of the current state action using a one-step TD value and the current state value. As discussed in Chapter 5, we use a copy of the original neural network that has weights w^- (w with superscript $-$). We use the loss to calculate the gradient of the agent (online/original) network's weight w and take a step in the negative direction of the gradient to reduce the loss. Please note that as discussed in Chapter 5, we keep the target network with weights w^- frozen and update these weights on a less frequent basis. To quote from the section on batch methods of DQN in Chapter 5:

> *Here we have used a different weight vector w_t^- to calculate the estimate of target. Essentially, we have two networks, one called online with weights "w" which is being updated as per equation (5.24) and second a similar network called target network but with a copy of the weight "w" called "w−". Weight vector "w− is updated less frequently say after every 100 updates of online network. This approach keeps the target network constant and allows us to use the machinery of supervised learning.*

The loss function is as follows:

$$L = \frac{1}{N} \sum_{i=1}^{N} \left[r_i + \left((1 - done_i).\gamma.\max_{a_i} \hat{q}(s_i', a_i'; w_t^-) \right) - \hat{q}(s_i, a_i; w_t) \right]^2 \quad (6.3)$$

We take a gradient (derivative) of **L** with regard to w and then use this gradient to update the weights w of the online network. The equations are as follows:

$$\nabla_w L = -\frac{1}{N} \sum_{i=1}^{N} \left[r_i + \left((1 - done_i).\gamma.\max_{a_i} \hat{q}(s_i', a_i'; w_t^-) \right) - \hat{q}(s_i, a_i; w_t) \right] \nabla \hat{q}(s_i, a_i; w_t) \quad (6.4)$$

$$w_{t+1} \leftarrow w_t - \alpha \nabla_w L \quad (6.5)$$

Combining the two, we get our familiar update in equation (6.2). However, in PyTorch and TensorFlow, we do not carry out the updates by directly coding them as it is not easy to calculate the gradients $\nabla \hat{q}(s_i, a_i; w_t)$. That's one of the primary reasons to use packages like PyTorch and TensorFlow, which automatically calculate gradients based on the operations performed to calculate the loss metric L. We just need a function to calculate that metric L. This is done by the function `compute_td_loss`. It takes in a batch of (`states, actions, rewards, next_states, done_flags`). It also takes in the discount parameter γ as well as the agent/online and target networks. The function then computes loss L as per equation (6.3). Listing 6-5 gives the implementation in PyTorch, and Listing 6-6 gives it in TensorFlow.

Listing 6-5. Compute TD Loss in PyTorch

```
def compute_td_loss(agent, target_network, states, actions, rewards, next_
states, done_flags,
                    gamma=0.99, device=device):
    # convert numpy array to torch tensors
    states = torch.tensor(states, device=device, dtype=torch.float)
    actions = torch.tensor(actions, device=device, dtype=torch.long)
    rewards = torch.tensor(rewards, device=device, dtype=torch.float)
    next_states = torch.tensor(next_states, device=device, dtype=torch.float)
    done_flags = torch.tensor(done_flags.astype('float32'),device=device,dt
ype=torch.float)

    # get q-values for all actions in current states
    # use agent network
    predicted_qvalues = agent(states)

    # compute q-values for all actions in next states
    # use target network
    predicted_next_qvalues = target_network(next_states)

    # select q-values for chosen actions
    predicted_qvalues_for_actions = predicted_qvalues[range(
        len(actions)), actions]

    # compute Qmax(next_states, actions) using predicted next q-values
    next_state_values,_ = torch.max(predicted_next_qvalues, dim=1)

    # compute "target q-values"
    target_qvalues_for_actions = rewards + gamma * next_state_values * (1-
done_flags)

    # mean squared error loss to minimize
    loss = torch.mean((predicted_qvalues_for_actions -
                      target_qvalues_for_actions.detach()) ** 2)

    return loss
```

Listing 6-6. Compute TD Loss in TensorFlow

```
def compute_td_loss(agent, target_network, states, actions, rewards, next_
states,
                        done_flags, gamma=0.99):

    # get q-values for all actions in current states
    # use agent network
    predicted_qvalues = agent(states)

    # compute q-values for all actions in next states
    # use target network
    predicted_next_qvalues = target_network(next_states)

    # select q-values for chosen actions
    row_indices= tf.range(len(actions))
    indices = tf.transpose([row_indices, actions])
    predicted_qvalues_for_actions = tf.gather_nd(predicted_qvalues, indices)

    # compute Qmax(next_states, actions) using predicted next q-values
    next_state_values = tf.reduce_max(predicted_next_qvalues, axis=1)

    # compute "target q-values"
    target_qvalues_for_actions = rewards + gamma * next_state_values * (1-
    done_flags)

    # mean squared error loss to minimize
    loss = tf.keras.losses.MSE(target_qvalues_for_actions, predicted_
    qvalues_for_actions)

    return loss
```

At this point, we have all the machinery to train the agent to balance the pole. First, we define some hyperparameters like `batch_size`, total training steps `total_steps`, and the rate at which exploration ε will decay. It starts at 1.0 and slowly reduces the exploration to 0.05 as the agent learns the optimal policy. We also define an `optimizer`, which can take in the loss L as created in the previous listing and helps us take a gradient step to adjust the weights, essentially implementing equations (6.4) and (6.5). Listing 6-7 gives the training code in PyTorch. Listing 6-8 gives the same code in TensorFlow.

Listing 6-7. Train the Agent in PyTorch

```
for step in trange(total_steps + 1):

    # reduce exploration as we progress
    agent.epsilon = epsilon_schedule(start_epsilon, end_epsilon, step, eps_
    decay_final_step)

    # take timesteps_per_epoch and update experience replay buffer
    _, state = play_and_record(state, agent, env, exp_replay, timesteps_
    per_epoch)

    # train by sampling batch_size of data from experience replay
    states, actions, rewards, next_states, done_flags = exp_replay.
    sample(batch_size)

    # loss = <compute TD loss>
    loss = compute_td_loss(agent, target_network,
                           states, actions, rewards, next_states, done_flags,
                           gamma=0.99,
                           device=device)

    loss.backward()
    grad_norm = nn.utils.clip_grad_norm_(agent.parameters(), max_grad_norm)
    opt.step()
    opt.zero_grad()

###Omitted code here###
### code to periodically evaluate the performance and plot some graphs
```

Listing 6-8. Train the Agent in TensorFlow

```
for step in trange(total_steps + 1):

    # reduce exploration as we progress
    agent.epsilon = epsilon_schedule(start_epsilon, end_epsilon, step, eps_
    decay_final_step)

    # take timesteps_per_epoch and update experience replay buffer
    _, state = play_and_record(state, agent, env, exp_replay, timesteps_
    per_epoch)
```

```
# train by sampling batch_size of data from experience replay
states, actions, rewards, next_states, done_flags = exp_replay.
sample(batch_size)

with tf.GradientTape() as tape:
    # loss = <compute TD loss>
    loss = compute_td_loss(agent, target_network,
                           states, actions, rewards, next_states, done_
                           flags,
                           gamma=0.99)

gradients = tape.gradient(loss, agent.model.trainable_variables)
clipped_grads = [tf.clip_by_norm(g, max_grad_norm) for g in gradients]
optimizer.apply_gradients(zip(clipped_grads, agent.model.trainable_
variables))
```

We now have a fully trained agent. We train the agent and plot the mean reward per episode periodically as we train the agent for 50,000 steps. In the left plot in Figure 6-2, the x-axis value of 10 corresponds to the 10,000[th] step. We also plot the TD loss every 20 steps, and that's why we have the x-axis on the right plot going from 0 to 2500, i.e., 0 to 2500x20=50,000 steps. Unlike supervised learning, the targets are not fixed. We keep the target network fixed for a short duration and update it periodically by refreshing the target network weights with the online network. Also, as discussed, nonlinear function approximation (neural networks) with off-policy learning (Q-learning) and bootstrapped targets (the target network being just an estimate of the actual value and the estimate formed using the current estimates of other q-values) has no convergence guarantee. The training may see losses going up and exploding or fluctuating. This loss graph is counterintuitive as compared to the loss graphs in the usual supervised learning. Figure 6-2 shows the graphs from the training DQN.

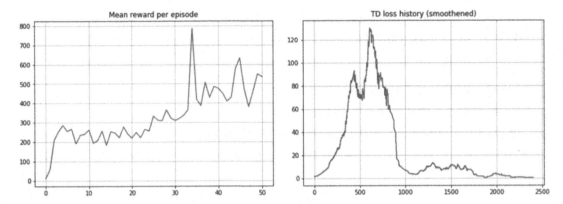

Figure 6-2. *Training curves for DQN*

The code notebooks listing6_1_dqn_pytorch.ipynb and listing6_1_dqn_tensorflow.ipynb have some more code to record the behavior of how the trained agent performs as a video file and then play the video to show the behavior.

This completes the implementation of a full DQN using deep learning to train an agent. It might look like overkill to use a complex neural network for such a simple network. The core idea was to focus on the algorithm and teach you how to write a DQN learning agent. We will now use the same implementation with minor tweaks so that the agent can play Atari games using the game image pixel values as the state.

Atari Game-Playing Agent Using DQN

In a 2013 seminal paper titled "Playing Atari with Deep Reinforcement Learning,"[1] the authors used a deep learning model to create a neural network–based Q-learning algorithm. They christened it Deep Q Networks. This is exactly what we implemented in the previous section. We will now briefly discuss the additional steps the authors took to train the agent to play Atari games. The main gist is the same as the previous section with two key differences: using game image pixel values as state inputs that require some preprocessing, and using convolutional networks inside an agent instead of linear layers that we saw in the previous section. The rest of the approach to calculate the loss L and carry out the training remains the same as the previous section. Please note that training with convolution networks takes a lot of time, especially on regular PCs/laptops. Get ready to watch the training code run for hours even on moderately powerful GPU-based machines.

---

[1]https://arxiv.org/pdf/1312.5602.pdf

You can find the complete code to train the agent in PyTorch in file `listing6_2_dqn_atari_pytorch.ipynb`. You can find the same code in TensorFlow in `listing6_2_dqn_atari_tensorflow.ipynb`. The Gym library has implemented many of the transformations needed on an Atari image, and wherever possible, we will be using the same thing.

Let's now talking about the image preprocessing done to get the image pixel values ready for feeding into the deep learning network. We will talk about this in the context of a game called Breakout in which there is a paddle at the bottom, and the idea is to move the paddle to ensure the ball does not fall below it. We need to use the paddle to hit and take out as many bricks as possible. Each time the ball misses the paddle, the player loses a life. The player has five lives to start. Figure 6-3 shows three frames of the game.

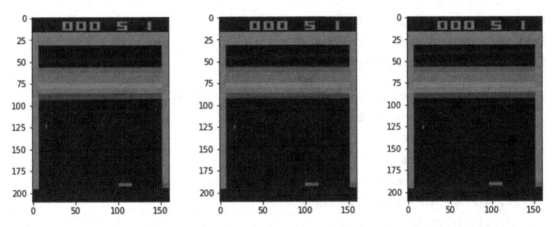

Figure 6-3. *Atari Breakout game images*

Atari game images are 210×160-pixel images with a 128-color palette. We will do preprocessing to prune down the image and make the convolutional network run faster. We scale down the images. We also remove some of the information from the sides, keeping just the relevant part of the images for training. We can convert the image to grayscale again to reduce the size of the input vector, with one channel of grayscale instead of three channel of colors for RGB (the Red, Green, Blue channels). A preprocessed single frame of the image of size (1×84×84 in PyTorch or 84×84×1 in TensorFlow) just gives the static state. The position of the ball or paddle does not tell us the direction in which both are moving. Accordingly, we will stack a few consecutive frames of the game images together to train the agent. We will stack four reduced-size grayscale images that will the state *s* feeding into the neural network. The input (i.e. state *s*) will be of size 4×84×84 in PyTorch and 84×84×4 in TensorFlow, where 4 refers to the four frames of the game images and 84×84 is the grayscale image size of each frame. Stacking four frames together will allow the agent network to infer the direction of movement of the ball and paddle. We use Gym's `AtariPreprocessing` to carry out image reduction from a 210×160×3 size array of color images to an 84×84 array of grayscale images. This function also scales down individual pixel values from the range (0,255) to (0.0, 1.0) by setting `scale_obs=True`. Next we use `FrameStack` to stack together four images as discussed earlier. Finally, in line with the original approach, we also clip the reward values to just -1 or 1. Listing 6-9 gives the code carrying out all these transformations.

Listing 6-9. Train the Agent in PyTorch

```
from gym.wrappers import AtariPreprocessing
from gym.wrappers import FrameStack
from gym.wrappers import TransformReward

def make_env(env_name, clip_rewards=True, seed=None):
    env = gym.make(env_name)
    if seed is not None:
        env.seed(seed)
    env = AtariPreprocessing(env, screen_size=84, scale_obs=True)
    env = FrameStack(env, num_stack=4)
    if clip_rewards:
        env = TransformReward(env, lambda r: np.sign(r))
    return env
```

The previous preprocessing step produces the final state that we will be feeding into the network. This will be of size 4×84×84 in PyTorch and 84×84×4 in TensorFlow, where 4 refers to the four frames of the game images and 84×84 is the grayscale image size of each frame. Figure 6-4 shows the input to the network.

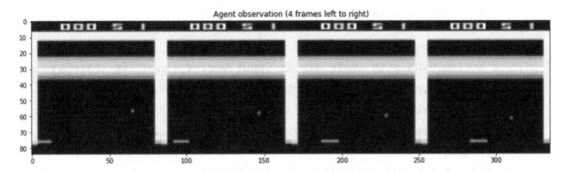

Figure 6-4. Processed image to be used as state input into the neural network

Next, we build the neural network that will take in the previous image, i.e., the state/observation *s*, and produce q-values for all four actions in this case. The actions for this game are ['NOOP', 'FIRE', 'RIGHT', 'LEFT'], using the spacebar to start, i.e., fire, pressing A on the keyboard to move the paddle left, pressing D to move the paddle right, and finally pressing Esc to quit the game. The following is the specification of the network we will build:

```
input: tensorflow: [batch_size, 84, 84, 4]
    pytorch:  [batch_size, 4, 84, 84]

1st hidden layer: 16 nos of 8x8 filters with stride 4 and ReLU
activation
2nd hidden layer: 32 nos of 4x4 filters with stride of 2 and ReLU
activation
3nd hidden layer: Linear layer with 256 outputs and ReLU activation
output layer: Linear with "n_actions" units with no activation
```

The rest of the code is similar to what we had earlier. Listing 6-10 and Listing 6-11 show the code of the modified DQN agents in PyTorch and TensorFlow, respectively.

Listing 6-10. DQN Agent in PyTorch

```
class DQNAgent(nn.Module):
    def __init__(self, state_shape, n_actions, epsilon=0):

        super().__init__()
        self.epsilon = epsilon
        self.n_actions = n_actions
```

```
        self.state_shape = state_shape

        state_dim = state_shape[0]
        # a simple NN with state_dim as input vector (inout is state s)
        # and self.n_actions as output vector of logits of q(s, a)
        self.network = nn.Sequential()
        self.network.add_module('conv1', nn.Conv2d(4,16,kernel_size=8,
        stride=4))
        self.network.add_module('relu1', nn.ReLU())
        self.network.add_module('conv2', nn.Conv2d(16,32,kernel_size=4,
        stride=2))
        self.network.add_module('relu2', nn.ReLU())
        self.network.add_module('flatten', nn.Flatten())
        self.network.add_module('linear3', nn.Linear(2592, 256)) #2592
        calculated above
        self.network.add_module('relu3', nn.ReLU())
        self.network.add_module('linear4', nn.Linear(256, n_actions))

        self.parameters = self.network.parameters

    def forward(self, state_t):
        # pass the state at time t through the newrok to get Q(s,a)
        qvalues = self.network(state_t)
        return qvalues

    def get_qvalues(self, states):
        # input is an array of states in numpy and outout is Qvals as numpy
        array
        states = torch.tensor(states, device=device, dtype=torch.float32)
        qvalues = self.forward(states)
        return qvalues.data.cpu().numpy()

    def sample_actions(self, qvalues):
        # sample actions from a batch of q_values using epsilon greedy policy
        epsilon = self.epsilon
        batch_size, n_actions = qvalues.shape
        random_actions = np.random.choice(n_actions, size=batch_size)
```

```
    best_actions = qvalues.argmax(axis=-1)
    should_explore = np.random.choice(
        [0, 1], batch_size, p=[1-epsilon, epsilon])
    return np.where(should_explore, random_actions, best_actions)
```

Listing 6-11. DQN Agent in TensorFlow

```
class DQNAgent:
    def __init__(self, state_shape, n_actions, epsilon=0):

        super().__init__()
        self.epsilon = epsilon
        self.n_actions = n_actions
        self.state_shape = state_shape

        # a simple NN with state_dim as input vector (inout is state s)
        # and self.n_actions as output vector of logits of q(s, a)
        self.model = tf.keras.models.Sequential()
        self.model.add(tf.keras.Input(shape=state_shape))
        self.model.add(tf.keras.layers.Conv2D(16, kernel_size=8, strides=4,
        activation='relu'))
        self.model.add(tf.keras.layers.Conv2D(32, kernel_size=4, strides=2,
        activation='relu'))
        self.model.add(tf.keras.layers.Flatten())
        self.model.add(tf.keras.layers.Dense(256, activation='relu'))
        self.model.add(tf.keras.layers.Dense(n_actions))

    def __call__(self, state_t):
        # pass the state at time t through the newrok to get Q(s,a)
        qvalues = self.model(state_t)
        return qvalues

    def get_qvalues(self, states):
        # input is an array of states in numpy and outout is Qvals as numpy
        array
        qvalues = self.model(states)
        return qvalues.numpy()
```

```
    def sample_actions(self, qvalues):
        # sample actions from a batch of q_values using epsilon greedy policy
        epsilon = self.epsilon
        batch_size, n_actions = qvalues.shape
        random_actions = np.random.choice(n_actions, size=batch_size)
        best_actions = qvalues.argmax(axis=-1)
        should_explore = np.random.choice(
            [0, 1], batch_size, p=[1-epsilon, epsilon])
        return np.where(should_explore, random_actions, best_actions)
```

You will notice the similarity in the code between PyTorch and TensorFlow in eager execution mode. You are well advised to focus on one framework and master the concepts. Once you have mastered one, it will be easy to port the code to the other framework. We will be using PyTorch in this book for the majority of the examples, with some TensorFlow versions here and there.

Except for these two changes, i.e., some problem-specific preprocessing and a problem-appropriate neural network, the rest of the code remains the same between CartPole and Atari. You can also use the Atari version to train the agent on any version of the Atari game. Further, except for these two changes, the same code can be used to train the DQN agent for any environment. You can look into the available Gym environments from the Gym library documentation and try to modify the code from listing6_1_dqn_pytorch.ipynb or listing6_1_dqn_atari_pytorch.ipynb to train the agents for different environments.

This completes the implementation and training of DQN. Now that we know how to train a DQN agent, we will look into some issues and various approaches we could take to modify the DQN. As we talked about at the beginning of the chapter, we will look at some recent and state-of-the-art variations.

Prioritized Replay

In the previous chapter, we saw how to use a batch version of updates in DQN that addresses some key issues that are there in the online version, with updates being done with each transition and a transition being discarded right after that one step of learning. The following are the key issues in the online versions:

- The training samples (transitions) are correlated, breaking i.i.d. (independent identically distributed) assumptions. With online learning, we have transitions coming in a sequence that are correlated. Each transition is linked to the previous one. This breaks the i.i.d. assumption that is required to apply gradient descent.

- As the agent learns and discards, it may never get to visit the initial exploratory transitions. If the agent goes down a wrong path, it will keep seeing examples from that part of the state space. It may settle on a very suboptimal solution.

- With neural networks, learning on a single transition basis is hard and inefficient. There will be too much variance for the neural networks to learn anything effective. Neural networks work best when they learn in batches of training samples.

These were addressed in DQN by using an experience replay where all transitions are stored. Each transition is a tuple of (`state`, `action`, `reward`, `next_state`, `done`). As the buffer gets full, we discard old samples to add new ones. We then sample a batch from the current buffer with each transition in the buffer having equal probability of being selected in a batch. It allows rare and more exploratory transitions to be picked multiple times from the buffer. However, a plain-vanilla *experience replay* does not have any way to choose the important transitions with some priority. Would it help to somehow assign an importance score to each transition stored in the replay buffer and sample the batch from the buffer using these importance scores as the probability of selection, assigning a higher probability of selection to important transitions as signified by their respective importance score?

This is what the authors of the paper "Prioritized Experience Replay"[2] from DeepMind explored in 2016. We will follow the main concepts of this paper to create

---

[2]https://arxiv.org/pdf/1511.05952.pdf

our own implementation of experience replay and apply it on the DQN agent for the CartPole environment. Let's start by talking a little bit about how these importance scores are assigned and how the loss L is modified.

The key approach of this paper is to assign importance scores to training samples in the buffer using their TD errors. When a batch of samples is picked from the buffer, we calculate the TD error as part of the loss L calculation. The TD error is given by this equation:

$$\delta_i = r_i + \left((1 - done_i).\gamma.\max_{a_i} \hat{q}\left(s_i', a_i'; w_t^-\right) \right) - \hat{q}(s_i, a_i; w_t) \tag{6.6}$$

It appears inside equation (6.3) where we calculate the loss. The error is squared and averaged over all samples to calculate the magnitude of updates to weight vectors as shown in equations (6.4) and (6.5). The magnitude of TD error δ_i denotes the contribution that the sample transition *(i)* would have on the update. The authors used this reasoning to assign an importance score p_i to each sample, where p_i is given by this equation:

$$p_i = |\delta_i| + \varepsilon \tag{6.7}$$

A small constant ε is added to avoid the edge case of p_i being zero when TD error δ_i is zero. When a new transition is added to the buffer, we assign it the max of p_i across all current transitions in the buffer. When a batch is picked for training, we calculate the TD error δ_i of each sample as part of the loss/gradient calculation. This TD error is then used to update the importance score of these samples back in the buffer.

There is another approach of rank-based prioritization that the paper talks about. Using that approach, $p_i = \dfrac{1}{rank(i)}$, where *rank(i)* is the rank of transition(i) when the replay buffer transitions are sorted based on $|\delta_i|$. In our code example, we will be using the first approach, which is called *proportional prioritization*.

Next, at the time of sampling, we convert p_i to probabilities by using the following equation:

$$P(i) = \frac{p_i^\alpha}{\sum_i p_i^\alpha} \tag{6.8}$$

Here, $P(i)$ denotes the probability of transition (i) in the buffer getting sampled and as part of the training batch. This assigns a higher sampling probability to the transitions that have a higher TD error. Here, α is a hyperparameter, which was tuned using grid search, and the authors found $\alpha = 0.6$ to be the best for the proportional variant that we will be implementing.

The previous approach of breaking the uniform sampling with some kind of sampling based on importance introduces bias. We need to correct the bias while calculating the loss L. In the paper, this was corrected using *importance sampling* by weighing each sample with weight w_i and then summing it up to get the revised loss function L. The equation for calculating weights is as follows:

$$w_i = \left(\frac{1}{N} \cdot \frac{1}{P(i)} \right)^{\beta} \tag{6.9}$$

Here, N is the number of samples in the training batch, and $P(i)$ is the probability of selecting a sample as calculated in the previous expression earlier. β is another hyperparameter for which we will use a value of 0.4 from the paper. The weights are further normalized by $\frac{1}{max_i w_i}$ to ensure that the weights stay within bounds.

$$w_i = \frac{1}{max_i w_i} w_i \tag{6.10}$$

With these changes in place, the loss L equation is also updated to weigh each transition in the batch with w_i as follows:

$$L = \frac{1}{N} \sum_{i=1}^{N} \left[\left(r_i + \left((1 - done_i).\gamma.\max_{a_i} \hat{q}\left(s_i', a_i'; w_t^-\right) \right) - \hat{q}\left(s_i, a_i; w_t\right) \right).w_i \right]^2 \tag{6.11}$$

Notice the w_i in the equation. After L is calculated, we follow the usual gradient step using back propagation of the loss gradient with respect to the online neural network weights w.

Remember, the TD error in the previous equation is used to update the importance score back in the replay buffer for these transitions in the current training batch. This completes the theoretical discussion on the prioritized replay. We will now look at the implementation. The complete code of training a DQN agent with prioritized replay is given in listing6_3_dqn_prioritized_replay.ipynb, which has two flavors, one in

PyTorch and another in TensorFlow. However, from this point on, we will only list the PyTorch versions. You are advised to study the code in detail along with the referenced paper after going through the explanations given next. The ability to follow the academic papers and match the details in the paper to working code is an important part of becoming a good practitioner. The explanation is to just get you started. For a firm grasp of the material, you should follow the accompanying code in detail. It will be even better if you try to code it yourself after absorbing how the code works.

Getting back to the explanation, we first look at the prioritized replay implementation, which is the major change in the code from the previous DQN training notebook. Listing 6-12 gives the code for prioritized replay. Most of the code is similar to that of the plain `ReplayBuffer` we saw earlier. We now have an additional array called `self.priorities` to hold the importance/priority score p_i for each sample. Function `add` is modified to assign p_i to the new sample being added. It is just the max of values in the array `self.priorities`. Function `sample` is the one where there is maximum change. The first probabilities are calculated using equation (6.8), and then the weights are calculated using (6.9) and (6.10). The function now returns additional two arrays: the array of weights `np.array(weights)` and the array of index `np.array(idxs)`. The array of indexes contains the indexes of the samples in the buffer that were sampled in the batch. This is required so that after the calculation of TD error in the loss step, we can update the priority/importance back in the buffer. Function `update_priorities(idxs, new_priorities)` is exactly for that purpose.

Listing 6-12. Prioritized Replay

```
class PrioritizedReplayBuffer:
    def __init__(self, size, alpha=0.6, beta=0.4):
        self.size = size #max number of items in buffer
        self.buffer =[] #array to holde buffer
        self.next_id = 0
        self.alpha = alpha
        self.beta = beta
        self.priorities = np.ones(size)
        self.epsilon = 1e-5

    def __len__(self):
        return len(self.buffer)
```

```python
def add(self, state, action, reward, next_state, done):
    item = (state, action, reward, next_state, done)
    max_priority = self.priorities.max()
    if len(self.buffer) < self.size:
        self.buffer.append(item)
    else:
        self.buffer[self.next_id] = item
    self.priorities[self.next_id] = max_priority
    self.next_id = (self.next_id + 1) % self.size

def sample(self, batch_size):
    priorities = self.priorities[:len(self.buffer)]
    probabilities = priorities ** self.alpha
    probabilities /= probabilities.sum()
    N = len(self.buffer)
    weights = (N * probabilities) ** (-self.beta)
    weights /= weights.max()

    idxs = np.random.choice(len(self.buffer), batch_size, p=probabilities)

    samples = [self.buffer[i] for i in idxs]
    states, actions, rewards, next_states, done_flags = \
    list(zip(*samples))
    weights = weights[idxs]

    return  (np.array(states), np.array(actions), np.array(rewards),
             np.array(next_states), np.array(done_flags),
             np.array(weights), np.array(idxs))

def update_priorities(self, idxs, new_priorities):
    self.priorities[idxs] = new_priorities+self.epsilon
```

Next, we look at the loss calculation. The code is almost similar to the TD loss computation we saw in Listing 6-5. There are two changes. The first is multiplying the TD error with weights, in line with equation (6.11). The second change is calling update_priorities from inside the function to update the priorities back in the buffer. Listing 6-13 shows the code for the revised TD_loss compute_td_loss_priority_replay computation.

Listing 6-13. TD Loss with Prioritized Replay

```
def compute_td_loss_priority_replay(agent, target_network, replay_buffer,
                                    states, actions, rewards, next_states,
done_flags, weights, buffer_idxs,
                                    gamma=0.99, device=device):
    # convert numpy array to torch tensors
    states = torch.tensor(states, device=device, dtype=torch.float)
    actions = torch.tensor(actions, device=device, dtype=torch.long)
    rewards = torch.tensor(rewards, device=device, dtype=torch.float)
    next_states = torch.tensor(next_states, device=device, dtype=torch.float)
    done_flags = torch.tensor(done_flags.astype('float32'),device=device,dt
    ype=torch.float)
    weights = torch.tensor(weights, device=device, dtype=torch.float)

    # get q-values for all actions in current states
    # use agent network
    predicted_qvalues = agent(states)

    # compute q-values for all actions in next states
    # use target network
    predicted_next_qvalues = target_network(next_states)

    # select q-values for chosen actions
    predicted_qvalues_for_actions = predicted_qvalues[range(
        len(actions)), actions]

    # compute Qmax(next_states, actions) using predicted next q-values
    next_state_values,_ = torch.max(predicted_next_qvalues, dim=1)

    # compute "target q-values"
    target_qvalues_for_actions = rewards + gamma * next_state_values * (1-
    done_flags)

    #compute each sample TD error
    loss = ((predicted_qvalues_for_actions - target_qvalues_for_actions.
    detach()) ** 2) * weights

    # mean squared error loss to minimize
```

```
loss = loss.mean()

# calculate new priorities and update buffer
with torch.no_grad():
    new_priorities = predicted_qvalues_for_actions.detach() - target_
    qvalues_for_actions.detach()
    new_priorities = np.absolute(new_priorities.detach().numpy())
    replay_buffer.update_priorities(buffer_idxs, new_priorities)

return loss
```

The training code remains the same as before. You can look at the `listing6_3_dqn_prioritized_replay_pytorch.ipynb` notebook to see the details. Like before, we train the agent, and we can see that the agent learns to balance the pole really well with this approach. Figure 6-5 shows the training curves.

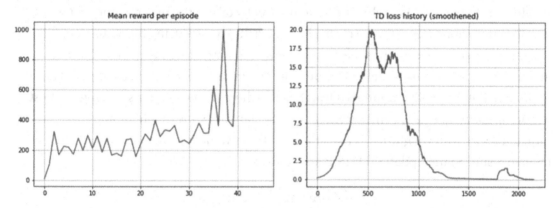

Figure 6-5. *Training curve for DQN agent with prioritized experience replay on CartPole*

This completes the section on prioritized replay. You are advised to refer to the original paper and code notebooks for further details.

Double Q-Learning

You saw in Chapter 5, that using the same network for selecting the maximizing action as well as the q-value for that maximum action leads to an overestimation bias, which in turn could lead to suboptimal policies. The authors of the paper "Deep Reinforcement

Learning with Double Q-Learning"[3] explore this bias, first mathematically and then in the context of DQN on Atari games.

Let's look at the max operation in the regular DQN. We calculate the TD target as follows:

$$Y^{DQN} = r + \gamma . \max_{a'} \hat{q}\left(s', a'; w_t^-\right)$$

We have simplified the equation a bit by dropping the subscript (i) as well as removing the (1-done) multiplier, which drops the second term for the terminal state. We have done so to keep the explanation uncluttered. Now, let's unwrap this equation by moving the "*max*" inside. The previous update can be equivalently written as follows:

$$r + \gamma . \hat{q}\left(s', argmax_{a'} \hat{q}\left(s', a'; w_t^-\right); w_t^-\right)$$

We have moved the max inside by first taking the max action and then taking the q-value for that max action. This is similar to directly taking the max q-value. In the previous unwrapped equation, we can clearly see that we are using the same network weight w_t^-, first for selecting the best action and then for getting the q-value for that action. This is what causes maximization bias. The authors of the paper suggested an approach that they called double DQN (DDQN) where the weight for selecting the best action, $argmax_a \hat{q}(s', a')$, comes from the online network with weight w_t and then the target network with weight w_t^- is used to select the q-value for that best action. This change results in the updated TD target as follows:

$$r + \gamma . \hat{q}\left(s', argmax_{a'} \hat{q}(s', a'; w_t); w_t^-\right)$$

Notice that now the inner network for selecting the best action is using online weights w_t. Everything else remains same. We calculate the loss as before and then use the gradient step to update the weights of the online network. We also periodically update the target network weights with the weights from the online network. The updated loss function that we use is as follows:

$$L = \frac{1}{N} \sum_{i=1}^{N} \left[r_i + \left((1 - done_i) . \gamma . \hat{q}\left(s_i', argmax_{a'} \hat{q}\left(s_i', a'; w_t\right); w_t^-\right)\right) - \hat{q}(s_i, a_i; w_t)\right]^2 \quad (6.12)$$

---

[3]https://arxiv.org/pdf/1509.06461v3.pdf

The authors show that the previous approach leads to significant reduction in overestimation bias, which in turn leads to better policies. Let's now look at the implementation details. The only thing that will change as compared to the DQN implementation is the way loss is calculated. We will now use equation 6.12 to calculate the loss. Everything else, including the DQN agent code, the replay buffer, and the way training is carried out to step through back propagation of gradients, will remain the same. Listing 6-14 gives revised loss function calculations. We calculate the current q-value with `q_s = agent(states)` and then, for each row, pick the q-value corresponding to the action a_i. We then use the agent network to calculate the q-values for the next states: `q_s1 = agent(next_states)`. This is used to find the best action for each row, and then we use the target network with the best action to find the target q-value.

```
q_s1 = agent(next_states).detach()
_,a1max = torch.max(q_s1, dim=1)
q_s1_target = target_network(next_states)
q_s1_a1max = q_s1_target[range(len(a1max)), a1max]
```

Listing 6-14. TD Loss with Double Q-Learning

```
def td_loss_ddqn(agent, target_network, states, actions, rewards, next_
states, done_flags,
                 gamma=0.99, device=device):
    # convert numpy array to torch tensors
    states = torch.tensor(states, device=device, dtype=torch.float)
    actions = torch.tensor(actions, device=device, dtype=torch.long)
    rewards = torch.tensor(rewards, device=device, dtype=torch.float)
    next_states = torch.tensor(next_states, device=device, dtype=torch.float)
    done_flags = torch.tensor(done_flags.astype('float32'),device=device,dt
ype=torch.float)

    # get q-values for all actions in current states
    # use agent network
    q_s = agent(states)

    # select q-values for chosen actions
    q_s_a = q_s[range(
        len(actions)), actions]
```

```
# compute q-values for all actions in next states
# use agent network (online network)
q_s1 = agent(next_states).detach()

# compute Q argmax(next_states, actions) using predicted next q-values
_,a1max = torch.max(q_s1, dim=1)

#use target network to calclaute the q value for best action chosen above
q_s1_target = target_network(next_states)

q_s1_a1max = q_s1_target[range(len(a1max)), a1max]

# compute "target q-values"
target_q = rewards + gamma * q_s1_a1max * (1-done_flags)

# mean squared error loss to minimize
loss = torch.mean((q_s_a - target_q).pow(2))

return loss
```

Running DDQN on CartPole produces the training graph given in Figure 6-6. You may not notice a big difference as CartPole is too simple a problem to show the benefits. In addition, we have been running the training algorithm for a small number of episodes to demonstrate the algorithms. For quantified benefits of the approach, you should look at the referenced paper.

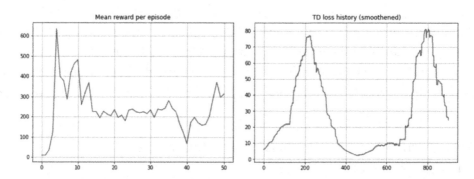

Figure 6-6. *Training curve for DDQN on CartPole*

This completes the discussion on DDQN. Next, we look at dueling DQN.

Dueling DQN

Up until now all our networks took in state S and produced the q-values $Q(S,A)$ for all actions A in the state S. Figure 6-1 shows a sample of such a network. However, many times in a particular state, there is no impact from taking any specific action. Consider the case that a car is driving in the middle of road and there are no cars around your car. In such a scenario, the action of taking a slight left or right, or speeding a bit or breaking a bit, has no impact; these actions all produce similar q-values. Is there a way to separate the average value in a state and the advantage of taking a specific action over that average? That's the approach that the authors of the paper titled "Dueling Network Architectures for Deep Reinforcement Learning"[4] took in 2016. They showed that it led to significant improvements, and the improvement was higher as the number of possible actions in a state grew.

Let's derive the computation that the dueling DQN network performs. We saw the definition of state-value and action-value functions in Chapter 2 in equations (2.9) and (2.10), which are reproduced here:

$$v_\pi(s) = E_\pi[G_t \mid S_t = s]$$

$$q_\pi(s,a) = E_\pi[G_t \mid S_t = s, A_t = a]$$

Then in Chapter 5 on function approximation, we saw these equations change a bit with the introduction of parameters w when we switched to representing the state/action values as parameterized functions.

$$\hat{v}(s,w) \approx v_\pi(s)$$

$$\hat{q}(s,a,w) \approx q_\pi(s,a)$$

Both sets of equations show us that v_π measures the value of being in a state in general, and q_π shows us the value of taking a specific action from the state S. If we subtract Q from V, we get something that is called *advantage A*. Please note that there is a bit of overload of notations. A inside $Q(S,A)$ represents action, and A_π on the left side of equation represents the advantage, not the action.

$$A_\pi(s,a) = Q_\pi(s,a) - V_\pi(s) \tag{6.13}$$

---

[4]https://arxiv.org/pdf/1511.06581.pdf

The authors created a network that like before takes in a state S as input and after a few layers of network produces two streams, one giving state value V and another giving advantage A with part of the network being individual sets of layers, one for V and one for A. Finally, the last layer combines advantage A and state value V to recover Q. To have better stability, however, they made an additional change of subtracting the average of advantage values from each output node of $Q(S,A)$. The equation that neural network implements is as follows:

$$\hat{Q}\left(s,a;w_1,w_2,w_3\right)=\hat{V}\left(s;w_1,w_2\right)+\left(\hat{A}\left(s,a;w_1,w_3\right)-\frac{1}{|A|}\sum_{a'}\hat{A}\left(s,a';w_1,w_3\right)\right) \qquad (6.14)$$

In the previous equation, weight w_1 corresponds to the initial common part of the network, w_2 corresponds to the part of the network that predicts state value $\hat{V}$, and finally w_3 corresponds to the part of network that predicts advantage $\hat{A}$. Figure 6-7 shows a representative network architecture.

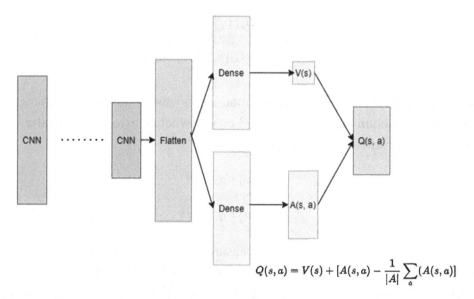

$$Q(s,a) = V(s) + [A(s,a) - \frac{1}{|A|}\sum_a (A(s,a)]$$

Figure 6-7. *Dueling network. The network has a common set of weights in the initial layers, and then it branches off to have one set of weights producing value V and another set producing advantage A*

The authors named this architecture *dueling networks* as it has two networks fused together with an initial common part. Since the dueling network is at the agent network level, it is independent of the other components like the type of replay buffer or the way the weights are learned (i.e., simple DQN or double DQN). Accordingly, we can use the dueling network independent of the type of replay buffer or the type of learning. In our walk-through, we will be using a simple replay buffer with uniform probability of selection for each transition in the buffer. Further, we will be using a DQN agent. Compared to listing6_1 for DQN, the only change will be the way the network is constructed. Listing 6-15 shows the code for the dueling agent network.

Listing 6-15. Dueling Network

```
class DuelingDQNAgent(nn.Module):
    def __init__(self, state_shape, n_actions, epsilon=0):

        super().__init__()
        self.epsilon = epsilon
        self.n_actions = n_actions
        self.state_shape = state_shape

        state_dim = state_shape[0]
        # a simple NN with state_dim as input vector (inout is state s)
        # and self.n_actions as output vector of logits of q(s, a)
        self.fc1 = nn.Linear(state_dim, 64)
        self.fc2 = nn.Linear(64, 128)
        self.fc_value = nn.Linear(128, 32)
        self.fc_adv = nn.Linear(128, 32)
        self.value = nn.Linear(32, 1)
        self.adv = nn.Linear(32, n_actions)

    def forward(self, state_t):
        # pass the state at time t through the newrok to get Q(s,a)
        x = F.relu(self.fc1(state_t))
        x = F.relu(self.fc2(x))
        v = F.relu(self.fc_value(x))
        v = self.value(v)
        adv = F.relu(self.fc_adv(x))
        adv = self.adv(adv)
        adv_avg = torch.mean(adv, dim=1, keepdim=True)
        qvalues = v + adv - adv_avg
        return qvalues
```

```
def get_qvalues(self, states):
    # input is an array of states in numpy and outout is Qvals as numpy
    array
    states = torch.tensor(states, device=device, dtype=torch.float32)
    qvalues = self.forward(states)
    return qvalues.data.cpu().numpy()

def sample_actions(self, qvalues):
    # sample actions from a batch of q_values using epsilon greedy policy
    epsilon = self.epsilon
    batch_size, n_actions = qvalues.shape
    random_actions = np.random.choice(n_actions, size=batch_size)
    best_actions = qvalues.argmax(axis=-1)
    should_explore = np.random.choice(
        [0, 1], batch_size, p=[1-epsilon, epsilon])
    return np.where(should_explore, random_actions, best_actions)
```

We have two layers of common network (self.fc1 and self.fc2). For V prediction, we have another two layers (self.fc_value and self.value) on top of fc1 and fc2. Similarly, for advantage estimation, we again have a separate set of two layers (self. fc_adv and self.adv) on top of fc1 and fc2. Then these outputs are combined to give the modified q-value as per equation (6.14). The rest of the code, e.g., the calculation of the TD loss and the gradient descent for the weight update, remains the same as DQN. Figure 6-8 shows the result of training the previous network on CartPole.

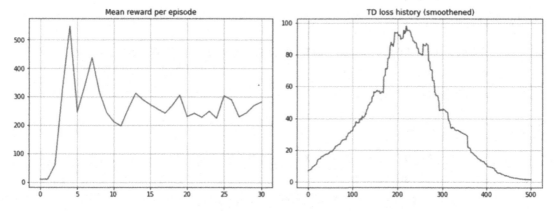

Figure 6-8. *Training curves for a dueling network*

Like we said, you could try to substitute `ReplayBuffer` with `PrioritizedReplayBuffer`. They could also use double DQN instead of DQN as a learning agent. This concludes the discussion on dueling DQN. We now look at a very different variant in the next section.

NoisyNets DQN

We need to explore parts of state space. We have been doing so using a ε-greedy policy. Under this exploration, we take the max q-value action with probability (1- ε), and we take a random action with probability ε. The authors of a recent 2018 paper titled "Noisy Networks for Exploration,"[5] used a different approach of adding random perturbations to linear layers as parameters, and like network weights, these are also learned.

The usual linear layers are affine transformations as given by the following:

$$y = wx + b$$

In noisy linear versions, we introduce random perturbations in the weights as given by the following:

$$y = \left(\mu^w + \sigma^w \odot \epsilon^w\right)x + \left(\mu^b + \sigma^b \odot \epsilon^b\right)$$

In the previous equation, μ^w, σ^w, μ^b, and σ^b are the weights of the network that are learned. ϵ^w and ϵ^b are random noises that introduce randomness leading to exploration. Figure 6-9 gives a schematic diagram of the noisy version of the linear layer, which explains the equation we just talked about in the previous paragraph.

---

[5]https://arxiv.org/pdf/1706.10295.pdf

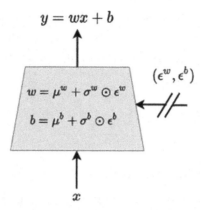

Figure 6-9. *Noisy linear layer. The weights and biases are a linear combination of mean and standard deviation, which are learned just like the weights and biases in a regular linear layer*

We will implement the factorized version as discussed in the paper where each element $\epsilon_{i,j}^w$ of the matrix is factored. Suppose we have p units of inputs and q units of output. Accordingly, we generate a p-size vector of Gaussian noise ϵ_i and a q-size vector of Gaussian noise ϵ_j. Each $\epsilon_{i,j}^w$ and ϵ_j^b can now be written as follows:

$$\epsilon_{i,j}^w = f(\epsilon_i)f(\epsilon_j)$$

$$\epsilon_j^b = f(\epsilon_j)$$

$$\text{where; } f(x) = sgn(x)\sqrt{|x|}$$

For factorized networks like the one we are using, we suggest you initialize the weights as follows:

- Each element $\mu_{i,j}$ of μ^w and μ^b is sampled from uniform distribution in the range $U\left[-\dfrac{1}{\sqrt{p}}, \dfrac{1}{\sqrt{p}}\right]$, where p is the number of input units.

- Similarly, each element $\sigma_{i,j}$ of σ^w and σ^b is initialized to a constant $\dfrac{\sigma_0}{\sqrt{p}}$ with the hyperparameter σ_0 set to 0.5.

We create a noisy layer along the lines of the linear layer provided by PyTorch. We do so by extending `nn.Module` from PyTorch. It is a simple and standard implementation where you create your weight vectors in the `init` function. Then you write a `forward` function to take an input and transform it through a set of noisy linear and regular linear layers. You will also need some additional functions. In our case, we wrote a function called reset_noise to generate the noise ϵ^w and ϵ^b. This function internally uses a helper function called _noise. We also have a function reset_parameters to reset the parameters following the strategy outlined earlier. We could use a noisy net with DQN, DDQN, dueling DQN, and prioritized replay in various combinations. However, for the purpose of the walk-through, we will focus on using a regular replay buffer with DQN. We also train using the regular DQN approach and not DDQN. Listing 6-16 gives the code for the noisy linear.

Listing 6-16. Noisy Linear Layer in PyTorch

```python
class NoisyLinear(nn.Module):
    def __init__(self, in_features, out_features, sigma_0 = 0.4):
        super(NoisyLinear, self).__init__()
        self.in_features  = in_features
        self.out_features = out_features
        self.sigma_0= sigma_0

        self.mu_w = nn.Parameter(torch.FloatTensor(out_features, in_
        features))
        self.sigma_w = nn.Parameter(torch.FloatTensor(out_features, in_
        features))
        self.mu_b = nn.Parameter(torch.FloatTensor(out_features))
        self.sigma_b = nn.Parameter(torch.FloatTensor(out_features))

        self.register_buffer('epsilon_w', torch.FloatTensor(out_features,
        in_features))
        self.register_buffer('epsilon_b', torch.FloatTensor(out_features))

        self.reset_noise()
        self.reset_params()

    def forward(self, x):
        if self.training:
            w = self.mu_w + self.sigma_w * self.epsilon_w
            b = self.mu_b + self.sigma_b * self.epsilon_b
        else:
            w = self.mu_w
```

```
        b = self.mu_b
    return F.linear(x, w, b)

def reset_params(self):
    k = 1/self.in_features
    k_sqrt = math.sqrt(k)
    self.mu_w.data.uniform_(-k_sqrt, k_sqrt)
    self.sigma_w.data.fill_(k_sqrt*self.sigma_0)
    self.mu_b.data.uniform_(-k_sqrt, k_sqrt)
    self.sigma_b.data.fill_(k_sqrt*self.sigma_0)

def reset_noise(self):
    eps_in = self._noise(self.in_features)
    eps_out = self._noise(self.out_features)
    self.epsilon_w.copy_(eps_out.ger(eps_in))
    self.epsilon_b.copy_(self._noise(self.out_features))

def _noise(self, size):
    x = torch.randn(size)
    x = torch.sign(x)*torch.sqrt(torch.abs(x))
    return x
```

The rest of the implementation remains same. The only difference now is that we have no ε-greedy selection in the function `sample_actions` of the DQN agent. We also have a `reset_noise` function to reset the noise after each batch. This is in line with the recommendations of the paper to decorrelate. Listing 6-17 contains the NoisyDQN version with the previous modifications. The rest of the implementation is similar to the vanilla DQN agent.

Listing 6-17. NoisyDQN Agent in PyTorch

```
class NoisyDQN(nn.Module):
    def __init__(self, state_shape, n_actions):
        super(NoisyDQN, self).__init__()
        self.n_actions = n_actions
        self.state_shape = state_shape
        state_dim = state_shape[0]
        # a simple NN with state_dim as input vector (inout is state s)
```

```python
        # and self.n_actions as output vector of logits of q(s, a)
        self.fc1 = NoisyLinear(state_dim, 64)
        self.fc2 = NoisyLinear(64, 128)
        self.fc3 = NoisyLinear(128, 32)
        self.q = NoisyLinear(32, n_actions)

    def forward(self, state_t):
        # pass the state at time t through the newrok to get Q(s,a)
        x = F.relu(self.fc1(state_t))
        x = F.relu(self.fc2(x))
        x = F.relu(self.fc3(x))
        qvalues = self.q(x)
        return qvalues

    def get_qvalues(self, states):
        # input is an array of states in numpy and outout is Qvals as numpy
        array
        states = torch.tensor(states, device=device, dtype=torch.float32)
        qvalues = self.forward(states)
        return qvalues.data.cpu().numpy()

    def sample_actions(self, qvalues):
        # sample actions from a batch of q_values using greedy policy
        batch_size, n_actions = qvalues.shape
        best_actions = qvalues.argmax(axis=-1)
        return best_actions

    def reset_noise(self):
        self.fc1.reset_noise()
        self.fc2.reset_noise()
        self.fc3.reset_noise()
        self.q.reset_noise()
```

Training a NoisyDQN in the CartPole environment produces the training curves, as given in Figure 6-10. We may not see any significant difference between this variant and DQN (or for that matter all the variants). The reason is that we are using a simple problem and training it for a short number of episodes. The idea in the book is to teach you the inner details of a specific variant. For a thorough study of the improvements and other observations, you are advised to refer to the original papers referenced. Also, once again we would like to emphasis that you should go through the accompanying Python notebooks in detail, and after you have grasped the details, you should try to code the example anew.

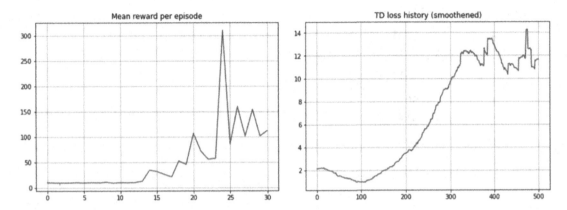

Figure 6-10. *NoisyNet DQN training graph*

You are also encouraged to try to code a noisy version of dueling DQN. Further, you could also try the DDQN variant of learning. In other words, with what we have learned so far, we could try following combinations:

- DQN

- DDQN (impacts how we learn)

- Dueling DQN (impacts the architecture of training)

- Dueling DDQN

- Replace vanilla ReplayBuffer with prioritized replay buffer

- Replace ε-exploration with NoisyNets in any of the previous approaches

- Code all combinations on TensorFlow

- Try many other Gym environments, making appropriate changes, if any, to the network

- Run some of them on Atari, especially if you have access to a GPU machine

Categorical 51-Atom DQN (C51)

In a 2017 paper titled "A Distributional Perspective on Reinforcement Learning,"[6] the authors argued in favor of the distributional nature of RL. Instead of looking at the expected values like the q-value, they looked at Z, a random distribution whose expectation is Q.

Up to now we have been outputting $Q(s, a)$ values for an input state s. The number of units in the output were of size n_action. In a way, the output values were the expected $Q(s, a)$ using the Monte Carlo technique of averaging over a number of samples to form an estimate $\hat{Q}(s,a)$ of the actual expected value $E[Q(s, a)]$.

In categorial 51-Atom DQN, for each $Q(s, a)$ (n_action of them), we now produce an estimate of the distribution of $Q(s, a)$ values: n_atom (51 to be precise) values for each $Q(s, a)$. The network is now predicting the entire distribution modeled as a categorical probability distribution instead of just estimating the mean value of $Q(s, a)$.

$$Q(s,a) = \sum_i z_i p_i(s,a)$$

$p_i(s, a)$ is the probability that the action value at (s, a) will be z_i.

We now have n_action * n_atom outputs, i.e., n_atom outputs for each value of n_action. Further, these outputs are probabilities. For one action, we have n_atom probabilities, and these are the probability of the q-value being in any one of the n_atom discrete values in the range V_min to V_max. You should refer to the previously mentioned paper for more details.

In the C51 version of distributional RL, the authors took i to be 51 atoms (support points) over the values -10 to 10. We will use the same setup in the code. As these values are parameterized in the code, you are welcome to change them and explore the impact.

After the Bellman updates are applied, the values shift and may not fall on the 51 support points. There is a step of projection to bring back the probability distribution to the support points of 51 atoms.

The loss is also replaced from the mean squared error to *cross-entropy* loss. The agent is trained using an ε-greedy policy, similar to DQN. The whole math is fairly involved, and it will be a good exercise for you to go through the paper together with the

---

[6]https://arxiv.org/pdf/1707.06887.pdf

code to link each code line with the specific detail in the paper. This is an important skill you as a practitioner of RL need to have.

Similar to the DQN approach, we have a class `CategoricalDQN`, which is the neural network through that takes the state s as input to produce the distribution Z of $Q(s, a)$. There is a function to calculate the TD loss: `td_loss_categorical_dqn`. As discussed earlier, we need a projection step to bring the values back to the n_atom support points, which is carried out in the function `compute_projection`. Function `compute_projection` is used inside `td_loss_categorical_dqn` while calculating the loss calculation. The rest of the training remains the same as before.

Figure 6-11 gives the training curves for running this through the `CartPole` environment.

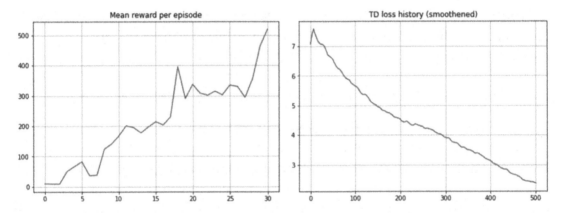

Figure 6-11. *Categorical 51 Atom DQN (C51) training graph*

Quantile Regression DQN

A little after the paper on the C51 algorithm was published in mid-2017, some of the original authors along with a few additional ones, all from DeepMind, came up with a variant that they called *quantile regression DQN* (QR-DQN). In a paper titled "Distributional Reinforcement Learning with Quantile Regression,"[7] the authors used a slightly different approach than the original C51, but still within the same focus area of distribution RL.

Similar to the C51 approach of distributional RL, the QR-DQN approach also depended on using quantiles to predict the distribution of $Q(s, a)$ instead of predicting

---

[7]https://arxiv.org/pdf/1710.10044.pdf

an estimate of the average of $Q(s, a)$. Both C51 and QR-DQN are variants of distributional RL and produced by scientists from DeepMind.

The C51 approach modeled the distribution of $Q^\pi(s, a)$ named $Z^\pi(s, a)$ as a categorical distribution of probability overfixed points in the range of V_{min} to V_{max}. The probability over these points was what was learned by the network. Such an approach resulted in the use of a *projection* step after the Bellman update to bring the new probabilities back to the fixed support points of n_atoms spread uniformly over V_{min} to V_{max}. While the result worked, there was a bit of disconnect with the theoretical basis on which the algorithm was derived.

In QR-DQN the approach is slightly different. The support points are still N, but now the probabilities were fixed to 1/N with the location of these points being learned by network. To quote the authors:

> We "transpose" the parametrization from C51: whereas the former uses N fixed locations for its approximation distribution and adjusts their probabilities, we assign fixed, uniform probabilities to N adjustable locations.

The loss used in DQ DQN is that of quantile regression loss mixed with huber loss. This is called *quantile huber loss*; equations 9 and 10 in the referenced paper give the details. We are not showing the code listings here as we want you to read the paper and match the equations in the paper with the code in the notebook listing6_8_qr_dqn_pytorch.ipynb. The paper is dense with mathematics, and unless you are comfortable with advanced math, you should try to focus on the higher-level details of the approach.

Figure 6-12 shows the training curve.

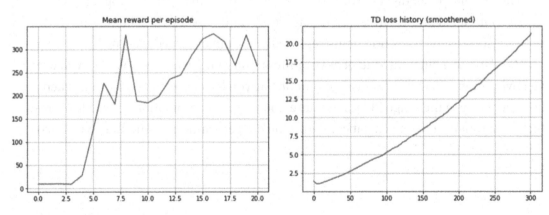

Figure 6-12. *Quantile regression DQN*

Hindsight Experience Replay

In the 2018 paper by OpenAI titled "Hindsight Experience Replay,"[8] the authors presented a sample efficient approach to learn in an environment where the rewards are sparse. The common approach is to shape the reward function in a way to guide the agents toward optimization. This is not generalizable.

Compared to RL agents, which learn from a successful outcome, humans seem to learn not just from that but also from unsuccessful outcomes. This is the basis of the idea proposed in the hindsight replay approach known as *hindsight experience replay* (HER). While HER can be combined with various RL approaches, in our code walk-through, we will use HER with dueling DQN, giving us HER-DQN.

In the HER approach, after an episode is played out, say an unsuccessful one, we form a secondary objective where the original goal is replaced with the last state before termination as a goal for this trajectory.

Say an episode has been played out: $s_0, s_1, \ldots s_T$. Normally we store in the replay buffer a tuple of $(s_t, a_t, r, s_{t+1}, done)$. Let's say the goal for this episode was g, which could not be achieved in this run. In the HER approach, we will store the following in the replay buffer:

- $(s_t||g, a_t, r, s_{t+1}||g, done)$

- $(s_t||g', a_t, r(s_t, a_t, g'), s_{t+1}||g', done)$: Other state transitions based on synthetical goals like the last state of the episode as a subgoal, say g'. The reward is modified to show how the state transition $s_t \rightarrow s_{t+1}$ was good or bad for the subgoal of g'.

The original paper discusses various strategies for forming these subgoals. We will use the one called *future*, which is a replay with k random states that come from the same episode as the transition being replayed and were observed after it.

We also use a different kind of environment from our past notebooks. We will use an environment of a bit-flipping experiment. Say you have a vector with n-bits, each being a binary in the range {0,1}. Therefore, there are 2^n combinations possible. At reset, the environment starts in a n-bit configuration chosen randomly, and the goal is also

---

[8]https://arxiv.org/pdf/1707.01495.pdf

randomly picked to be some different n-bit configuration. Each action is to flip a bit. The bit to be flipped is the policy $\pi(a|s)$ that the agent is trying to learn. An episode ends if the agent is able to find the right configuration matching the goal or when the agent has exhausted **n** actions in an episode. Listing 6-18 shows the code for the environment. The complete code is in notebook `listing6_9_her_dqn_pytorch.ipynb`.

Listing 6-18. Bit-Flipping Environment

```
class BitFlipEnvironment:

    def __init__(self, bits):
        self.bits = bits
        self.state = np.zeros((self.bits, ))
        self.goal = np.zeros((self.bits, ))
        self.reset()

    def reset(self):
        self.state = np.random.randint(2, size=self.bits).astype(np.float32)
        self.goal = np.random.randint(2, size=self.bits).astype(np.float32)
        if np.allclose(self.state, self.goal):
            self.reset()
        return self.state.copy(), self.goal.copy()

    def step(self, action):
        self.state[action] = 1 - self.state[action]  # Flip the bit on
        position of the action
        reward, done = self.compute_reward(self.state, self.goal)
        return self.state.copy(), reward, done

    def render(self):
        print("State: {}".format(self.state.tolist()))
        print("Goal : {}\n".format(self.goal.tolist()))

    @staticmethod
    def compute_reward(state, goal):
        done = np.allclose(state, goal)
        return 0.0 if done else -1.0, done
```

We have implemented our own `render` and `step` functions so that the interface of our environment remains similar to the ones in Gym and so that we can use our previously developed machinery. We also have a custom function `compute_reward` to return the `reward` and `done` flags when given the input of a state and a goal.

The authors show that with a regular DQN, where the state (configuration of n-bits) is represented as a deep network, it is almost impossible for a regular DQN agent to learn beyond 15-digit combinations. However, coupled with the HER-DQN approach, the agent is able to learn easily even for large-digit combinations like 50 or so. In Figure 6-13 we give the complete pseudocode from the paper with certain modifications to make it match with our notations.

HINDSIGHT EXPERIENCE REPLAY (HER)

Input:

    An off-policy algorithm (e.g. DQN or its variants)

    A strategy of sampling goals for replay (*future, episode, random*)

    A reward function (e.g., 0 if goal not met and 1 if goal met)

Initialize:

    Initialize neural network A

    Initialize Replay Buffer R

Loop for each episode in $(1, M)$:

    Start episode with s_0 (non terminal) and goal g

    for $t = 0, T - 1$:

        Select a_t using a behavior policy (e.g. ε-greedy)

$$a_t \leftarrow \pi_b \left(s_t \,\|\, g \right)$$

        Take action a_t and observe reward r_t next state s_{t+1}

        Record transition $(s_t, a_t, r_t, s_{t+1}, done_t)$ in a temporary array ET

    For $t = 0. T - 1$:

        Store $(s_t\|g, a_t, r_t, s_{t+1}\|g, done_t)$ in R

        Sample additional goals using sampling strategy, e.g., (future)

        for $\_ in 0, k$:

            select a transition k from trajectory in future

            $g' \leftarrow s'_k$, next state from kth transition in trajectory array

            Calculate new reward r' and $done'$ flag using (s_t, a_t, g')

            Store transition $(s_t\|g', a_t, r', s_{t+1}\|g', done')$ in R

    For $t = 1, N$:

    Sample a batch from replay buffer

    Perform one step of gradient descent

Figure 6-13. *HER using a future strategy*

We use dueling DQN. The most interesting part of the code is the implementation of the HER algorithm as per the pseudocode given in Figure 6-13. Listing 6-19 is a line-by-line implementation of that pseudocode.

Listing 6-19. Hindsight Experience Replay Implementation

```python
def train_her(env, agent, target_network, optimizer, td_loss_fn):

    success_rate = 0.0
    success_rates = []

    exp_replay = ReplayBuffer(10**6)

    for epoch in range(num_epochs):
        # Decay epsilon linearly from eps_max to eps_min
        eps = max(eps_max - epoch * (eps_max - eps_min) / int(num_epochs *
        exploration_fraction), eps_min)
        print("Epoch: {}, exploration: {:.0f}%, success rate: {:.2f}".
        format(epoch + 1, 100 * eps, success_rate))
        agent.epsilon = eps
        target_network.epsilon = eps

        successes = 0
        for cycle in range(num_cycles):

            for episode in range(num_episodes):

                # Run episode and cache trajectory
                episode_trajectory = []
                state, goal = env.reset()

                for step in range(num_bits):

                    state_ = np.concatenate((state, goal))
                    qvalues = agent.get_qvalues([state_])
                    action = agent.sample_actions(qvalues)[0]
                    next_state, reward, done = env.step(action)

                    episode_trajectory.append((state, action, reward, next_
                    state, done))
```

```
        state = next_state
        if done:
            successes += 1
            break

    # Fill up replay memory
    steps_taken = step
    for t in range(steps_taken):

        # Usual experience replay
        state, action, reward, next_state, done = episode_
        trajectory[t]
        state_, next_state_ = np.concatenate((state, goal)),
        np.concatenate((next_state, goal))
        exp_replay.add(state_, action, reward, next_state_, done)

        # Hindsight experience replay
        for _ in range(future_k):
            future = random.randint(t, steps_taken)  # index of
            future time step
            new_goal = episode_trajectory[future][3]  # take
            future next_state from (s,a,r,s',d) and set as goal
            new_reward, new_done = env.compute_reward(next_
            state, new_goal)
            state_, next_state_ = np.concatenate((state, new_
            goal)), np.concatenate((next_state, new_goal))
            exp_replay.add(state_, action, new_reward, next_
            state_, new_done)

# Optimize DQN
for opt_step in range(num_opt_steps):
    # train by sampling batch_size of data from experience replay
    states, actions, rewards, next_states, done_flags = exp_
    replay.sample(batch_size)
    # loss = <compute TD loss>
    optimizer.zero_grad()
    loss = td_loss_fn(agent, target_network,
```

```
                              states, actions, rewards, next_states,
                              done_flags,
                              gamma=0.99,
                              device=device)
            loss.backward()
            optimizer.step()

        target_network.load_state_dict(agent.state_dict())

    success_rate = successes / (num_episodes * num_cycles)
    success_rates.append(success_rate)

# print graph
plt.plot(success_rates, label="HER-DQN")

plt.legend()
plt.xlabel("Epoch")
plt.ylabel("Success rate")
plt.title("Number of bits: {}".format(num_bits))
plt.show()
```

In the code, we use the previously coded td_loss_dqn function to compute the TD loss and take a gradient step. We also start with a very exploratory behavior policy with $\varepsilon=0.2$ and slowly reduce it to zero, halfway through the training. The rest of the code matches line by line with the pseudocode in Figure 6-13.

Figure 6-14 shows the training curve. For a 50-bit BitFlipping environment, the agent with HER is able to successfully solve the environment 100 percent of the time. Remember, the environment starts with a random combination of 50 bits as a starting point and another random combination as the goal. The agent has a maximum of 50 flipping moves to reach the goal combination. An exhaustive search would require the agent to try each of the 2^{50} combinations except the one it started with initially.

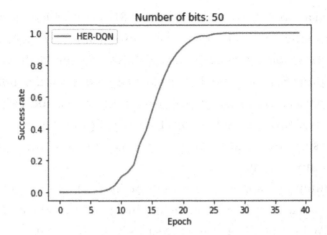

Figure 6-14. *Success rate graph: bit flipping environment with HER using a future strategy*

This brings us to the end of discussion on HER as well as to the end of chapter.

Summary

This was a fairly long chapter where we looked at DQN and most of its popular and recent variants.

We started with a quick recap of Q-learning and the derivation of the update equation for DQN. We then looked at the implementation of DQN in both PyTorch and TensorFlow for a simple `CartPole` environment. After this we looked at the Atari games, the original inspiration in 2013, to be able to use deep learning in the context of reinforcement learning. We looked at the additional preprocessing steps and changes in the network from a linear one to one based on convolutional layers.

Next, we talked about prioritized replay where the samples from the buffer are picked based on a certain importance score assigned to them proportional to the magnitude of the TD error.

Following this, we revisited double Q-learning in the context of DQN, known as double DQN. This is an approach that impacts the way learning takes place and attempts to reduce the maximization bias.

We then looked at dueling DQN in which two networks with an initial shared network were used. This was followed by NoisyNets in which ε-greedy exploration was replaced by noisy layers.

Next, we looked at two flavors of distributional RL under which the network produced Z, a distribution of q-values. Instead of producing the expected action-value $Q(S, A)$, it outputs the whole distribution, specifically a categorical distribution. We also saw the use of the projection step and losses like *cross entropy* and *quantile huber loss*.

The last section was on hindsight experience replay, which addresses learning in environments with sparse rewards. Previous learning approaches were centered around learning only from successful outcomes, but hindsight replay allows us to learn from unsuccessful outcomes as well.

Many of algorithms and approaches we saw in this chapter are state-of-the-art research. You will gain a lot by looking at the original papers as well as going through the code line by line. We have also suggested the various combinations that you could try to code to further cement the concepts in your mind.

This chapter concludes our exploration of value-based methods where we learn a policy by first learning with V or Q functions and then using these to find an optimal policy. In the next chapter, we will switch to policy-based methods where we find the optimal policy without the involvement of the intermediary step of learning V/Q functions.

## CHAPTER 7

Policy Gradient Algorithms

Up to now we have been focusing on model-based and model-free methods. All the algorithms using these methods estimated the action values for a given current policy. In a second step, these estimated values were used to find a better policy by choosing the best action in a given state. These two steps were carried out in a loop again and again until no further improvement in values was observed. In this chapter, we will look at a different approach for learning optimal policies by directly operating in the policy space. We will improve the policies without explicitly learning or using state or state-action values.

We will also see that the policy-based approach and the value-based approach are not two disjoint approaches. There are approaches that combine the value-based and policy-based approaches such as the actor-critic methods.

The core of the chapter will be to establish the definition and mathematically derive the key parts of policy-based optimization. The policy-based approach is currently one of the most popular family of approaches for solving large and continuous space problems in reinforcement learning.

Introduction

We started our journey by first looking at simple model-based approaches wherein we solved small, discrete state space problems by iterating over Bellman equations. Following this, we discussed a model-free setup using the Monte Carlo and temporal difference approaches. We then extended the analysis to cover large or continuous state space using function approximation. In particular, we looked at DQN and many of its variants as the way to go for policy learning.

© Nimish Sanghi 2021
N. Sanghi, *Deep Reinforcement Learning with Python*, https://doi.org/10.1007/978-1-4842-6809-4_7

The core idea of all these approaches was to first learn the value of the current policy and then make iterative improvements to the policy to get better rewards. This was done using the general framework of *Generalized Policy Iteration* (GPI). If you think for a minute, you will realize that our real objective was to learn a good policy, and we used value functions as an intermediary step to guide us in finding a good policy.

This approach of learning value functions to improve a policy is an indirect one. It is not always easy to learn values as compared to learning good policies directly. Consider the case of you encountering a bear on a jogging trail. What comes to your mind first? Does your brain try to evaluate the state (the bear in front of you) and the action values for possible actions ("freeze," "pet the bear," "run for your life," or "attack the bear")? Or do you "run" with almost certainty, i.e., follow a policy of `action="run"` with a probability of 1.0? I am sure the answer is the latter. Let's take another example of playing a game of Atari Breakout, the one we used in the DQN examples in the previous chapter. Consider the situation where the ball is almost near the right edge of your paddle and moving away from the paddle (the "state"). As a human player, what do you do? Do you try to evaluate $Q(s, a)$, the state-action values for the two actions and then decide whether the paddle needs to move right or left? Or do you just look at the state and learn to move the paddle right to avoid having the ball fall? Again, I am sure the answer is the second one. In both these examples, the latter and easier alternative was that of learning to act directly instead of learning the value first followed by using the state value to find the best action among the possible choices.

Pros and Cons of Policy-Based Methods

The previous examples show that in many cases, it is easier to learn the policy (what action to take in a given state) as compared to learning the value functions and then using them to learn a policy. Why then did we go through the approach of value methods like SARSA, Q-learning, DQN, etc., at all? Well, the policy learning, while easier, is not a bed of roses. It has its own set of challenges, especially based on our current knowledge and available algorithms, which are listed here:

- Advantages

  - Better convergence

  - Effective in high-dimensional and continuous action spaces

  - Learns stochastic policies

- Disadvantages
  - Usually convergences to local maximum instead of global ones
  - Policy evaluation inefficient and with high variance

Elaborating on these points, remember the DQN learning curves? We saw how the value of policy varied a lot during trainings. In the "cart pole" problem, we saw the score (as shown in the left graph of all the training progress diagrams in the previous chapter) fluctuate a lot. There was no steady convergence toward a better policy. Policy-based methods, especially with some additional controls that we will talk about toward the end of the chapter, ensure a fairly smooth and steady progress toward better policies as we move through the learning process.

Our action space has always been a small set of possible actions. Even in the case of function approximation coupled with deep learning like DQN, we had action spaces that were limited to single digits. The actions were unidimensional. Imagine trying to control various joins of a walking robot together. We would need to make decisions about each of the joints of the robot, and these individual choices together would make a complete action in a given state of the robot. Further, the individual actions of each joint are not going to be discrete ones. Most likely, the actions, such as speed of motors or angles by which an arm or a leg needs to move, are going to be in a continuous range. Policy-based methods are more suited to handle these actions.

In all the value-based methods we have seen so far, we always learned an optimal policy—a deterministic one where we knew with certainty the best action to take in a given state. Actually, we had to introduce the concept of exploration to try different actions using ε-greedy policies, with a reduction of exploration probability as the agent learned to act with better actions. The final output was always a deterministic policy. However, deterministic policies are not always *optimal*. There are situations where the optimal policy is to take multiple actions with some probability distribution, especially in multi-agent environments. If you have some experience with game theory, you will realize this immediately from setups like prisoner's dilemma and the corresponding Nash equilibrium. Anyway, let's look at a simple situation.

Have you ever played the game of rock-paper-scissors? It is a two-player game. In a single turn, each player has to choose one of the three options of scissors, rock, or paper. Both the players do so at the same time and reveal their choice at the same time. The rules state that scissors beats paper because scissors can cut paper, rock beats scissors because a rock can be used to smash the scissors, and paper beats rock because the paper can cover the rock.

What is the best policy? There are no clear winners. If you always choose, let's say, rock, then I as your opponent will exploit that knowledge and always choose paper. Can you think of any other deterministic policy (i.e., of choosing one of the three all the time)? To avoid the opponent from exploiting your strategy, you have to be completely random in making the choice. You have to choose scissors or rock or paper randomly with equal probability, i.e., a stochastic policy. Deterministic policies are a specialized form of stochastic policies in which one choice has a probability of 1.0 with all other actions having a zero probability. Stochastic policies are more general, and that's what the policy-based approach learns.

Here is the deterministic policy:

$$a = \pi_\theta(s)$$

In other words, this is the specific action a to be taken when in state s.

Here is the stochastic policy:

$$a \sim \pi_\theta(a|s)$$

In other words, this is the distribution of action probability in a given state s.

There are disadvantages as well. Policy-based approaches, while having good convergence, can converge into local maxima. The second big disadvantage is that policy-based methods do not learn any direct representation of value functions, making evaluating the value of a given policy inefficient. Evaluating the policy usually requires playing out multiple episodes of an agent using a policy and then using those outcomes to calculate the policy values, essentially the MC approach, which comes with the issue of high variance in estimated policy values. We will see a way to address this concern by combining the best of both worlds of value-based methods and policy-based methods. This is known as the *actor-critic* family of algorithms.

Policy Representation

In the previous chapter, which covered model-free setups with function approximation, we represented value functions in equation (5.1) as follows:

$$\hat{v}(s;w) \approx v_\pi(s)$$

$$\hat{q}(s,a;w) \approx q_\pi(s,a)$$

We had a model (a linear model or a neural network) with weights w. We represented the state value v and state-action value q with functions parameterized by weights w. Instead, we will now parameterize the policy directly as follows:

$$\pi(a|s;\theta) \approx \pi_\theta(a|s)$$

Discrete Case

For not too large a discrete action space, we will actually parameterize another function $h(s, a; \theta)$ for the state-action pairs. The probability distribution will be formed using a soft-max of h.

$$\pi(a|s;\theta) = \frac{e^{h(s,a;\theta)}}{\sum_b e^{h(s,b;\theta)}}$$

The value $h(s, a; \theta)$ is known as *logits* or *action preferences*. It is similar to the approach we take in the supervised classification case. In supervised learning, we input X, the observations, and here in RL we input the state S to the model. The outputs of the model in supervised cases are the logits of input X belonging to different classes. And in RL, the output of the model is *action preference h* for taking that specific action a.

Continuous Case

In continuous action spaces, the Gaussian representation of a policy is a natural choice. Suppose our action space is continuous and multidimensional with a dimension of, say, d. Our model will take state S as input and produce the multidimensional mean vector $\in R^d$. Variance $\sigma^2 I_d$ can also be parameterized or can be kept constant. The policy the agent will follow is a Gaussian policy with mean μ and a variance $\sigma^2 I_d$.

$$\pi(a|s;\theta) \sim N(\mu, \sigma^2 I_d)$$

Policy Gradient Derivation

The approach to deriving a policy-based algorithm is similar to what we do in supervised learning. Here is the outline of steps we will follow to come up with the algorithm:

1. We form an objective that we want to maximize, just like supervised learning. It will be total reward received by following a policy. That will be the objective we want to maximize.

2. We will derive the gradient update rule to carry out the gradient ascent. We are doing gradient ascent and not gradient descent as our objective is to maximize the total average reward.

3. We will need to recast the gradient update formula into an expectation so that the gradient update can approximated using samples.

4. We will formally convert the update rule into an algorithm that can be used with auto-differentiation libraries like PyTorch and TensorFlow.

Objective Function

Let's start with the objective we want to maximize. As highlighted in the first bullet in the previous list, it will be the value of the policy, i.e., the reward an agent can get by following a policy. There are many variations to the expected reward representation. We will look at some of these and talk briefly about the context of when to use which representation. However, the detailed derivation of the algorithm will be done using one of the variants as the derivations for other reward formulations are pretty similar. The reward function and its variants are as follows:

- *Episodic undiscounted*: $J(\theta) = \sum_{t=0}^{T-1} r_r$

- *Episodic discounted*: $J(\theta) = \sum_{t=0}^{T-1} \gamma^t r_t$

- *Infinite horizon discounted*: $J(\theta) = \sum_{t=0}^{\infty} \gamma^t r_t$

- *Average reward*: $J(\theta) = \lim_{T \to \infty} \frac{1}{T} \sum r_t$

Most of our derivation will follow an episodic undiscounted structure of reward just to keep the math simple and focus on the key aspects of the derivation.

I also want to give you a feel for the discount factor γ. The discount is used in infinite formulation to keep the sum bounded. Usually, we use a discount value of 0.99 or something similar to get the sum to stay theoretically bounded. In some formulations, the discount factor also plays the role of interest—i.e., a reward today is worth more than the same reward tomorrow. Using a discount factor brings in the concept of favoring the reward today. The discount factor is also used to reduce the variance in the estimation by providing a soft cutoff of the time horizon.

Suppose you get a reward of 1 at every time step and you use the discount factor of γ. The sum of this infinite series is $\dfrac{1}{1-\gamma}$. Let's say we have $\gamma = 0.99$. The infinite series sum is then equal to 100. Therefore, you could think of discount of 0.99 as limiting your horizon to 100 steps in which you collected a reward of 1 in each of the 100 steps to give you a total of 100.

To summarize, a discount of γ implies a time horizon of $\dfrac{1}{1-\gamma}$ steps.

Using γ also ensures that the impact of changing policy actions in the initial part of the trajectory has higher impact on the overall quality of the policy versus the impact of decisions in the later part of the trajectory.

Moving back to derivation, let's now calculate the gradient update for improving a policy. The agent follows a policy as parameterized by θ.

The policy is parameterized by θ.

$$\pi_\theta(a|s) \tag{7.1}$$

The agent follows the policy and generates the trajectory τ as follows:

$$s_1 \rightarrow a_1 \rightarrow s_2 \rightarrow a_2 \rightarrow \ldots \rightarrow s_{T-1} \rightarrow a_{T-1} \rightarrow s_T \rightarrow a_T$$

Here, s_T is not necessarily the terminal state but some time horizon T up to which we are considering the trajectory.

The probability of trajectory τ depends on the transition probabilities $p(s_{t+1}|s_t, a_t)$ and the policy $\pi_\theta(a_t|s_t)$. It is given by the following expression:

$$p_\theta(\tau) = p_\theta(s_1, a_1, s_2, a_2, \ldots, s_T, a_T) = p(s_1)\prod_{t=1}^{T}\pi_\theta(a_t|s_t)p(s_{t+1}|s_t, a_t) \tag{7.2}$$

The expected return from following the policy π is given by the following:

$$J(\theta) = E_{\tau \sim p_\theta(\tau)}\left[\sum_t r(s_t, a_t)\right]$$ (7.3)

We want to find the θ that maximizes the expected reward/return $J(\theta)$. In other words, the optimal $\theta = \theta*$ is given by the following expression:

$$\theta^* = \arg\max_\theta \ E_{\tau \sim p_\theta(\tau)}\left[\sum_t r(s_t, a_t)\right]$$ (7.4)

Before we move forward, let's see how we will evaluate the objective $J(\theta)$. We convert the expectation in (7.3) to an average over samples; i.e., we run the agent through policy multiple times collecting N trajectories. We calculate the total reward in each trajectory and take an average of the total reward across N trajectories. This is Monte Carlo (MC) estimation of the expectation. This is what we meant when we talked about evaluating a policy. The expression we obtain is the following:

$$J(\theta) \approx \frac{1}{N}\sum_{i=1}^{N}\sum_{t=1}^{T} r(s_t^i, a_t^i)$$ (7.5)

Derivative Update Rule

Moving on, let's try to find the optimal θ. To keep the notations easier to understand, we will replace $\sum_t r(s_t, a_t)$ with $r(\tau)$. Rewriting (7.3), we get the following:

$$J(\theta) = E_{\tau \sim p_\theta(\tau)}\left[r(\tau)\right] = \int p_\theta(\tau) r(\tau)\, d\tau$$ (7.6)

We take the gradient/derivative of the previous expression with respect to θ.

$$\nabla_\theta J(\theta) = \nabla_\theta \int p_\theta(\tau) r(\tau)\, d\tau$$ (7.7)

Using linearity, we can move the gradient inside the integral.

$$\nabla_\theta J(\theta) = \int \nabla_\theta p_\theta(\tau)\ r(\tau)\, d\tau$$ (7.8)

With the log derivative trick, we know that $\nabla_x f(x) = f(x)\nabla_x \log f(x)$. Using this, we can write the previous expression (7.8) as follows:

$$\nabla_\theta J(\theta) = \int p_\theta(\tau)\left[\nabla_\theta \log p_\theta(\tau) r(\tau)\right]\, d\tau$$ (7.9)

We can now write the integral back as the expectation, which gives us the following expression:

$$\nabla_\theta J(\theta) = E_{\tau \sim p_\theta(\tau)} \left[\nabla_\theta \log p_\theta(\tau) r(\tau) \right] \tag{7.10}$$

Let's expand the term $\nabla_\theta \log p_\theta(\tau)$ by writing out the full expression of $p_\theta(\tau)$ from equation (7.2).

$$\nabla_\theta \log p_\theta(\tau) = \nabla_\theta \log \left[p(s_1) \prod_{t=1}^{T} \pi_\theta(a_t|s_t) p(s_{t+1}|s_t,a_t) \right] \tag{7.11}$$

We know that the log of the product of terms can be written as a sum of the log of terms. In other words:

$$\log \prod_i f_i(x) = \sum_i \log f_i(x) \tag{7.12}$$

Substituting (7.12) in equation (7.11), we get the following:

$$\nabla_\theta \log p_\theta(\tau) = \nabla_\theta \left[\log p(s_1) + \sum_{t=1}^{T} \{ \log \pi_\theta(a_t|s_t) + \log p(s_{t+1}|s_t,a_t) \} \right] \tag{7.13}$$

The only term in (7.13) dependent on θ is $\pi_\theta(a_t|s_t)$. The other two terms $\log p(s_1)$ and $\log p(s_{t+1}|s_t, a_t)$ do not depend on θ. Accordingly, we can simplify the previous expression (7.13) as follows:

$$\nabla_\theta \log p_\theta(\tau) = \sum_{t=1}^{T} \nabla_\theta \log \pi_\theta(a_t|s_t) \tag{7.14}$$

Substituting equation (7.14) into the expression for $\nabla_\theta J(\theta)$ in equation (7.10), as well as expanding $r(\tau)$ as $\sum_t r(s_t, a_t)$, we get the following:

$$\nabla_\theta J(\theta) = E_{\tau \sim p_\theta(\tau)} \left[\left(\sum_{t=1}^{T} \nabla_\theta \log \pi_\theta(a_t|s_t) \right) \left(\sum_{t=1}^{T} r(s_t,a_t) \right) \right] \tag{7.15}$$

We can now replace the outer expectation with an estimate/average over multiple trajectories to get the following expression for the *gradient of policy objective*:

$$\nabla_\theta J(\theta) \approx \frac{1}{N} \sum_{i=1}^{N} \left[\left(\sum_{t=1}^{T} \nabla_\theta \log \pi_\theta(a_t^i|s_t^i) \right) \left(\sum_{t=1}^{T} r(s_t^i,a_t^i) \right) \right] \tag{7.16}$$

where superscript index i denotes the ith trajectory.

To improve the policy, we take a +ve step in the direction of $\nabla_\theta J(\theta)$.

$$\theta = \theta + \alpha \nabla_\theta J(\theta) \qquad (7.17)$$

Summarizing, we design a model that takes state s as input and produces the policy distribuion $\pi_\theta(a|s)$ as the output of the model. We use a policy as determined by current model parameters θ to generate trajectories, calculate the total return of each trajectory. We calculate $\nabla_\theta J(\theta)$ using (7.16) and then change the model parameters θ using the expression $\theta = \theta + \alpha \nabla_\theta J(\theta)$ in (7.17).

Intuition Behind the Update Rule

Let's develop some intuition behind equation (7.16). Let's explain the equation in words. We carry out an average over N trajectories, and that is the outermost sum. What do we average over the trajectories? For each trajectory, we look at the total reward we obtained in that trajectory and multiply it by the sum of log probabilities of all the actions along that trajectory.

Now suppose the total reward $r(\tau^i)$ of a trajectory was +ve. Each gradient inside the first inner sum—i.e., $\nabla_\theta \log \pi_\theta\left(a_t^i|s_t^i\right)$, the gradient of the log probability of that action— gets multiplied by the total reward $r(\tau^i)$. It results in an individual *gradient-log* term being amplified by the total reward of the trajectory, and in equation (7.17), its contribution is to move the model parameters θ in the +ve direction of $\nabla_\theta \log \pi_\theta\left(a_t^i|s_t^i\right)$, i.e., increase the probability of taking action a_t^i when the system is in state s_t^i. However, if $r(\tau^i)$ was a -ve quantity, equations (7.16) and (7.17) lead to moving θ in the -ve direction, resulting in a decrease of the probability of taking action a_t^i when the system is in state s_t^i.

We could summarize the whole explanation by saying that policy optimization is all about trial and error. We roll out multiple trajectories. The probability of all the actions along the trajectory is increased for those trajectories that are good. For the trajectories that are bad, the probability of all the actions along those bad trajectories are reduced, as depicted in Figure 7-1.

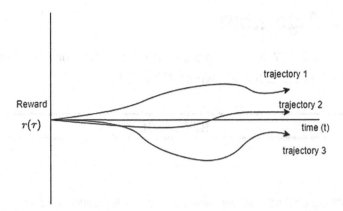

Figure 7-1. *Trajectory rollouts. Trajectory 1 is good, and we would like the model to produce more of these. Trajectory 2 is neither good nor bad, and the model should not worry too much about it. Trajectory 3 is bad, and we would want the model to reduce the probability of it*

Let's look at the same interpretation by comparing the expression in (7.17) with that of maximum likelihood. If we just wanted to model the probability of seeing the trajectories we saw, we would get the maximum likelihood estimation—we observe some data (trajectories), and we want to build a model with the highest probability of producing the observed data/trajectory. This is the maximum likelihood model building. Under that, we would get an equation as follows:

$$\nabla_\theta J_{ML}(\theta) \approx \frac{1}{N} \sum_{i=1}^{N} \left[\left(\sum_{t=1}^{T} \nabla_\theta \log \pi_\theta \left(a_t^i | s_t^i \right) \right) \right] \tag{7.18}$$

In equation (7.18), we are just increasing the probability of actions to increase the overall probability of trajectories. We are doing the same in policy gradients in (7.16), just that we are weighing the log probability gradients with the reward so that good trajectories are increased and bad trajectories probabilities are decreased—instead of increasing the probability of all the trajectories.

Before we conclude this section, one observation we would like to make is around the Markov property and partial observability. We have not really used the Markov assumption in the derivation. At the end, equation (7.16) just says to increase the probability of good stuff and reduce the probability of bad stuff. We have not used Bellman equations so far. A policy gradient can work for non-Markovian setups as well.

REINFORCE Algorithm

We now convert equation (7.16) into an algorithm for policy optimization. We give the basic algorithm in Figure 7-2. It is known as REINFORCE.

REINFORCE

Input:

    A model with parameters θ taking state S as input and producing $\pi_\theta(a|s)$

    Other parameters: step size α

Initialize:

    Initialize weights $\boldsymbol{\theta}$

Loop:

    Sample $\{\tau^i\}$, a set of N trajectories from current policy $\pi_\theta(a_t|s_t)$

    Update model parameters θ:

$$\nabla_\theta J(\theta) \approx \frac{1}{N}\sum_{i=1}^{N}\left[\left(\sum_{t=1}^{T}\nabla_\theta \log \pi_\theta\left(a_t^i|s_t^i\right)\right)\left(\sum_{t=1}^{T}r\left(s_t^i,a_t^i\right)\right)\right]$$

$$\theta = \theta + \alpha\nabla_\theta J(\theta)$$

Figure 7-2. *REINFORCE algorithm*

    Let's look at some implementation-level details. Suppose you use a neural network as a model that takes a state value as input and produces the logit (log probability) of taking all possible actions in that state. Figure 7-3 shows a diagram of such a model.

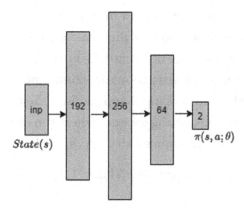

Figure 7-3. *Neural network model for predicting policy*

We use auto-differentiation libraries such as PyTorch or TensorFlow. We do not explicitly calculate the differentiation. Equation (7.16) gives us the expression for $\nabla_\theta J(\theta)$. With PyTorch or TensorFlow, we need an expression $J(\theta)$. The neural network model will take state S as input and produce $\pi_\theta(a_t | s_t)$. We need to use this output and carry out further computation to arrive at an expression for $J(\theta)$. The auto-differential packages like PyTorch or TensorFlow will automatically calculate the gradient $\nabla_\theta J(\theta)$ from the expression for $J(\theta)$. The correct expression for $J(\theta)$ is as follows:

$$\tilde{J}(\theta) = \frac{1}{N} \sum_{i=1}^{N} \left[\left(\sum_{t=1}^{T} \log \pi_\theta \left(a_t^i | s_t^i \right) \right) \left(\sum_{t=1}^{T} r \left(s_t^i, a_t^i \right) \right) \right] \qquad (7.19)$$

You can check and confirm that the gradient of this expression will give us the correct value for $\nabla_\theta J(\theta)$, as shown in (7.16).

The expression in (7.19) is known as a *pseudo-objective*. This is the expression we need to implement in auto-diff libraries like PyTorch and TensorFlow. We calculate the log probabilities $\log \pi_\theta \left(a_t^i | s_t^i \right)$, weigh the probabilities with the total reward of the trajectory $\left(\sum_{t=1}^{T} r \left(s_t^i, a_t^i \right) \right)$, and then calculate the negative log likelihood (NLL, or cross entropy loss) of the weighted quantity, giving us the expression in (7.20). It is similar to the approach we take for training a multiclass classification model in a supervised learning setup. The only difference is weighing of log probability by the trajectory reward. This is the approach we will take when actions are discrete. The loss we implement in PyTorch/TensorFlow is as follows:

$$L_{cross-entropy}(\theta) = -1 * \frac{1}{N} \sum_{i=1}^{N} \left[\left(\sum_{t=1}^{T} \log \pi_\theta \left(a_t^i | s_t^i \right) \right) \left(\sum_{t=1}^{T} r \left(s_t^i, a_t^i \right) \right) \right] \qquad (7.20)$$

Please note that PyTorch and TensorFlow minimize the loss by taking a step in negative direction of the loss. And also note that the -ve gradient of (7.20) is a +ve gradient of (7.19) due to the presence of a factor of -1 in (7.20).

Next, we look at the situation when actions are continuous. As discussed, the model parameterized by θ will take state S as input and produce the mean μ of a multivariate normal distribution. We are considering the case where the variance of the normal distribution is known and fixed to some small value, say $\sigma^2 I_d$.

$$\pi\left(a|s;\theta\right) \sim N\left(\mu, \sigma^2 I_d\right)$$

Let's say for state s_t^i the mean that the model produces is $\mu_\theta\left(s_t^i\right)$. The value of $\log \pi_\theta\left(a_t^i|s_t^i\right)$ is then given by the following:

$$\log \pi_\theta\left(a_t^i|s_t^i\right) = \log \frac{1}{\sqrt{2\pi}\sigma} e^{-\frac{1}{2\sigma^2}\left(a_t^i - \mu_\theta\right)^2}$$

$$= -\frac{1}{2}\log 2\pi - \log\sigma - \frac{1}{2\sigma^2}\left(a_t^i - \mu_\theta\right)^2 \qquad (7.20)$$

The only value in the previous expression that depends on model parameters θ is $\mu_\theta\left(s_t^i\right)$. Let's take a gradient of (7.20) with regard to θ. We obtain the following:

$$\nabla_\theta \log \pi_\theta\left(a_t^i|s_t^i\right) = const \; x \left(a_t^i - \mu_\theta\right) \nabla_\theta \; \mu_\theta\left(s_t^i\right)$$

To implement this in PyTorch or TensorFlow, we will form a modified mean squared error, just like the approach we took for the previous discrete actions. We weigh the mean squared error with the trajectory return. The loss equation we implement in PyTorch or TensorFlow is given in (7.21).

$$L_{MSE}\left(\theta\right) = \frac{1}{N}\sum_{i=1}^{N}\left[\left(\sum_{t=1}^{T}\left(a_t^i - \mu_\theta\right)^2\right)\left(\sum_{t=1}^{T}r\left(s_t^i, a_t^i\right)\right)\right] \qquad (7.21)$$

Again, note that using gradient $L_{MSE}(\theta)$ and then taking a step in the -ve direction of the gradient will produce the following:

$$-\nabla_\theta L_{MSE}\left(\theta\right) = \frac{1}{N}\sum_{i=1}^{N}\left[\left(\sum_{t=1}^{T}\left(a_t^i - \mu_\theta\right)\nabla_\theta \; \mu_\theta\left(s_t^i\right)\right)\left(\sum_{t=1}^{T}r\left(s_t^i, a_t^i\right)\right)\right] \qquad (7.22)$$

A step in the direction of $-\nabla_\theta L_{MSE}(\theta)$ is a step in the direction of $\nabla \tilde{J}(\theta)$, as given in (7.19). This is a step that is trying to increase the value of $\tilde{J}(\theta)$, i.e., maximizing the return from the policy.

To summarize, implementations in PyTorch or TensorFlow require us to form cross entropy loss in discrete action space or mean squared loss in the case of continuous action space with each loss term weighted by the total return of the trajectory from which the pair $\left(s_t^i, a_t^i\right)$ came. This is similar to the approach we take in supervised learning except for the extra step of weighing by the trajectory return $r(\tau^i) = \left(\sum_{t=1}^{T} r\left(s_t^i, a_t^i\right)\right)$.

Please also note that *weighted cross entropy loss* or *weighted mean squared loss* has no meaning or significance. It is just a convenient expression that allows us to use PyTorch and TensorFlow's auto-diff capabilities to calculate the gradients using back propagation and then take a step to improve the policy. Compared to this, in supervised learning, the losses do signify the quality of prediction. There is no such inference or meaning that can be attached in the case of the policy gradient scenario. That's why we call them pseudo-loss/objective.

Variance Reduction with Reward to Go

The expression we derived in equation (7.16), if used in its current form, has an issue. It has high variance. We will now leverage the temporal nature of the problem to do some variance reduction.

When we roll out the policy (i.e., take actions as per the policy) to produce a trajectory, we calculate the total reward of the trajectory $r(\tau^i)$. Next, each of the action probability terms for the actions in the trajectory are weighted by this trajectory reward.

However, the action taken in a time step, say t', can only impact the reward we see after that action. The reward we see prior to time step t' is not impacted by the action we take at time step t' or any subsequent actions. The reason is that the world is causal. Future actions cannot impact the past rewards. We will use this property to drop certain terms in (7.16) and reduce the variance. Given are the steps that derive the revised formula. Please note that it is not a rigorous mathematical proof.

We start with equation (7.15).

$$\nabla_\theta J(\theta) = E_{\tau \sim p_\theta(\tau)}\left[\left(\sum_{t=1}^{T} \nabla_\theta \log \pi_\theta\left(a_t | s_t\right)\right)\right]$$

We change the index of summation for the reward term from t to t' and also move that sum inside the first summation over π_θ. This gives us the following expression:

$$\nabla_\theta J(\theta) = E_{\tau \sim p_\theta(\tau)} \left[\left(\sum_{t=1}^T \left(\nabla_\theta \log \pi_\theta(a_t|s_t) \sum_{t'=1}^T r(s_{t'}, a_{t'}) \right) \right) \right]$$

In the summation term for the sum over index t, we drop the reward terms that came before time t. At time t, the action we take can only impact the reward that comes at time t and later. This leads to changing the second inner sum going from $t' = t$ to T instead of going from $t' = 1$ to T. In other words, the start index is now $t' = t$ and not $t = 1$. The revised expression is as follows:

$$\nabla_\theta J(\theta) = E_{\tau \sim p_\theta(\tau)} \left[\left(\sum_{t=1}^T \left(\nabla_\theta \log \pi_\theta(a_t|s_t) \sum_{t'=t}^T r(s_{t'}, a_{t'}) \right) \right) \right]$$

The inner sum $\sum_{t'=t}^T r(s_{t'}, a_{t'})$ is no longer the total reward of the tracjectory. Rather, it is the reward of the remaining trajectory that we see from *time* = t to T. As you recall, this is nothing but the q-value. The q-value is the expected reward we get at from time t onward until the end, after we take a step/action a_t at time t while in state s_t. We can also call it *reward to go*. Since the expression $\sum_{t'=t}^T r(s_{t'}, a_{t'})$ is for only one trajectory, we denote it is an estimate of the expected reward to go. The updated gradient equations are as follows:

$$\hat{Q}_t^i = \sum_{t'=t}^T r(s_{t'}^i, a_{t'}^i)$$

$$\nabla_\theta J(\theta) = \frac{1}{N} \sum_{i=1}^N \sum_{t=1}^T \nabla_\theta \log \pi_\theta(a_t^i|s_t^i) \hat{Q}_t^i \tag{7.23}$$

To use this equation in PyTorch or TensorFlow, we just need to make a minor modification. Instead of weighing each log probability term with the total trajectory reward, we will now weigh it with the remaining rewards from that time step; in other words, we weigh it with a reward-to-go value. Figure 7-4 shows a revised REINFORCE algorithm using reward to go.

REINFORCE WITH REWARD TO GO

Input:

    A model with parameters θ taking state S as input and producing $\pi_\theta(a|s)$

    Other parameters: step size α

Initialize:

    Initialize weights $\boldsymbol{\theta}$

Loop:

    Sample $\{\tau\}$, a set of N trajectories from current policy $\pi_\theta(a_t|s_t)$

    Calculate the reward to go $\hat{Q}_t^i = \sum_{t'=t}^{T} r\left(s_{t'}^i, a_{t'}^i\right)$

    Update model parameters θ:

$$\nabla_\theta J(\theta) \approx \frac{1}{N} \sum_{i=1}^{N} \sum_{t=1}^{T} \nabla_\theta \log \pi_\theta\left(a_t^i|s_t^i\right) . \hat{Q}_t^i$$

$$\theta = \theta + \alpha \nabla_\theta J(\theta)$$

Figure 7-4. *REINFORCE algorithm using reward to go*

We have been doing a lot of theory so far in this chapter, and there is a bit of overload of mathematical formula. We have tried to keep it minimal, and if there is one takeaway from the chapter this far, it is that of the REINFORCE algorithm in Figure 7-4. Let's now put this equation into practice. We will implement REINFORCE from Figure 7-4 to our usual `CartPole` problem with continuous state space and discrete actions.

Before, we do, let's introduce a last mathematical term. The exploration of state-action space in policy gradient algorithms comes from the fact that we learn a stochastic policy that assigns a probability to all the actions for a given state instead of choosing the best possible action using DQN. To ensure that exploration is maintained and to ensure that $\pi_\theta(a|s)$ does not collapse to a single action with high probability, we introduce a regularization term known as *entropy*. Entropy of a distribution is defined as follows:

$$H(X) = \sum_x -p(x) . \log p(x)$$

To keep enough exploration, we will want the probability to have a spread-out distribution and not let the probability distribution peak around a single value or a small region too soon. The bigger the spread of a distribution, the higher the entropy H(x) of a distribution. Accordingly, the term fed into the PyTorch/TensorFlow minimizer is as follows:

$$Loss(\theta) = -J(\theta) - H\left(\pi_\theta\left(a_t^i|s_t^i\right)\right)$$

$$= -\frac{1}{N}\sum_{i=1}^{N}\left[\sum_{t=1}^{T}\left(\log\pi_\theta\left(a_t^i|s_t^i\right)\sum_{t'=t}^{T}\gamma^{t'-t}r\left(s_{t'}^i,a_{t'}^i\right)\right) - \beta\sum_{a_i}\pi_\theta\left(a_t^i|s_t^i\right).\log\pi_\theta\left(a_t^i|s_t^i\right)\right]$$

In our code example, we are taking only one trajectory, i.e., $N = 1$. We will, however, average it over the number of actions to get the average loss. The function we will actually implement is as follows:

$$Loss(\theta) = -J(\theta) - H\left(\pi_\theta\left(a_t|s_t\right)\right)$$

$$= -\frac{1}{T}\sum_{t=1}^{T}\left(\log\pi_\theta\left(a_t|s_t\right)G(s_t) - \beta\sum_{a_i}\pi_\theta\left(a_t|s_t\right).\log\pi_\theta\left(a_t|s_t\right)\right)$$

where,

$$G(s_t) = \sum_{t'=t}^{T}\gamma^{t-t'}r\left(s_{t'}^i,a_{t'}^i\right)$$

Please note that we have reintroduced the discount factor γ in the previous expressions.

Let's now walk through the implementation. You can find the complete listing of the code in `listing7_1_reinforce_pytorch.ipynb`. We also have a TensorFlow version of the code in `listing7_1_reinforce_tensorflow.ipynb`. However, we will go through only the PyTorch version. The TensorFlow version follows pretty much the same steps except for minor differences in the way we define the network or calculate the loss and step through the gradients. In our code we have used TensorFlow 2.0 in eager execution mode.

We explained the environment `CartPole` earlier. It has a four-dimensional continuous state space and a discrete action space of two actions: "move left" and "move right." Let's first define a simple policy network with one hidden layer of 192 units and ReLU activation. The final output has no activation. Listing 7-1 shows the code.

Listing 7-1. Policy Network in PyTorch

```
model = nn.Sequential(
          nn.Linear(state_dim,192),
          nn.ReLU(),
          nn.Linear(192,n_actions),
)
```

Next, we define a generate_trajectory function that takes the current policy to generate a trajectory of (states, actions, rewards) for one episode. It uses a helper function predict_probs to do so. Listing 7-2 gives the code. It starts with initializing the environment and then successively takes steps following the current policy, returning the (states, actions, rewards) of the trajectory it unrolled.

Listing 7-2. generate_trajectory in PyTorch

```
def generate_trajectory(env, n_steps=1000):
    """

    Play a session and genrate a trajectory
    returns: arrays of states, actions, rewards
    """

    states, actions, rewards = [], [], []

    # initialize the environment
    s = env.reset()

    #generate n_steps of trajectory:
    for t in range(n_steps):
        action_probs = predict_probs(np.array([s]))[0]
        #sample action based on action_probs
        a = np.random.choice(n_actions, p=action_probs)
        next_state, r, done, _ = env.step(a)

        #update arrays
        states.append(s)
        actions.append(a)
        rewards.append(r)
```

```
        s = next_state
        if done:
            break

    return states, actions, rewards
```

We also have another helper function to convert the individual step returns $r(s_{t'}, a_{t'})$

to reward to go as per the expression $G(s_t) = \sum_{t'=t}^{T} \gamma^{t-t'} r\left(s_{t'}^i, a_{t'}^i\right)$. Listing 7-3 contains the implementation of this function.

Listing 7-3. get_rewards_to_go in PyTorch

```
def get_rewards_to_go(rewards, gamma=0.99):

    T = len(rewards) # total number of individual rewards
    # empty array to return the rewards to go
    rewards_to_go = [0]*T
    rewards_to_go[T-1] = rewards[T-1]

    for i in range(T-2, -1, -1): #go from T-2 to 0
        rewards_to_go[i] = gamma * rewards_to_go[i+1] + rewards[i]

    return rewards_to_go
```

We are now ready to implement the training. We build the loss function that we are going to feed into the PyTorch optimizer. As explained, we going to implement the following expression:

$$Loss(\theta) = -\frac{1}{T} \sum_{t=1}^{T} \left(\log \pi_\theta(a_t|s_t) G(s_t) - \beta \sum_{a_i} \pi_\theta(a_t|s_t).\log \pi_\theta(a_t|s_t) \right)$$

Listing 7-4 contains the code of the loss calculation.

Listing 7-4. Training for One Trajectory in PyTorch

```
#init Optimizer
optimizer = torch.optim.Adam(model.parameters(), lr=1e-3)

def train_one_episode(states, actions, rewards, gamma=0.99, entropy_
coef=1e-2):
```

```
# get rewards to go
rewards_to_go = get_rewards_to_go(rewards, gamma)

# convert numpy array to torch tensors
states = torch.tensor(states, device=device, dtype=torch.float)
actions = torch.tensor(actions, device=device, dtype=torch.long)
rewards_to_go = torch.tensor(rewards_to_go, device=device, dtype=torch.
float)

# get action probabilities from states
logits = model(states)
probs = nn.functional.softmax(logits, -1)
log_probs = nn.functional.log_softmax(logits, -1)

log_probs_for_actions = log_probs[range(len(actions)), actions]

#Compute loss to be minized
J = torch.mean(log_probs_for_actions*rewards_to_go)
H = -(probs*log_probs).sum(-1).mean()

loss = -(J+entropy_coef*H)

optimizer.zero_grad()
loss.backward()
optimizer.step()

return np.sum(rewards) #to show progress on training
```

We are now ready to carry out the training. Listing 7-5 shows how we can train the agent for 10,000 steps, printing the average episode reward after 100 steps of trajectory training. We also stop the training once we achieve a mean reward of 300.

Listing 7-5. Training the Agent in PyTorch

```
total_rewards = []
for i in range(10000):
    states, actions, rewards = generate_trajectory(env)
    reward = train_one_episode(states, actions, rewards)
    total_rewards.append(reward)
```

```
    if i != 0 and i % 100 == 0:
        mean_reward = np.mean(total_rewards[-100:-1])
        print("mean reward:%.3f" % (mean_reward))
        if mean_reward > 300:
            break
env.close()
```

By the end of training, the agent has learned to balance the pole well. You will also notice that the program took a lot fewer iterations and less time to achieve this result as compared to the DQN-based approach.

Please note that REINFORCE is an *on-policy* algorithm.

Further Variance Reduction with Baselines

We started with original policy gradient update expression in (7.15) and converted the expectation to an estimate using the average in (7.16). Following this, we showed how the variance could be reduced by considering rewards to go instead of full trajectory rewards. The expression with this rewards to go was given in equation (7.23).

In this section, we look at yet another change that makes the policy gradient even more stable. Let's consider the motivation. Assume you have done three rollouts of the trajectory following a policy. And let's say the reward was 300, 200, and 100. To keep the explanation simple, please consider the case of total rewards and total trajectory probability version of the gradient update equation as given in equation (7.10), reproduced here:

$$\nabla_\theta J(\theta) = E_{\tau \sim p_\theta(\tau)} \left[\nabla_\theta \log p_\theta(\tau) r(\tau) \right]$$

So, what will the gradient update do? It will weigh the gradient of the log probability of the first trajectory with 300, the second trajectory with 200, and the third trajectory with 100. This means that the probability of each of the three trajectories is being increased by some different amount. Let's look at a pictorial representation of it, given in Figure 7-5.

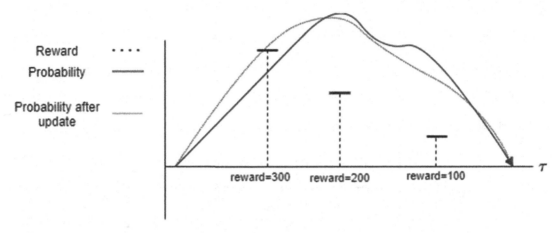

Figure 7-5. *The gradient update for a policy with actual trajectory rewards*

As you can see from the diagram, we are increasing the probability of all three trajectories with different weighting factors, all +ve weights, making the probability of all trajectories go up. Ideally, we would have loved to increase the probability of the trajectory with a reward of 300 and reduce the probability of the trajectory with a reward of 100 as it is not a very good trajectory. We would want the policy to change such that it does not generate the trajectory with a reward of 100 too often. However, using the current approach, the revised probability curve is becoming flatter as it is trying to increase the probability of all three trajectories and the total area under the probability curve has to be 1.

Let's consider a scenario in which we subtract the average reward of three trajectories, $\dfrac{300+200+100}{3}=200$, from each of the three rewards. We get the revised trajectory rewards of 100, 0, and -100 (300-200; 200-200; 100-200). Let's use the revised trajectory rewards as the weights to carry out the gradient update. Figure 7-6 shows the outcome of such an update. We can see that the probability curve is becoming narrower and sharper as it's spread reduces along the x-axis.

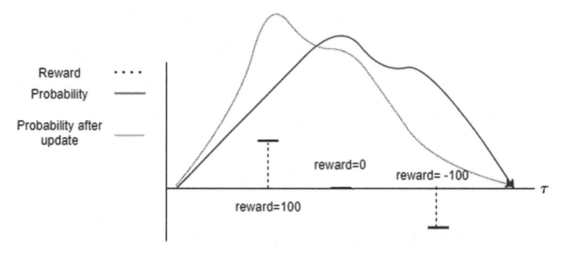

Figure 7-6. *The gradient update for a policy with trajectory rewards reduced by a baseline*

Reducing the rewards with a baseline reduces the variance of the update. In the limit, whether we use or do not use a baseline, the outcome will be same. The introduction of a baseline does not alter the optimal solution. It just reduces the variance and thereby speeds up the learning. We will show mathematically that the introduction of a baseline does not alter the expected value of the gradient update. The baseline can be a fixed baseline across all trajectories and all steps in the trajectory, or it can be a changing quantity that depends on the state. *However, it cannot depend on the action.* Let's first go through the derivation in which the baseline is a function of the state s_t^i.

Let's update the equation in (7.15) to introduce a baseline.

$$\nabla_\theta J(\theta) = E_{\tau \sim p_\theta(\tau)} \left[\left(\sum_{t=1}^{T} \nabla_\theta \log \pi_\theta (a_t|s_t) \right) (r(\tau) - b(s_t)) \right]$$

Let's separate out the term of $b(s_t)$ and evaluate what the expectation would be.

$$E_{\tau \sim p_\theta(\tau)} \left[\left(\sum_{t=1}^{T} \nabla_\theta \log \pi_\theta (a_t|s_t) \right) b(s_t) \right]$$

Let's move the first inner sum out due to the property of linearity of expectation to obtain the expression.

$$\sum_{t=1}^{T} E_{a_t \sim \pi_\theta(a_t|s_t)} \left[\nabla_\theta \log \pi_\theta (a_t|s_t) b(s_t) \right]$$

We have switched the expectation from $\tau \sim p_\theta(\tau)$ to $a_t \sim \pi_\theta(a_t|s_t)$. This is because we moved the first inner sum outside the expectation, and after that the only term that depends on a probability distribution is the action a_t with probability $\pi_\theta(a_t|s_t)$.

Let's just focus on the inner expectation: $E_{\tau \sim p_\theta(\tau)}\left[\nabla_\theta \log \pi_\theta(a_t|s_t)b(s_t)\right]$. We can write this as integral, as shown here:

$$E_{a_t \sim \pi_\theta(a_t|s_t)}\left[\nabla_\theta \log \pi_\theta(a_t|s_t)b(s_t)\right]$$

$$= \int \pi_\theta(a_t|s_t)\left(\nabla_\theta \log \pi_\theta(a_t|s_t)\right)b(s_t)\,da_t$$

$$= \int \pi_\theta(a_t|s_t)\frac{\nabla_\theta \pi_\theta(a_t|s_t)}{\pi_\theta(a_t|s_t)}\,b(s_t)\,da_t$$

$$= \int \nabla_\theta \pi_\theta(a_t|s_t)\,b(s_t)\,da_t$$

$$= b(s_t)\nabla_\theta \int \pi_\theta(a_t|s_t)\,da_t$$

As $b(s_t)$ does not depend on a_t, we can take it out. Again, due to the linearity of the integral, we can swap the gradient and integral. Now the integral will evaluate to 1 as that is the total probability using the curve for $\pi_\theta(a_t|s_t)$. Accordingly, we get the following:

$$E_{a_t \sim \pi_\theta(a_t|s_t)}\left[\nabla_\theta \log \pi_\theta(a_t|s_t)b(s_{t'})\right]$$

$$= b(s_t)\nabla_\theta(1) = b(s_t).0$$

$$= 0$$

The previous derivation shows us that subtracting a baseline that depends on the state or could be a constant will not change the expectation. *The condition is that it should not depend on the action a_t.*

Therefore, REINFORCE with the baseline will go through the updates as follows:

$$\nabla_\theta J(\theta) = E_{\tau \sim p_\theta(\tau)}\left[\left(\sum_{t=1}^{T}\nabla_\theta \log \pi_\theta(a_t|s_t)\right)\left(r(\tau) - \mathrm{b}(s_t)\right)\right] \qquad (7.24)$$

We can modify the rewards to go given in (7.23) with a baseline to get the following:

$$\hat{Q}(s_t^i, a_t^i) = \sum_{t'=t}^{T}\gamma^{t'-t}r(s_{t'}^i, a_{t'}^i)$$

$$\nabla_\theta J(\theta) = \frac{1}{N}\sum_{i=1}^{N}\sum_{t=1}^{T}\nabla_\theta \log \pi_\theta(a_t^i|s_t^i)\left[\hat{Q}^i(s_t, a_t) - \mathrm{b}^i(s_t)\right] \qquad (7.25)$$

Equation 7.25 is REINFORCE with a baseline and rewards to go. We have used two tricks to reduce the variance of the vanilla REINFORCE. We used a temporal structure to remove the rewards that are in the past and not impacted by the actions in the present. Then we used the baseline to have the bad policies get -ve rewards and to have the good policies get +ve rewards to make the policy gradient show a lower variation as we go through the learning.

Please note that REINFORCE and all its variations are *on-policy algorithms*. After the weights of the policy are updated, we need to roll out new trajectories. The old trajectories are no more representative of the old policy. This is one of the reasons why that, like the value-based on-policy methods, REINFORCE is also sample inefficient. We cannot use transitions from earlier policies. We have to discard them and generate new transitions after each weight update.

Actor-Critic Methods

In this section, we will further refine the algorithm by combining the policy gradient with the value functions to get something called the *actor-critic* family of algorithms (A2C/A3C). Let's first define a term called *advantage* $A(s, a)$.

Defining Advantage

Let's first talk about the expression $\hat{Q}\left(s_t^i, a_t^i\right)$ in equation (7.25). It is the reward to go in a given trajectory (i) and in a given state s_t.

$$\hat{Q}\left(s_t^i, a_t^i\right) = \sum_{t'=t}^{T} r\left(s_{t'}^i, a_{t'}^i\right)$$

To evaluate the $\hat{Q}$ value using the previous expression, we are using Monte Carlo simulation. In other words, we are adding up all the rewards from that time step t until the end, i.e., until T. It will again have high variance as it is only one trajectory estimate of the expectation. In the previous chapter on model-free policy learning, we saw that MC methods have zero bias but high variance. Comparatively, TD methods have some bias but low variance and can lead to faster convergence due to lower variance. Could we do something similar here also? What is this reward to go? What is the expectation of the expression $\hat{Q}\left(s_t^i, a_t^i\right)$? It is nothing but the q-value of the state-action pair (s_t, a_t).

If we had access to the q-value, we could replace the summation of individual rewards with the q-estimate.

$$\hat{Q}^i\left(s_t,a_t\right)=q\left(s_t,a_t;\phi\right) \tag{7.26}$$

Let's roll the value of $q(s_t, a_t)$ by one time step. This is similar to the TD(0) approach we saw in Chapter 5. We can write $\hat{Q}^i\left(s_t,a_t\right)$ as follows:

$$\hat{Q}\left(s_t^i,a_t^i\right)=r\left(s_{t'}^i,a_{t'}^i\right)+V\left(s_{t+1}\right) \tag{7.27}$$

This is the undiscounted rollout. As discussed at the beginning of the chapter, we will do all the derivations in the context of the finite horizon undiscounted setting. The analysis can be easily extended to other settings. We will switch to a more general case in the final pseudocode for the algorithm while restricting our analysis to the undiscounted case.

Looking at equation (7.25) again, can you think of a good baseline $b^i(s_t)$ that could be used? How about using the state value $V(s_t)$? As explained, we can use any value as the baseline as long as it does not depend on the action a_t. $V(s_t)$ is one such quantity that depends on the state s_t but does not depend on the action a_t.

$$b^i\left(s_t\right)=V\left(s_t\right) \tag{7.28}$$

Using the previous expression:

$$\hat{Q}\left(s_t^i,a_t^i\right)-b^i\left(s_t\right)=\hat{Q}^i\left(s_t,a_t\right)-V\left(s_t\right) \tag{7.29}$$

The right side is known as the *advantage $A(s_t, a_t)$*. It is the extra benefit/reward we get by following a policy at state s_t to take step a_t, which gives a reward of $\hat{Q}\left(s_t^i,a_t^i\right)$ versus the average reward we get in state s_t as denoted by $V(s_t)$. We can now substitute equation (7.27) in (7.29) to get the following:

$$\hat{A}\left(s_t^i,a_t^i\right)$$

$$=\hat{Q}\left(s_t^i,a_t^i\right)-b^i\left(s_t\right)$$

$$=\hat{Q}\left(s_t^i,a_t^i\right)-V\left(s_t\right)$$

$$=r\left(s_{t'}^i,a_{t'}^i\right)+V\left(s_{t+1}\right)-V\left(s_t\right) \tag{7.30}$$

Advantage Actor Critic

Continuing from the previous section, let's rewrite the gradient update given in equation (7.25) in terms of the previous expressions.

Here is the original gradient update from equation (7.25):

$$\nabla_\theta J(\theta) = \frac{1}{N}\sum_{i=1}^{N}\sum_{t=1}^{T}\nabla_\theta \log \pi_\theta\left(a_t^i|s_t^i\right)\left[\hat{Q}^i\left(s_t,a_t\right)-b^i\left(s_t\right)\right]$$

Substituting, $b^i(s_t) = V(s_t)$ from (7.28), we get the following:

$$\nabla_\theta J(\theta) = \frac{1}{N}\sum_{i=1}^{N}\sum_{t=1}^{T}\nabla_\theta \log \pi_\theta\left(a_t^i|s_t^i\right)\left[\hat{Q}\left(s_t^i,a_t^i\right)-V\left(s_t\right)\right]$$

Using the MC approach, we get this:

$$\hat{Q}\left(s_t^i,a_t^i\right)=\sum_{t'=t}^{T}r\left(s_{t'}^i,a_{t'}^i\right)$$

Or, using the TD(0) approach, we get this:

$$\hat{Q}\left(s_t^i,a_t^i\right)=r\left(s_{t'}^i,a_{t'}^i\right)+V\left(s_{t+1}\right)-V\left(s_t\right) \tag{7.31}$$

Look at the inner expression $\hat{Q}\left(s_t^i,a_t^i\right)-V\left(s_t\right)$ in the previous expression. Q is the value of following a specific step a_t using the current policy. In other words, the "actor" and V are the average values of the following curent policy, i.e., the "critic." The actor is trying to maximize the reward, and the critic is telling the algorithm how good or bad that specific step was as compared to the average. The *actor-critic* approach is a family of algorithms with an *actor* that is changing policy gradients to improve actions, and a *critic* informing the algorithm about the goodness of an action using the current policy.

We can rewrite (7.30) in the form of an advantage to get the following:

$$\nabla_\theta J(\theta) = \frac{1}{N}\sum_{i=1}^{N}\sum_{t=1}^{T}\nabla_\theta \log \pi_\theta\left(a_t^i|s_t^i\right)\left[\hat{A}^i\left(s_t,a_t\right)\right] \tag{7.32}$$

This expression is the reason we also call it *advantage actor critic* (A2C). Please note that the actor critic is a family of approaches, with A2C and A3C being two specific instances of it. Sometimes in literature actor critic is also interchangeably referred to as A2C. At the same time, some papers refer to A2C as a synchronous version of A3C, which we will talk about shortly in the next section.

We can further combine (7.32) with (7.30) to express the following:

$$MC\ approach: \hat{A}\left(s_t^i, a_t^i\right) = \sum_{t'=t}^{T} r\left(s_{t'}^i, a_{t'}^i\right) - V\left(s_t\right)$$

$$TD(0)\ approach: \hat{A}\left(s_t^i, a_t^i\right) = r\left(s_{t'}^i, a_{t'}^i\right) + V\left(s_{t+1}\right) - V\left(s_t\right)$$

The revised update rule using actor critic is as follows:

$$MC: \nabla_\theta J(\theta) = \frac{1}{N} \sum_{i=1}^{N} \sum_{t=1}^{T} \nabla_\theta \log \pi_\theta\left(a_t^i | s_t^i\right) \left[\sum_{t'=t}^{T} r\left(s_{t'}^i, a_{t'}^i\right) - V\left(s_t\right) \right]$$

$$TD: \nabla_\theta J(\theta) = \frac{1}{N} \sum_{i=1}^{N} \sum_{t=1}^{T} \nabla_\theta \log \pi_\theta\left(a_t^i | s_t^i\right) \left[r\left(s_{t'}^i, a_{t'}^i\right) + V\left(s_{t+1}\right) - V\left(s_t\right) \right] \qquad (7.33)$$

We need two networks, one network to estimate the state-value function $V(s_t)$ parameterized by parameters ϕ and another network to output the policy $\pi_\theta(a_t | s_t)$ parameterized by θ. Figure 7-7 shows the complete pseudocode for the actor critic (also known as A2C for advantage actor critic).

ADVANTAGE ACTOR-CRITIC ALGORITHM

Input:

A model with parameters θ taking state S as input and producing $\pi_\theta(a|s)$

A model with parameters ϕ taking state S as input and producing $V_\emptyset(s)$

Other parameters: step sizes α, β

Initialize:

Initialize weights $\boldsymbol{\theta}$, $\boldsymbol{\phi}$

Loop:

Sample $\{\tau\}$, a set of N trajectories from current policy $\pi_\theta(a_t|s_t)$

Calculate the reward to go $\hat{Q}_t^i = \sum_{t'=t}^{T} r\left(s_{t'}^i, a_{t'}^i\right)$

Fit Value function $V_\emptyset(s)$ to $\hat{Q}_t^i$ by forming mean square error:

$$L = \left(V_\emptyset(s) - \hat{Q}_t^i\right)^2$$

Carried out stochastic gradient step on L to adjust ϕ:

$$\phi = \phi - \beta * \nabla_\emptyset L$$

Update policy model parameters θ:

Calculate the pseudo cross-entropy-loss: $L_{CE}(\theta) = -J(\theta)$:

$$J(\theta) = \frac{1}{N} \sum_{i=1}^{N} \sum_{t=1}^{T} \log \pi_\theta\left(a_t^i | s_t^i\right) . \left(r\left(s_t^i, a_t^i\right) + V_\emptyset\left(s_{t+1}\right) - V_\emptyset\left(s_t\right)\right)$$

Carry out gradient step on θ:

$$\theta = \theta + \alpha \nabla_\theta J(\theta)$$

Figure 7-7. *Advantage actor-critic algorithm*

Please note that in the previous pseudocode, we have used one-step undiscounted return for advantage $\hat{A}\left(s_t^i, a_t^i\right)$.

$$r\left(s_t^i, a_t^i\right) + V_{\varnothing}\left(s_{t+1}\right) - V_{\varnothing}\left(s_t\right)$$

The discounted one-step version will be as follows:

$$r\left(s_t^i, a_t^i\right) + \gamma V_{\varnothing}\left(s_{t+1}\right) - V_{\varnothing}\left(s_t\right)$$

Similarly, the discounted n-step return version will be as follows:

$$\left(\sum_{t'=t}^{t+n-1} \gamma^{t'-t} r\left(s_{t'}^i, a_{t'}^i\right)\right) + \gamma^n V_{\varnothing}\left(s_{t+n}\right) - V_{\varnothing}\left(s_t\right)$$

And using the MC approach of directly using rewards to go, the advantage would be as follows:

$$\hat{A}\left(s_t^i, a_t^i\right) = \sum_{t'=t}^{T} \gamma^{t'-t} r\left(s_{t'}^i, a_{t'}^i\right) - V\left(s_t\right)$$

This is the version we will implement in our code.

Implementation of the A2C Algorithm

Let's look at the implementation details of the pseudocode in Figure 7-7. We need two networks/model—one for the policy network (the actor) with the parameter vector θ and another value estimation network (the critic) with the parameter vector φ. In the actual design, the policy network and value estimation network can share some initial weights. This is similar to the dueling network architecture we saw in the previous chapter. It is actually a desirable design choice for faster convergence. Figure 7-8 gives a schematic of the combined model.

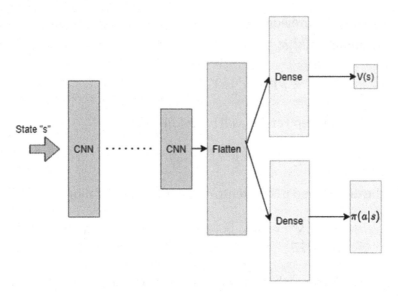

Figure 7-8. *Actor critic network with common weights in the initial layers*

In our code walk-through, we will make the following changes to the actor-critic algorithm given in Figure 7-7:

- We will use the MC discounted version of the advantage.

$$\hat{A}\left(s_t^i, a_t^i\right) = \sum_{t'=t}^{T} \gamma^{t'-t} r\left(s_{t'}^i, a_{t'}^i\right) - V\left(s_t\right)$$

- Like REINFORCE, we will introduce the entropy regularizer.

- Instead of training two separate loss training steps of the first fitting V(s) and then doing the policy gradient, we will form a single loss objective that will carry out the V(s) fitting as well as the policy gradient step together with the entropy regularizer.

The loss using actor critic with the previous modifications is as follows:

$$Loss(\theta, \phi) = -J(\theta, \phi) - H\left(\pi_\theta\left(a_t^i | s_t^i\right)\right)$$

$$= -\frac{1}{N} \sum_{i=1}^{N} \left[\sum_{t=1}^{T} \left(\log \pi_\theta\left(a_t^i | s_t^i\right) \left[\hat{Q}\left(s_t^i, a_t^i\right) - V_\phi\left(s_t^i\right) \right] \right) - \beta \sum_a \pi_\theta\left(a | s_t^i\right) . \log \pi_\theta\left(a | s_t^i\right) \right]$$

Like with REINFORCE, we will carry out weight updates after each trajectory. Therefore, $N = 1$. We will, however, average it over the number of actions to get the average loss. So, the function we will actually implement is as follows:

$$Loss(\theta,\phi) = -\frac{1}{T}\left[\sum_{t=1}^{T}\left(\log \pi_\theta(a_t|s_t)\left[\hat{Q}(s_t,a_t) - V_\phi(s_t)\right]\right) - \beta\sum_a \pi_\theta(a|s_t).\log \pi_\theta(a|s_t)\right]$$

This is the loss we will implement. You can find the complete code for implementing actor critic in PyTorch in `listing7_2_actor_critic_pytorch.ipynb`. The code repository also has a TensorFlow version given in `listing7_2_actor_critic_tensorflow.ipynb`. The implementation will pretty much follow the same steps that we had in REINFORCE. There are only some minor changes: the network construction and the loss calculation as per the previous expression.

Let's first talk about the network. We will have a joint network with shared weights, one producing the policy action probabilities and another the value of state. For `CartPole`, it is a fairly simple network and is given in Figure 7-9.

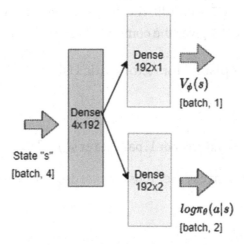

Figure 7-9. *Actor-critic network for the CartPole enviroment*

Listing 7-6 shows the implementation in PyTorch. It is a straight implementation of the network, as shown in Figure 7-9.

Listing 7-6. Actor-Critic Network in PyTorch

```
class ActorCritic(nn.Module):
    def __init__(self):
        super(ActorCritic, self).__init__()
        self.fc1 = nn.Linear(state_dim, 128)
        self.actor = nn.Linear(128,n_actions)
        self.critic = nn.Linear(128,1)

    def forward(self, s):
        x = F.relu(self.fc1(s))
        logits = self.actor(x)
        state_value = self.critic(x)
        return logits, state_value

model = ActorCritic()
```

The other change is the way we implement the training code for one episode. It is similar to the code in Listing 7-4 for REINFORCE with a minor change to introduce $V(s_t)$ as a baseline value. Listing 7-7 gives the complete code for `train_one_episode`.

Listing 7-7. train_one_episode for Actor Critic Using MC Rewards to Go in PyTorch

```
#init Optimizer
optimizer = torch.optim.Adam(model.parameters(), lr=1e-3)

def train_one_episode(states, actions, rewards, gamma=0.99, entropy_
coef=1e-2):

    # get rewards to go
    rewards_to_go = get_rewards_to_go(rewards, gamma)

    # convert numpy array to torch tensors
    states = torch.tensor(states, device=device, dtype=torch.float)
    actions = torch.tensor(actions, device=device, dtype=torch.long)
    rewards_to_go = torch.tensor(rewards_to_go, device=device,
    dtype=torch.float)

    # get action probabilities from states
```

```
logits, state_values = model(states)
probs = nn.functional.softmax(logits, -1)
log_probs = nn.functional.log_softmax(logits, -1)

log_probs_for_actions = log_probs[range(len(actions)), actions]

advantage = rewards_to_go - state_values.squeeze(-1)

#Compute loss to be minized
J = torch.mean(log_probs_for_actions*(advantage))
H = -(probs*log_probs).sum(-1).mean()

loss = -(J+entropy_coef*H)

optimizer.zero_grad()
loss.backward()
optimizer.step()

return np.sum(rewards) #to show progress on training
```

Please note that the code to train over multiple trajectories is the same as before. When we run the code, we see that compared to REINFORCE, the training using A2C happens faster with fairly steady progress toward a better policy.

Please note that actor critic is also an *on-policy* approach, just like REINFORCE.

Asynchronous Advantage Actor Critic

In 2016, the authors of the paper "Asynchronous Methods for Deep Reinforcement Learning,"[1] introduced the asynchronous version of A2C. The basic idea is simple. We have a global server that is the "parameter" server providing the network parameters: θ, ϕ. There are multiple actor-critic agents running in parallel. Each actor-critic agent obtains the parameter from the server, carries out trajectory rollouts, and does the gradient descent on θ, ϕ. The agent updates the parameter back to the server. It allows for faster learning, especially in an environment where we use simulators, e.g., robotic environments. We can first train an algorithm using A3C on multiple instances of the simulator. A subsequent learning would be to further fine-tune/train the algorithm on a physical robot in the real environment.

---

[1]https://arxiv.org/pdf/1602.01783.pdf

Figure 7-10 shows a high-level schematic of A3C. Please note that it is a simplistic explanation of the approach. For actual implementation details, you are advised to refer to the referenced paper in detail.

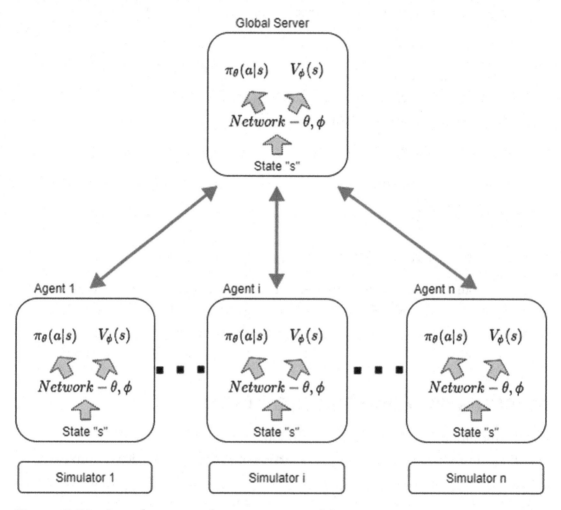

Figure 7-10. *Asynchronous advantage actor critic*

As explained, some papers refer to the synchronous version with multiple agents training together as the A2C version of A3C, i.e., A3C without the asynchronous part. However, at times the actor critic with one agent is also referred to as *advantage actor critic* (A2C). In the end, the actor critic is a family of algorithms where we use two networks together: a value network to estimate the $V(s)$ and a policy network to estimate the policy $\pi_\theta(a|s_t)$. We are leveraging the best of both worlds: value-based methods and policy gradient methods.

Trust Region Policy Optimization Algorithm

The method we have detailed so far in this chapter is also known as *vanilla policy gradient* (VPG). The policy we trained using VPG is a stochastic one that offers exploration on its own without explicitly using an ε-greedy exploration. As the training progresses, the policy distribution becomes sharper, centering around optimal actions. This reduces the exploration, making the algorithm exploit more and more what it has learned. It can cause the policy to get stuck at a local maxima. We tried to address this issue by introducing the regularizer, but that's not the only approach.

As we saw in the policy gradient approach in previous sections, we update the policy parameters by a small amount given by the following equation:

$$\theta_{new} = \theta_{old} + \alpha \nabla_\theta J(\theta)\big|_{\theta=\theta_{old}}$$

In other words, the gradient is evaluated at the old policy parameter $\theta = \theta_{old}$ and then updated by taking a small step determined by the step size α. VPG tries to keep the new and old policies near to each other in the parameter space by restricting the change in policy parameters from θ_{old} to θ_{new} using a learning rate α. However, just because policy parameters are nearby, it does not guarantee that old and new policies (i.e., action probability distribution) are actually close to each other. A small change in parameter θ could lead to significant divergence in the policy probabilities. Ideally, we would like to keep the old and new policies close to each other in the probability space and not in the parameter space. This is the key insight as detailed by authors of the 2015 paper titled "Trust Region Policy Optimization."[2] Before we dive into the details, let's spend a few minutes talking about a metric called Kullback-Liebler divergence (KL-divergence). It is a measure of how different two probabilities are. It comes from the field of information theory, and diving deep into it would require a book of its own. We will only attempt to give the formula and some intuition behind it without getting into the mathematical proof.

Suppose we have two discrete probability distributions P and Q defined over some range of values (called *support*). Let the support be "x" going from 1 to 6. $P_X(X = x)$

---

[2]https://arxiv.org/pdf/1502.05477.pdf

defines the probability of X=x using the probability distribution P. Similarly, we have another probability distribution Q defined over the same support. As an example, consider a die with six faces with probability distribution.

x	1	2	3	4	5	6
P(x)	1/6	1/6	1/6	1/6	1/6	1/6
Q(x)	2/9	1/6	1/6	1/6	1/6	1/9

The die Q is loaded to show less of 6 and more of 1, while P is a fair die with equal probabilities of showing any face of the dice.

The KL-divergence between P and Q is expressed as follows:

$$D_{KL}(P\|Q) = \sum_x P(x)\log\frac{P(x)}{Q(x)} \tag{7.34}$$

Let's calculate $D_{KL}(P\|Q)$ for the previous table.

$$D_{KL}(P\|Q) = \frac{1}{6}\log\frac{1/6}{2/9} + \frac{1}{6}\log\frac{1/6}{1/6} + \frac{1}{6}\log\frac{1/6}{1/6} + \frac{1}{6}\log\frac{1/6}{1/6} + \frac{1}{6}\log\frac{1/6}{1/6} + \frac{1}{6}\log\frac{1/6}{1/9}$$

$$= \frac{1}{6}\log\frac{3}{4} + \frac{1}{6}\log 1 + \frac{1}{6}\log 1 + \frac{1}{6}\log 1 + \frac{1}{6}\log 1 + \frac{1}{6}\log\frac{3}{2}$$

$$= \frac{1}{6}\log\frac{3}{4} + \frac{1}{6}x\,0 + \frac{1}{6}x\,0 + \frac{1}{6}x\,0 + \frac{1}{6}x\,0 + \frac{1}{6}\log\frac{3}{2}$$

$$= \frac{1}{6}\left(\log\frac{3}{4} + \log\frac{3}{2}\right)$$

$$= \frac{1}{6}\log\left(\frac{3}{4}x\frac{3}{2}\right)$$

$$= \frac{1}{6}\log\left(\frac{9}{8}\right) = 0.0196$$

You can satisfy yourself by putting P = Q to obtain $D_{KL}(P\|Q) = 0$. When two probabilities are equal, the KL divergence is 0. For any other two unequal probability distributions, you will get a +ve KL divergence. The farther apart the distribution is, the higher the KL divergence value. There is a rigorous mathematical proof to show that KL divergence is always +ve and zero only when the two distributions are equal.

Also note that KL divergence is not symmetric.

$$D_{KL}(P\|Q) \neq D_{KL}(Q\|P)$$

KL divergence is a kind of pseudomeasure of distance between two probability distributions in probability space. The KL divergence formula for continuous probability distributions is given as follows:

$$D_{KL}(P\|Q) = \int P(x)\log\frac{P(x)}{Q(x)}dx \tag{7.35}$$

Coming back to TRPO, we want to keep the new and old policies close to each other not in parameter space but in probability space. This is the same as saying that we want the KL-divergence to be bounded in each update step to ensure that the new and old policies do not diverge too far.

$$D_{KL}(\theta\|\theta_k) \leq \delta$$

Here, θ_k is the current policy parameter, and θ is the parameter for the updated policy.

Let's now turn our attention to the objective that we are trying to maximize. Our previous metric $J(\theta)$ did not have any explicit dependence on new and old policy parameters, say θ_{k+1} and θ_k, respectively. There is an alternative formulation for the policy objective using importance sampling. We will state this without mathematical derivation, as shown here:

$$J(\theta, \theta_k) = E_{a\sim\pi_{\theta_k}(a|s)}\left[\frac{\pi_\theta(a|s)}{\pi_{\theta_k}(a|s)}A^{\pi_{\theta_k}}(s,a)\right] \tag{7.36}$$

Here, θ is the parameter of the revised/updated policy, and θ_k is the parameter of the old policy. We are trying to take the maximum possible steps to go from the old policy parameter θ_k to the revised policy with the parameter θ such that the KL-divergence between the new and old policies do not diverge too much. Rephrasing, to find a new policy that increases the objective to the maximum extent without going out of the trust region around the old policy is defined by $D_{KL}(\theta\|\theta_k) \leq \delta$. In mathematical terms, we can summarize the maximization problem as follows:

$$\theta_{k+1} = \arg\max_\theta J(\theta, \theta_k)$$

$$s.t. D_{KL}\left(\theta \,\|\, \theta_k\right) \le \delta$$

$$where, J\left(\theta, \theta_k\right) = E_{a \sim \pi_{\theta_k}(a|s)}\left[\frac{\pi_\theta(a|s)}{\pi_{\theta_k}(a|s)} A^{\pi_{\theta_k}}(s,a)\right] \tag{7.37}$$

The advantage $A^{\pi_{\theta_k}}(s,a)$ is defined as before:

$$A^{\pi_{\theta_k}}(s,a) = Q^{\pi_{\theta_k}}(s,a) - V^{\pi_{\theta_k}}(s)$$

Or, when we roll out by one step and V is parameterized by another network with parameter ϕ, here is the equation:

$$A^{\pi_{\theta_k}}(s_t, a_t) = r(s_t, a_t) + V^{\pi_{\theta_k}}(s_{t+1}; \phi) - V^{\pi_{\theta_k}}(s_t; \phi)$$

This is the theoretical representation of the objective maximization in TRPO. However, using the Taylor series expansion of the objective $\theta_{k+1} = \arg \max_\theta J\left(\theta, \theta_k\right)$ and the KL constraint $D_{KL}(\theta\|\theta_k) \le \delta$, coupled with Lagrangian duality using convex optimization, we can get an approximate update expression. The approximation can break the guarantee of KL-divergence being bounded, for which a backtracking line search is added to the update rule. Lastly, it involves the inversion of an ***nxn*** matrix, which is not easier to compute. In that case, the conjugate gradient algorithm is used. At this point, we have a practical algorithm to calculate the update using TRPO.

We are not getting into the details of these derivations or giving the full algorithm. We want you to understand the basic setup. Most of the time we will not be implementing these algorithms by our own hand.

Proximal Policy Optimization Algorithm

Proximal policy optimization (PPO) is also motivated by the same question as TRPO. "How can we take the maximum possible step size in policy parameters without going too far and getting to a worse policy than the original one before the update?"

The PPO-clip variant that we will detail does not have KL-divergence. It depends on clipping the gradients in the objective function such that the update has no incentive to move the policy too far from the original step. PPO is simpler to implement and has empirically been shown to perform as good as TRPO. The details are in the 2017 paper titled "Proximal Policy Optimization Algorithms."[3]

The objective using the PPO-clip variant is as follows:

$$J(\theta,\theta_k) = min\left(\frac{\pi_\theta(a|s)}{\pi_{\theta_k}(a|s)}A^{\pi_{\theta_k}}(s,a),g\left(\epsilon,A^{\pi_{\theta_k}}(s,a)\right)\right)$$

where:

$$g(\epsilon,A) = \begin{cases} (1+\epsilon)A, A \geq 0 \\ (1-\epsilon)A, A < 0 \end{cases} \tag{7.38}$$

Let's rewrite $J(\theta,\theta_k)$, when advantage A is +ve, as shown here:

$$J(\theta,\theta_k) = min\left(\frac{\pi_\theta(a|s)}{\pi_{\theta_k}(a|s)},(1+\epsilon)\right)A^{\pi_{\theta_k}}(s,a)$$

When the advantage is +ve, we want to update the parameters so that the new policy $\pi_\theta(a|s)$ is higher than the old policy $\pi_{\theta_k}(a|s)$. But instead of increasing it too far, we clip the gradients to ensure that the new policy increase is within 1+ε times the old policy.

Similarly, when the advantage is -ve, we get the following:

$$J(\theta,\theta_k) = min\left(\frac{\pi_\theta(a|s)}{\pi_{\theta_k}(a|s)},(1-\epsilon)\right)A^{\pi_{\theta_k}}(s,a)$$

In other words, when the advantage is -ve, we want the parameters to be updated such that we decrease the policy probability for that (s, a) pair. However, instead of decreasing all the way, we clip the gradients so that the new policy probability does not go down below (1-ε) times the old policy probability.

In other words, we are clipping the gradients to ensure that policy updates leave the policy probability distribution to be within (1-ε) to (1+ε) times the old probability distribution. ε acts as a regularizer. It is pretty easy to implement PPO as compared to TRPO. We can follow the same pseudocode as given in Figure 7-7 for A2C with just one change to swap the objective J(θ) in Figure 7-7 with the objective given in (7.38).

This time, instead of coding it ourselves, we will use a library. OpenAI has a library called Baselines (https://github.com/openai/baselines). It has implementations

---

for many of the popular and newest algorithms. There is another library that is based on Baselines called Stable Baselines 3. You can read more about it at `https://stable-baselines3.readthedocs.io/en/master/`.

Our code will follow the same pattern as before, except that we will not be explicitly defining the policy network. We will also not write the training step of calculating loss and stepping through the gradient ourselves. You can find the complete code to train and record the performance of `CartPole` training using PPO in `listing7_3_ppo_baselines3.ipynb`. We will now walk through the code snippet of creating an agent, training it on `CartPole`, and evaluating the performance, as given in Listing 7-8.

Listing 7-8. PPO Agent for CartPole Using a Stable Baselines 3 Implementation

```
from stable_baselines3 import PPO
from stable_baselines3.ppo.policies import MlpPolicy
from stable_baselines3.common.evaluation import evaluate_policy

#create enviroment
env_name = 'CartPole-v1'
env = gym.make(env_name)

# build model
model = PPO(MlpPolicy, env, verbose=0)

# Train the agent for 30000 steps
model.learn(total_timesteps=30000)

# Evaluate the trained agent
mean_reward, std_reward = evaluate_policy(model, env, n_eval_episodes=100)
print(f"mean_reward:{mean_reward:.2f} +/- {std_reward:.2f}")
```

That's it. It took just a few lines of code to train the agent with PPO. The Python notebook contains additional code to record the performance of the trained agent and play the video. We are not going to get into the code details for it. Interested readers are advised to use the previous links to dive deep into OpenAI Baselines as well as Stable Baselines.

We would also to use this opportunity to stress once more the point of getting to know the popular RL libraries well. While walking through the implementations of various algorithms in this book, you should note that it is equally important to get comfortable with the popular RL implementations and learn to use them for your specific needs. The code accompanying this book is to help you understand the concepts better. It is by no means the production code. Libraries like Baselines have highly optimized code with the ability to leverage the GPU and multiple cores to run many agents in parallel.

Summary

This chapter introduced you to the alternate approach of directly learning a policy instead of going through the learning state/action values first and then using those to find the optimal policy.

We looked at the derivation of REINFROCE, the most basic of the policy gradient methods. After the initial derivation, we looked at a couple of variance reduction techniques such as rewards to go and the use of baselines.

This led us to look at the actor-critic family in which we combined value-based methods to learn state values acting as baselines using REINFORCE. The policy network (actor) with the state value network (critic) gave us the ability to combine the best of value-based methods and policy gradient methods. We briefly touched upon the asynchronous version known as A3C.

Finally, we looked at a couple of advanced policy optimization techniques such as trust region policy optimization (TRPO) and proximal policy optimization (PPO). We talked about the key motivations and approaches using each of these two techniques. We also saw the use of libraries to train an agent using PPO.

## CHAPTER 8

Combining Policy Gradient and Q-Learning

So far in this book, in the context of deep learning combined with reinforcement learning, we have looked at deep Q-learning with its variants in Chapter 6 and at policy gradients in Chapter 7. Neural network training requires multiple iterations, and Q-learning, an off-policy approach, enables us to use transitions multiple times, giving us sample efficiency. However, Q-learning can be unstable at times. Further, it is an indirect way of learning. Instead of learning an optimal policy directly, we first learn q-values and then use these action values to learn the optimal behavior. In Chapter 7, we looked at the approach of learning a policy directly, giving us much better improvement guarantees. However, all the policies we looked at Chapter 7 were on-policy. We used a policy to interact with the environment and make updates to the policy weights to increase the probability of good trajectories/actions while reducing the probability of bad ones. However, we carried out the learning on-policy as the previous transitions become invalid after the update to policy weights.

In this chapter, we will look at combining the benefits of both the approaches, i.e., off-policy learning and learning the policy directly. We will first talk about the trade-offs of Q-learning versus policy gradient methods. After this, we will look at three popular approaches of combining Q-learning with policy gradients: deep deterministic policy gradients (DDPG), twin delayed DDPG (TD3), and soft actor critic (SAC). We will largely follow the notations, approach, and sample code as documented in the OpenAI Spinning Up library.[1]

---

[1]https://spinningup.openai.com/

© Nimish Sanghi 2021
N. Sanghi, *Deep Reinforcement Learning with Python*, https://doi.org/10.1007/978-1-4842-6809-4_8

Trade-Offs in Policy Gradient and Q-Learning

In Chapter 7 we looked at DQN, the deep learning version of Q-learning. In Q-learning, an off-policy method, we collect transitions from an exploratory behavior policy and then use these transitions in a batch stochastic gradient update to learn the q-values. As we learn the q-values, we improve the policy by taking the max over the q-values of all possible actions in a state to choose the best action. This was the equation we followed:

$$w_{t+1} = w_t + \alpha . \frac{1}{N} \sum_{i=1}^{N} \left[r_i + \gamma \, max_{a_i} \tilde{q}\left(s_i', a_i'; w_t^-\right) - \hat{q}\left(s_i, a_i; w\right) \right].\nabla_w \, \hat{q}\left(s_i, a_i; w\right) \qquad (8.1)$$

Please note the max. By taking max i.e., $max_{a_i} \tilde{q}\left(s_i', a_i'; w_t^-\right)$, we are improving the target value $r_i + \gamma \, max_{a_i} \tilde{q}\left(s_i', a_i'; w_t^-\right)$, and that forces the current state-action q-value $\hat{q}\left(s_i, a_i; w\right)$ to update the weights to reach the higher target. This is the Bellman optimality equation that we are forcing our network weights to satisfy. The whole learning is off-policy because the Bellman optimality equations hold for the optimal policy no matter what policy was followed. It needs to be satisfied for all the (s, a, r, s') transitions, no matter which policy these were generated using. We are able to reuse the transitions with the replay buffer, which makes this learning very sample efficient. However, there are a few issues that Q-learning suffers from.

The first one is about using Q-learning in its current form for continuous actions. Please look at $max_{a_i} \tilde{q}\left(s_i', a_i'; w_t^-\right)$. All the examples we saw in Chapter 6 were the ones with discrete actions. Do you know why? How do you think you will perform *max* when the action space is continuous and multidimensional, e.g., moving multiple joints of a robot together?

When the actions are discrete, it is easy to take *max*. We input state s to the model, and we get $Q(s, a)$ for all the possible actions. With a limited number of discrete actions, choosing the *max* is easy. Figure 8-1 shows a sample model.

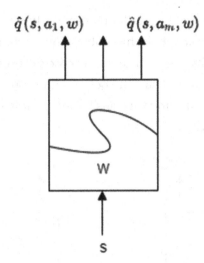

$$\hat{q}(s,a_1,w) \qquad \hat{q}(s,a_m,w)$$

W

S

Figure 8-1. *Generic model for DQN learning with discrete actions*

Now imagine the actions being continuous! How would you take the maximum? To find $\max_{a_i} \tilde{q}\left(s_i',a_i';w_t^-\right)$ for each s_i', we will have to run another optimization algorithm to find the max. This will be an expensive process as it needs to be carried out for every transition in the batch as part of policy improvement.

The second issue is that of learning the wrong objective. We actually want an optimal policy, but we do not do so directly under DQN. We learn the action-value functions and then use *max* to find the optimal q-value/optimal action.

The third issue is that DQN is also not stable at times. There are no theoretical guarantees, and we are trying to update the weights using the semi-gradient update that we talked about in Chapter 5. We are essentially trying to follow the process of supervised learning with changing targets. What we learn can impact the new trajectory generation, which in turn can impact our quality of learning. All the progress graphs we saw for DQN with the average reward did not continually improve. They were very choppy and required careful adjustment of hyperparameters to ensure that the algorithm settled toward a good policy.

Finally, the fourth issue is that DQN learns a deterministic policy. We use an exploratory behavior policy to generate and explore what the agent learns in a deterministic policy. Experiments especially in robotics have shown that some amount of stochastic policy is better as the modeling of the world and manipulations we do with joints are not always perfect. We need to have some amount of randomness to adjust for imperfect modeling or conversion of action values to actual robot joint movements. Also, deterministic policies are a limiting case of a stochastic policies.

Let's turn our attention to policy gradient methods. In policy gradient methods, we input the state and the output we get is the probability of actions for discrete actions or the parameters of a probability distribution in the case of continuous actions. We can see that policy gradients allowed us to learn the policies for both discrete and continuous actions. However, learning continuous actions in not feasible in DQN. Figure 8-2 shows the model used in policy gradients.

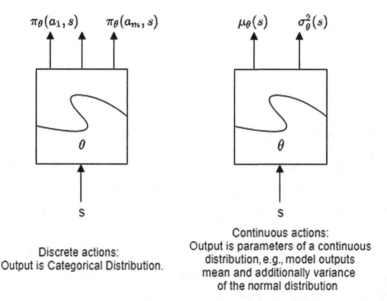

Discrete actions:
Output is Categorical Distribution.

Continuous actions:
Output is parameters of a continuous distribution, e.g., model outputs mean and additionally variance of the normal distribution

Figure 8-2. *Policy networks for policy gradient methods. In Chapter 7, we saw discrete actions, but the process works out fine for continuous actions as explained in that chapter*

Further, using the policy gradient approach, we directly learn to improve the policy instead of the roundabout way of first learning the value functions and then using them to find the optimal policy. The vanilla policy gradient did suffer from a collapse to a bad region, and we saw approaches like TRPO and PPO controlling the step size to improve the guarantee of policy gradients, leading to a better policy.

Policy gradients, unlike DQN, learn a stochastic policy, and thereby exploration is built into the policy we are trying to learn. However, the biggest lacuna in the policy gradient method was that it is an on-policy approach. Once we use the transitions to calculate the gradient update, the model has moved to a new policy. The earlier transitions are not relevant anymore in this updated policy world. We need to discard the previous transitions after an update and generate new trajectory/transitions to train the model on. This makes the policy learning very sample inefficient.

We did use value learning as part of policy gradients using the actor-critic methods in which the policy network was the actor trying to learn the best actions, and the value network was the critic informing the policy network of how good or bad the actions are. However, even using the actor-critic methods, the learning was on-policy. We used the critic to guide the actor, but we still needed to discard all the transitions after an update to the policy (and/or value) networks.

Is there a way we could learn the policy directly but somehow leverage Q-learning to learn off-policy? And could we do so for the continuous action space? This is what we will talk about in this chapter. We will combine Q-learning with policy gradients to come up with algorithms that are off-policy and work well for continuous actions.

General Framework to Combine Policy Gradient with Q-Learning

We will look at continuous action policies. We will have two networks. One is for learning the optimal action for a given state, the actor network. Suppose the policy network is parameterized by θ, and the network learns a policy that produces the action a = $\mu_\theta(s)$, which maximizes $Q(s, a)$. In mathematical notations:

$$\max_{a'} Q^*\left(s',a'\right) \approx Q^*\left(s',\mu_\theta\left(s\right)\right)$$

The second network, the critic network, will again take state (s) as one input and the optimal action from the first network, $\mu_\theta(s)$, as the other input to produce the q-value $Q_\phi(s, \mu_\theta(s))$. Figure 8-3 shows the interaction of the networks conceptually.

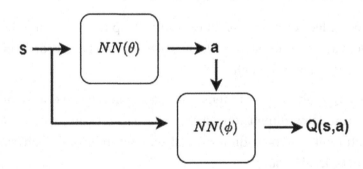

Figure 8-3. *Combining the policy and Q-learning. We learn directly the policy as well as Q using two networks in which the action output from the first network (actor) is fed into the second network (critic), which learns Q(s, a)*

To ensure exploration, we want to take action *a*, which is exploratory. This is similar to the approach we took in Q-learning where we learned a deterministic policy but generated transitions from an exploratory ε-greedy policy. Similarly, here, while we learn a, we add a bit of randomness $\epsilon \sim N(0, \sigma^2)$ and use the $a + \epsilon$ action to explore the environment and generate trajectories.

Like Q-learning, we will use a replay buffer to store the transitions and reuse the previous transitions to learn. This is one of the big benefits of all the approaches we will see in this chapter. They will make policy learning off-policy and hence sample efficient.

In Q-learning, we had to use a target network that was a copy of the Q-network. The reason was to provide some kind of stationery target while learning q-values. You can revisit the discussion of target networks in Chapter 5 and Chapter 6. In those approaches, the target network weights were updated with the online/agent network weights periodically. Here also we will use a target network. However, the approach for updating the target network weights for algorithms in this chapter will be that of *polyak averaging* (*exponential averaging*), as given by the following equation:

$$\phi_{target} \leftarrow \rho\phi_{target} + (1 - \rho)\phi \tag{8.2}$$

We will also be using a target network for the policy network. This is for the same reason as providing the stable target q-values, which allows us to carry out the supervised learning style of gradient descent and adjust the weights to the approximate $Q(s, a)$.

With this background, we are ready to look at our first algorithm: deep deterministic policy gradient.

Deep Deterministic Policy Gradient

In 2016, in a paper titled "Continuous Control with Deep Reinforcement Learning,"[2] authors from DeepMind introduced the DDPG algorithm. The authors had the following points to make about their approach:

- While DQN solves high-dimensional state space, it can only handle discrete and low-dimensional action space. DQN cannot be applied to continuous and high-dimensional action domains, e.g., physical control tasks like robots.

---

[2]https://arxiv.org/pdf/1509.02971.pdf

- Discretizing action space is not an option due to the *curse of dimensionality*. Assume that you have a robot with seven joints and each joint can move in the range $(-k, k)$. Let's do a coarse discretization of each joint having three possible values $\{-k, 0, k\}$. Even with this coarse discretization, the total combinations of discrete actions in all seven dimensions work out to $3^7 = 2187$. Instead, if we decide to divide the discrete range for each joint in 10 possible values within the range $(-k, k)$, we get $10^7 = 10$ *million* options. This is the *curse of dimensionality* where the set of possible action combinations grows exponentially with each new dimension/joint.

- DDPG is an algorithm that is as follows:

  - *Model free*: We do not know the model. We learn it from the interaction of the agent with the environment.

  - *Off-policy*: DDPG, like DQN, uses an exploratory policy to generate transitions and learns a deterministic policy.

  - *Continuous and high-dimensional action space*: DDPG works only for a continuous action domain and works well with high-dimensional action spaces.

  - *Actor-critic*: This means we have an actor (policy network) and critic, the action-value (q-value) network.

  - *Replay buffer*: Like DQN, DDPG uses a replay buffer to store transitions and uses them to learn. This breaks the temporal dependence/correlation of training examples, which could otherwise mess up the learning.

  - *Target network*: Like DQN, it uses a target network to provide fairly stable targets for the q-value to learn. However, unlike DQN, it does not update the target network by copying over the weights of online/agent/main network periodically. Rather, it uses the polyak/exponential average to keep moving the target network a little bit after every update to the main network.

Let's now turn our attention to the network architecture and losses we calculate. First let's look at the Q-learning part, and then we will look at the policy learning network.

Q-Learning in DDPG (Critic)

In DQN, we calculated a loss that was minimized by gradient descent. The loss is given by equation (6.3), reproduced here:

$$L = \frac{1}{N}\sum_{i=1}^{N}\left[r_i + \left((1-done_i).\gamma.\max_{a_i}\hat{q}\left(s_i^{'},a_i^{'};w_t^{-}\right)\right) - \hat{q}\left(s_i,a_i;w_t\right)\right]^2 \quad (8.3)$$

Let's rewrite the equation. We will drop subindex **i** and **t** to reduce the clutter of notation. We will change the summation to expectation to emphasize that what we usually want is an expectation, but it is estimated by average over samples under Monte Carlo. Eventually in the code we have sums, but they are Monte Carlo estimations of some expectation. We will also replace w_t^- , the target network weights, with ϕ_{targ}. Similarly, we will replace the main weights w_t with ϕ. Further, we will move the weights from inside the function parameter to the sub-indices on the function, i.e., $Q_\phi(...) \leftarrow Q(....; \phi)$. With all these symbol changes, equation (8.3) looks like this:

$$L(\phi,D) = \underset{(s,a,r,s^{'},d)\sim D}{E}\left[\left(Q_\phi(s,a) - \left(r + \gamma(1-d)\max_{a'}Q_{\phi_{targ}}(s',a')\right)\right)^2\right] \quad (8.4)$$

This is still the DQN formulation where we take a max of discrete actions in state $(s^{'})$ to get $\max_{a'}Q_{\phi_{targ}}(s',a')$. In continuous space we cannot take *max*, and hence we have another network (actor) to take input state *s* and produce the action, which maximizes $Q_{\phi_{targ}}(s',a')$; i.e., we replace $\max_{a'}Q_{\phi_{targ}}(s',a')$ with $Q_{\phi_{target}}\left(s^{'},\mu_{\theta_{targ}}(s^{'})\right)$ where $a' = \mu_{\theta_{targ}}(s^{'})$ is the target policy. The updated loss expression is as follows:

$$L(\phi,D) = \underset{(s,a,r,s^{'},d)\sim D}{E}\left[\left(Q_\phi(s,a) - \left(r + \gamma(1-d)Q_{\phi_{target}}\left(s^{'},\mu_{\theta_{targ}}(s^{'})\right)\right)\right)^2\right] \quad (8.5)$$

This is the updated mean squared Bellman error (MSBE) that we will implement in code and then do back propagation to minimize the loss function. Please note that this is only a function of ϕ and so the gradient of $L(\phi, D)$ is with respect to ϕ. As discussed earlier, in the code we will replace the expectation with the sample average being the MC estimate of the expectation.

Next let's look at the policy learning part.

Policy Learning in DDPG (Actor)

In the policy learning part, we are trying to learn $a = \mu_\theta(s)$, a deterministic policy that gives the action that maximizes $Q_\phi(s, a)$. As the action space is continuous and we assume that the Q function is differentiable with respect to the action, we can just perform gradient ascent with respect to the policy parameters to solve.

$$\max_\theta J(\theta, D) = \max_\theta \underset{s \sim D}{E} \left[Q_\phi \left(s, \mu_\theta(s) \right) \right] \qquad (8.6)$$

As the policy is deterministic, the expectation in (8.6) does not depend on the policy, which is different than what we saw in stochastic gradients in the previous chapter. The expectation operator there depended on policy parameters because the policy was stochastic, which in turn impacted the expected q-value.

We can take the gradient of J with regard to θ to get the following:

$$\nabla_\theta J(\theta, D) = \underset{s \sim D}{E} \left[\nabla_a Q_\phi(s, a) \big|_{a = \mu_\phi(s)} \nabla_\phi \mu_\phi(s) \right] \qquad (8.7)$$

This is straight application of chain rule. Please also note that we do not get any $\nabla \log (\ldots)$ terms inside the expectation as the state s over which the expectation is being taken is coming from the replay buffer, and it has no dependence on the parameter θ with respect to which gradient is being taken.

Further, in a 2014 paper titled "Deterministic Policy Gradient Algorithms,"[3] the authors showed that equation (8.7) is the policy gradient, i.e., the gradient of the policy's performance. You are advised to read through both of these papers to get a deeper theoretical understanding of the math behind DDPG.

As discussed earlier, to aid in exploration, while we learn a deterministic policy, we will use a noisy exploratory version of the learned policy to explore and generate transitions. We do so by adding a mean zero Gaussian noise to the learning policy.

Pseudocode and Implementation

At this point, we are ready to give the complete pseudocode. Please refer to Figure 8-4 for this.

---

[3]http://proceedings.mlr.press/v32/silver14.pdf

DEEP DETERMINISTIC POLICY GRADIENT

1. Input initial policy parameters θ, Q-function parameters ϕ, empty replay buffer D.

2. Set the target parameters equal to the online parameters $\theta_{targ} \leftarrow \theta$ and $\phi_{targ} \leftarrow \phi$.

3. **Repeat.**

4.   Observe state s and select the action.

$$a = clip(\mu_\theta(s) + \epsilon, a_{Low}, a_{High}), \text{ where } \epsilon \sim N$$

5.   Execute action a in the environment and observe the next state s', reward r, and done signal d.

6.   Store (s, a, r, s', d) in the replay buffer D.

7.   if s' is the terminal state, reset the environment.

8.   If it's time to update, **then**:

9.   For as many updates as required:

10.   Sample a batch $B = \{(s, a, r, s', d)\}$ from replay buffer D.

11.   Compute targets.

$$y(r, s', d) = r + \gamma(1 - d)Q_{targ}\left(s', \mu_{\theta_{targ}}(s')\right)$$

12.   Update the Q function with one-step gradient descent on ϕ.

$$\nabla_\phi \frac{1}{|B|} \sum_{(s,a,r,s',d)\in B} \left(Q_\phi(s,a) - y(r,s',d)\right)^2$$

13.   Update the policy with one-step gradient ascent on θ.

$$\nabla_\theta \frac{1}{|B|} \sum_{s\in B} Q_\phi\left(s, \mu_\theta(s)\right)$$

14.   Update the target networks using polyak averaging.

$$\phi_{targ} \leftarrow \rho\phi_{targ} + (1-\rho)\phi$$

$$\theta_{targ} \leftarrow \rho\theta_{targ} + (1-\rho)\theta$$

Figure 8-4. *Deep deterministic policy gradient algorithm*

Gym Environments Used in Code

Turning to the implementation, we will be using two environments in this chapter to run the code. The first one is a pendulum swing environment called Pendulum-v0. Here the state is a three-dimensional vector giving the angle of the pendulum (i.e., its *cos* and *sin* components), with the third dimension being the angular velocity (theta-dot): $\left[cos(\theta), sin(\theta), \dot{\theta}\right]$. The action is a single value, with the torque being applied to the pendulum. The idea is to balance the pendulum in an upright position for as long as possible. See Figure 8-5.

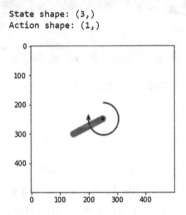

Figure 8-5. *Pendulum environment from the OpenAI Gym library*

After we train the network on this simple continuous action environment with one-dimensional action space, we will look into another environment called a lunar-lander continuous one: LunarLanderContinuous-v2. In this environment, we try to land the lunar module on the moon between the flags. The state vector is eight-dimensional: [x_pos, y_pos, x_vel, y_vel, lander_angle, lander_angular_vel, left_leg_ground_contact_flag, right_leg_ground_contact_flag].

The action is two-dimensional floats: [main engine, left-right engines].

- *Main engine*: -1..0 is engine off, and range (0,1) is the engine throttle from 50% to 100% power. The engine can't work with less than 50 percent power.

- *Left right*: range(-1.0, -0.5) fires the left engine, range(+0.5, +1.0) fires the right engine, and range(-0.5, 0.5) is both engines off.

Figure 8-6 shows a snapshot of the environment.

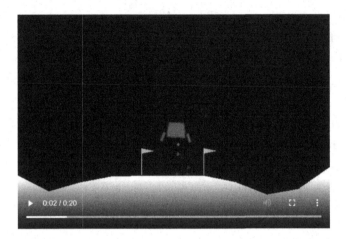

Figure 8-6. *Lunar-lander continuous from the OpenAI Gym library*

Code Listing

Let's now turn our attention to the actual code for implementing the DDPG pseudocode given in Figure 8-4. The code is from file `listing8_1_ddpg_pytorch.ipynb`. We also have a complete implementation in TensorFlow 2.0 in the file `listing8_1_ddpg_tensorflow.ipynb`. All code walk-throughs will borrow snippets from these two files. We will first be talking about the Q and policy networks, followed by loss calculation and then the training loop. Finally, we will talk about the code to run and test the performance of the trained agent.

Policy Network Actor (PyTorch)

First let's look at the *actor/policy* network. Listing 8-1 shows the policy network code in PyTorch. We define a simple neural network with two hidden layers of size 256, each with ReLU activation. If you look at the function forward, you will notice that the final layer (self.actor) is passed through the tanh activation. Tanh is a squashing function; it re-maps the values in $(-\infty, \infty)$ to a squashed range, (-1,1). We then multiply this squashed value with the action limit (self.act_limit) so that the continuous output from MLPActor is within the valid range of action values that the environment accepts. We create our network class by extending the PyTorch nn.Module class, which requires us to define a forward function with input state S as a parameter producing the action value as the network output.

Listing 8-1. Policy Network in PyTorch

```
class MLPActor(nn.Module):
    def __init__(self, state_dim, act_dim, act_limit):
        super().__init__()
        self.act_limit = act_limit
        self.fc1 = nn.Linear(state_dim, 256)
        self.fc2 = nn.Linear(256, 256)
        self.actor = nn.Linear(256, act_dim)

    def forward(self, s):
        x = self.fc1(s)
        x = F.relu(x)
        x = self.fc2(x)
        x = F.relu(x)
        x = self.actor(x)
        x = torch.tanh(x)  # to output in range(-1,1)
        x = self.act_limit * x
        return x
```

Policy Network Actor (TensorFlow)

Listing 8-2 contains the same function in TensorFlow 2.0. It is pretty much similar to the PyTorch implementation except that we subclass `tf.keras.Model` instead of `nn.Module`. We implement the network forward logic in a function called `call` instead of the function `forward`. And then there are minor differences in the way layers are named such as `dense` versus `linear` as well as the way the dimensions of the layers are passed.

Listing 8-2. Policy Network in TensorFlow

```python
class MLPActor(tf.keras.Model):
    def __init__(self, state_dim, act_dim, act_limit):
        super().__init__()
        self.act_limit = act_limit
        self.fc1 = layers.Dense(256, activation="relu")
        self.fc2 = layers.Dense(256, activation="relu")
        self.actor = layers.Dense(act_dim)

    def call(self, s):
        x = self.fc1(s)
        x = self.fc2(x)
        x = self.actor(x)
        x = tf.keras.activations.tanh(x)   # to output in range(-1,1)
        x = self.act_limit * x
        return x
```

Q-Network Critic Implementation

Next we look at the Q-network (*critic*). This is also a simple two-layer hidden network with ReLU activation and then a final layer with a number of outputs equal to one. The final layer does not have any activation, enabling the network to produce any value as output of the network. This network is outputting the q-value, and that is why we need to have a possible range of $(-\infty, \infty)$.

PyTorch

Listing 8-3 shows the code for the critic network in PyTorch, and Listing 8-4 shows the code in TensorFlow. They are pretty similar to the implementation of the actor/policy network except for the minor differences as discussed earlier.

Listing 8-3. Q/Critic Network in PyTorch

```
class MLPQFunction(nn.Module):
    def __init__(self, state_dim, act_dim):
        super().__init__()
        self.fc1 = nn.Linear(state_dim+act_dim, 256)
        self.fc2 = nn.Linear(256, 256)
        self.Q = nn.Linear(256, 1)

    def forward(self, s, a):
        x = torch.cat([s,a], dim=-1)
        x = self.fc1(x)
        x = F.relu(x)
        x = self.fc2(x)
        x = F.relu(x)
        q = self.Q(x)
        return torch.squeeze(q, -1)
```

TensorFlow

Listing 8-4 shows the code for the critic network in TensorFlow.

Listing 8-4. Q/Critic Network in TensorFlow

```
class MLPQFunction(tf.keras.Model):
    def __init__(self, state_dim, act_dim):
        super().__init__()
        self.fc1 = layers.Dense(256, activation="relu")
        self.fc2 = layers.Dense(256, activation="relu")
        self.Q = layers.Dense(1)

    def call(self, s, a):
```

```
x = tf.concat([s,a], axis=-1)
x = self.fc1(x)
x = self.fc2(x)
q = self.Q(x)
return tf.squeeze(q, -1)
```

Combined Model-Actor Critic Implementation

Once both the networks are defined, we combine them into a single class that allows us to manage the online and target networks in a more modular way. This is just for better code organization and nothing more. The class combining the two networks is implemented as MLPActorCritic. In this class, we also define a function get_action, which takes the state and a noise scale. It passes the state through the policy network to get $\mu_\theta(s)$, and then it adds a noise (zero mean Gaussian noise) to give a noisy action for exploration. This is the function that implements step 4 of the algorithm:

$$a = clip\left(\mu_\theta\left(s\right)+\epsilon, a_{Low}, a_{High}\right), \text{where } \epsilon \sim N$$

Listing 8-5 shows the implementation of MLPActorCritic in PyTorch, and Listing 8-6 shows the TensorFlow version. The implementations are pretty similar except for the individual nuances like which class to subclass. The other difference is that in PyTorch you need to convert NumPy arrays to torch tensors before you can pass them through the network, while in TensorFlow we can directly pass NumPy arrays to the model.

Listing 8-5. MLPActorCritic in PyTorch

```
class MLPActorCritic(nn.Module):
    def __init__(self, observation_space, action_space):
        super().__init__()
        self.state_dim = observation_space.shape[0]
        self.act_dim = action_space.shape[0]
        self.act_limit = action_space.high[0]

        #build Q and policy functions
        self.q = MLPQFunction(self.state_dim, self.act_dim)
        self.policy = MLPActor(self.state_dim, self.act_dim, self.act_limit)

    def act(self, state):
```

```
    with torch.no_grad():
        return self.policy(state).numpy()

def get_action(self, s, noise_scale):
    a = self.act(torch.as_tensor(s, dtype=torch.float32))
    a += noise_scale * np.random.randn(self.act_dim)
    return np.clip(a, -self.act_limit, self.act_limit)
```

Listing 8-6. MLPActorCritic in TensorFlow

```
class MLPActorCritic(tf.keras.Model):
    def __init__(self, observation_space, action_space):
        super().__init__()
        self.state_dim = observation_space.shape[0]
        self.act_dim = action_space.shape[0]
        self.act_limit = action_space.high[0]

        #build Q and policy functions
        self.q = MLPQFunction(self.state_dim, self.act_dim)
        self.policy = MLPActor(self.state_dim, self.act_dim, self.act_limit)

    def act(self, state):
        return self.policy(state).numpy()

    def get_action(self, s, noise_scale):
        a = self.act(s.reshape(1,-1).astype("float32")).reshape(-1)
        a += noise_scale * np.random.randn(self.act_dim)
        return np.clip(a, -self.act_limit, self.act_limit)
```

Experience Replay

Like with DQN, we use experience replay. And it is the same version from DQN that we use in DDPG for both PyTorch and TensorFlow. It is implemented using NumPy arrays, and the same code works for both PyTorch and TensorFlow. As it is the same implementation borrowed from DQN, we are not giving the code for it. To review the code for ReplayBuffer, please check the implementations in the Jupyter Notebooks.

Q-Loss Implementation

Next, we look into the Q-loss calculation. We are essentially implementing the equations from steps 11 and 12 of the pseudocode.

$$y(r,s',d) = r + \gamma(1-d)Q_{targ}\left(s', \mu_{\theta_{targ}}(s')\right)$$

$$\nabla_\phi \frac{1}{|B|} \sum_{(s,a,r,s',d)\in B} \left(Q_\phi(s,a) - y(r,s',d)\right)^2$$

PyTorch

Listing 8-7 gives the PyTorch implementation. We first convert the batch of (s, a, r, s', d) into PyTorch tensors. Next we calculate $Q_\phi(s, a)$ using the batch of (s, a) and pass it through the *policy* network. Following this, we calculate the target $y(r, s', d)$ as per the previous expression. We use with torch.no_grad() to stop the gradient calculation while computing the target as we do not want to adjust the target network weights using auto-diff from PyTorch. We will adjust the target network weights manually using polyak averaging. Stopping the calculation of unwanted gradients can speed up the training, and also it ensures that you do not have any unintended side effects of a gradient step impacting the weights that you want to keep frozen or adjust manually. Finally, we calculate the loss.

$$Q_{Loss} = \frac{1}{|B|} \sum_{(s,a,r,s',d)\in B} \left(Q_\phi(s,a) - y(r,s',d)\right)^2$$

PyTorch carries out the back propagation to calculate the gradient. We do not need to calculate the gradient explicitly in the code.

Listing 8-7. Q-Loss Computation in PyTorch

```
def compute_q_loss(agent, target_network, states, actions, rewards,
next_states, done_flags,
                gamma=0.99):

    # convert numpy array to torch tensors
    states = torch.tensor(states, dtype=torch.float)
    actions = torch.tensor(actions, dtype=torch.float)
    rewards = torch.tensor(rewards, dtype=torch.float)
```

```
next_states = torch.tensor(next_states, dtype=torch.float)
done_flags = torch.tensor(done_flags.astype('float32'),dtype=torch.float)

# get q-values for all actions in current states
# use agent network
predicted_qvalues = agent.q(states, actions)

# Bellman backup for Q function
with torch.no_grad():
    q_next_state_values = target_network.q(next_states, target_
    network.policy(next_states))
    target = rewards + gamma * (1 - done_flags) * q_next_state_values

# MSE loss against Bellman backup
loss_q = ((predicted_qvalues - target)**2).mean()

return loss_q
```

TensorFlow

The TensorFlow version is similar, and Listing 8-8 lists the complete implementation.
The main difference from PyTorch is that we do not convert the NumPy arrays to tensors.
However, we cast the data type to float32 to make it compatible with the default data
type for network weights. Please remember that for all TensorFlow implementations
we are using eager execution mode, and similar to PyTorch, we use with tape.stop_
recording() to stop the gradient computation in the target network.

Listing 8-8. Q-Loss Computation in TensorFlow

```
def compute_q_loss(agent, target_network, states, actions, rewards,
next_states, done_flags,
                   gamma, tape):

    # convert numpy array to proper data types
    states = states.astype('float32')
    actions = actions.astype('float32')
    rewards = rewards.astype('float32')
    next_states = next_states.astype('float32')
    done_flags = done_flags.astype('float32')
```

```
# get q-values for all actions in current states
# use agent network
predicted_qvalues = agent.q(states, actions)

# Bellman backup for Q function
with tape.stop_recording():
    q__next_state_values = target_network.q(next_states, target_
    network.policy(next_states))
    target = rewards + gamma * (1 - done_flags) * q__next_state_values

# MSE loss against Bellman backup
loss_q = tf.reduce_mean((predicted_qvalues - target)**2)

return loss_q
```

Policy Loss Implementation

Next, we calculate the policy loss as per step 13 of the pseudocode.

$$Policy_{Loss} = -\frac{1}{|B|}\sum_{s \in B}Q_{\phi}\left(s, \mu_{\theta}(s)\right)$$

This is a straightforward computation. It is just a three-line code implementation, both in PyTorch and in TensorFlow. Listing 8-9 contains the PyTorch version, and Listing 8-10 contains the TensorFlow version. Please note the -ve sign in the loss. Our algorithm needs to do gradient ascent on the policy objective, but auto-differentiation libraries like PyTorch and TensorFlow implement gradient descent. Multiplying the policy objective by -1.0 makes it a loss, and gradient descent on a loss is the same as gradient ascent on a policy objective.

Listing 8-9. Policy-Loss Computation in PyTorch

```
def compute_policy_loss(agent, states):

    # convert numpy array to torch tensors
    states = torch.tensor(states, dtype=torch.float)

    predicted_qvalues = agent.q(states, agent.policy(states))

    loss_policy = - predicted_qvalues.mean()

    return loss_policy
```

Listing 8-10. Policy-Loss Computation in TensorFlow

```
def compute_policy_loss(agent, states, tape):

    # convert numpy array to proper data type
    states = states.astype('float32')

    predicted_qvalues = agent.q(states, agent.policy(states))

    loss_policy = - tf.reduce_mean(predicted_qvalues)

    return loss_policy
```

One Step Update Implementation

Next we define a function called one_step_update that gets a batch of (s, a, r, s', d) and computes the Q-loss followed by back propagation and then a similar step of policy-loss computation followed by the gradient step. It finally carries out an update to the target network weights using polyak averaging. Essentially, this step with the previous two functions compute_q_loss and compute_policy_loss implements steps 11 to 14 of the pseudocode.

Listing 8-11 shows the PyTorch version of one_step_update. The first step is to calculate the Q-loss and carry out gradient descent on the critic/Q network weights. We then freeze the Q-network weights so that gradient descent on the policy network does not impact the weights of the Q-network. This is followed by computing the policy loss and gradient descent on the actor/policy network weights. We again unfreeze the Q-network weights. Lastly, we update the target network weights using polyak averaging.

Listing 8-11. One-Step Update in PyTorch

```
def one_step_update(agent, target_network, q_optimizer, policy_optimizer,
                    states, actions, rewards, next_states, done_flags,
                    gamma=0.99, polyak=0.995):

    #one step gradient for q-values
    q_optimizer.zero_grad()
    loss_q = compute_q_loss(agent, target_network, states, actions,
    rewards, next_states, done_flags,
                    gamma)
    loss_q.backward()
```

```
q_optimizer.step()

#Freeze Q-network
for params in agent.q.parameters():
    params.requires_grad = False

#one setep gradient for policy network
policy_optimizer.zero_grad()
loss_policy = compute_policy_loss(agent, states)
loss_policy.backward()
policy_optimizer.step()

#UnFreeze Q-network
for params in agent.q.parameters():
    params.requires_grad = True

# update target networks with polyak averaging
with torch.no_grad():
    for params, params_target in zip(agent.parameters(), target_
    network.parameters()):
        params_target.data.mul_(polyak)
        params_target.data.add_((1-polyak)*params.data)
```

Listing 8-12 gives the TensorFlow version of one_step_update, which is similar to the PyTorch implementation flow. The differences are in the way the gradient is calculated, in the way the gradient step is taken in each of these libraries, in the way weights are frozen and unfrozen, and in the way the target network weights are updated. The logic is the same; it's just a difference of which library function to call and what parameters to pass—basically the syntax difference between two libraries.

Listing 8-12. One-Step Update in TensorFlow

```
def one_step_update(agent, target_network, q_optimizer, policy_optimizer,
                    states, actions, rewards, next_states, done_flags,
                    gamma=0.99, polyak=0.995):

    #one step gradient for q-values
    with tf.GradientTape() as tape:
```

```
    loss_q = compute_q_loss(agent, target_network, states, actions,
    rewards, next_states, done_flags,
                gamma, tape)

    gradients = tape.gradient(loss_q, agent.q.trainable_variables)
    q_optimizer.apply_gradients(zip(gradients, agent.q.trainable_
    variables))

#Freeze Q-network
agent.q.trainable=False

#one setep gradient for policy network
with tf.GradientTape() as tape:
    loss_policy = compute_policy_loss(agent, states, tape)
    gradients = tape.gradient(loss_policy, agent.policy.trainable_
    variables)
    policy_optimizer.apply_gradients(zip(gradients, agent.policy.
    trainable_variables))

#UnFreeze Q-network
agent.q.trainable=True

# update target networks with polyak averaging
updated_model_weights = []
for weights, weights_target in zip(agent.get_weights(), target_network.
get_weights()):
    new_weights = polyak*weights_target+(1-polyak)*weights
    updated_model_weights.append(new_weights)
target_network.set_weights(updated_model_weights)
```

DDPG: Main Loop

The final step is the implementation of the DDPG algorithm, which uses the earlier one_step_update function. It creates the optimizers and initializes the environment. It keeps stepping through the environment using the current online policy. Initially, for the first start_steps=10000, it takes a random action to explore the environment, and once enough transitions are collected, it uses the current policy with noise to selection actions. The transitions are added to the ReplayBuffer, dropping the earliest one from

273

buffer if the buffer has reached full capacity. update_after tells the algorithm to start doing a gradient update only after update_after=1000 transitions are collected in the buffer. The code runs the loop multiple times as defined by parameter epoch=5. We have used epoch=5 for demonstration purposes. You may want to run it a lot longer, say, something like 100 epochs or so. That is definitely recommended for the lunar-lander environment. We are giving the listing for only the PyTorch version in Listing 8-13.

Listing 8-13. DDPG Outer Training Loop in PyTorch

```python
def ddpg(env_fn, seed=0,
         steps_per_epoch=4000, epochs=5, replay_size=int(1e6), gamma=0.99,
         polyak=0.995, policy_lr=1e-3, q_lr=1e-3, batch_size=100, start_
         steps=10000,
         update_after=1000, update_every=50, act_noise=0.1, num_test_
         episodes=10,
         max_ep_len=1000):

    torch.manual_seed(seed)
    np.random.seed(seed)

    env, test_env = env_fn(), env_fn()

    ep_rets, ep_lens = [], []

    state_dim = env.observation_space.shape
    act_dim = env.action_space.shape[0]

    act_limit = env.action_space.high[0]

    agent = MLPActorCritic(env.observation_space, env.action_space)
    target_network = deepcopy(agent)

    # Freeze target networks with respect to optimizers (only update via
    polyak averaging)
    for params in target_network.parameters():
        params.requires_grad = False

    # Experience buffer
    replay_buffer = ReplayBuffer(replay_size)

    #optimizers
```

```python
q_optimizer = Adam(agent.q.parameters(), lr=q_lr)
policy_optimizer = Adam(agent.policy.parameters(), lr=policy_lr)

total_steps = steps_per_epoch*epochs
state, ep_ret, ep_len = env.reset(), 0, 0

for t in range(total_steps):
    if t > start_steps:
        action = agent.get_action(state, act_noise)
    else:
        action = env.action_space.sample()

    next_state, reward, done, _ = env.step(action)
    ep_ret += reward
    ep_len += 1

    # Ignore the "done" signal if it comes from hitting the time
    # horizon (that is, when it's an artificial terminal signal
    # that isn't based on the agent's state)
    done = False if ep_len==max_ep_len else done

    # Store experience to replay buffer
    replay_buffer.add(state, action, reward, next_state, done)

    state = next_state

    # End of trajectory handling
    if done or (ep_len == max_ep_len):
        ep_rets.append(ep_ret)
        ep_lens.append(ep_len)
        state, ep_ret, ep_len = env.reset(), 0, 0

    # Update handling
    if t >= update_after and t % update_every == 0:
        for _ in range(update_every):
            states, actions, rewards, next_states, done_flags = replay_
            buffer.sample(batch_size)

            one_step_update(
```

```
                    agent, target_network, q_optimizer, policy_
                    optimizer,
                    states, actions, rewards, next_states, done_flags,
                    gamma, polyak
        )

    # End of epoch handling
    if (t+1) % steps_per_epoch == 0:
        epoch = (t+1) // steps_per_epoch

        avg_ret, avg_len = test_agent(test_env, agent, num_test_
        episodes, max_ep_len)
        print("End of epoch: {:.0f}, Training Average Reward: {:.0f},
        Training Average Length: {:.0f}".format(epoch, np.mean(ep_
        rets), np.mean(ep_lens)))
        print("End of epoch: {:.0f}, Test Average Reward: {:.0f}, Test
        Average Length: {:.0f}".format(epoch, avg_ret, avg_len))
        ep_rets, ep_lens = [], []

return agent
```

The TensorFlow version is pretty similar except for minor differences in which library functions to call and how to pass the parameters. In the TensorFlow version, we have an extra bit of code to initialize the network weights so that we can freeze the target network weights right before we start training. The way we have architected the model, the model is not built until the first step of training, and hence we need to have this extra bit of code in TensorFlow to force the building of the models. We are not giving the code listing for the TensorFlow version.

The rest of the code is to train the agent and then record the performance of the trained agent. We run the algorithm first for the pendulum environment and then for the lunar-lander Gym environment. These code versions are interesting to read, but as they are incidental to our objective of learning about DDPG, we will not dive into the details of these code implementations. However, interested readers may want to check out the relevant library documentations and step through the code.

This completes the code implementation walk-through. We can see that even after five epochs of training, the agent is able to perform very well on the simpler pendulum environment and is able to perform decently well on more complex lunar-lander environment.

Next, we will look at twin delayed DDPG, also known as TD3. It has some other enhancements and tricks to address some of the stability and convergence speed issues seen in DDPG.

Twin Delayed DDPG

Twin delayed DDPG was proposed in 2018 in a paper titled "Addressing Function Approximation Error in Actor-Critic Methods."[4] DDPG suffers from the overestimation bias that we saw in Q-learning in Chapter 4 (in the section "Maximization bias and Double Q learning"). We saw the approach of double DQN in Chapter 6 to address the bias by decoupling the maximizing action and maximum q-value. In the previously mentioned paper, the authors show that DDPG also suffers from the same overestimation bias. They propose a variant of double Q-learning, which addresses this overestimation bias in DDPG. The approach uses the following modifications:

- *Clipped double Q-learning*: TD3 uses two independent Q-functions and takes the minimum of the two while forming targets under Bellman equations, i.e., the targets in step 11 of the DDPG pseudocode in Figure 8-4. This modification is the reason the algorithm is called *twin*.

- *Delayed policy updates*: TD3 updates the policy and target networks less frequently as compared to the Q-function updates. The paper recommends one update to the policy and target networks for every two updates of the Q function. It means carrying out updates in steps 13 and 14 of the DDPG pseudocode in Figure 8-4 once for every two updates of the Q-function in steps 11 and 12. This modification is the reason to call this algorithm *delayed*.

- *Target policy smoothing*: TD3 adds noise to the target action, making it harder for the policy to exploit Q-function estimation errors and control the overestimation bias.

---

[4]https://arxiv.org/pdf/1802.09477.pdf

Target-Policy Smoothing

The action used to calculate the target $y(r, s', d)$ is based on the target networks. In DDPG, we calculated $a'(s') = \mu_{\theta_{targ}}(s')$ in step 11 of Figure 8-4. However, in TD3 we carry out the target policy smoothing by adding a noise to the action. To the deterministic action $\mu_{\theta_{targ}}(s')$, we add a mean zero Gaussian noise with some clip ranges. The action is then further clipped using *tanh* and multiplied with max_action_range to make sure that action values fit within the range of accepted action values.

$$a'(s') = \text{clip}\left(\mu_{\theta_{targ}}(s') + \text{clip}(\epsilon, -c, c), a_{Low}, a_{High}\right), \quad \epsilon \sim \mathcal{N}(0, \sigma) \tag{8.8}$$

Q-Loss (Critic)

We use two independent Q-functions and learn them from a common target that uses the minimum of the two independent Q-functions. Expressing the target mathematically looks like this:

$$y(r, s', d) = r + \gamma(1-d)\min_{i=1,2} Q_{\phi_{targ,i}}(s', a'(s')) \tag{8.9}$$

We are first using equation (8.8) to find the noisy target action $a'(s')$. This in turn is used to calculate the target q-values: the q-value of the first and second Q target networks: $Q_{\phi_{targ,1}}(s', a'(s'))$ and $Q_{\phi_{targ,2}}(s', a'(s'))$.

The common target in (8.9) is used next to find the losses for both the Q-networks, as shown here:

$$Q_{Loss,1} = \frac{1}{B} \sum_{(s,a,r,s',d) \in B} \left(Q_{\phi_1}(s,a) - y(r,s',d)\right)^2$$

and here:

$$Q_{Loss,2} = \frac{1}{B} \sum_{(s,a,r,s',d) \in B} \left(Q_{\phi_2}(s,a) - y(r,s',d)\right)^2 \tag{8.10}$$

The losses are added together and then minimized independently to train the Q_{ϕ_1} and Q_{ϕ_2} networks (i.e., two online critic networks).

$$Q_{Loss} = \sum_{i=1,2} Q_{Loss,i} \qquad (8.11)$$

Policy Loss (Actor)

The policy loss calculation remains unchanged, the same as what was used in DDPG.

$$Policy_{Loss} = -\frac{1}{B} \sum_{s \in B} Q_{\phi_1}\left(s, \mu_\phi\left(s, \mu_\theta(s)\right)\right) \qquad (8.12)$$

Please note that we use only Q_{ϕ_1} in the equation. Like DDPG, please also note the -ve sign. We need to do gradient ascent, but PyTorch and TensorFlow do gradient descent. We convert the ascent to descent using a -ve sign.

Delayed Update

We update the online policy and agent network weights in a delayed manner, i.e., one update for every two update of the online Q networks Q_{ϕ_1} and Q_{ϕ_2}.

Pseudocode and Implementation

At this point we are ready to give the complete pseudocode. Please refer to Figure 8-7.

TWIN DELAYED DDPG

1. Input initial policy parameters θ, Q-function paramters ϕ_1 and ϕ_2, and empty replay buffer D.

2. Set the target parameters equal to the online parameters $\theta_{targ} \leftarrow \theta$, $\phi_{targ,1} \leftarrow \phi_1$, and $\phi_{targ,2} \leftarrow \phi_2$.

3. **Repeat**.

4.   Observe state s and select the action.

$$a = clip\left(\mu_\theta(s) + \epsilon, a_{Low}, a_{High}\right), \text{where } \epsilon \sim N$$

5.   Execute a in the environment and observe next state s', reward r, and done signal d.

6.   Store (s, a, r, s', d) in the replay buffer D.

7.   If s' is terminal state, reset the environment.

8.   If it's time to update, **then**:

9.   For j in range (as many updates as required):

10.   Sample a batch $B = \{(s, a, r, s', d)\}$ from replay buffer D.

11.   Compute the target actions.

$$a'(s') = clip\left(\mu_{\theta_{targ}}(s') + clip(\epsilon, -c, c), a_{Low}, a_{High}\right), \quad \epsilon \sim \mathcal{N}(0, \sigma)$$

12.   Compute the targets.

$$y(r, s', d) = r + \gamma(1 - d)\min_{i=1,2} Q_{\phi_{targ,i}}\left(s', a'(s')\right)$$

13.   Update the Q function with the one-step gradient descent on ϕ.

$$\nabla_\phi \frac{1}{B} \sum_{(s,a,r,s',d)\in B} \left(Q_{\phi_i}(s,a) - y(r,s',d)\right)^2, \quad \text{for } i = 1,2$$

14.   If j mod policy_update == 0:

15.   Update the policy with a one-step gradient ascent on θ:

$$\nabla_\theta \frac{1}{|B|} \sum_{s\in B} Q_{\phi_i}\left(s, \mu_\theta(s)\right)$$

16.   Update the target networks using *polyak* averaging.

$$\phi_{targ} \leftarrow \rho\phi_{targ} + (1 - \rho)\phi$$

$$\theta_{targ} \leftarrow \rho\theta_{targ} + (1 - \rho)\theta$$

Figure 8-7. *Twin delayed DDPG algorithm*

Code Implementation

Let's now walk through the code implementation. Like DDPG we will run the algorithm on pendulum and lunar lander. Most of the code is similar to that of DDPG except for the three modifications that we talked about earlier. Accordingly, we will only walk through just the highlights of these changes, both in the PyTorch and TensorFlow versions. You can find the complete code for the PyTorch version in the file listing8_2_td3_pytorch. ipynb and the TensorFlow version in listing8_2_td3_tensorflow.ipynb.

Combined Model-Actor Critic Implementation

We first look at the agent networks. The individual Q-network (critic) MLPQFunction and policy-network (actor) MLPActor are the same as before. However, the agent where we combine the actor and critic together, i.e., MLPActorCritic, sees a minor change. We now have two Q-networks in line with the "twin" part of TD3. Listing 8-14 contains the code for MLPActorCritic, both in PyTorch and TensorFlow.

Listing 8-14. MPLActorCritic in PyTorch and TensorFlow

```
#################PyTorch#################
class MLPActorCritic(nn.Module):
    def __init__(self, observation_space, action_space):
        super().__init__()
        self.state_dim = observation_space.shape[0]
        self.act_dim = action_space.shape[0]
        self.act_limit = action_space.high[0]

        #build Q and policy functions
        self.q = MLPQFunction(self.state_dim, self.act_dim)
        self.policy = MLPActor(self.state_dim, self.act_dim, self.act_limit)

    def act(self, state):
        with torch.no_grad():
            return self.policy(state).numpy()

    def get_action(self, s, noise_scale):
        a = self.act(torch.as_tensor(s, dtype=torch.float32))
        a += noise_scale * np.random.randn(self.act_dim)
        return np.clip(a, -self.act_limit, self.act_limit)
```

```
################# TensorFlow #################
class MLPActorCritic(tf.keras.Model):
    def __init__(self, observation_space, action_space):
        super().__init__()
        self.state_dim = observation_space.shape[0]
        self.act_dim = action_space.shape[0]
        self.act_limit = action_space.high[0]

        #build Q and policy functions
        self.q1 = MLPQFunction(self.state_dim, self.act_dim)
        self.q2 = MLPQFunction(self.state_dim, self.act_dim)
        self.policy = MLPActor(self.state_dim, self.act_dim, self.act_limit)

    def act(self, state):
        return self.policy(state).numpy()

    def get_action(self, s, noise_scale):
        a = self.act(s.reshape(1,-1).astype("float32")).reshape(-1)
        a += noise_scale * np.random.randn(self.act_dim)
        return np.clip(a, -self.act_limit, self.act_limit)
```

Q-Loss Implementation

The replay buffer remains the same. The next change is in the way Q-loss is calculated. We implement target policy smoothing and clipped double Q-learning as per equations (8.8) to (8.11). Listing 8-15 contains the code for compute_q_loss in PyTorch. This time we are not explicitly listing the code for TensorFlow, which can be explored further in file listing8_2_td3_tensorflow.ipynb.

Listing 8-15. Q-Loss in PyTorch

```
def compute_q_loss(agent, target_network, states, actions, rewards, next_
states, done_flags,
                    gamma, target_noise, noise_clip, act_limit, tape):

    # convert numpy array to proper data types
    states = states.astype('float32')
    actions = actions.astype('float32')
    rewards = rewards.astype('float32')
```

```
next_states = next_states.astype('float32')
done_flags = done_flags.astype('float32')

# get q-values for all actions in current states
# use agent network
q1 = agent.q1(states, actions)
q2 = agent.q2(states, actions)

# Bellman backup for Q function
with tape.stop_recording():

    action_target = target_network.policy(next_states)

    # Target policy smoothing
    epsilon = tf.random.normal(action_target.shape) * target_noise
    epsilon = tf.clip_by_value(epsilon, -noise_clip, noise_clip)
    action_target = action_target + epsilon
    action_target = tf.clip_by_value(action_target, -act_limit, act_limit)

    q1_target = target_network.q1(next_states, action_target)
    q2_target = target_network.q2(next_states, action_target)
    q_target = tf.minimum(q1_target, q2_target)
    target = rewards + gamma * (1 - done_flags) * q_target

# MSE loss against Bellman backup
loss_q1 = tf.reduce_mean((q1 - target)**2)
loss_q2 = tf.reduce_mean((q2 - target)**2)
loss_q = loss_q1 + loss_q2

return loss_q
```

Policy-Loss Implementation

Policy loss calculation remains the same except that we use only one of the Q-networks, which is actually the first one with weights ϕ_1.

One-Step Update Implementation

The implementation of the one_step_update function is also pretty similar except for the fact that we need to carry out the gradient of q-loss with respect to the combined network weights of the Q1 and Q2 networks passed into the function as q_params. Further, we need to freeze and unfreeze the network weights for both q1 and q2.

Listing 8-16 contains the implementation of one_step_update in PyTorch, and Listing 8-17 contains the code in TensorFlow. Please pay special attention to how the weights are frozen and unfrozen and how gradient updates are calculated as well as how the weights are updated to the target network. These operations have some nuances between PyTorch code and TensorFlow code.

Listing 8-16. One-Step Update in PyTorch

```
def one_step_update(agent, target_network, q_params, q_optimizer, policy_
optimizer,
                    states, actions, rewards, next_states, done_flags,
                    gamma, polyak, target_noise, noise_clip, act_limit,
                    policy_delay, timer):

    #one step gradient for q-values
    q_optimizer.zero_grad()
    loss_q = compute_q_loss(agent, target_network, states, actions,
    rewards, next_states, done_flags,
                    gamma, target_noise, noise_clip, act_limit)
    loss_q.backward()
    q_optimizer.step()

    # Update policy and target networks after policy_delay updates of
    Q-networks
    if timer % policy_delay == 0:
        #Freeze Q-network
        for params in q_params:
            params.requires_grad = False

        #one setep gradient for policy network
        policy_optimizer.zero_grad()
        loss_policy = compute_policy_loss(agent, states)
        loss_policy.backward()
        policy_optimizer.step()

        #UnFreeze Q-network
```

```
for params in q_params:
    params.requires_grad = True

# update target networks with polyak averaging
with torch.no_grad():
    for params, params_target in zip(agent.parameters(),
    target_network.parameters()):
        params_target.data.mul_(polyak)
        params_target.data.add_((1-polyak)*params.data)
```

Listing 8-17 shows the TensorFlow version in the one-step update.

Listing 8-17. One-Step Update in TensorFlow

```
def one_step_update(agent, target_network, q_params, q_optimizer,
policy_optimizer,
                    states, actions, rewards, next_states, done_flags,
                    gamma, polyak, target_noise, noise_clip, act_limit,
                    policy_delay, timer):

    #one step gradient for q-values
    with tf.GradientTape() as tape:
        loss_q = compute_q_loss(agent, target_network, states, actions,
        rewards, next_states, done_flags,
                    gamma, target_noise, noise_clip, act_limit, tape)

        gradients = tape.gradient(loss_q, q_params)
        q_optimizer.apply_gradients(zip(gradients, q_params))

    # Update policy and target networks after policy_delay updates of
    Q-networks
    if timer % policy_delay == 0:
        #Freeze Q-network
        agent.q1.trainable=False
        agent.q2.trainable=False

        #one setep gradient for policy network
        with tf.GradientTape() as tape:
            loss_policy = compute_policy_loss(agent, states, tape)
```

```
gradients = tape.gradient(loss_policy, agent.policy.trainable_
variables)
policy_optimizer.apply_gradients(zip(gradients, agent.policy.
trainable_variables))
```

```
#UnFreeze Q-network
agent.q1.trainable=True
agent.q2.trainable=True
```

```
# update target networks with polyak averaging
updated_model_weights = []
for weights, weights_target in zip(agent.get_weights(), target_
network.get_weights()):
    new_weights = polyak*weights_target+(1-polyak)*weights
    updated_model_weights.append(new_weights)
target_network.set_weights(updated_model_weights)
```

TD3 Main Loop

The next change is the frequency of updates. Unlike DDPG, in TD3 we update the online policy and target weights once for every two updates of Q-networks. It is a minor change to the DDPG code, and hence we are not listing it here.

We now run TD3 first for the pendulum environment and then for the lunar-lander Gym environment. We can see that after five episodes, the pendulum gets well balanced in the upright condition. The training quality of the lunar lander, just like DDPG, is kind of mediocre. The lunar-lander environment is a complex one, and hence we need to run the training for a higher number of epochs, like 50 or 100.

We may also not see any appreciable difference in the quality of learning between DDPG and TD3. However, if we could run it on more complex environments, we would see the relative higher performance of TD3 over DDPG. Interested readers can refer to the original paper of TD3 to check out the benchmark studies that the authors of TD3 did with respect to other algorithms.

Soon we will look at our last algorithm in this chapter, an algorithm called *soft actor critic*. Before we do, we will take a short detour to understand something called the *reparameterization trick* that SAC uses.

Reparameterization Trick

The reparameterization trick is a change in the variable approach that is used in variational auto-encoders (VAEs). There it is needed to propagate gradients through nodes, which are stochastic. Reparameterization is also used to bring down the variance of gradient estimates. And this second reason is the one we will explore here. This deep dive follows a blog post by Goker Erdogan[5] with additional analytical derivations and explanations.

Suppose we have a random variable x, which follows a normal distribution. Let the distribution be parameterized by θ as follows:

$$x \sim p_\theta(x) = N(\theta,1) = \frac{1}{\sqrt{2\pi}} e^{-\frac{1}{2}(x-\theta)^2} \tag{8.13}$$

We draw samples from it and then use those samples to find the minimum of the following:

$$J(\theta) = E_{x \sim p_\theta(x)}\left[x^2\right]$$

We do so using gradient descent. Our focus is on finding two different approaches for determining the estimate of the derivate/gradient $\nabla_\theta J(\theta)$.

Score/Reinforce Way

First we will follow the log trick, which is what we did while talking about REINFORCE using policy gradient. We saw that it has high variance, and that's what we hope to demonstrate for a simple example distribution as shown earlier.

We take the derivative of $J(\theta)$ with respect to θ.

$$\nabla_\theta J(\theta)$$

$$= \nabla_\theta E_{x \sim p_\theta(x)}\left[x^2\right]$$

$$= \nabla_\theta \int p_\theta(x) x^2 dx$$

$$= \int \nabla_\theta p_\theta(x) x^2 dx$$

---

[5]http://gokererdogan.github.io/2016/07/01/reparameterization-trick/

$$= \int \frac{p_\theta(x)}{p_\theta(x)} \nabla_\theta p_\theta(x) x^2 dx$$

$$= \int p_\theta(x) \frac{\nabla_\theta p_\theta(x)}{p_\theta(x)} x^2 dx$$

$$= \int p_\theta(x) \nabla_\theta log \, p_\theta(x) x^2 dx$$

$$= E_{x \sim p_\theta(x)} \left[\nabla_\theta log \, p_\theta(x) x^2 \right]$$

Next, we use Monte Carlo to form an estimate of $\nabla_\theta J(\theta)$ using samples.

$$\widehat{\nabla_\theta J(\theta)} = \frac{1}{N} \sum_{i=1}^{N} \nabla_\theta log \, p_\theta(x_i) x_i^2$$

Substituting the expression for $p_\theta(x)$ from earlier and taking a log followed by gradient wrt θ, we get the following:

$$\widehat{\nabla_\theta J(\theta)} = \frac{1}{N} \sum_{i=1}^{N} (x_i - \theta) x_i^2 \tag{8.14}$$

Reparameterization Trick and Pathwise Derivatives

The second approach is that of the reparameterization trick. We will redefine x as a composition of a constant and a normal distribution that has no parameter θ. Let x be defined as follows:

$$x = \theta + \epsilon \quad \text{where} \quad \epsilon \sim N(0,1)$$

We can see that the previous reparameterization leaves the distribution for x unchanged.

$$p_\theta(x) = N(\theta,1)$$

Let's calculate $\nabla_\theta J(\theta) = \nabla_\theta E_{x \sim p_\theta(x)} \left[x^2 \right]$.

$$\nabla_\theta J(\theta)$$

$$= \nabla_\theta E_{x \sim p_\theta(x)} \left[x^2 \right]$$

$$= \nabla_\theta E_{\epsilon \sim N(0,1)}\left[\left(\theta + \epsilon\right)^2\right]$$

As the expectation does not depend on θ, we can move the gradient inside without running into the `log` issue (i.e. finding log inside the derivate) shown in the previous method.

$$= \nabla_\theta \int p(\epsilon)(\theta + \epsilon)^2 \, d\epsilon$$

$$= \int p(\epsilon) \nabla_\theta (\theta + \epsilon)^2 \, d\epsilon$$

$$= \int p(\epsilon) 2(\theta + \epsilon) d\epsilon$$

$$= E_{\epsilon \sim N(0,1)}\left[2(\theta + \epsilon)\right]$$

Next, we convert the expectation to the MC estimate to get the following:

$$\widehat{\nabla_\theta J(\theta)} = \frac{1}{N}\sum_{i=1}^{N} 2(\theta + \epsilon_i) \tag{8.15}$$

Experiment

We use equations (8.14) and (8.15) to calculate the mean and variance of the estimates using two approaches. We do so using different values of N to calculate (8.14) and (8.15), and we repeat the experiment 10,000 times for each value of N to calculate the mean and variance of the gradient estimates as given in (8.14) and (8.15). Our experiment will show that the mean is the same for both equations. In other words, they estimate the same value, but the variance of the estimate in (8.14) is higher than that in (8.15) by almost one order of magnitude. It's higher by a factor of 21.75 in our case.

Let's freeze this:

$$\theta = 2$$

- We generate samples for $x \sim N(\theta, 1)$ and use these samples in equation (8.14) to calculate the REINFORCE estimate of $\nabla_\theta J(\theta)$.

- We generate samples for $\epsilon \sim N(0, 1)$ and use these samples in equation (8.15) to calculate the reparameterized estimate of $\nabla_\theta J(\theta)$.

Please see the details of the experiment and code in `listing8_3_reparameterization.ipynb`. In the notebook, we also calculate the analytical solution to derive the results, as shown next.

For the REINFORCE gradient using (8.14), the gradient has the following:

$$mean = 4$$

$$variance = \frac{87}{N}$$

For the REPARAMETERIZED gradient using (8.15), the gradient has the following:

$$mean = 4$$

$$variance = \frac{4}{N}$$

We can see that the gradient estimate has the same mean under both approaches. However, the variance in the reparametrized approach is a lot smaller, by one order of magnitude. This is exactly what our code run confirms.

To summarize, suppose we have a policy network that takes state s as input, and the network is parameterized by θ. The policy network produces the mean and variance of the policy, i.e., a stochastic policy with normal distribution whose mean and variance are the outputs of the network, as shown in Figure 8-8.

Continuous actions:
Output is parameters of a continuous
distribution e.g. model outputs
mean and additionally variance
of the Normal distribution

Figure 8-8. *Stochastic policy network*

We define the action a as follows:

$$a \sim N\left(\mu_\theta(s), \sigma_\theta^2(s)\right) \tag{8.16}$$

We reparametrize action a to decompose the deterministic and stochastic part out such that the stochastic part does not depend on the network parameters θ.

$$a = \mu_\theta(s) + \sigma_\theta^2(s).\varepsilon$$

$$\text{where: } \epsilon \sim N(0,1) \tag{8.17}$$

The reparameterization allows us to calculate the policy gradients that have lower variance as compared to using a nonparametrized approach. In addition, reparameterization allows us an alternative way to flow the gradient back through the network by separating out the stochastic part into a nonparameterized part. We will use this approach in the soft actor-critic algorithm.

Entropy Explained

Just one more thing before we start digging into the details of SAC: let's revisit entropy. We talked about entropy as a regularizer as part of the REINFORCE code walk-through in the previous chapter. We will be doing something similar. Let's understand what entropy is.

Suppose we have a random variable x following some distribution $P(x)$. The entropy of the x is defined as follows:

$$H(P) = \underset{x \sim P}{E}\left[-logP(x)\right] \tag{8.18}$$

Suppose we have a coin with $P(H) = \rho$ and $P(T) = 1 - \rho$. We calculate the entropy H for different values of $\rho \, \varepsilon \, (0, 1)$.

$$H(x) = -\left[\rho \, log\rho + (1-\rho)\log(1-\rho)\right]$$

We can plot the curve of $H(x)$ versus ρ as shown in Figure 8-9.

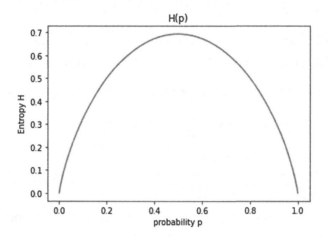

Figure 8-9. *Entropy of a Bernoulli distribution as a function of p, which is the probabililty of getting 1 in a trial*

We can see that entropy H is the maximum for $\rho = 0.5$, i.e., when we have maximum uncertainty between getting a 1 or a 0. In other words, by maximizing the entropy we are ensuring that the stochastic action policy has a broad distribution and does not collapse to a sharp peak too early. A sharp peak will reduce the exploration.

Soft Actor Critic

The soft actor critic came about around the same time as TD3. Like DDPG and TD3, SAC also uses an actor-critic construct with off-policy learning for continuous controls. However, unlike DDPG and TD3, SAC learns a stochastic policy. Hence, SAC forms a bridge between the deterministic policy algorithms like DDPG and TD3 with the stochastic policy optimization. The algorithm was introduced in a 2018 paper titled "Soft Actor-Critic: Off-Policy Maximum Entropy Deep Reinforcement Learning with a Stochastic Actor."[6]

---

[6]https://arxiv.org/abs/1801.01290 and https://arxiv.org/pdf/1812.05905.pdf

It uses the clipped double-Q trick like TD3, and due to its learning stochastic policy, it indirectly benefits from the target policy smoothing without explicit need of adding noise to the target policy.

A core feature of SAC is use of entropy as part of maximization. To quote the authors of the paper:

"In this framework, the actor aims to simultaneously maximize expected return and entropy; that is, to succeed at the task while acting as randomly as possible."

SAC vs. TD3

This is what is similar in both:

- Both use mean squared Bellman error (MSBE) minimization toward a common target.

- A common target is calculated using target Q networks that are obtained using polyack averaging.

- Both use clipped double Q, which consists of a minimum of two q-values to avoid overestimation.

This is what is different:

- SAC uses entropy regularization, which is absent in TD3.

- The TD3 target policy is used to calculate the next-state actions, while in SAC we use the current policy to get actions for the next states.

- In TD3, the target policy uses smoothing by adding random noise to actions. However, in SAC the policy learned is a stochastic one that provides a smoothing effect without any explicit noise addition.

Q-Loss with Entropy-Regularization

Entropy measures randomness in the distribution. The higher the entropy, the flatter the distribution. A sharp peaked policy has all its probability centered around that peak, and hence it will have low entropy. With entropy regularization, the policy is trained to maximize a trade-off between the expected return and entropy with α controlling the trade-off. The policy is trained to maximize a trade-off between the expected return and entropy, a measure of randomness in the policy.

$$\pi^* = \arg\max_{\pi} \; E_{\tau \sim \pi} \left[\sum_{t=0}^{\infty} \gamma^t \left(R(s_t,a_t,s_{t+1}) + \alpha H\left(\pi(\cdot|s_t)\right) \right) \right] \tag{8.19}$$

In this setting, V^π is changed to include the entropy from every time step.

$$V^\pi(s) = E_{\tau \sim \pi} \left[\sum_{t=0}^{\infty} \gamma^t \left(R(s_t,a_t,s_{t+1}) + \alpha H\left(\pi(\cdot|s_t)\right) \right) \Big| s_0 = s \right] \tag{8.20}$$

In addition, Q^π is changed to include the entropy bonuses from every timestep except the first.

$$Q^\pi(s,a) = E_{\tau \sim \pi} \left[\sum_{t=0}^{\infty} \gamma^t R(s_t,a_t,s_{t+1}) + \alpha \sum_{t=1}^{\infty} \gamma^t H\left(\pi(\cdot|s_t)\right) \Big| s_0 = s, a_0 = a \right] \tag{8.21}$$

With these definitions, V^π and Q^π are connected by the following:

$$V^\pi(s) = E_{a \sim \pi} \left[Q^\pi(s,a) + \alpha H\left(\pi(\cdot|s)\right) \right] \tag{8.22}$$

The Bellman equation for Q^π is as follows:

$$Q^\pi(s,a) = E_{s' \sim P, a' \sim \pi} \left[R(s,a,s') + \gamma \left(Q^\pi(s',a') + \alpha H\left(\pi(\cdot|s')\right) \right) \right]$$

$$= E_{s' \sim P} \left[R(s,a,s') + \gamma V^\pi(s') \right] \tag{8.23}$$

The right side is an expectation that we convert into a sample estimate.

$$Q^\pi(s,a) \approx r + \gamma \left(Q^\pi(s',\tilde{a}') - \alpha \log \pi(\tilde{a}'|s') \right), \quad \tilde{a}' \sim \pi(\cdot|s') \tag{8.24}$$

Above, (s, a, r, s') come from the replay buffer, and $\tilde{a}'$ comes from sampling the online/agent policy. *In SAC, we do not use target network policy at all.*

Like TD3, SAC uses clipped double Q and minimizes the mean squared Bellman error (MSBE). Putting it all together, the loss functions for the Q-networks in SAC are as follows:

$$L(\phi_i, D) = E_{(s,a,r,s',d) \sim D} \left[\left(Q_{\phi_i}(s,a) - y(r,s',d) \right)^2 \right], \quad i = 1,2 \tag{8.25}$$

where the target is given by the following:

$$y(r,s',d) = r + \gamma(1-d)\left(\min_{i=1,2} Q_{\phi_{\text{targ},i}}\left(s',\widetilde{a}'\right) - \alpha\log\pi_\theta\left(\widetilde{a}'|s'\right)\right), \ \widetilde{a}' \sim \pi_\theta\left(\cdot|s'\right) \tag{8.26}$$

We convert expectations to sample averages.

$$L(\phi_i,\mathcal{D}) = \frac{1}{|B|}\sum_{(s,a,r,s',d)\in B}\left(Q_{\phi_i}(s,a) - y(r,s',d)\right)^2, \quad \text{for } i=1,2 \tag{8.27}$$

The final Q-loss we will minimize is as follows:

$$Q_{Loss} = L(\phi_1,\mathcal{D}) + L(\phi_2,\mathcal{D}) \tag{8.28}$$

Policy Loss with Reparameterization Trick

The policy should choose actions to maximize the expected future return and future entropy, i.e., $V^\pi(s)$.

$$V^\pi(s) = \mathop{E}_{a\sim\pi}\left[Q^\pi(s,a) + \alpha H\left(\pi(\cdot|s)\right)\right]$$

We rewrite this as follows:

$$V^\pi(s) = \mathop{E}_{a\sim\pi}\left[Q^\pi(s,a) - \alpha\log\pi(a|s)\right] \tag{8.29}$$

The authors of the paper use reparameterization along with the squashed Gaussian policy.

$$\widetilde{a}_\theta(s,\xi) = \tanh\left(\mu_\theta(s) + \sigma_\theta(s)\odot\xi\right), \ \xi\sim\mathcal{N}(0,I) \tag{8.30}$$

Combining the previous two equations (8.29) and (8.30) and also noting that our policy network is parameterized by θ, the policy network weights, we get the following:

$$\mathop{E}_{a\sim\pi_\theta}\left[Q^{\pi_\theta}(s,a) - \alpha\log\pi_\theta(a|s)\right] = \mathop{E}_{\xi\sim\mathcal{N}}\left[Q^{\pi_\theta}\left(s,\widetilde{a}_\theta(s,\xi)\right) - \alpha\log\pi_\theta\left(\widetilde{a}_\theta(s,\xi)|s\right)\right] \tag{8.31}$$

Next, we substitute the function approximator for Q, taking the minimum of the two Q-functions.

$$Q^{\pi_\theta}\left(s,\widetilde{a}_\theta(s,\xi)\right) = \min_{i=1,2} Q_{\phi_i}\left(s,\widetilde{a}_\theta(s,\xi)\right) \tag{8.32}$$

The policy objective is accordingly transformed to the following:

$$\max_{\theta} \; E_{\substack{s \sim \mathcal{D} \\ \xi \sim \mathcal{N}}} \left[\min_{i=1,2} Q_{\phi_i}\left(s, \widetilde{a}_{\theta}(s, \xi)\right) - \alpha \log \pi_{\theta}\left(\widetilde{a}_{\theta}(s, \xi) | s\right) \right] \qquad (8.33)$$

Like before, we use minimizers in PyTorch/TensorFlow. Accordingly, we introduce a -ve sign to convert maximization to a loss minimization.

$$Policy_{Loss} = - E_{\substack{s \sim \mathcal{D} \\ \xi \sim \mathcal{N}}} \left[\min_{i=1,2} Q_{\phi_i}\left(s, \widetilde{a}_{\theta}(s, \xi)\right) - \alpha \log \pi_{\theta}\left(\widetilde{a}_{\theta}(s, \xi) | s\right) \right] \qquad (8.34)$$

We also convert the expectation to an estimate using samples to get the following:

$$Policy_{Loss} = -\frac{1}{|B|} \sum_{s \in B} \left(\min_{i=1,2} Q_{\phi_i}\left(s, \widetilde{a}_{\theta}(s)\right) - \alpha \log \pi_{\theta}\left(\widetilde{a}_{\theta}(s) | s\right) \right) \qquad (8.35)$$

Pseudocode and Implementation

At this point we are ready to give the complete pseudocode. Please refer to Figure 8-10.

SOFT ACTOR CRITIC

1. Input initial policy parameters θ, Q-function parameters ϕ_1 and ϕ_2, and empty replay buffer D.

2. Set the target parameters equal to the online parameters $\phi_{targ,1} \leftarrow \phi_1$ and $\phi_{targ,2} \leftarrow \phi_2$.

3. **Repeat**

4. Observe state s and select action $a \sim \pi_\theta(\cdot|s)$.

5. Execute action a in the environment and observe next state s', reward r, and done signal d.

6. Store (s, a, r, s', d) in the replay buffer D.

7. if s' is terminal state, reset the environment.

8. If it's time to update, **then**:

9.   For j in range (as many updates as required):

10.   Sample a batch $B = \{(s, a, r, s', d)\}$ from replay buffer D.

11.   Compute target for Q functions:

$$y(r,s',d) = r + \gamma(1-d)\left(\min_{i=1,2} Q_{\phi_{targ,i}}\left(s',\widetilde{a}'\right) - \alpha\log\pi_\theta\left(\widetilde{a}'|s'\right)\right)$$

$$\widetilde{a}' \sim \pi_\theta\left(\cdot|s'\right)$$

12.   Update the Q function with one-step gradient descent on ϕ.

$$\nabla_{\phi_i}\frac{1}{|B|}\sum_{(s,a,r,s',d)\in B}\left(Q_{\phi_i}(s,a) - y(r,s',d)\right)^2, \quad \text{for } i = 1,2$$

13.   Update policy by one step of gradient ascent using:

$$\nabla_\theta\frac{1}{|B|}\sum_{s\in B}\left(\min_{i=1,2} Q_{\phi_i}\left(s,\widetilde{a}_\theta(s)\right) - \alpha\log\pi_\theta\left(\widetilde{a}_\theta(s)|s\right)\right)$$

where $\widetilde{a}_\theta(s)$ is a sample from $\pi_\theta(\cdot|s)$, which is differentiable with regard to θ via the reparameterization trick.

14.   Update the target networks using polyak averaging.

$$\phi_{targ,i} \leftarrow \rho\phi_{targ,i} + (1-\rho)\phi_i, \quad \text{for } i = 1,2$$

Figure 8-10. *Soft actor critic algorithm*

Code Implementation

With all the mathematical derivations and pseudocode, it is time to dive into the implementation in PyTorch and TensorFlow. The implementation using PyTorch is in file `listing_8_4_sac_pytorch.ipynb`. Like before, we train the agent using SAC on the pendulum and lunar-lander environments. The TensorFlow 2.0 implementation is in file `listing_8_4_sac_tensorflow.ipynb`.

Policy Network-Actor Implementation

We first look at the actor network. This time, the actor implementation takes the state as input, which is the same as before. However, the output has two components.

- Either squashed (i.e., passing the action value through tanh) deterministic action a, which is $\mu_\theta(s)$, or a sample action a from the distribution $N\big(\mu_\theta(s), \sigma_\theta^2(s)\big)$. The sampling uses the reparameterization trick, and PyTorch implements this for you as `distribution.rsample()`. You can read about it at `https://pytorch.org/docs/stable/distributions.html` under the topic "Pathwise derivative."

- The second output is the log probability that we will need for calculating entropy inside the Q-loss as per equation (8.26). Since we are using squashed/tanh transformation, the log probability needs to apply a change of variables for random distribution using the following:

$$f_Y(y) = f_X\big(g^{-1}(y)\big)\left|\frac{d}{dy}\big(g^{-1}(y)\big)\right|$$

The code uses some tricks to calculate a numerically stable version. You can find more details in the original paper.

Listing 8-18 lists the code for `SquashedGaussianMLPActor` as discussed earlier. The neural network continues to be the same as before: two hidden layers of size 256 units with ReLU activations.

Listing 8-18. SquashedGaussianMLPActor in PyTorch

```python
LOG_STD_MAX = 2
LOG_STD_MIN = -20

class SquashedGaussianMLPActor(nn.Module):
    def __init__(self, state_dim, act_dim, act_limit):
        super().__init__()
        self.act_limit = act_limit
        self.fc1 = nn.Linear(state_dim, 256)
        self.fc2 = nn.Linear(256, 256)
        self.mu_layer = nn.Linear(256, act_dim)
        self.log_std_layer = nn.Linear(256, act_dim)
        self.act_limit = act_limit

    def forward(self, s, deterministic=False, with_logprob=True):
        x = self.fc1(s)
        x = F.relu(x)
        x = self.fc2(x)
        x = F.relu(x)
        mu = self.mu_layer(x)
        log_std = self.log_std_layer(x)
        log_std = torch.clamp(log_std, LOG_STD_MIN, LOG_STD_MAX)
        std = torch.exp(log_std)

        # Pre-squash distribution and sample
        pi_distribution = Normal(mu, std)
        if deterministic:
            # Only used for evaluating policy at test time.
            pi_action = mu
        else:
            pi_action = pi_distribution.rsample()

        if with_logprob:
            # Compute logprob from Gaussian, and then apply correction for
            Tanh squashing.
            # NOTE: The correction formula is a little bit magic. To get an
            understanding
```

```
            # of where it comes from, check out the original SAC paper
            (arXiv 1801.01290)
            # and look in appendix C. This is a more numerically-stable
            equivalent to Eq 21.
            # Try deriving it yourself as a (very difficult) exercise. :)
            logp_pi = pi_distribution.log_prob(pi_action).sum(axis=-1)
            logp_pi -= (2*(np.log(2) - pi_action - F.softplus(-2*pi_
            action))).sum(axis=1)
        else:
            logp_pi = None

        pi_action = torch.tanh(pi_action)
        pi_action = self.act_limit * pi_action

        return pi_action, logp_pi
```

Listing 8-19 shows the TensorFlow version. For reparameterization, we sample it explicating using the following code line:

```
pi = mu + tf.random.normal(tf.shape(mu)) * std
```

The core TensorFlow package does not have functions to calculate the log likelihood that we need for entropy. We implement our own small function `gaussian_likelihood` to do it. An alternative to all this would have been to use the TensorFlow distributions package: `tfp.distributions.Distribution`. The rest of the implementation of the actor is similar to what we saw in PyTorch.

Listing 8-19. SquashedGaussianMLPActor in TensorFlow

```
LOG_STD_MAX = 2
LOG_STD_MIN = -20

EPS = 1e-8

def gaussian_likelihood(x, mu, log_std):
    pre_sum = -0.5 * (((x-mu)/(tf.exp(log_std)+EPS))**2 + 2*log_std +
    np.log(2*np.pi))
    return tf.reduce_sum(pre_sum, axis=1)

def apply_squashing_func(mu, pi, logp_pi):
```

```python
# Adjustment to log prob
# NOTE: This formula is a little bit magic. To get an understanding of where it
# comes from, check out the original SAC paper (arXiv 1801.01290) and look in
# appendix C. This is a more numerically-stable equivalent to Eq 21.
# Try deriving it yourself as a (very difficult) exercise. :)
logp_pi -= tf.reduce_sum(2*(np.log(2) - pi - tf.nn.softplus(-2*pi)), axis=1)

# Squash those unbounded actions!
mu = tf.tanh(mu)
pi = tf.tanh(pi)
return mu, pi, logp_pi

class SquashedGaussianMLPActor(tf.keras.Model):
    def __init__(self, state_dim, act_dim, act_limit):
        super().__init__()
        self.act_limit = act_limit
        self.fc1 = layers.Dense(256, activation="relu")
        self.fc2 = layers.Dense(256, activation="relu")
        self.mu_layer = layers.Dense(act_dim)
        self.log_std_layer = layers.Dense(act_dim)
        self.act_limit = act_limit

    def call(self, s):
        x = self.fc1(s)
        x = self.fc2(x)
        mu = self.mu_layer(x)
        log_std = self.log_std_layer(x)
        log_std = tf.clip_by_value(log_std, LOG_STD_MIN, LOG_STD_MAX)
        std = tf.exp(log_std)

        pi = mu + tf.random.normal(tf.shape(mu)) * std
        logp_pi = gaussian_likelihood(pi, mu, log_std)
        mu, pi, logp_pi = apply_squashing_func(mu, pi, logp_pi)
```

```
mu *= self.act_limit
pi *= self.act_limit

return mu, pi, logp_pi
```

Q-Network, Combined Model, and Experience Replay

The Q-function network MLPQFunction, which combines the actor and critic together into an agent in class MLPActorCritic, and ReplayBuffer implementations are the same, or at least pretty similar. Accordingly, we do not list these parts of the code here.

Q-Loss and Policy-Loss Implementation

Next we look at compute_q_loss and compute_policy_loss. This is a straight implementation of steps 11 to 13 of the pseudocode in Figure 8-10. If you compare these steps with steps 11 to 14 of TD3 in Figure 8-7, you will see lots of similarities except for the fact that the action is sampled from the online network and SAC has an additional term of entropy in both the losses. These changes are minor, and hence we are not listing the code explicitly in the text here.

One-Step Update and SAC Main Loop

Again, the code for one_step_update and the overall training algorithm follows a similar pattern as before.

Once we run and train the agent, we see similar outcomes as DDPG and TD3. As discussed, we are using simple environments, and hence all three continuous control algorithms (DDPG, TD3, and SAC) in this chapter behave well. Please refer to the various papers referenced in this chapter to dive deep into the official performance comparisons of these various approaches.

This brings us to the end of this chapter of continuous control in actor-critic settings. By now we have seen model-based policy iteration approaches, deep learning–based Q-learning (DPN) approaches, policy gradients for discrete actions, and policy gradients for continuous control. This covers most of the popular approaches of reinforcement learning. We have one more major topic to consider before we finish our journey: that of using model learning in a model-free world and efficient model exploration for environments where we know the model but it is too complex or vast to be explored exhaustively.

Summary

In this chapter, we looked at actor-critic methods for continuous control where we combined off-policy Q-learning types with policy gradients to derive off-policy continuous control actor-critic methods.

We first looked at deep deterministic policy gradients, which was introduced in 2016. It was our first continuous control algorithm. DDPG is an actor-critic method with deterministic continuous control policies.

Next, we looked at twin delayed DDPG, which came out in 2018 and addressed some of the stability and inefficiency challenges found in DDPG. Like DDPG, it also learned a deterministic policy in off-policy setting with the actor-critic architecture.

Lastly, we looked at soft actor critic, which bridged the DDPG style of learning with stochastic policy optimization using entropy. SAC is an off-policy stochastic policy optimization using the actor-critic setup. We also saw the reparameterization trick to get lower variance estimates of the gradients.

CHAPTER 9

Integrated Planning and Learning

Studying topics separately followed by learning about them together has been a recurring theme in this book. We first looked at model-based algorithms in Chapter 3. Using this setup, we knew the model dynamics of the world in which the agent was operating. The agent used the knowledge of model dynamics along with Bellman equations to first carry out the evaluation/prediction task to learn the state or state-action values. It then followed this up by improving the policy to get the optimal behavior, which was called *policy improvement/policy iteration*. Once we know the model, we can plan ahead to carry out the evaluation/improvement steps. This is called the *planning phase*.

We started by exploring a model-free regime in Chapter 4. *Model-free* means we do not know the model. We learn the model by interacting with it. We call this *learning*. In a model-free setup, we looked separately at the Monte Carlo (MC) and temporal difference (TD) methods. We compared and contrasted the merits and demerits of using both approaches. Next, we combined MC and TD into a single unified approach using *n-step* and *eligibility traces*.

In Chapter 6, we extended the methods from Chapter 4 to nontabular continuous space large-scale problems using function approximation and deep learning. All the methods covered in Chapters 3 to 6 were called *value-based methods* wherein the state or state-action values were learned followed by policy improvement using these learned state/state-action values.

Chapter 7 was focused on an alternate approach, namely, *policy-based methods*. This method means learning the optimal policy directly without going through the intermediary step of learning the state/action values. Initially, it gave an impression that the value-based and policy-based methods were distinct. However, just like combining MC and TD into one under eligibility traces, in Chapter 8 we combined value-based

305

© Nimish Sanghi 2021
N. Sanghi, *Deep Reinforcement Learning with Python*, https://doi.org/10.1007/978-1-4842-6809-4_9

Q-learning and policy learning to get the best of both worlds under actor-critic (AC) methods like DDPG, TD3, and SAC.

In this chapter, we will combine the model-based approaches and model-free approaches to make our algorithms more powerful and sample efficient by leveraging the best of both of them. This is the main emphasis of this chapter.

We will also study the exploration-exploitation dilemma in more detail to go beyond just blindly following e-greedy policies. We will look at simpler setups to gain a stronger understanding of the exploration-exploitation dilemma. This will be followed by a deep dive into a "guided forward looking tree search approach," called *Monte Carlo tree search* (MCTS).

Model-Based Reinforcement Learning

What is model-free RL? In model-free RL, we do not know the model. Rather, we learn the value function and/or policy by having the agent interact with the environment, i.e., *learning by experience*. This is what we saw in Chapters 4 to 8 of this book. In comparison, the model-based RL we are talking about now is the one under which we learn the model by having the agent interact with the environment, i.e., again *learning by experience*. The learned model is used to plan the value function and policy—something similar to what we saw in Chapter 3. In Chapter 3, we assumed prior knowledge of the model, and we also assumed it to be perfect. However, in model-based RL, we learn the model and then use that knowledge. However, the knowledge may be incomplete; in other words, we may not know the exact transition probabilities or complete distribution of rewards. We learn parts of the system dynamics that we experience as the agent interacts with the environment. We are basing our knowledge on limited interaction, and hence without an exhaustive interaction covering all the possibilities, our knowledge of the model is incomplete.

What do we mean by model here? This means to have estimates of the transition probabilities $P(s_t, a_t)$ and the reward $R(s_t, a_t)$. The agent interacts with the world/environment and forms an impression of the world. Pictorially it can be represented as shown in Figure 9-1.

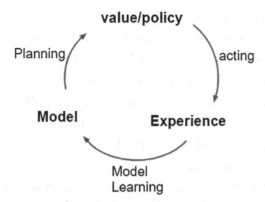

Figure 9-1. *Model-based reinforcement learning. The agent learns the model based on its interaction with the environment, and then that model is used for planning*

The advantages are that learning becomes sample efficient. We can use the learned model to plan effectively as compared to the model-free approach. Further, the model interaction is all about taking an action a_t while in state s_t and observing the outcome of the next state s_{t+1} and the reward r_{t+1}. We can use supervised learning machinery to learn from the interactions with the real world, where a given (s_t, a_t) is the sample input and s_{t+1} and/or r_{t+1} are the sample targets.

$$s_1, a_1 \rightarrow r_2, s_2$$

$$s_2, a_2 \rightarrow r_3, s_3$$

$$: : :$$

$$s_{T-1}, a_{T-1} \rightarrow r_T, s_T$$

Like any other regular supervised machine learning setup, we can learn from the previous samples that the agent gathers from its interaction with the environment.

- Learning $s_t, a_t \rightarrow r_{t+1}$ is a regression problem with a loss like mean squared loss.

- Learning the transition dynamics $s_t, a_t \rightarrow s_{t+1}$ is a density estimation problem. We could learn a discrete categorical distribution, a Gaussian, or a mixture of Gaussian model parameters. The loss could be a KL-divergence loss.

If we extend the learning to Bayesian learning, then we can also reason about the model uncertainties, i.e., how sure or unsure we are about the learned model transitions and reward functions. The Bayesian approach to learning produces not just a point estimate but a whole distribution of the estimate that gives us the capability to reason about the strength of the estimation. A narrow probability distribution for the estimate means that a large part of probability is centered around the peak; i.e., we have a strong confidence in the estimate. Conversely, a broad distribution for the estimate reflects a higher uncertainty about the estimate.

However, nothing comes free in life. This two-step approach of first learning an imperfect representation of the model followed by using this imperfect representation to plan or find optimal policy introduces two sources of error. First, our learned representation of the model dynamics may be inaccurate. Second, learning a value function from an imperfect model may have its own inaccuracies.

The learned model could be represented as a "table lookup" (similar to what we saw in Chapters 2 and 3), linear expectation model, or linear Gaussian model. There can be even more complex model representations like the Gaussian process model or deep belief network models. It depends on the nature of problem, ease of data collection, etc. Deciding on the right representation requires domain expertise. Let's look at a simple example of learning a table lookup model.

First, we look at the expressions that we will use to learn the reward and transition dynamics. It is a simple averaging method that we will use here. To estimate the transition probability, we take the average of the number of times the transition $(s_t, a_t) \rightarrow s_{t+1}$ was seen and divided it by the total number of times the agent saw itself in (s_t, a_t).

$$\hat{p}(s,a) = \frac{1}{N(s,a)} \sum_{t=1}^{T} \mathbb{1}\left(S+t=s, A_t=a, S_{t+1}=s'\right) \tag{9.1}$$

Here, $\mathbb{1}\left(S+t=s, A_t=a, S_{t+1}=s'\right)$ is an indicator function. Indicator functions take a value of 1 when their condition inside the brackets is true and a value of zero otherwise. In summary, this indicator function is counting the number of times (s, a) leads to a transition to the next state, $S_{t+1}=s'$.

Similarly, we can define the reward learning as an average as well.

$$\hat{r}(s,a) = \frac{1}{N(s,a)} \sum_{t=1}^{T} \mathbb{1}(S_t=s, A_t=a)R_t \tag{9.2}$$

Let's look at a simple environment in which there are only two states and we observe a set (eight) of the agent's interaction with the environment. We assume no discounting, i.e., $\gamma = 1$.

Suppose we see $(A, 0, B, 0)$. This means that the agent starts in state A, observes a reward of zero, and sees itself in state B, which is again followed by a reward of 0 and finally followed by a transition to the terminal state.

Let's say the eight transitions/interactions collected by the agent are as follows:

A, 0, B, 0

B, 1

B, 1

B, 1

B, 1

B, 1

B, 1

B, 0

We apply equations (9.1) and (9.2) to construct the model as follows:

- We saw only one transition from A to B, and we got a reward of 0. So, we conclude that $P(B|A)$ is 1 and $R(state = A) = 0$. Please note that in the previous example we are not explicitly showing actions to keep things simple. You could think of this as taking a random action in each state or could think of this as a Markov reward process (MRP) instead of a full-blown MDP.

- We saw eight transitions from B, all of them leading to the terminal state. In two instances, the reward was zero while in the remaining six cases it was 1. This can be modeled as saying that $P(Terminal|B) = 1$. The reward $R(B) = 1$ with 0.75 (6/8) probability and $R(B) = 0$ with 0.25 probability.

Figure 9-2 shows the model we learned from these eight interactions.

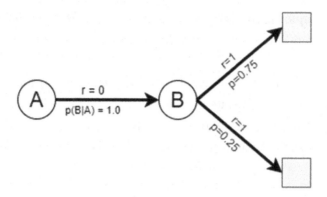

Figure 9-2. *Table lookup model learned from the environment interaction*

This is one of the many parameterized model representations where we explicitly learned the model dynamics and then discarded the sample interactions with the real world. However, there is another approach that was used in DQN: the nonparameterized model. In the nonparameterized model, we stored the interactions in a buffer, and then we sampled from the buffer. An example from the previous eight interactions would be to store tuples of (state, reward, next_state) in a list (remember in this example we do not have actions as it is an MRP).

$$D = [(A,0,B), (B,0,T), (B,1,T), (B,1,T), (B,1,T), (B,1,T), (B,1,T), (B, 0,T)]$$

The first two values in buffer D come from one transition, i.e., *A*, 0, *B*, 0. The rest of the seven entries in the buffer are the remaining seven transitions from the previous example.

A broad categorization of model learning is as follows:

- *Parameterized*:

  - Table lookup model

  - Linear expectation model

  - Linear Gaussian model

  - Gaussian process model

  - Deep belief network model

- *Nonparameterized*: Store all interactions (s, a, r, s') in a buffer and then later do sampling from this buffer to generate example transitions.

Planning with a Learned Model

Once we know the model, we can use it to carry out planning using the value or policy iteration that we saw in Chapter 3. In these methods, we do one-step rollouts using Bellman equations.

However, there is another way the learned model can be used. We can sample from it and use these samples under the MC or TD approach of learning. While carrying out the MC or TD style of learning in this case, the agent does not interact with the real environment. Rather, it interacts with the *model of the environment* that it has approximated from past experiences. To an extent, it is still called *planning*. We are using the model learned to plan and not planning from direct interaction with the real world.

Please remember that the model we learn is an approximation. It is based on a partial interaction our agent has had with the environment. It is usually not complete or exhaustive. We discussed this in the preceding section. The inaccuracies in the learned model would limit the quality of learning. The algorithms optimize the learning with respect to the model we have formed and not the real-world model. This can limit the quality of learning. If our confidence in the learned model is not too high, we could go back to the model-free RL methods that we saw earlier. Or we could use the Bayesian approach to reason about the model uncertainties. The Bayesian approach is not something we will explore further in this book. Interested readers can check out various advanced RL texts and papers to explore this further.

So far, we have seen that model-based RL offers the advantage of learning the model and thereby making learning more sample efficient. However, it comes at a cost of the model estimates not being accurate, which in turn limits the quality of learning. Is there a way to combine the model-based and model-free learning into a single unified framework and leverage the best of both approaches? This is what we will explore now.

Integrating Learning and Planning (Dyna)

We saw two types of experiences: a real experience where the agent interacts with the real environment to get the next state and reward, s_{t+1}, r_{t+1}; and a simulated experience where the agent uses the learned model to generate additional simulated experiences.

A simulated experience is cheaper and easy to generate, especially in the field of robotics. We have fast robot simulators to generate the samples that may not be 100 percent accurate in the real world but that help us generate and simulate agent behavior at a fast pace compared to the real-world interaction of robots. However, the simulations may not be accurate, which is where additional learning from real-world experiences would help. We can modify the diagram from Figure 9-1 to introduce this step, as shown in Figure 9-3.

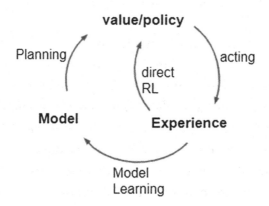

Figure 9-3. *Dyna architecture*

In Dyna, the agent interacts with the environment (acting) to produce real experiences. These real experiences are used to learn the model of the world and directly improve the value/policy like a model-free RL setup. This is the same as what we saw in Chapters 4 to 8. The model learned from real-world interactions is used to generate simulated transitions. These simulated transitions are used to further improve the value/policy. We call this step *planning* as we are using the model of the world to generate the experiences. We can carry out the planning step by using the simulated experience multiple times for each step of "acting" to generate the new samples from the real world.

Let's look at a concrete implementation of Dyna, i.e., Tabular Dyna Q. In this, we assume that the state and actions are discrete and form a small set so that we can use a tabular representation for the $Q(s, a)$, which are the q-values. We use the q-learning approach under TD to learn and improve policies. This is similar to the approach we saw in Figure 4-14 of Q-learning, the off-policy TD control. We will have some additional steps to learn from the simulated experience as well. In Figure 4-14, we only used the real experiences to learn q-values, but we will now learn the model and use that to generate additional simulated experiences to learn from. Figure 9-4 gives the complete algorithm.

TABULAR DYNA Q

Initialize:

State-action values $Q(s, a) = 0$ for all s € S and a € A.

Initialize the model (s, a) for all s € S and a € A.

Policy $\pi = \varepsilon - greedy$ policy with some small ε€[0, 1]

Learning rate (step size) α€[0, 1]

Discount factor γ€[0, 1]

Loop for each episode:

Start state S

Loop for each step till episode end:

Choose action A based on $\varepsilon - greedy$ policy

Take action A and observe reward R and next state S'

If S' not terminal:

$Q(S,A) \rightarrow Q(S,A) + \alpha * [R + \gamma * \max_{a'} Q(S', a') - Q(S,A)]$

else:

$Q(S,A) \rightarrow Q(S,A) + \alpha * [R - Q(S,A)]$

Model $(S, A) \leftarrow R, S'$ (we are assuming deterministic env)

$S \leftarrow S'$

Loop repeat n times:

S $\leftarrow$ a random previously seen state

$A \leftarrow$ random action previously taken in S

$R, S' \leftarrow Model(S, A)$

$$Q(S,A) \leftarrow Q(S,A) + \alpha * \left[R + \gamma * max_a Q(S',a') - Q(S,A) \right]$$

Return policy π based on final Q values.

Figure 9-4. *Tabular Dyna Q*

You can see from the pseudocode in Figure 9-4 that tabular Dyna Q is similar to the tabular Q-learning of Figure 4-14 except that in Dyna Q for every step in the real environment, we also carry out additional *n* steps using a simulated experience, i.e., in this case, sampling from the previous transitions seen in the real world. As we increase *n*, the number of episodes required to converge and learn an optimal value will decrease.

Consider a case where the maze has zero rewards for every transition except for the last terminal/goal state transition with a reward value of 1. An example of such a maze would be the maze on the left side of Figure 9-5. Let's also assume that the initial q-values are zero for every (s, a) pair. In regular Q-learning, we will learn the goal value of 1 when the first episode terminates. Then the value of 1 will propagate slowly—one cell/level per episode to eventually reach from start state. The q-values and optimal policy will start to converge over additional episodes after that. However, in the case of Dyna Q, we will generate *n* additional examples per the real step in the environment. This will speed up the convergence. We will see policy convergence much before the vanilla q-learning approach. Refer to Chapter 8 of the book *Reinforcement Learning: An Introduction*[1] for a more theoretical and detailed explanation of this faster convergence.

Let's apply the previous tabular Dyna Q pseudocode to the same environment we saw in Chapter 4. We will modify Listing 4-4 to incorporate model learning and then *n* steps of planning (*learning from a simulated experience*) for each step of direct RL-based learning from actual experience. The complete code is given in `listing9_1_dynaQ. ipynb`. In the walk-through, we will highlight the key differences between Dyna Q code and Q-learning code from Chapter 4.

First, we rename the agent from `QLearningAgent` to `DynaQAgent`. It's just a name change, and the code remains same except for an additional dictionary to store the seen real-world transitions. We add the following two lines of code to the `__init__` function:

```
self.buffer = {}
self.n = n # the number of planning steps to be taken from simulated exp
```

Second, we add logic to follow the planning part of the pseudocode from Figure 9-4, shown here:

Loop repeat *n* times:

$S \leftarrow$ a random previously seen state

$A \leftarrow$ random action previously taken in S

$R, S' \leftarrow Model(S, A)$

$$Q(S,A) \leftarrow Q(S,A) + \alpha * \left[R + \gamma * max_{a'} Q(S',a') - Q(S,A) \right]$$

This is added in the function `train_agent` where we train the agent. Listing 9-1 shows the revised implementation of the function.

Listing 9-1. Train_agent Using Dyna Q

```
#training algorithm
def train_agent(env, agent, episode_cnt = 10000, tmax=10000, anneal_eps=True):
    episode_rewards = []
    for i in range(episode_cnt):
        G = 0
        state = env.reset()
        for t in range(tmax):
            action = agent.get_action(state)
            next_state, reward, done, _ = env.step(action)
            agent.update(state, action, reward, next_state, done)
            G += reward
            if done:
                episode_rewards.append(G)
                # to reduce the exploration probability epsilon over the
                # training period.
                if anneal_eps:
                    agent.epsilon = agent.epsilon * 0.99
                break
        # add the experience to agent's buffer (i.e. agent's model
        estimate)
        agent.buffer[(state,action)] = (next_state, reward, done)
        state = next_state
        # plan n steps through simulated experience
```

```
for j in range(agent.n):
    state_v, action_v = random.choice(list(agent.buffer))
    next_state_v, reward_v, done_v = agent.
    buffer[(state_v,action_v)]
    agent.update(state_v, action_v, reward_v, next_state_v,
    done_v)

return np.array(episode_rewards)
```

Next, we run Dyna Q against the maze as well as the taxi world environment from OpenAI Gym. Looking at the training curves in the Python notebook, we note that convergence takes fewer episodes under Dyna Q when compared to vanilla Q-learning. This establishes the claim that Dyna Q (or in general any Dyna architecture) is sample efficient.

Dyna Q and Changing Environments

Let's now consider the case where we first learn the optimal policy for a maze using Dyna Q. After some steps, we change the environment and make it harder, as shown in Figure 9-5. The left figure has the original grid for which the agent learns to navigate from start S to goal G through the opening on the right side of the gray brick wall. After the agent has learned the optimal behavior, the grid is changed. The opening on the right side is closed, and a new opening is made on the left side. The agent when trying to navigate to the goal through the earlier learnt path now sees the original path blocked i.e., opening on right side of the original maze. It is due to the change we just made.

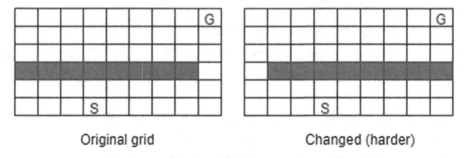

Original grid   Changed (harder)

Figure 9-5. *Dyna Q with grid made more difficult midway after the agent learns to navigate through the opening on the right side. The agent learns to navigate the grid through the new opening on the left side of the brick wall*

Sutton and Barto in their book *Reinforcement Learning: An Introduction* show that Dyna Q will take a while to learn the changed environment. Once the environment is changed midway, there are a number of episodes in which the agent keeps going to the right but finds the path blocked, and hence it needs lots of additional steps under the ε-greedy policy to learn the alternate route of taking the opening on the left side to reach the goal.

Let's consider the second case that they show in their book. In the second case, the environment is changed midway and made simpler; i.e., a new opening is introduced to the right without closing the original opening on the left. Figure 9-6 shows the maze before and after the change.

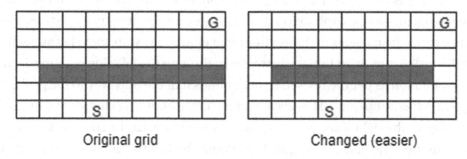

Original grid   Changed (easier)

Figure 9-6. *Dyna Q with grid made simpler after the agent has learned the optimal policy for the left grid. The Dyna Q agent fails to discover the shorter path through the new right gap*

By running a Dyna Q learning algorithm on this setup, we can show that Dyna Q does not learn the new opening on the right side of the brick wall. The new path through the right of the brick wall if followed will offer a shorter path to the goal state. Dyna Q has already learned the optimal policy, and it has no incentive to explore for a changed environment. A random/chance exploration of the new opening depends on the exploratory policy, which in turn depends on the ε exploration.

There is a revised algorithm to fix this problem known as Dyna Q+, as explained in the following section.

Dyna Q+

Dyna Q+ is a typical example of the exploration/exploitation dilemma that needs to be well thought in all reinforcement learning setups. We talked about it earlier. If we start to exploit the knowledge (i.e., the model or the policy) early, we risk the chance of not getting to know better paths. The agent greedily becomes happy with whatever it has managed to learn. On the other hand, if the agent explores too much, it is wasting time looking at suboptimal paths/options even when it has already got the most optimal solution. Unfortunately, the agent has no direct way of knowing that it has reached the optimal policy, and hence it needs to use other heuristics/ways to balance the exploration-exploitation dilemma.

In Dyna Q+, we encourage the exploration of unseen states by adding a reward to the states over and above what we observed. This additional reward term encourages exploration for the states that have not been visited in the real world in a while.

In the simulated planning part, we add $\kappa\sqrt{\tau}$ to the reward; i.e., the reward r becomes $r + \kappa\sqrt{\tau}$ where κ is a small constant and τ is the time since the transition under question was seen in the real-world exploration. It encourages the agent to try these transitions and hence catch the changes in the environment effectively, with some lag as controlled by κ. In Figure 9-6, the agent initially learns to go through the left-side opening. It carries out the exploration as per the revised term but finds that the only way to the goal is through the left-side opening. However, after the environment is changed by making a new opening on the right side, the agent on the subsequent exploration of this part of maze will discover the new opening and eventually the fact that it is a shorter path to the goal. The agent will revise its optimal behavior to follow the opening on the right side. As the time of the last visit to a part of grid increases, the $\kappa\sqrt{\tau}$ term in the reward grows and at some stage may grow so much that it overshadows the reward from the current optimal behavior, forcing the agent to explore the unvisited part once more.

Expected vs. Sample Updates

We have seen various ways to combine learning and planning. We can see that learning and planning are both about the way the value functions are updated. The first dimension is about what is being updated, whether a state value (v) or an action value (q). The other dimension is the width of the update. In other words, does the update happen based on a single sample seen (sample update), or is the update based on all possible transitions (expected update) using the transition probabilities for the next state given the current state and action, i.e., $p(s_t, a_t)$? The third and last dimension is whether the update is carried out for any arbitrary policy v_π, q_π or for the optimal policy v_*, q_*. Let's look at various combinations and map them back to what we have seen so far in the book.

- $v_\pi(s)$ updated using the expected update. The update is for a value function. It is an expected update covering all the possible transitions from a given state using the transition probability distribution $p(s', r|s, a)$. The action is carried out using the current policy agent.

  This is policy evaluation using dynamic programming, as shown in equation (3.6).

  $$v_{k+1}(s) \leftarrow \sum_a \pi(a|s) \sum_{s',r} p(s',r|s,a)\left[r + \gamma\, v_k(s')\right]$$

- $v_\pi(s)$ updated using the sample update. The update is for the value function and is based on the sample the agent sees following a policy π.

  This is policy evaluation under TD(0), as shown in equation (4.4). The value of state (s) is updated based on the action taken by the agent as per policy π, the subsequent reward (r), and the next state (s') seen by the agent.

  $$v_{k+1}(s) \leftarrow v_k(s) + \alpha\left[r + \gamma v_k(s') - v_k(s)\right]$$

- $v*(s)$ updated using max over all the possible actions. The value of state (s) is updated based on the expectation of all the possible next states and rewards. The update is done by taking the max over all the possible actions, i.e., the optimal action at a given point in time and not based on the current policy the agent is following.

  This is value iteration using dynamic programming as per equation (3.8).

  $$v_{k+1}(s) \leftarrow \max_a \sum_{s',r} p(s',r|s,a)\left[r + \gamma\, v_k(s')\right]$$

- $q_\pi(s, a)$ updated using expected update. The value being updated is q-value and is updated in the expectation based on all the next states and rewards possible from a given state-action pair. The update is based on the current policy the agent is following.

This is q-policy evaluation using dynamic programming, i.e., equation (3.2) expressed in iterative form.

$$q_{k+1}(s,a) \leftarrow \sum_{s',r} p(s',r|s,a)\left[r+\gamma \sum_{a'} \pi(a'|s')q_k(s',a')\right]$$

- $q_\pi(s, a)$ updated using the samples. The update for the q-value is based on the samples and on the current policy the agent is following, i.e., on-policy update.

- This is q-value iteration using dynamic programming. Here is the iterative version of equation (3.4):

$$q_{k+1}(s,a) \leftarrow \sum_{s',r} p(s',r|s,a)\left[r+\gamma \, max_{a'} q_k(s',a')\right]$$

- $q_*(s, a)$ updated using all the possible states and max over all the possible actions in the next state. This is an update for the q-value and based on the expectation of all possible following state and action pairs. It is updating by taking a max over actions and hence updating for an optimal policy and not the policy the agent is currently following.

This is SARSA using a model-free setup, as shown in equation (4.6). It has been rewritten to match the notations in this section.

$$q_{k+1}(s,a) \leftarrow q_k(s,a)+\alpha\left[r+\gamma q_k(s',a')-q_k(s,a)\right]$$

- $q_*(s, a)$ updated using the sample action and then taking the max over all the possible actions from the next state. This is updating the q-value using a sample. The update is based on a *max* over all possible action, i.e., an off-policy update and not the update for the current policy the agent is following.

This is the Q-learning that we studied in Chapter 4 and then extended to deep networks under DQN. This is equation (4.10) rewritten to match the notations in this chapter.

$$q_{k+1}(s,a) \leftarrow q_k(s,a)+\alpha\left[r+\gamma max_{a'} \, q_k(s',a')-q_k(s,a)\right]$$

The previous explanation shows how DP and model-free worlds are linked. In DP, since we know the model dynamics, we do a wide sweep over all the possible transitions $p(s_t, a_t)$. And in the model-free world, we do not know the model, and hence we do sample-based MC or TD updates. The difference between DP and model-free is all about the update being done over the expectation or done over samples.

It also goes to show that once we start learning model dynamics, we can mix and match any of the previous approaches under the Dyna setup. Just like earlier, we have combined the model-free and model-based approaches in a unified single setup. This is similar to what we did by combining value-based DQN and policy gradient into a unified approach under actor critic as well as the way we combined a one-step sample (TD) and a multistep sample (MC) into a single framework using eligibility traces.

Another way to organize the RL algorithms is to look at a two-dimensional world where the vertical axis is the length/depth of update, with TD(0) being at one end and MC at other end. The second/horizontal dimension could be looked at as the width of the update with the dynamic programming expected updates at one end and the sample-based MC/TD updates at the other end. Figure 9-7 shows this distinction.

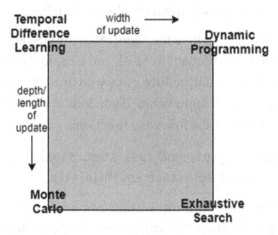

Figure 9-7. *Reinforcement learning approaches in a nutshell*

We can further refine this unification by adding more dimensions. A third possible dimension, orthogonal to the width and depth of the update, would be off-policy versus on-policy updates. We could also add a fourth dimension, which is the purely value-based approach or purely policy-learning approach or a mix of both, i.e., actor critic.

Up to now we have looked at combining learning and planning in what is called the *backward view*. We used planning (e.g., Dyna Q) to update the value functions, but there is no planning involved while choosing an action in the real world. It is kind of a passive planning approach, where planning was used to generate additional steps/synthetic examples to train and improve the model/policy/value functions. In a following section, we will look at *forward planning* in which we carry out planning at decision time. In other words, we use the model knowledge (learned or given) to look ahead and then take an action based on what we think is the best action. We will look at this approach in the context of the Monte Carlo tree search algorithm (MCTS). However, before we do, let's revisit the exploration versus exploitation issue in the next section.

Exploration vs. Exploitation

In reinforcement learning, we always need to balance between using current knowledge and exploring more to gain new knowledge. Initially we have no or very little knowledge about the world (environment). We can explore a lot more and start improving our belief about the world. As our belief improves and strengthens, the agent starts exploiting that belief along with gradually reducing its exploration.

Up until now we have looked at exploration in different forms.

- ε-greedy strategies are where the agent takes the best action based on its current belief with probability $(1-\varepsilon)$, and it explores randomly with probability ε. We gradually reduce ε as we go through the steps. We saw this in all the DQN approaches. If you look at the notebooks for Chapter 6, you will see the following function:

```
def epsilon_schedule(start_eps, end_eps, step, final_step):
    return start_eps + (end_eps-start_eps)*min(step, final_step)/ final_step
```

- We always started with epsilon=1.0 and over a period reduced it to 0.05. The previous function implemented the epsilon reduction schedule.

- We also saw exploration in the form of learning stochastic policies in policy gradient methods where we always learned a policy distribution $\pi_\theta(a|s)$. We did not take any *max* over actions to learn a single optimal action, which was the case in DQN. This ensures that we are not learning the deterministic action. Different nonzero probabilities for all the actions ensured exploration.

- We also saw use of entropy regularization in policy gradient and actor-critic methods that forced enough exploration to ensure that the agent does not prematurely commit to exploitation without doing enough exploration of unknown parts of the policy/action space. Please refer to Chapter 7's Listing 7-1 for a quick sample of this approach.

In this section, we will look a simple setup to study more formally the trade-offs between exploration versus exploitation and the various strategies for efficient exploration.

Multi-arm Bandit

We will consider an environment that is known as *multi-arm bandit* based on the concept of multiple casino slot machines stacked together. The agent does not know the individual reward amount of success rates for each slot machine. The agent's job is to choose a machine and pull the slot machine lever to receive a reward. This cycle repeats for as long as we want. The agent needs to explore to try all the machines and form a belief about the individual reward distribution for each of the machines. As its belief gets stronger, it must start exploiting its knowledge/belief more to pull the best machine's lever and reduce exploration. Figure 9-8 shows the setup.

Figure 9-8. *Noncontextual multi-arm bandit*

The reason we study multi-arm bandit is that it is a simple setup. Further, it can be extended to contextual multi-arm bandit in which the distribution of rewards for each slot machine is not fixed. Rather, it depends on the context at a given point in time, e.g., the "current state" of the agent. The contextual multi-arm bandit has many practical use cases. We will consider one such example here.

Suppose you have 10 advertisements, and you want to show one advertisement to the user in the browser window based on the context (e.g., content) of the page. The current page is the context, and showing one of the 10 advertisement is the action. When the user clicks the advertisement, the user gets a reward of 1; otherwise, the reward is 0. The agent has the history of how many times a user clicked a shown advertisement within the same context, i.e., clicking the shown advertisement on a web page with similar content. The agent wants to take a series of actions with a goal to increase/maximize the chances of users clicking the shown advertisement. This is an example of contextual multi-arm bandit.

Another example is an online store showing other product recommendations based on what a user is currently viewing. The online store hopes that the user will find some of the recommendations interesting and may click them. Yet another example would be choosing a drug out of K possible options, administering the drug to a patient to choose the best one, and reaching that conclusion over a maximum of T tries.

We can further extend the bandit framework to consider full-scale MDPs. But each extension makes the formal analysis all the more laborious and cumbersome. Accordingly, we will study here the simplest setup of noncontextual bandit to help you appreciate the basics. Interested readers can study this further with many good resources available on the Web.

Regret: Measure of Quality of Exploration

Next, we define the quality of exploration. Consider that the system is in state S. In noncontextual bandit, it is a frozen initial state that is nonchanging and remains the same every time. And for contextual bandit, the state S may change over time. Further, suppose we follow a policy $\pi_t(s)$ at time t to choose an action. Also, consider that you know the optimal policy $\pi_*(s)$.

The regret at time t, i.e., the regret of choosing an action from the nonoptimal policy, is defined as follows:

$$regret = E_{a\sim\pi^*(s)}\left[r(s,a)\right] - E_{a\sim\pi_t(s)}\left[r(s,a)\right] \tag{9.3}$$

It is the expected reward from following an optimal policy minus the reward from following a specific policy.

We can sum it over all timesteps to get the total regret over T steps as follows:

$$\eta = \sum_{t=1}^{T}\left(E_{a\sim\pi^*(s)}\left[r(s,a)\right] - E_{a\sim\pi_t(s)}\left[r(s,a)\right]\right) \tag{9,4}$$

Since we are looking at noncontextual bandit where the state (s) remains the same at every time step, i.e., remains fixed as the initial state. We can simplify (9.4) as shown here:

$$\eta = T.\ E_{a\sim\pi^*(s)}\left[r(s,a)\right] - \sum_{t=1}^{T}\left(E_{a\sim\pi_t(s)}\left[r(s,a)\right]\right) \tag{9.5}$$

We will use (9.5) to compare various sampling strategies. We will look at three commonly used exploration strategies in the following sections. We will do so with the help of code examples. You can find the complete code in listing9_2_exploration_ exploitation.ipynb.

Let's first describe the setup we will use. Consider that the multi-arm bandit has K actions. Each of this action has a fixed probability θ_k of producing a reward of 1 and a $(1 - \theta_k)$ probability of producing a reward of 0. The optimal action is the value of k (lowercase k), which has a maximum probability of success.

$$\theta^* = \theta_k$$

Listing 9-2 shows the code for the bandit. We store k as self.n_actions and all the θ_k as self._probs. Function pull takes as input the action k, returning a reward of 1 or 0 based on the probability distribution of the action, i.e., θ_k. Function optimal_reward returns the max of self._probs.

Listing 9-2. Bandit Environment

```
class Bandit:
    def __init__(self, n_actions=5):
        self._probs = np.random.random(n_actions)
        self.n_actions = n_actions

    def pull(self, action):
        if np.random.random() > self._probs[action]:
            return 0.0
        return 1.0

    def optimal_reward(self):
        return np.max(self._probs)
```

Next, we will look at three exploration strategies starting with the ε-greedy exploration strategy.

Epsilon Greedy Exploration

This is similar to the ϵ-greedy strategy we saw in previous chapters. The agent tries different actions and forms an estimate $\hat{\theta}_k$ of the unknown actual success probabilities θ_k for the bandit environment's different actions. It takes the action k with $\hat{\theta}^* = \max \hat{\theta}_k$ with the $(1 - \epsilon)$ probability. In other words, it exploits the knowledge gained so far to take the action that it considers best based on $\hat{\theta}_k$ estimates. Further, it takes a random action with the probability ϵ to explore.

We will keep $\epsilon = 0.01$ as the exploration probability and will keep it constant throughout the experiment. Listing 9-3 shows the code implementing this strategy. First, we define RandomAgent as the base class. We have two arrays to store the cumulative count of success and failure outcomes of each action. We store these counts in arrays: self.success_cnt and self.failure_cnt.

Function update(self, action, reward) updates these counts based on which action was taken and what was the outcome. Function reset(self) resets these counts. We do so to run the same experiment multiple times and plot the average values to smoothen out the randomness. Function get_action(self) is where the exploration strategy is implemented. It will use different approaches to balance the explore versus exploit based on the type of strategy. For RandomAgent, the actions are always selected at random from the set of possible actions.

Next, we implement the ε-exploration agent in the class EGreedyAgent. This is implemented by extending RandomAgent and overriding the function get_action(self). As explained, the action with the highest probability is chosen with the probability $(1 - \epsilon)$, and a random action is chosen with the probability ϵ.

Listing 9-3. Epsilon Greedy Exploration Agent

```python
class RandomAgent:
    def __init__(self, n_actions=5):
        self.success_cnt = np.zeros(n_actions)
        self.failure_cnt = np.zeros(n_actions)
        self.total_pulls = 0
        self.n_actions = n_actions

    def reset(self):
        self.success_cnt = np.zeros(n_actions)
        self.failure_cnt = np.zeros(n_actions)
        self.total_pulls = 0

    def get_action(self):
        return np.random.randint(0, self.n_actions)

    def update(self, action, reward):
        self.total_pulls += 1
        self.success_cnt[action] += reward
        self.failure_cnt[action] += 1 - reward

class EGreedyAgent(RandomAgent):
    def __init__(self, n_actions=5, epsilon=0.01):
        super().__init__(n_actions)
        self.epsilon = epsilon

    def get_action(self):
        estimates = self.success_cnt / (self.success_cnt+self.failure_cnt+1e-12)
        if np.random.random() < self.epsilon:
            return np.random.randint(0, self.n_actions)
        else:
            return np.argmax(estimates)
```

In our setup, we are not changing the ε value, and hence the agent never learns to execute a perfect optimal policy. It continues to explore with the ε probability forever. Therefore, the regret will never go down to zero, and we expect the cumulative regret as given by (9.5) to grow linearly with the slop of growth defined by the value of ε. The bigger the ε value, the steeper the slope of growth.

Upper Confidence Bound Exploration

We will now look at the strategy called *upper confidence bound* (UCB). In this approach, the agent tries different actions and records the number of successes (α_k) or failures (β_k).

It calculates the estimates of success probabilities that will be used to see which action has the highest success estimate.

$$exploit = \hat{\theta}_k = \frac{\alpha_k}{\alpha_k + \beta_k}$$

It also calculates the exploration need that favors the least visited actions, as shown here:

$$explore = \sqrt{\frac{2.\log t}{\alpha_k + \beta_k}}$$

where t is the total number of steps taken so far.

The agent then picks the action with the maximum (explore + exploit) score, as shown here:

$$score = \frac{\alpha_k}{\alpha_k + \beta_k} + \lambda \sqrt{\frac{2.\log t}{\alpha_k + \beta_k}} \tag{9.6}$$

where λ controls the relative importance of explore versus exploit. We will use $\lambda = 1$ in our code.

The approach in UCB is to compute an upper confidence bound (upper confidence interval) to ensure that we have a 0.95 (or any other confidence level) probability that the actual estimate is within the UCB value. As the number of trials increases, and as we take a particular action again and again, the uncertainty in our estimate reduces. The score in (9.6) will approach the estimate $\hat{\theta}_k$. The actions that have not been visited at all will have the score = ∞ because of $(\alpha_k + \beta_k) = 0$ in equation (9.6). The UCB is shown to have a close to optimal growth bound. We will not go into the mathematical proof of this. You can refer to advanced texts on bandit problems.

Let's walk through the implementation of a UCB agent. Listing 9-4 gives the code. As explained, we again extend the RandomAgent class shown in Listing 9-3 and override the get_action function to choose the action as per the UCB equation (9.6). Please note that to avoid dividing by zero, we add a small constant 1e-12 in the denominators where self.success_cnt+self.failure_cnt appears.

Listing 9-4. UCB Exploration Agent

```
class UCBAgent(RandomAgent):
    def get_action(self):
        exploit = self.success_cnt / (self.success_cnt+self.failure_cnt+1e-12)
        explore = np.sqrt(2*np.log(np.maximum(self.total_pulls,1)))/(self.
        success_cnt+self.failure_cnt+1e-12))
        estimates =  exploit + explore
        return np.argmax(estimates)
```

Thompson Sampling Exploration

Next, we look at our final strategy, that of Thompson sampling. This is based on the idea of choosing an action based on the probability of it being the one that maximizes the expected reward. While UCB is based on the frequentist notion of probability, Thompson sampling is based on a Bayesian idea.

Initially, we have no prior knowledge of which is a better action, i.e., which action has the highest success probability θ_k. Accordingly, we form an initial belief that all the θ_k values are uniformly distributed in range $(0,1)$. This is called *prior* in Bayesian terminology. We express this with a beta distribution[2] of $\hat{\theta}_k \sim Beta(\alpha=1, \beta=1)$. The agent samples a value for each action k and chooses the action with the maximum sampled $\hat{\theta}_k$.

Next, it plays out that action (i.e., calls the function pull to perform the chosen action) and observes the outcome. Based on the outcome, it updates the posterior distribution of $\hat{\theta}_k$. As the success and failure counts are updated in each step, the agent updates its belief of the $\hat{\theta}_k$.

$$\hat{\theta}_k \sim Beta(\alpha=\alpha_k+1, \beta=\beta_k+1) \tag{9.7}$$

---

[2]https://en.wikipedia.org/wiki/Beta_distribution

329

The cycle goes on. As we go through multiple steps, α_k and β_k increase. The *Beta* distribution becomes narrower with a peak around the mean value of $\dfrac{\alpha_k}{\alpha_k + \beta_k}$.

Let's look at the implementation of Thompson sampling in code, as given in Listing 9-5. Like before, we extend the `RandomAgent` class and override the `get_action` method to implement equation (9.7).

Listing 9-5. Thompson Sampling Exploration

```
class ThompsonAgent(RandomAgent):
    def get_action(self):
        estimates = np.random.beta(self.success_cnt+1, self.failure_cnt+1)
        return np.argmax(estimates)
```

Comparing Different Exploration Strategies

We implement a function `get_regret` to take `n_steps=10000` steps using the bandit environment and a chosen exploration strategy. We carry out the experiment `n_trials=10` times and store the average cumulative regret as a function of the step number. Listing 9-6 gives the code that implements `get_regret`.

Listing 9-6. get_regret Function

```
def get_regret(env, agent, n_steps=10000, n_trials=10):
    score = np.zeros(n_steps)
    optimal_r = env.optimal_reward()

    for trial in range(n_trials):
        agent.reset()
        for t in range(n_steps):
            action = agent.get_action()
            reward = env.pull(action)
            agent.update(action, reward)
            score[t] += optimal_r - reward
    score = score / n_trials
    score = np.cumsum(score)
    return score
```

We run the experiment for the three agents: ε-greedy, UCB, and Thompson exploration. We plot the cumulative reward, as shown in Figure 9-9.

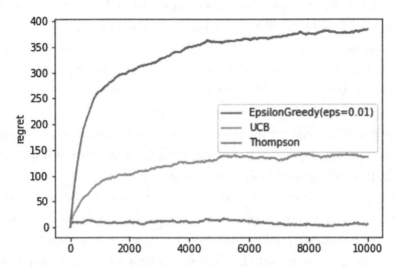

Figure 9-9. *Regret curve for different exploration strategies*

We can see that UCB and Thompson have sublinear growth, while ε-greedy regret continues to grow at a faster pace (actually at a linear growth with a rate of growth determined by the value of ε).

Let's now move back to the discussion of Monte Carlo tree search where we will use UCB as a way to carry out explore versus exploit decisions. The choice of UCB in MCTS is based on the current trends shown in popular MCTS implementations.

Planning at Decision Time and Monte Carlo Tree Search

The way Dyna uses planning is called *background planning*. The model learned is used to generate simulated samples that are then fed to the algorithm, just like real samples. These additional simulated samples help to improve the value estimates further over and above the estimates done using real-world interactions. When an action has to be selected in, say, state S_t, there is no planning at this decision time.

The other way to plan is to begin and end the plan while in state S_t to look ahead, kind of like playing out the various scenarios in your head using the model learned so far and using this plan to decide on action A_t to be taken at time t. Once the action A_t is taken, the agent finds itself in a new state S_{t+1}. The agent again looks ahead, plans, and takes a step. This cycle goes on. This is called *decision-time planning*. Depending on the time available, the further/deeper the agent can plan from the current state, the more powerful and helpful the plan will be in making a decision on what action to take at time t. Hence, decision-time planning is most helpful in cases where fast responses are not required. In board games like Chess and Go, the decision-time plan can look, say, a dozen of moves ahead before deciding on what action to take. However, if a fast response is required, then background planning is most suitable.

These forward search algorithms select the best possible action by looking ahead. They build a search tree of possible options starting from the current state S_t that the agent is in. The possible options in a given state-action pair may depend on the model of the MDP the agent has learned from prior interactions, or it may be based on the model of MDP given to the agent in the beginning. For example, in the case of board games like Chess and Go, we have clearly defined the rules of the game, and therefore we know the environment in complete exact detail. Figure 9-10 shows an example of a search tree.

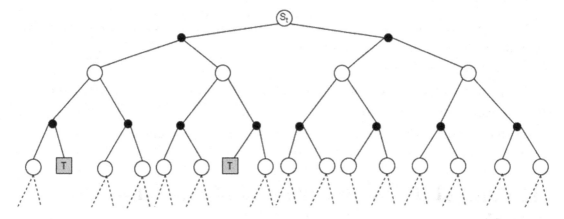

Figure 9-10. *Search tree starting from current state S_t*

However, if the branching factor is high, we cannot build an exhaustive search tree. In the game of Go, the average branching factor is around 250. Even if you build a three-level deep exhaustive tree, the third level will have $250^3 = 15,625,000$ nodes, i.e., 15 million nodes. And to take possible advantage of looking far ahead, we want to go a lot deeper than two or three levels. That is where a *simulation-based search tree* is formed instead of an exhaustive one. We use a policy called a *rollout policy* to simulate multiple trajectories and form an MC estimate of action values. These estimates are used to choose the best action at root state S_t. This helps in improving the policy. After the best action is taken, the agent finds itself in a new state, and it starts all over again to roll out the simulation tree from that new state. This cycle goes on. The number of rollout trajectories tried depends on the time constraint within which the agent needs to decide on an action.

MCTS is an example of decision time planning. MCTS is exactly as described earlier with some additional enhancements to accumulate value estimates and direct the search to the most rewarding part of the tree. The basic version of MCTS consists of four steps.

1. *Selection/tree traversal*: Starting from the root node, use a tree policy to traverse the tree and reach a leaf node.

2. *Expansion*: Add child nodes (actions) to the leaf node and choose one of them.

3. *Simulation/rollout*: Play the game until termination, starting from previously selected child node. We use a fixed rollout policy to play this out, and it could be a random rollout policy as well.

4. *Back propagation*: Use the results of playout to update all the nodes from termination to all the way up to the root node by following (backtracking) the path that was traversed.

The cycle is repeated multiple times, always starting from the current root node until we run out of time allotted for search or we run it for a fixed number of iterations. At this point, an action with the highest value is selected based on the accumulated statistics. Figure 9-11 shows a schematic of MCTS.

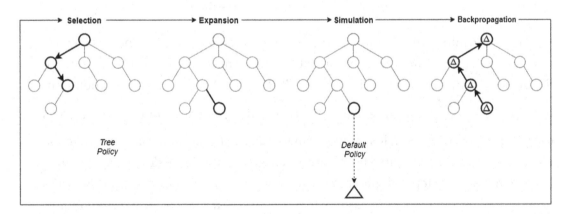

Figure 9-11.   *One iteration of MCTS consisting of four steps*

Next, the agent performs the chosen action in a real environment. This moves the agent to a new state, and the previous MCTS cycle starts once more, this time with the new state being the root state from which the simulated based tree is built.

Let's look at a simple made-up example. We will use the UCB measure of the following:

$$UCB1\left(S_i\right) = \underline{V_i} + C\sqrt{\frac{lnN}{n_i}},\, where\, C = 2$$

$UCB1$ will be used to decide which node to choose from in the expansion phase. We start with the root node S_0, and for each node we keep two statistics, the total score and the number of visits to that node. The initial setup is as follows:

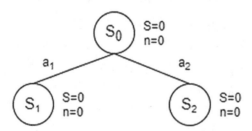

We expand the tree at the root node by adding all the available actions from S_0, let's say a_1 and a_2. These actions lead us to two new states, S_1 and S_2, respectively. We initialize the score and count statistics for these two nodes. The tree at this point looks like this:

This is the initial tree. We now start executing the steps of MCTS. The first step is tree traversal using $UCB1$ values. We are at S_0, and we need to choose a child node with the highest $UCB1$ value. Let's calculate the $UCB1$ for S_1. As $n = 0$, the exploration term in $UCB1$, i.e., $\sqrt{\frac{lnN}{n}}$, is infinite. This is the case with S_2. As part of our tree policy, let's choose the node with a smaller subindex in the case of ties, which leads to a selection of S_1. As S_1 has not been visited ever before, i.e., as $n = 0$ for S_1, we do not expand and instead move on to step 3 of rollout. We use a rollout policy to simulate random actions from S_1 until termination. Let's assume that we observe a value of 20 at termination as shown here:

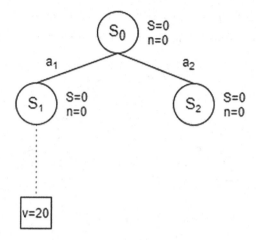

The next step is the fourth one, i.e., to back propagate the value from the terminal state all the way up to the root node. We update the visit count and total score for all the nodes falling in the path from the terminal state to the root node. And then we erase the rollout part from S_1. At this point, the tree looks like the one shown. Please notice the updated statistics for nodes S_1 and S_0.

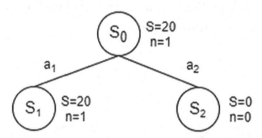

This brings us to the end of the first iteration of MCTS steps. We will now run one more iteration of MCTS steps, again starting from S_0. The first step is a tree traversal starting from S_0. We need to select one of the two nodes, i.e., S_1 or S_2 based on which has a higher $UCB1$ value. For S_1, the $UCB1$ value is given by the following:

$$UCB(S_1) = \frac{20}{1} + 2.\sqrt{\frac{ln1}{1}} = 20$$

The 1 in $ln\ 1$ comes from the value of n at the root node, which tells us the total number of trials so far. And the 1 in the denominator inside the square root comes from the value of n for node S_1. The $UCB(S_2)$ continues to be ∞ as the n for S_2 is still 0. So, we choose node S_2. That ends the tree traversal step since S_2 is a leaf node. We carry out a rollout from S_2. Let's assume that the rollout from S_2 produces a terminal value of 10. That completes the rollout phase. The tree at this point looks like this:

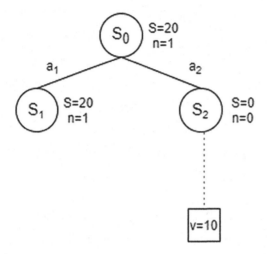

The next step is to back propagate the terminal value of 10 all the way back to root state and in the process update the statistics of all the nodes in the path, i.e., S_2 and S_0 in this case. We then erase the rollout part. At the end of back propagation step, the updated tree looks like the one shown here:

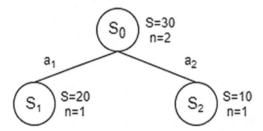

Let's carry out one more iteration of MCTS, and this will be the final iteration. We again start from S_0 and recalculate the $UCB1$ values of child nodes.

$$UCB(S_1) = \frac{20}{1} + 2.\sqrt{\frac{ln2}{1}} = 21.67$$

$$UCB(S_2) = \frac{10}{1} + 2.\sqrt{\frac{ln2}{1}} = 11.67$$

As the UCB value of S_1 is higher, we choose that. We have reached a leaf node, and that ends the tree traversal part step of MCTS. We are at S_1, and it has been visited before, so we now expand S_1 by simulating all possible actions from S_1 and the resulting states we end up in. The tree at this point looks like this:

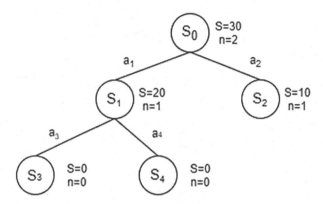

We need to choose a leaf node between S_3 and S_4 followed by rollout from that chosen node. As before, the $UCB1$ for both S_3 and S_4 is ∞. As per our tree policy, we chose the node with a lower subindex in the case of a tie. This means we choose S_3 and do a rollout from S_3. Let's assume that the terminal state at the end of the rollout produces a terminal value of 0. This completes the rollout step of MCTS. The tree looks like this:

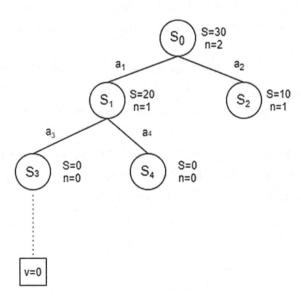

The final step is to back propagate the value of zero all the way back to the root node. We update the statistics of nodes in the path, i.e., nodes S_3, S_1, and S_0. The tree looks like this:

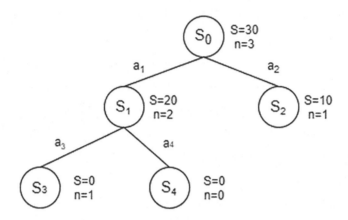

At this point, let's say we have run out of time. The algorithm now needs to choose the best action at S_0 and take that step in the real world. At this point, we will only compare the average values, and for S_1 and S_2 both the average values are 10. It is a tie. We can have additional rules to break the tie. However, let's say we always choose a random action to break a tie while making the final choice of the best action. And let's say we randomly selected S_1. The agent takes action a_1 and lands at S_1 assuming a deterministic setup. We now make S_1 the new root node and carry out multiple iterations of MCTS from S_1, eventually choosing the best action to take at S_1. This way we step through the real world.

This is the essence of MCTS. There are many variations of MCTS that we will not go into. The main objective was to help you familiarize yourself with a simple and basic MCTS setup as well as walk you through the computations to solidify your understanding.

Before we conclude this chapter, we will briefly talk about a recent and famous use case of MCTS, i.e., of AlphaGo and AlphaGo Zero, which helped design an algorithm to have a computer beat human experts in the game of Go.

AlphaGo Walk-Through

AlphaGo was architected by Deep Mind in 2016[3] to beat human experts in the game of Go. A standard search tree would test everything possible from a given position. However, games with high branching factors cannot use this approach. If a game has a branching factor of b (i.e., the number of legal moves at any position is b) and the total game length (i.e., depth or number of sequential moves until the end) is d, then there are b^d possible sequences of moves. Evaluating all the options is not feasible for any moderate board game. Considering the game of chess with ($b \approx 35, d \approx 50$) or the game of Go with ($b \approx 250, d \approx 150$), an exhaustive search is impossible. But the effective search space can be reduced with two general approaches.

- You can reduce the depth with position evaluation. After expanding the search tree for some depth, replace the state at a leaf node with an approximate evaluation function $v(s) \approx v^*(s)$. This approach worked for board games such as chess, checkers, and Othello but did not work for Go due to Go's complexity.

- The second approach is to reduce the breadth of the tree from full expansion at a node with sampling actions from a policy $p(s)$. Monte Carlo rollouts do not branch at all; they play out an episode from a leaf node and then use the average return as an estimate of $v(s)$. We saw this approach in MCTS in which the rollout values were used to estimate the v(s) of the leaf node and the policy was further improved by using the revised estimate of $v(s)$.

In the previous academic paper, the authors combined MCTS with deep neural networks to achieve super-human performance. They passed the board image as a 19×19-pixel image to a convolutional neural network (CNN) and used this to construct the representation of the board position, i.e., the *state*.

They used expert human moves to carry out supervised learning and learn two policies, i.e., $p(s)$.

---

[3]https://deepmind.com/research/case-studies/alphago-the-story-so-far

- *SL policy network (p_σ):* The authors used the supervised policy learning network p_σ. This was trained using the CNN-style network with 19×19 board positions as the input state (s) with the board positions being based on expert human moves.

- *Rollout policy (p_π):* The same data was also used to train another network called *fast policy* p_π, which acted as the rollout policy in the "rollout" phase of MCTS.

Next the authors trained a reinforcement learning (RL) network p_ρ, initialized from the SL policy network, which tries to improve the SL policy network to have more winnings, i.e., using policy optimization to improve with the objective of more wins. It is similar to what we saw in Chapter 7.

Lastly, another network v_θ is trained to predict the value of a state $v(s)$ for self-plays by the RL policy network p_ρ. Figure 9-12 shows a high-level diagram of the neural network training.

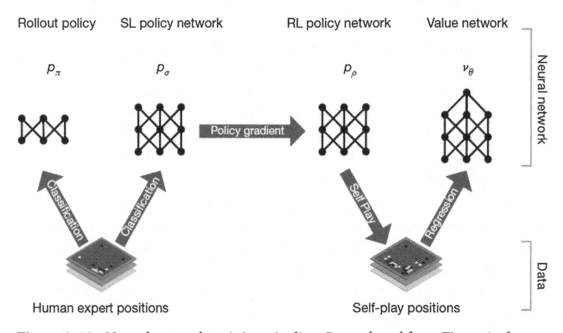

Figure 9-12. *Neural network training pipeline. Reproduced from Figure 1 of AlphaGo paper[4]*

---

[4]https://deepmind.com/research/case-studies/alphago-the-story-so-far

Finally, the policy network and the value network are combined to implement MCTS and to carry out forward search. The authors used a UCB-like approach to traverse the expanded part of the tree. Once a leaf node (S_L) was reached, they used one sample from the SL policy network p_σ to expand the leaf node (step 2 of MCTS). The leaf node was evaluated in two ways: one by using value network $v_\theta(S_L)$ and another by a fast rollout until termination using the rollout network p_π to get outcome z_L. These two values were combined using a mixing parameter λ.

$$V(S_L) = (1 - \lambda)v_\theta(s_L) + \lambda z_L$$

The fourth step of MCTS is carried out to update the score and visit counts at each node as we saw in the example in the previous section.

Once the search is complete, the algorithm chooses the best action from the root node, and then the cycle of MCTS goes on from the new state.

Subsequently, a year later, in 2017 the authors came out with a further refinement called "Mastering the game of Go without human knowledge,"[5] which trains to play without any human expert board positions, starting from random plays and improving upon it. Please refer to the paper for more details.

This brings us to the end of this chapter. It was the final chapter in this book in which we took a deep dive on some specific aspect of reinforcement learning. The Alpha Go explanation was at a conceptual level. Interested readers may want to refer to the original paper.

Summary

In this chapter, we carried out the last unification, that of combining model-based planning with model-free learning. First, we studied model-based RL where we learn the model and use that to plan. Next, we looked at integrating planning and learning into a single architecture under Dyna. Then, we looked at a specific version of Dyna with Q-learning in Dyna Q. We also briefly touched upon Dyna Q+ to engineer exploration for states not visited for a long time. This helped us manage learning in a changing environment. Next, we explored in detail the various ways state or action values could be updated either in expectation or via sample based updates.

---

[5]https://deepmind.com/research/case-studies/alphago-the-story-so-far

We then talked about the exploration versus exploitation dilemma in a simplified setting of multi-arm bandits. We looked at various exploration strategies such as ϵ-greedy exploration, upper confidence bound exploration, and Thomson sampling exploration. With the help of an experiment, we saw their relative performance on cumulative regret.

In the last part of the chapter, we studied forward looking and tree-based search. We took a deep dive into Monte Carlo tree search and walked through its use in solving the game of Go.

The next and final chapter will take a broad sweep over topics that we did not touch upon in this book.

## CHAPTER 10

Further Exploration and Next Steps

This is the last chapter of the book. Throughout the book, we have dived deep into many foundational aspects of reinforcement learning (RL). We looked at MDP and at planning in MDP using dynamic planning. We looked at model-free value methods. We talked about scaling up solution techniques using function approximation specifically by using deep learning–based approaches such as DQN. We looked at policy-based methods such as REINFORCE, TRPO, PPO, etc. We unified value and policy optimization methods in the actor-critic (AC) approach. Finally, we looked at how to combine the model-based and model-free methods in the previous chapter.

Most of these approaches are foundational to mastering reinforcement learning. However, reinforcement learning is a quickly expanding area with lots of specialized use cases in autonomous vehicles, robotics, and similar other fields. These go beyond the problem setup we used throughout this book to explain the concepts. We could not have covered all the emerging aspects as part of the core topics. That would have made the book very bulky; in addition, many of the areas are seeing new approaches almost every day.

In this last chapter, we will cover some of the topics that we think you should be aware of at a high level. We will keep the discussion at a conceptual level with links to some of the popular research/academic papers, where applicable. You can use these references to extend your knowledge horizon based on your individual interest area in the field of RL. Unlike in previous chapters, you will not always find the detailed pseudocode or actual code implementations. This has been done on purpose to provide a whirlwind tour of some emerging areas and new advances. You should use this chapter to get a 30,000-foot understanding of different topics. Based on your specific interest, you should dive deep into specific topics using the references given here as a starting point.

We will also talk about some popular libraries and ways to continue learning.

© Nimish Sanghi 2021
N. Sanghi, *Deep Reinforcement Learning with Python*, https://doi.org/10.1007/978-1-4842-6809-4_10

Model-Based RL: Additional Approaches

In the previous chapter, we looked at model-based RL wherein we learned the model by having the agent interact with the environment. The learned model was then used to generate additional transitions, i.e., to augment the data gathered by the agent through actual interaction with the real world. This was the approach that the Dyna algorithm took.

While Dyna helps in speeding up the learning process and addresses some of the sample inefficiency issues seen in model-free RL, it is mostly used for problems with simple function approximators. It has not been successful in deep learning function approximators that require lots of samples to get trained; too many training samples from simulators could degrade the quality of learning due to imperfections of the simulators' ability to model the world accurately. In this section, we will look at some recent approaches of combining the learned model with model-free methods within the context of deep learning.

World Models

In a 2018 paper titled "World Models,"[1] the authors proposed an approach to building a generative neural network model, which is a compressed representation of the spatial and temporal aspects of the environment, and using it to train the agent.

We humans develop a mental model of the world we see around us. We do not store all the smallest possible details of the environment. Rather, we store an abstract higher-level representation of the world that compresses spatial aspects as well as temporal aspects of the world and the relationships between the different entities of the world. We store only part of the world that we have been exposed to or is relevant for us.

We look at the current state or the context of the task at hand, think of the action we want to take, and predict the state that the action will take us into. Based on this predictive thinking, we choose the best action. Think of a baseball batter. He has milliseconds to act, swinging the bat at the right time and in right direction to connect with the ball. How do you think he does it? With years of practice, the batter has developed a strong internal model in which he can predict the future trajectory of the

---

[1]https://worldmodels.github.io/; https://arxiv.org/pdf/1803.10122.pdf

ball and can start swinging the bat at present to reach that exact point in the trajectory milliseconds later. The difference between a good player and a bad player largely boils down to this predictive capability of the player based on his internal model. Years of practice makes the whole thing intuitive without a lot of conscious planning in the mind.

In the paper, the authors show the way they achieved this predictive internal model using a large/powerful recurrent neural network (RNN) model that they called the *world model* and using a small controller model. The reason for the small controller model is to keep the credit assignment problem within bounds and have policies iterate faster during training. At the same time, the large "world model" allows it to retain all the spatial and temporal expressiveness required to have a good model of the environment and have a small controller model to keep the policy search focused on fast iterations during training.

The authors explore the ability to train agents on generated world models, completely replacing the interaction with the real world. Once the agent is well trained on the internal model representation, the learned policy is transferred to the real world. They also show the benefit of adding a small random noise to the internal world model to ensure that the agent does not over-exploit the imperfections of the learned model.

Let's next look at the breakdown of the model that was used. Figure 10-1 gives a high-level overview of the pipeline. At each instant, the agent receives an observation from the environment.

The world model consists of two modules.

- The vision model (V) encodes the high-dimensional image (observation vector) into a low-dimensional latent vector using a variational auto encoder (VAE) from deep learning. The latent vector z, the output of module V, compresses the spatial information of the observation into a smaller vector.

- The latent vector z is fed into a memory RNN (M) module to capture the temporal aspects of the environment. The M model, being an RNN network, compresses what happens over time and serves as a predictive model. Because many complex environments are stochastic and also because of the imperfections in our learning, the M model is trained to predict a distribution of the next state $P(Z_{t+1})$ instead of predicting a deterministic value Z_{t+1}. It does so by predicting the distribution of the next latent vector Z_{t+1} based on the current and past (the RNN part) as a mixture of Gaussian distribution $P(z_{t+1}|a_t, z_t, h_t)$, where h_t, the hidden state of RNN, captures the history. That is why it is called a *mixture density model based on a recurrent neural network* (MDM-RNN).

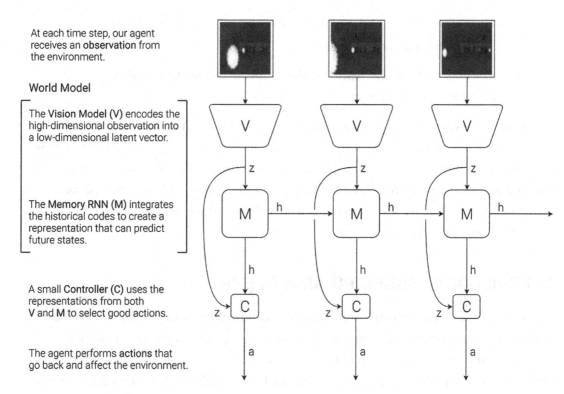

At each time step, our agent receives an **observation** from the environment.

World Model

The **Vision Model (V)** encodes the high-dimensional observation into a low-dimensional latent vector.

The **Memory RNN (M)** integrates the historical codes to create a representation that can predict future states.

A small **Controller (C)** uses the representations from both V and M to select good actions.

The agent performs **actions** that go back and affect the environment.

Figure 10-1. *Overview of the agent model in used in the "world view." Reproduced from Ha and Schmidhuber, "Recurrent World Models Facilitate Policy Evolution," 2018*[2]

The controller model is responsible for taking the spatial information (z_t) and temporal information (h_t), concatenating them together, and feeding them into a single-layer linear model. The overall flow of the information is as follows:

1. The agent gets an observation at time t. The observation is fed into the V model, which codifies it into a smaller latent vector z_t.

2. Next the latent vector is fed into an M model that predicts the z_{t+1}, i.e., h_t.

3. The outputs of the V and M model are concatenated and fed into the C controller, which produces the action a_t. In other words, using z_t and z_{t+1}, predict a_t.

[2]https://worldmodels.github.io/

4. The action is fed into the real world as well as it is used by the M model to update its hidden state.

5. The action in the real world produces the next state/observation, and the next cycle begins.

For other details like the pseudocode, the implementation details of the networks used, and the losses used in training, please refer to the previously referenced paper. In the paper, the authors also talk about how they used the predictive power to come up with hypothetical scenarios by feeding back the prediction z_{t+1} as the next real-world observation. They further show how they were able to train an agent in "dream world" and then transfer the learning to the real world.

Imagination-Augmented Agents (I2A)

As discussed earlier, Dyna proposed a way to combine the *model-free* and *model-based* approaches. The model-free methods have higher scalability in terms of complex environments and has been seen to work well with deep learning. However, these are not sample efficient as deep learning requires a large number of training samples to be effective. Even a simple Atari game policy training could take millions of examples to get trained. Model-based, on the other hand, is sample efficient. Dyna provided a way to combine the two advantages. Apart from using the real-world transitions to train the agent, the real-world transitions are also used to learn a model that is used to generate/simulate additional training examples. The problem, however, is that *model learning may not be perfect*, and unless this fact is accounted for, direct use of Dyna in a complex deep learning combined reinforcement learning does not give good results. The poor model knowledge can lead to over-optimism and poor agent performance.

Like the previous approach of using world models, the method *imagination augmented agents* (I2A) combines model-based and model-free approaches in a way to make the combined approach work well for complex environments. I2A forms an approximate environment model and leverages it by "learning to interpret" the learned model imperfections. It provides an end-to-end learning approach to extract useful information gathered from model simulations without relying exclusively on the simulated returns. The internal model is used by agents, also referred to as *imagining*, to seek positive outcomes while avoiding adverse outcomes. The authors from DeepMind, in their 2018 paper titled "Imagination-Augmented Agents for Deep Reinforcement

Learning,"[3] show that this approach can learn better with less data and imperfect models.

Figure 10-2 details the I2A architecture as explained in the referenced paper.

- The environment model in Figure 10-2(a), given the present information, makes predictions about the future. The imagination core (IC) has a policy net $\hat{\pi}$, which takes the current observation o_t or $\hat{o}_t$ (real or imagined) as input and produces a rollout action $\hat{a}_t$. The observation o_t or $\hat{o}_t$ and rollout action $\hat{a}_t$ are fed into the environment model, an RNN-based network, to predict the next observation $\hat{o}_{t+1}$ and reward $\hat{r}_{t+1}$.

- Many such ICs are strung together feeding the output of the previous IC to the next IC and producing an *imaged rollout trajectory* of length τ as shown in Figure 10-2(b). n such trajectories $\hat{T}_1 ... \hat{T}_i ... \hat{T}_n$ are produced. As the learned model cannot be assumed to be perfect, depending solely on the predicted rewards may not be a good idea. Also, the trajectories may contain information beyond the reward sequence. Therefore, each rollout is encoded by sequentially processing the output to get an embedding on each trajectory, as shown on the right side of Figure 10-2(b).

- Finally, the aggregator in Figure 10-2(c) combines these individual n rollouts and feeds them as an additional context to the policy network along with the model-free path of feeding the observation directly.

[3]https://arxiv.org/pdf/1707.06203.pdf

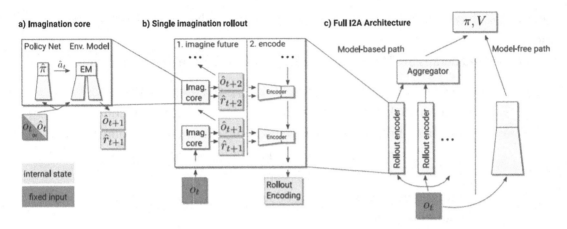

Figure 10-2. *I2A architecture. It depicts the IC in (a), the single imagination rollout in (b), and the full I2A architecture in (c). Reproduced from the paper "Imagination-Augmented Agents for Deep Reinforcement Learning," 2018[4]*

The authors of the paper show that learning the rollout encoder in step (b) plays a significant role in being able to handle the imperfect model learning well.

Model-Based RL with Model-Free Fine-Tuning (MBMF)

In a 2017 paper titled "Neural Network Dynamics for Model-Based Deep Reinforcement Learning with Model-Free Fine-Tuning," the authors demonstrate yet another way to combine model-free and model-based RL. They looked at the domain of locomotion tasks. The model-free methods of training robots for locomotion suffer from high sample complexity, something we have seen in all deep learning–based models. The authors combined the model-free and model-based approaches to come up with sample efficient models to learn the dynamics of locomotion with varying task goals using medium complexity neural networks.

The problem assumes that reward function $r_t = r(s_t, a_t)$ is given. The paper gives examples of the reward functions used for *moving forward* and *trajectory following*. Trajectory is shown by sparse *waypoints* that define the path the robot needs to follow. Waypoints are points on a given trajectory that, when connected with lines, approximate the given trajectory, as shown in Figure 10-3. For more details on how waypoints are used for trajectory planning, please refer to any text on autonomous vehicles and robots.

---

[4]https://arxiv.org/pdf/1707.06203.pdf

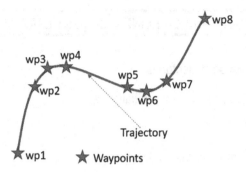

Figure 10-3. *Trajectory and waypoints*

At any point the robot's projected sequence of actions is considered. For each action, the line segment joining the current state $\hat{s}_t$ and estimated next state $\hat{s}_{t+1} = \hat{f}_\theta(\hat{s}_t, a_t)$ is projected on the closest line segment joining two consecutive waypoints of the trajectory. The reward is positive if the robot's movement is along the waypoints line segment and negative for a movement perpendicular to the waypoint line segment. Similarly, they have another set of reward function for the *moving forward* goal.

The neural network is learning the dynamics $\hat{s}_{t+1} = \hat{f}_\theta(\hat{s}_t, a_t)$. However, instead of predicting s_{t+1}, the network takes in (s_t, a_t) and predicts the difference $s_{t+1} - s_t$. Predicting the difference instead of the whole new state amplifies the changes and allows for small changes also to be captured.

The reward function and dynamics model are fed into a *model predictive controller* (MPC). MPC takes in the reward and next state to plan ahead for H steps using predicted s_{t+1} as the new input to predict s_{t+2} and so on. K randomly generated action sequences, each of length H steps, are evaluated to find the best action at initial time step t based on the highest cumulative reward among the K sequences. The robot then takes the action a_t. At this point, the sample sequences are dropped, and complete replanning of next K sequences, each of length H, is done at time $t + 1$. The use of this model's predictive controller (instead of an open loop approach) ensures that errors are not propagated forward. There is a replanning at each step. Figure 10-4 gives the complete algorithm.

MODEL-BASED REINFORCEMENT LEARNING

Gather dataset D_{RAND} of random trajectories.

Initialize empty dataset D_{RL}, and randomly initialize $\hat{f}_\theta$.

for iter=1 **to** max_iter **do**

    Train $\hat{f}_\theta(s,a)$ by performing gradient descent.

$$\text{Loss}(\theta) = \frac{1}{|D|} \sum (s_t, a_t, s_{t+1}) \in D^{\frac{1}{2}} \left\| (s_{t+1} - s_t) - \hat{f}_\theta(s_t, a_t) \right\|^2$$

$$\text{where } D = D_{RAND} \cup D_{RL}$$

    for $t = 1$ **to** T **do**

        Get agent's current state s_t.

        Use $\hat{f}_\theta$ to estimate optimal action sequence

            (explained earlier)

        Execute first action a_t from selected action sequence $A_t^{(H)}$.

        Add (s_t, a_t, s_{t+1}) to D_{RL}.

Figure 10-4. *MBMF algorithm*

Once the model is trained, to further improve the model, the authors fine-tuned it by initializing a model-free agent with the model-based learner trained as shown earlier. The model-free training can be done using any of the previous approaches we learned. This is the reason for naming it *model-based with model-free fine-tuning* (MBMF).

Model-Based Value Expansion (MBVE)

In a 2018 paper titled "Model-Based Value Expansion for Efficient Model-Free Reinforcement Learning,"[5] the authors take the approach of combining the model-based and model-free approaches with a known reward function to get a more disciplined approach to value estimation.

---

[5]https://arxiv.org/pdf/1803.00101.pdf

The algorithm learns the system dynamics $\hat{s}_{t+1} = \hat{f}_\theta\left(\hat{s}_t, a_t\right)$ to simulate the short-term horizon of trajectory and Q-learning to estimate the long-term value. This improves the Q-learning by providing higher-quality target values for training.

The authors show the performance of combining MBVE with DDPG versus vanilla DDPG and demonstrate significant improvement by combining MBVE with DDPG.

Imitation Learning and Inverse Reinforcement Learning

There is another branch of learning that is called *imitation learning*. With it we record the interactions of an expert and then use a supervised setting to learn a behavior that can mimic the expert.

As shown in Figure 10-5, we have an expert who looks at states s_t and produces the actions a_t. We use this data in a supervised setting with the states s_t as input to the model and the actions a_t as targets to learn a policy $\pi_\theta(a_t|s_t)$, as shown in the middle of Figure 10-5. This is the easiest way to learn a behavior, called *behavior cloning*. It's even simpler than the whole discipline of reinforcement learning. The system/learner does not analyze or reason about anything; it just blindly learns to mimic the behavior of the expert.

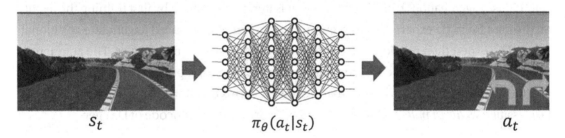

s_t $\pi_\theta(a_t|s_t)$ a_t

Figure 10-5. *Expert demonstration*

However, the learning is not perfect. Suppose you learn a near-perfect policy with some minor errors, and suppose you start in a state s_1. You follow the learned policy to take action a_1, which, say, is a minor deviation from what an expert would have taken. You keep taking these actions in a sequence, some matching the expert and some deviating a little bit from what an expert would have done. These deviations over multiple actions can add up and bring your vehicle (Figure 10-5) to the edge of the road. Now, most likely the expert would not have driven so badly to get to the edge of the road. The expert training data never saw what the expert would have done in this situation.

The policy has not been trained with these kinds of situations. The learned policy will most likely take an action that could be random and definitely not designed to correct the error to bring the vehicle back toward the center of the road.

This is an *open loop problem*. Errors from every action are getting compounded to make the actual trajectory drift from the expert trajectory, as shown in Figure 10-6.

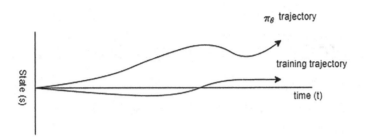

Figure 10-6. *Drift in trajectory over time*

This is also known as *distributional shift*. In other words, the distribution of states in the policy training is different from the distribution of states the agent sees when it just executes the policy in an open loop with no corrective feedback.

In cases like this, with additive errors, there is an alternative algorithm known as *DAgger* (for "dataset aggregation"), in which the agent is iteratively trained by first training the agent on the data from the expert demonstration. The trained policy is used to generate additional states. The expert then provides the correct action for these generated states. The augmented data along with the original data are again used to fine-tune the policy. This cycle goes on, and the agent gets closer and closer to the expert in terms of following the behavior. This can be classified as *direct policy learning*. Figure 10-7 gives the pseudocode of DAgger.

DAGGER

Do until tired:

  Train $\pi_\theta(a_t| s_t)$ from human data $D = \{s_1, a_1, ..., s_N, a_N\}$.

  Run $\pi_\theta(a_t| s_t)$ to get dataset $D_\pi = \{s_1, s_2, ..., s_N\}$.

  Ask human/expert to label D_π with actions $\{a_1, a_2, ..., a_N\}$.

  Aggregate: $D \leftarrow D \cup D_\pi$.

Figure 10-7. *DAgger for behavior cloning*

DAgger has a human expert label the unseen states as the Figure 10-7 policy is played out, which trains the agent to recover from mistakes/drifts. DAgger is simple and efficient. However, it is just behavior cloning and not reinforcement learning. It does not reason about anything other than trying to learn a behavior to follow the expert actions. If the expert covers a large part of the state space that the agent is likely to see, this algorithm can help the agent learn a good behavior. However, anything requiring long-term planning is not suited for DAgger.

If it is not reinforcement learning, why are we talking about it here? It turns out that in many cases, having an expert give a demonstration is a good way to understand the objective that the agent is trying to achieve. When coupled with other enhancements, imitation learning is a useful approach. We will talk about one such issue.

Up to now, in this book we have studied various algorithms to train the agent. With some algorithms, we knew the dynamics and transitions like the model-based setups, in others we learned in a model-free setup without explicitly learning the model, and finally in others we learned the model from interaction with the world to augment model-free learning. However, in all these cases, we considered the reward to be something simple, intuitive, and well known. In some other cases, we could handcraft a simple reward function, e.g., learing to follow a trajectory using MBMF. But all real-world cases are not so simple. The reward at times is ill defined and/or sparse. None of the previous algorithms will work in the absence of a well-defined reward.

Consider a case where you are trying to train a robot to pick up a jug of water and pour the water in a glass. What will the reward be for each action in the whole sequence? Will it be 1 when the robot is able to pour the water into a glass without spilling any on the table or breaking/dropping the jug/glass? Or will you define a range of rewards based on how much water was spilled? How will you induce a behavior to have the robot learn smooth actions like a human? Can you think of a reward that can provide correct feedback to the robot on what is a good move and what is a bad move?

Now look at the alternate scenario. The robot gets to watch a human carry out the task of pouring water. It, instead of learning a behavior, first learns a reward function noting all actions matching the human behavior as good and others as bad, with goodness depending on the extent of the deviation from what it saw humans do. It can then use the learned reward function to, as a next step, learn a policy/sequence of actions to perform similar actions. This is the domain of *inverse reinforcement learning (inverse RL) coupled with imitation learning*.

Table 10-1 compares behavior cloning, direct policy learning, and inverse RL.

Table 10-1. *Types of Imitation Learning*

	Direct Policy Learning	Reward Learning	Access to Environment	Interactive Demonstrator/ Expert	Pre-collected Demonstrations
Behavioral cloning	Yes	No	No	No	Yes
Direct policy learning	Yes	No	Yes	Yes	Optional
Inverse reinforcement learning	No	Yes	Yes	No	Yes

Inverse reinforcement learning is the MDP setup where we know the model dynamics but we have no knowledge of the reward function. Mathematically, we can express it as follows:

$$Given: D = \left\{ \tau_1, \tau_2, \ldots, \tau_m \right\} = \left\{ \left(s_0^i, a_0^i, \ldots s_T^I, a_T^i \right) \right\} \sim \pi^*$$

The goal is to learn a reward function r^* so that

$$\pi^* = argmax_\pi E_\pi \left[r^*(s,a) \right]$$

Figure 10-8 shows the high-level pseudocode for inverse RL. We collect sample trajectories from the expert, and we use them to learn the reward function. Next, using the learned reward function, we learn a policy that maximizes the reward. The learned policy is compared with the expert, and the difference is used to tweak the learned reward. This cycle goes on.

INVERSE RL

Expert/human data $D = \{s_1, a_1, \ldots, s_N, a_N\}$.

Do until tired:

    Learn reward function: $r_\theta(s_t, a_t)$.

    Learn policy given reward function (RL).

    Compare learned policy with the expert.

Figure 10-8. *Inverse reinforcement learning*

Please note that the inner *do loop* has a step (step 2, "Learn policy given reward function") of learning the policy iteratively. It is actually a loop abstracted to a single line of pseudocode. To scale this when the state space is continuous and high dimensional and also when the system dynamics are unknown, we need tweaks to make the previous approach work. In a 2016 paper titled "Guided Cost Learning: Deep Inverse Optimal Control via Policy Optimization,"[6] the authors used a sample-based approximation of MaxEntropy Inverse RL[7]. You can look at the previously referenced papers for further details. Figure 10-9 shows the high-level diagram of the approach.

---

[6]https://arxiv.org/pdf/1603.00448.pdf

[7]https://www.aaai.org/Papers/AAAI/2008/AAAI08-227.pdf

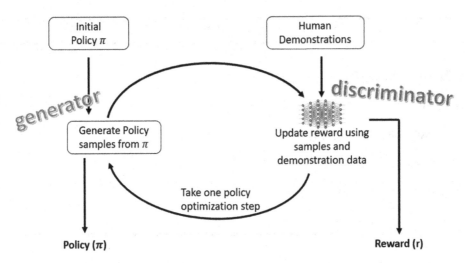

Figure 10-9. *Guided cost learning: deep inverse optimal control via policy optimization*

The architecture can be compared to *generative adversarial networks* (GANs) from deep learning. In GAN, a *generator network* tries to generate synthetic examples, and a *discriminator network* tries to give a high score to actual samples while giving a low score to synthetic examples. The generator tries to get better in generating examples that iteratively get harder to distinguish from "real-world examples," and the discriminator gets better and better in making a distinction between synthetic versus real-world examples.

In the same way, the guided cost learning as given in Figure 10-9 can be thought of as a GAN setup where the discriminator is getting better in giving a high reward to human observations while giving a low one to the actions/trajectories generated by the policy network. The policy network gets better and better in producing actions similar to a human expert.

The uses of inverse learning coupled with imitation learning are many.

- *Making characters in animation movies*: You can move the face and lips in sync with the words the characters are speaking. The face/lip movements of a human expert are first recorded (expect demonstrations), and a policy is trained to make a character's face/lips move like a human.

- *Part of speech tagging*: This is based on some expert/human labels.

- *Smooth imitation learning*: To have an autonomous camera follow a game like basketball, similar to what a human operation would do, to follow the ball across the court, zoom, and pan based on certain events.

- *Coordinated multi-agent imitation learning*: To look at recordings of, say, a soccer game (human expert demonstrations) and then learn a policy to predict the next place for the players to be based on the sequence.

Imitation learning is a quickly expanding area. We have barely touched the surface to just introduce the topic. There are tons of good places to start exploring these topics. A good place to start this is the ICML2018 tutorial on imitation learning.[8] It is a two-hour video tutorial with slides given by two experts from Caltech.

Derivative-Free Methods

Let's move back to the regular model-free RL that we saw in major parts of the book. In this section, we will briefly talk about the methods that allow us to improve policies without taking derivatives of policy $\pi_\theta(a|s)$ with respect to policy parameters θ.

We will look at *evolutionary methods*. Why are they evolutionary? Because they work like natural evolution. Things that are better/fitter survive, and things that are weaker fade away.

The first method we look at is called the *cross-entropy method*. It is embarrassingly simple.

1) Pick a random/stochastic policy.

2) Roll out a few sessions.

3) Pick some percentage of sessions with higher rewards.

4) Improve the policy to increase the probability of selecting those actions.

---

[8]https://sites.google.com/view/icml2018-imitation-learning/

Figure 10-10 gives the pseudocode of the cross-entropy method for training a continuous action policy, which is assumed to be a normal distribution with d-dimensional action space. Any other distribution could also be used, but for many domains, it has been shown that normal distribution is the best in terms of balancing the expressibility of the distribution and the number of parameters of the distribution.

CROSS-ENTROPY METHOD

Initialize $\mu \in R^d, \sigma \in R^d_{>0}$, where μ and σ are the mean and standard deviation of the normal distribution: $N\left(\mu \in R^d, \sigma \in R^d_{>0}\right)$.

For iteration = 1, 2, ...

   Sample n parameters $\theta_i \sim N(\mu, diag(\sigma^2))$.

   For each θ_i, perform one rollout to get return $R(\tau_i)$.

   Select the top k% of θ, and fit a new diagonal Gaussian to

   those samples using the maximum-likelihood. Update μ, σ.

Figure 10-10. *Cross-entropy method*

A similar approach called the *covariance matrix adaptation evolutionary strategy* (CMA-ES) is popular in the graphics world for an optimal gait of characters. In the cross-entropy method, we fit a diagonal Gaussian to the top k% of rollouts. However, in CMA-ES, we optimize the covariance matrix, and it amounts to the second-order model learning as compared to the first-order in the usual derivative methods.

A major drawback of the cross-entropy methods is that they work well for a relatively low-dimensional action space such as the CartPole, LunarLander, etc. Can the evolutionary strategy (ES) be made to work for deep net policies with high-dimensional action spaces? In a 2017 paper titled "Evolution Strategies as a Scalable Alternative to Reinforcement Learning,"[9] the authors show that ES can reliably train neural network policies, in a fashion well suited to be scaled up to modern distributed computer systems for controlling robots in the MuJoCo physics simulator.

---

[9]https://arxiv.org/pdf/1703.03864.pdf

Let's conceptually walk through the approach that was taken in this paper. Consider a probability distribution of policy parameters: $\theta \sim P_\mu(\theta)$. Here, θ means the parameters of the policy, and these parameters follow some probability distribution $P_\mu(\theta)$ parameterized by μ.

Our goal is to find the policy parameter θ such that it generates trajectories that maximize the cumulative return. This is similar to the objective we had for the policy gradient approach.

$$Goal : maximize E_{\theta \sim P_\mu(\theta), \tau \sim \pi_\theta} \left[R(\tau) \right]$$

Like with policy gradient, we do a stochastic gradient ascent, but unlike policy gradient, we do not do so in θ, rather in μ space.

$$\nabla_\mu E_{\theta \sim P_\mu(\theta), \tau \sim \pi_\theta} \left[R(\tau) \right] = E_{\theta \sim P_\mu(\theta), \tau \sim \pi_\theta} \left[\nabla_\mu \log P_\mu(\theta) R(\tau) \right] \qquad (10.1)$$

The previous expression is similar to what we saw in policy gradients. However, there is a subtle difference. We are not doing a gradient step in θ. Hence, we do not worry about $\pi_\theta(a|s)$. We ignore most of the information about a trajectory, i.e., states, actions, and rewards. We only worry about the policy parameter θ and total trajectory reward $R(\tau)$. This in turn enables very scalable distributed training similar to the A3C approach of running multiple workers, as shown in Figure 7-10.

Let's take a concrete example. Suppose $\theta \sim P_\mu(\theta)$ is a Gaussian distribution with a mean of μ and a convariance matrix of σ^2. I. Then $logP_\mu(\theta)$ given inside the "expectation" in (10.1) can be expressed as follows:

$$logP_\mu(\theta) = -\frac{\|\theta - \mu\|^2}{2\sigma^2} + const$$

Taking the gradient of the previous expression with regard to μ, we have this:

$$\nabla_\mu logP_\mu(\theta) = \frac{\theta - \mu}{\sigma^2}$$

Let's say we draw two parameter samples θ_1 and θ_2 and obtain two trajectories: τ_1 and τ_2.

$$E_{\theta \sim P_\mu(\theta), \tau \sim \pi_\theta}\left[\nabla_\mu log P_\mu(\theta) R(\tau)\right] \approx \frac{1}{2}\left[R(\tau_1)\frac{\theta_1 - \mu}{\sigma^1} + R(\tau_2)\frac{\theta_2 - \mu}{\sigma^2}\right] \qquad (10.2)$$

This merely converts the expectation in (10.1) to an estimate based on two samples. Can you interpret equation (10.2)? The analysis is similar to what we did in Chapter 7. If a reward of trajectory is +ve, we adjust the mean μ to get closer to that θ. If the trajectory reward is -ve, we move μ away from that sampled θ. In other words, like with policy gradient, we adjust μ to increase the proability of good trajectories and reduce the probability of bad trajectories. However, we do so by making adjustments directly to the distribution from which parameters came and not by adjusting the θ on which the policy depends. This allows us to ignore the details of states and actions, etc.

The previously referenced paper uses *antithetic sampling*. In other words, it samples a pair of policies with mirror noise ($\theta_+ = \mu + \sigma\epsilon$, $\theta_- = \mu - \sigma\epsilon$) and then samples the two trajectories τ_+ and τ_- to evaluate (10.2). Substituting these in (10.2), the expression can be simplified as follows:

$$\nabla_\mu E\left[R(\tau)\right] \approx \frac{\epsilon}{2\sigma}\left[R(\tau_+) + R(\tau_-)\right]$$

The previous manipulation allows efficient parameter passing between workers and parameter servers. At the beginning, μ is known, and only ϵ needs to be communicated, which reduces the number of parameters that need to be passed back and forth. It brings significant scalability in making the approach parallel.

Figure 10-11 shows the parallelized evolution strategy pseudocode.

PARALLELIZED EVOLUTION STRATEGIES

Input:

Learning rate α, noise standard deviation σ, initial policy paramters θ_0

Initialize:

n workers with known random seeds, and initial parameters θ_0

for t = 0, 1, 2, ... **do**

    for each worker i = 1, ..., n do

        Sample $\epsilon_i \sim N(0, I)$

        Compute returns $F_i = F(\theta_t + \sigma \epsilon_i)$

    end for

    Send all scalar returns F_i from each worker to every other worker.

    for each worker i = 1, ..., n **do**

        Reconstruct all perturbations ϵ_j for j = 1, ..., n.

        Set $\theta_{t+1} \leftarrow \theta_t + \alpha \dfrac{1}{n\sigma} \sum_{j=1}^{n} F_j \epsilon_j$

    end for

end for

***Figure 10-11.** Parallelized evolution strategies algorithm 2[10]*

The authors of the paper reported the following:

- They found that the use of virtual batch normalization and other reparameterizations of the neural network policy greatly improve the reliability of evolution strategies.

---

[10]https://arxiv.org/pdf/1703.03864.pdf

- They found the evolution strategies method to be highly parallelizable (as discussed earlier). In particular, using 1,440 workers, it was able to solve the MuJoCo 3D humanoid task in less than 10 minutes.

- The data efficiency of evolution strategies was surprisingly good. One-hour ES results require about the same amount of computation as the published one-day results for asynchronous advantage actor critic (A3C). On MuJoCo tasks, we are able to match the learned policy performance of TRPO.

- ES exhibited better exploration behavior than policy gradient methods like TRPO. On the MuJoCo humanoid task, ES has been able to learn a wide variety of gaits (such as walking sideways or walking backward). These unusual gaits are never observed with TRPO, which suggests a qualitatively different exploration behavior.

- The found the evolution strategies method to be robust.

If you are interested, you should read through the reference paper to get into the details and see how it compares with other methods.

Transfer Learning and Multitask Learning

In the previous chapters, we looked at using DQN and the policy gradient algorithms to train agents to play Atari games. If you check out the papers that showcase these experiments, you will notice that some Atari games are easier to train, while some are harder to train. If you look at the Atari game Breakout versus Montezuma's Revenge, as shown in Figure 10-12, you will notice that it is easier to train on Breakout as compared to training for Montezuma. Why is this?

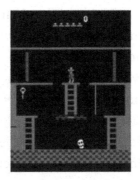

Breakout
(easy)

Montezuma's revenge
(hard)

Figure 10-12. *Easy and hard to learn Atari games*

Breakout has simple rules. However, Montezuma's Revenge on the right side of Figure 10-12 has some complex rules. They are not easy to learn. As a human, even if we are playing it for the first time and have no prior knowledge of the exact rules, we know that "keys" are something we usually pick to open new things and/or get big rewards. We know "ladders" can be used to climb up or down and that "skulls" are something to be avoided. In other words, our past experience of having played other games or having read about treasure hunts or having watched some movies gives us the context, or the previous learning, to quickly perform new tasks that we may never have seen before.

Prior understanding of the problem structure can help us solve new complex tasks quickly. When an agent solves prior tasks, it acquires useful knowledge that can help the agent solve new tasks. But where is this knowledge stored? The following are some possible options:

- *Q-function*: They tell us what a good state and action are.

- *Policy*: They tell us which actions are useful and which are not.

- *Models*: They codify the learned knowledge about how the world operates such as the laws of physics such as Newton's laws, friction, gravity, momentum, etc.

- *Features/hidden states*: The hidden layers of neural networks abstract higher-level constructs and knowledge that can be generalized across different domains/tasks. We see this in computer vision in supervised learning.

The ability to use the experience from one set of tasks to get faster and more effective performance on a new task is called *transfer learning*, i.e., transfer knowledge gained from past experiences to tackle new tasks. We see this significantly used in supervised learning, especially in the domain of computer vision when popular convolutional network architectures like ResNet trained on an ImageNet dataset are used as pretrained networks to train on new vision tasks. We will briefly look at how this technique can be applied in the field of reinforcement learning. Let's define some terminology that is commonly found in transfer learning literature.

- *Task*: In RL, the MDP problem that we are trying to train the agent to solve.

- *Source domain*: The problem on which the agent is trained first.

- *Target domain*: The MDP that we hope to solve faster by leveraging the knowledge from "source domain."

- *Shot*: The number of attempts in the target domain.

- *0-shot*: Run a policy trained on the source domain directly on the target domain.

- *1-shot*: Retrain the source domain trained agent just once on the target domain.

- *Few-shot*: Retrain the source domain's trained agent just a few times on the target domain.

Next let's look how we can transfer the knowledge gained from the source domain to the target domain in the context of reinforcement learning. At this point, three broad classes of approaches have been tried.

- *Forward transfer*: Train on one task and transfer to a new task.

- *Multitask transfer*: Train on many tasks and transfer to a new task.

- *Transfer models and value functions*.

We will briefly talk about each of these approaches. *Forward transfer* is one of the most common ways to transfer knowledge in supervised learning, especially in computer vision. One model, like the popular architecture ResNet, is trained to classify images on the ImageNet dataset. This is called *pretraining*. The trained model is then changed by replacing the last layer or last few layers. The network is retrained on a new task called *fine-tuning*. However, forward transfer in reinforcement learning could face some issues of domain shift. In other words, the representations learned in the source domain may not work well in the target domain. In addition, there is a difference in the MDP. In other words, certain things are possible in the source domain that are not possible in the target domain. There are also fine-tuning issues. For example, the policies trained on the source domain could have sharp peaks in probability distribution, almost close to being deterministic. Such a pekad distribution could hamper exploration while fine-tuning on target domain.

The transfer learning in supervised learning seems to work well probably because the large set of varied images in the ImageNet dataset helps the network learn very good generalized representation, which can then be fine-tuned to specific tasks. However, in reinforcement learning, the tasks are generally much less diverse, which makes it harder for the agent to learn the high-level generalizations. Further, there is the issue of policies being too deterministic, which hampers exploration for better convergence during fine-tuning. This issue can be handled by making the policies learn on a source domain with an objective that has an entropy regularizer term, something we have seen in a few examples in previous chapters such as soft actor critic (SAC) in Chapter 8. The entropy regularization ensures that the policies learned on the source system retain enough stochasticity to allow for exploration during fine-tuning.

There is another approach to make learning on the source domain more generic. We can add some randomization to the source domain. Say we are training a robot to do some task; we could instantiate many versions of the source domain with a different mass of each arm for the robot, or the friction coefficients. This will induce the agent to learn the underlying physics instead of memorizing to do well in a specific configuration. In another real-world setup involving images, we could again borrow from the "image augmentation" practice from computer vision, wherein we augment the training images with some random rotation, scaling, etc.

Next, we look at multitask transfer, the second way to approach to transfer learning. There are two key ideas to this: accelerate learning of all the tasks together that are executed together, and solve multiple tasks to provide better pre-training for the target domain.

One easy approach to train an agent on multiple tasks is to augment the state with a code/indicator signifying the specific task, e.g., extending state S as ($S + Indicator$). When an episode starts, the system chooses an MDP (task) at random and then chooses the initial state based on the initial state distribution. The training then runs like any other MDP. Figure 10-13 shows a schematic of this approach. This kind of approach can be tough at times. Imagine a policy getting better at solving a specific MDP; the optimization will start prioritizing the learning of that MDP at the cost of others.

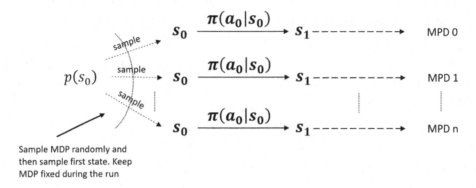

Figure 10-13. *Solving multiple tasks together*

We could also train the agents to solve different tasks separately and then combine these learnings to solve a new task. We need to combine/distill the policies learned for different tasks to a single one in some way. There are various approaches for this, and we will not get into the details here.

Let's look at another variation of multitask transfer: *that of a single agent learning two different tasks in the same environment.* An example would be a robot learning to do laundry as well as wash utensils. In this approach, we augment the state to add the context of the task and train the agent. This is known as *contextual policies.* Using this approach, the state is represented as follows:

$$\tilde{s} = \begin{bmatrix} s \\ \omega \end{bmatrix}$$

We learn the policies as follows:

$$\pi_\theta(a|s,\omega)$$

Here, ω is the context, i.e., the task.

Lastly, there is a third approach of transfer learning, that of transferring models or value functions. In this setting, we assume that the dynamics $p(s_{t+1}|s_t, a_t)$ is same in both the source and target domains. However, the reward functions are different; for example, the autonomous car learns to drive to a small set of places (source domain). It then has to navigate to a new destination (target domain). We could transfer either of the three: the model, the value functions, or the policies. Models are a logical choice and simple to transfer since the model $p(s_{t+1}|s_t, a_t)$ in principle is independent of the reward function. Transferring policies is usually done via contextual policies but otherwise not easy to do so as policies $\pi_\theta(a|s)$ contain the least information about the dynamics function. Value function transfer is also not so simple. Value functions couple dynamics, rewards, and policies.

$$Q^\pi(s, a) = \underbrace{r(s, a)}_{reward} + \gamma E_{\underbrace{s' \sim p(s'|s, a)}_{dynamics}, \underbrace{a' \sim \pi(a|s)}_{policy}}[Q^\pi(s', a')]$$

We can do value transfer using successor features and representation, the details of which can be found in texts detailing transfer learning.

Meta-Learning

We have looked at various approaches to making agents learn from experiences. But is that the way humans learn? Current AI systems excel at mastering a single skill. We have agents like AlphaGo that have beaten the best human Go player. IBM Watson beat the best human Jeopardy player. But can AlphaGo play the card game of Bridge? Can the Jeopardy agent hold an intelligent chat? Can an expert helicopter controller for aerobatics be used to carry out a rescue mission? Comparatively, humans learn to act intelligently in many new situations, drawing on their past experience or current expertise.

If we want agents to be able to acquire many skills across different domains, we cannot afford to train agents for each specific task in a data-inefficient way—the way current RL agents are. To get true AI, we need agents to be able to learn new tasks quickly by leveraging their past experiences. This approach of *learning to learn* is called *meta-learning*. And it is a key step to make RL agents human-like, always learning and improving based on experience and learning across varied tasks efficiently.

Meta-learning systems are trained on many different tasks (meta-training set) and then tested on new tasks. The terms *meta-learning* and *transfer-learning* could be confusing. These are evolving disciplines, and the terms are used inconsistently. However, one easy way to distinguish them would be to think of meta-learning as learning to optimize hyperparameters (e.g., number of nodes, architecture) of the model and think of transfer learning as fine-tuning an already tuned network.

During meta-learning, there are two optimizations at play: the learner, which learns (optimizes) the tasks; and the meta-learner, which trains (optimizes) the agents. There are three broad categories of meta-learning methods.

- *Recurrent models*: This approach trains a recurrent model like long short-term memory (LSTM) through episodes of tasks in the meta-training set.

- *Metric learning*: In this approach, the agent learns a new metric space in which learning is efficient.

- *Learning optimizers*: In this approach, there are two networks: the meta-learning and the learner. The meta-learner learns to update the learner network. The meta-learner can be thought of learning to optimize the hyperparameters of the model, and the learner network can be thought of as the regular network that is used to predict the action.

It is an interesting area of study with a lot of potential. Interested readers can refer to a great tutorial from the International Conference on Machine Learning (ICML-2019).[11]

Popular RL Libraries

We will briefly look at the popular libraries that are used in reinforcement learning. There are typical three categories: libraries that implement some popular environments, libraries that take care of deep learning, and libraries that implement many of the popular RL algorithms that we have seen in this book.

OpenAI Gym[12] is by far the most popular library when it comes to the RL environments. There are different types of environments ranging from simple classic control to Atari games to robotics. If you want to use Atari games, you will require additional installation. There is a popular library for continuous control tasks using a physics simulator known as MuJoCo. MuJoCo[13] requires a paid license. However, it offers a free trial license as well as a free student license. Atari games also require additional installation but are free.

---

[11]https://sites.google.com/view/icml19metalearning
[12]https://gym.openai.com/
[13]http://www.mujoco.org/index.html

We have tried a few environments from Gym. As part of your next steps, you should look at many other environments and try various learning algorithms, either handcrafted ones or implementations in the popular RL libraries.

Next are deep learning libraries. There are quite a few, but the most popular ones are TensorFlow from Google and PyTorch from Facebook. Another library, Sonnet from Deep Mind,[14] is built on top of TensorFlow to abstract common patterns. Apache MXNet is another popular library. There are some more, but the mentioned ones are by far the most popular ones. We advise you to master one of the popular ones and then branch off to learning the other popular deep learning libraries. At the moment, PyTorch is gaining significant traction over TensorFlow. You can choose either of these two as your first deep learning library and master it first before branching out to other ones.

The last category is the popular libraries implementing common RL algorithms. We list the popular ones here:

- *OpenAI Spinning Up*[15]: This is an ideal choice to further extend your knowledge and dive deep into the basics of implementations. Some of our code walk-throughs in this book are modified versions of the Spinning Up implementations.

- *OpenAI Baselines*[16]: OpenAI Baselines is a set of high-quality implementations of the reinforcement learning algorithms. These algorithms make it easier for the research community to replicate, refine, and identify new ideas, and then create good baselines to build research on top of.

- *Stable Baselines*[17]: Stable Baselines is a set of improved implementations of RL algorithms based on OpenAI Baselines.

- *Garage*[18]: Garage is a toolkit for developing and evaluating reinforcement learning algorithms. It has an accompanying library of state-of-the-art implementations built using that toolkit.

---

[14]https://github.com/deepmind/sonnet

[15]https://spinningup.openai.com/en/latest/

[16]https://github.com/openai/baselines

[17]https://stable-baselines.readthedocs.io/en/master/

[18]https://github.com/rlworkgroup/garage

- *Keras RL*[19]: Keras RL implements some state-of-the art deep reinforcement learning algorithms in Python and seamlessly integrates with the deep learning library Keras. Furthermore, Keras RL works with OpenAI Gym out of the box. This means that evaluating and playing around with different algorithms is easy.

- *TensorForce*[20]: TensorForce is an open source deep reinforcement learning framework, with an emphasis on modularized flexible library design and straightforward usability for applications in research and practice. TensorForce is built on top of Google's TensorFlow framework and requires Python 3.

There are probably many more, and new ones are always showing up. However, the previous list is already pretty large. As we said, you should choose one deep learning library, one environment framework, and one of the RL implementations. To start, we recommend either PyTorch of TensorFlow with Gym and Spinning Up.

How to Continue Studying

Deep reinforcement learning is seeing a lot of growth, and this is the most favored approach today to get agents to learn from experiences to behave intelligently. We hope that this book is just a start for you. We hope that you will continue to learn about this exciting field. You can use the following resources to continue learning:

- Look for courses and online videos to extend the knowledge. MIT, Stanford, and UC Berkeley have many online courses that would be the next logical choice to dive deeper into this discipline. There are some YouTube videos from Deep Mind and other experts in this field.

- Make it a habit to visit the OpenAI and Deep Mind websites regularly. They have a ton of material supplementing the research papers and are the basis of many of the algorithms we saw in this book.

---

[19]https://github.com/keras-rl/keras-rl
[20]https://github.com/tensorforce/tensorforce

- Set up a Google alert for new papers in the field of reinforcement learning and try to follow along with the papers. Reading research papers is an art, and Professor Andrew Ng of Stanford has some useful tips on what it takes to master a subject; see `https://www.youtube.com/watch?v=733m6qBH-jI`.

Finally, it goes without saying: please follow along with the algorithms we have talked about in this book. Dive deep into the papers that form the basis of these algorithms. Try to reimplement the code yourself either following the code given in the notebooks accompanying this book or look at the implementations, especially in the Open AI Spinning Up library.

Summary

This chapter was a whirlwind tour of various emerging topics in and around reinforcement learning that we could not dive deep into in the core chapters of the book.

We covered a lot in the previous chapters. However, there is an equally large number of topics that we could not cover in the earlier chapters. The purpose of this chapter was to give readers a quick 360-degree view of reinforcement learning by talking about these left-out topics. As we had a lot to cover, the focus was to provide a high-level overview with pointers for a further deep dive.

Index

A

Action value functions, 40
Actor-critic (AC) methods, 306, 343
    A2C, 234, 237
    advantage, 232, 233
    asynchronous advantage, 241, 242
    implementing A2C, 238–240
Advantage actor critic (A2C), 234
AlphaGo, 339
    branching factor, 339
    general approaches, 339
    MCTS, 341
    neural network training, 340
    policies, 339, 340
    RL network, 340
    SL policy network, 341
    standard search tree, 339
Artificial intelligence (AI), 2, 3
Atari games, 168, 169, 361, 362, 367
Auto-differentiation libraries, 218, 219
Autonomous vehicles (AVs), 9

B

Background planning, 331, 332
Back propagation, 177, 333, 336
Backup diagrams, 38, 39, 42
Baselines, 227, 247

Bayesian approach, 308, 311
Behavior cloning, 353, 354
Behavior policy, 92
Bellman equation, 41–43, 78, 121, 311
    algorithms, 47
    MDP, 46
    optimal, 44–46
    transition dynamics, 47
Bias, 83, 84
Bootstrapping, 93, 147, 177

C

CartPole environment, 24
Categorial 51-Atom DQN, 195, 196
Cliff-walking, 96
compute_projection function, 196
compute_reward function, 200
Convolutional neural network (CNN), 339
Covariance matrix
        adaptation-evolutionary
        strategy (CMA-ES), 360
Cross-entropy method, 359, 360

D

DAgger, 354, 355
Decision-time planning, 332
Deep belief network models, 308, 310

© Nimish Sanghi 2021
N. Sanghi, *Deep Reinforcement Learning with Python*, https://doi.org/10.1007/978-1-4842-6809-4

MCTS, 331

noncontextual bandit, 325

nonoptimal policy, 325

regret curve, 331

setup, 325

strategies, 325

Thompson sampling, 329, 331

total regret, 325

UCB, 328, 329

F

Factorized networks, 190

Fine-tuning, 350, 352, 367

forward function, 190, 263

Function approximation

approaches, 127

batch methods (DQN), 149–151

challenges, 131

coarse coding, 128, 129

convergence, 146, 147

deep learning libraries, 153

definition, 126

geometry, 124

gradient temporal difference
learning, 148, 149

incremental control

evaluation, 137

q-value, 136

SARSA on-policy, 138, 140–143

SARSA(λ), 143, 145, 146

linear least squares method,
151, 152

MC, TD, TD(λ), 132, 133, 135

minimizing loss function, 126

nonstationarity, 126

tile encoding, 129, 130

training data, 126

G

Garage, 371

Generalized policy iteration (GPI), 73, 84,
132, 137, 208

generate_trajectory function, 225

Generative adversarial
networks (GANs), 358

Gradient temporal difference learning, 148

Greedy in the limit with infinite
exploration (GLIE), 87

ε-greedy policy, 85, 86, 98, 103

GridworldEnv, 54

Gym library documentation, 174

H

Hindsight experience replay (HER),
48, 198, 202, 205

I, J

Imagination-Augmented
Agents (I2A), 348–350

Imitation learning, 353

DAgger, 354, 355

expert demonstration, 353

expert training data, 353

learned policy, 354

model-based setups, 355

model-free setups, 355

near-perfect policy, 353

open loop problem, 354

reward function, 355

robot, 355

trajectory drift, 354

types, 356

uses, 358

Printed in the United States
by Baker & Taylor Publisher Services